J.S. Gordon is a surveyor by profession and is otherwise currently researching for a PhD. He has been a serious researcher into the philosophies and mystery traditions of ancient cultures and civilizations for many years. He has written several books and regularly gives lectures on the .... related subjects, endeavouring .... ctive for a wider range of audie ....

Also by J.S. Gordon:

Egypt, Child of Atlantis

Khemmea – The Sacred Wisdom Tradition of Ancient Egypt

THE RISE & FALL OF
ATLANTIS

and the Mysterious Origins of Human Civilization

J.S. Gordon

WATKINS PUBLISHING

LONDON

Distributed in the USA and Canada by Sterling Publishing Co., Inc.
387 Park Avenue South, New York, NY 10016

This edition first published in the UK and USA 2008 by
Watkins Publishing, Sixth Floor, Castle House,
75–76 Wells Street, London W1T 3QH

1 3 5 7 9 10 8 6 4 2

Designed and typeset by Paul Saunders
Printed and bound in Great Britain

Library of Congress Cataloging-in-Publication Data Available

ISBN 13: 978-1-905857-24-1
ISBN 10: 1-905857-24-1

www.watkinspublishing.co.uk

For information about custom editions, special sales, premium and
corporate purchases, please contact Sterling Special Sales
Department at 800-805-5489 or specialsales@sterlingpub.com.

*This book is dedicated to the two Helenas –
one past and one present, but both with the same
passion for true knowledge.*

ACKNOWLEDGEMENTS

For material used as reference in this book or otherwise derived from advice, I am particularly grateful to Richard Milton, Jeremy Naydler, Michael Cremo and Richard Thompson; the Earth Sciences library at the Natural History Museum in London, the British Museum, the Lamont Doherty Earth Observatory at Columbia University, New York; Wood's Hole Oceanographic Center in Connecticut; the office of Marie Tharp, Charles Hapgood's son and trustee; the Peabody Museum of Archaeology and Ethnology at Harvard University; the British Library; plus the Society for Psychical Research and the library of the Theosophical Society in London. Further thanks are due to Michael Mann for his helpful advice in making the text rather more approachable for prospective readers of the book who might perhaps be unfamiliar with some of the concepts treated in it. I am similarly grateful to Peter Bently, my editor, for steering me through the rocky shallows of rendering the text more user-friendly to all whilst also suggesting several useful insertions by way of extra explanation.

I have otherwise tried to ensure that all due consents, references and attributions have been properly sought and obtained. If any have been overlooked by oversight, my apologies are due and I shall endeavour to incorporate any corrections or additions in future editions.

J.S. Gordon

CONTENTS

Part Four CULTURE

LIST OF ILLUSTRATIONS

PREFACE

The subtitle to this book refers to 'the mysterious origins of human civilization' – something one might not normally expect to find in conjunction with the subject of Atlantis. However, it is quite deliberate and, as will rapidly become obvious, this aspect of the book actually plays a much bigger part in the story that is about to unfold than Plato's island ever could on its own. That is because it is, in truth, far more intriguing.

The majority of books on Atlantis tend to approach it merely from the angle of a mysterious island with an even more mysterious civilization, destroyed by a one-off cataclysm at some time c12,000 years ago. However, as we shall see, it is the question mark which has historically hung over the Atlanteans themselves which is of far greater interest than the cataclysm. But since the genesis of the Atlanteans lies far back in the dim mists of ancient prehistory, long before the cataclysm, so we must first establish these origins, using whatever reasonable sources are available, before we start to concern ourselves with the small remaining island of Plato's story. Nevertheless, this book will also look very closely at the causes and aftermath of the cataclysm described by Plato, with the aim of showing quite clearly that the supposedly 'rational' idea that it is a mere myth is entirely mistaken.

The Structure of this Book

This book is structured in four parts. The relatively brief first part sets out to explain the rationale behind Plato's story, as well as its hidden esoteric allegory. The second part then goes on to deal with the 'mechanics and dynamics' of the way in which our planet itself functions – in a manner, as we will see, fundamentally misconstrued by modern scientific orthodoxy. This should then help to explain the general nature of the evolutionary process which led to the appearance of 'Atlantean humankind' in the first place.

This second part also serves as a general background explanation on the issue of such vast cataclysms as the one which supposedly destroyed the homeland of Plato's Atlanteans, supposedly within the space of 24 hours. However, it also goes much further, in questioning the very basis of some areas of modern scientific reasoning, particularly in the fields of associated anthropology, geology, geophysics and astrophysics. For those not particularly interested in the background science and philosophy, parts of this can be skipped. However, those who take the trouble to read this carefully will find that their effort repays real dividends by presenting to them a much broader and better overall perspective.

The third part deals with Atlantis itself and its supposedly also mythic continental predecessors (Lemuria and Hyperborea) plus their peoples, whose successors comprised not only Plato's Atlantean island but the lands and peoples of our own 'Fifth Race' of modern humanity. This part also deals very specifically with Plato's cataclysm and its after-effects on the civilizations surrounding the Mediterranean.

The fourth part finally considers particular aspects of what we today perhaps believe (or like to speculate) about Atlantean civilization and culture, including its religion and its 'magical' traditions. It also looks back more generally at the technology of ancient times – something which is rarely approached on an objective and consolidated basis.

Finally, the epilogue concludes with some speculations about the future, based upon the same 'unorthodox' approach.

The Issue of Supporting References

With regard to the various references used in the book – apart from Plato's own statements in the *Timaeus* and *Critias* – the following background comments may perhaps be found useful:

Even to begin to understand the background to the concept of an Atlantean continent and people, one must first of all openly question (and sometimes discard) a number of modern scientific theories elsewhere in the fields of the Earth sciences and anthropology. Thus a first main area of reference comes from the quite recent works of the best-selling scientific journalist Richard Milton. Although modern proponents of Christian 'Creationism' have since rather selectively appropriated some of his ideas and turned them into a supposedly self-justifying bandwagon trundling all across the internet, it was Milton who, in his original (1990) tour-de-force work *Shattering the Myths of Darwinism*, almost single-handedly took apart the morass of modern scientific concepts in the fields of geochronology and evolution. In doing so, he showed how and where the whole edifice of popularly accepted theory in these and other associated areas is actually built on highly unstable foundations and held together by a mass of none-too-safe assumptions.

A major benefit of Richard Milton's work is that it allows me to demonstrate in this book that Creationist theory and Darwinian theory are *not* the only two options available for consideration in dealing with the thorny question of evolution on our planet. There is another quite different approach. This – avoiding all suggestion of the involvement of extraterrestrials or of 'God' *per se* – not only has a fully rational basis to it but also explains the original source of the fundamentally misunderstood and comprehensively misrepresented biblical Creation story itself. That concept is outlined here in Chapter Three onwards and it provides the background to the whole rationale of an ethnologically different Atlantean people and their culture.

A second main body of references – particularly of an anthropological nature – is drawn from *The Secret Doctrine*, the magnum opus of H.P. Blavatsky (1831–91). Those who have taken the trouble to really study this amazing and altogether unique literary compendium and the sources from which it draws its material,[1] will already understand their value. They will also be grateful for the fact that, in this book, I have put those sources in a rather more immediately chronological order. *The Secret Doctrine* itself could not be considered entirely sequential in its approach to the vast multitude of subjects (whether ancient or modern) which it covers in the fields of literature and science on the one hand, and philosophy, theology and mysticism on the other.

Those who have never examined *The Secret Doctrine* objectively, on the grounds that Blavatsky was supposed to have been a clever fraud or merely a plagiarist, merely display their own ignorance and lazy prejudice. She openly admitted in the foreword to the book that none of the information contained in it was her own anyway. Even though the book's immense (and generally acknowledged) erudition and scholarship otherwise speak for themselves, Blavatsky's genius was seen as flawed or compromised in the public view by a single event related to the phenomenal display of her psychic powers. At the time, that event was considered (by a single, untrained and unsupervised representative of the Society for Psychical Research) to be untrustworthy. However, in 1999 the very same SPR vindicated Blavatsky when it had the original evidence reviewed by a world expert in the field of forensic science.[2] The 1999 SPR report came to the unqualified conclusion that the first report (of 1885) was based upon not only thoroughly unreliable but – because fundamentally wrong – also wholly unsupportable evidence. Regrettably, however, mud sticks; and the lazy worlds of modern journalism and myopic academia have merely continued to retail the original story with due lack of discrimination or up-to-date qualification.

The usefulness of Blavatsky's work in relation to this present book is twofold. First of all, her information provides a detailed and sourced indication of the geographical whereabouts and extent of ancient continents mentioned in various ancient texts and traditions, together with reasons as to when and why they disappeared. Secondly, it provides the one and only self-consistently logical explanation of human evolution, which is described in terms of a sevenfold sequence of 'Root Races', derived from a process of psycho-spiritual unfoldment of consciousness.

As we shall see, *when explained properly and in the correct scientific context*, this provides the long-looked-for bridge between the co-existent irrationalities of both Darwinism and Creationism, whilst simultaneously providing a rational basis for human psychology in the round. It should perhaps be added that some of the ideas and information put forward by Blavatsky were so far ahead of their time that they could not be proved by the science of her day, or even for several decades after that. However, as we demonstrate in later chapters, the last century has seen the development of various technologies which have proved her far-sightedness and accuracy beyond all controversy.

A third area of reference comes from the works of the great 19th-century explorers and anthropologists le Plongeon, de Bourbourg and von Humboldt, whose exploratory travels all over the world opened up fields of scientific and scholarly study in all sorts of areas which few others had even considered. These included the issue of ancient prehistoric continents in the various oceans and also the peoples associated with them.

A fourth body of supporting references comes from the research opus of Michael Cremo and Richard Thompson – *The Hidden History of the Human Race*. This is another amazing compendium of reports, this time gleaned from those many and varied archaeological and palaeontological discoveries of the 19th and early 20th centuries. These, because not fitting comfortably within the self-established orthodoxy of the time, were quietly shelved and more or less forgotten about until Cremo and Thompson came on the scene.

The rediscovery and structured revival of these reports, and the altogether startling prehistoric perspectives which they open up, have lent scientifically based credence and support to the concept of an intelligent and creative humanity existing over ten million years before the earliest date that modern science is currently prepared to admit as remotely possible. This is notwithstanding the fact that mid- to late-19th-century scientific researchers, contemporary with Darwin, were themselves widely certain from the evidence before them that such quite clearly had to be the case.

Cremo and Thompson's work is thus of considerable importance in providing a proper background of modern scientific evidence. This supports the anciently reported scenarios of primordial civilizations and cultures living on ancient continents which, although no longer extant, we have learned to associate with 'Atlantis' and 'Lemuria'. However, the reaction of modern scientific opinion has in the main been somewhat akin to that resulting from Blavatsky's

book in her time – stunned silence. The interlocking structures and substructures of current scientific opinion, spanning all sorts of disciplines from
archaeology to anthropology, to biology, geology and palaeontology, have
been unable to come up with a single reasoned counter-response.

Even blatantly prejudiced criticism has been limited because Cremo and
Thompson have merely used records which were themselves already in the
public and scientific domains. However, because of the direct threat of one
admission leading to another and then another, thereby causing or at least
threatening the unwinding of many of the substructures of modern scientific
thought and historical scholarship in these and other related fields, a pall of
silence has fallen over the whole spectrum, as the 'ostrich mentality' has again
quietly prevailed. Nevertheless, an appreciable number of archaeologists and
palaeontologists have quietly and gratefully acknowledged the fact that Cremo
and Thompson's work has reopened a field of enquiry which should never
have been shut in the first place.

In 2003 Cremo and Thompson presented their latest work, *Human Devolu-
tion – A Vedic Alternative to Darwinian Theory*, which I have only recently
come across. This, I am delighted to note, cross-corresponds with my own
suggestions in this book as to man's psycho-spiritual nature and origin
needing to be much better understood by scientists, and the public generally.

A fifth area of ancillary quotations and references is derived from the Egyptian *Hermetica*. According to modern scholarship this is, supposedly, a tract
of Neoplatonic philosophy; but to anyone who has studied esotericism in its
own terms, it is quite clearly a work reflecting the fundamentally practical
nature of ancient mystic and occult thought in general. In fact, it has been
described not as a Neoplatonic composition but a Neoplatonic *compilation*,
taken from one or more of the 42 sacred 'Books of Djehuty', the god-figure
(also known by the Greek name Thoth) symbolizing All-knowledge. These
encompassed the canon of all ancient Egyptian occult knowledge and esoteric
philosophy.

The fact that the *Hermetica* proceeds in the same line as Plato's own philosophical thought (hence the claim that it is a Neoplatonist writing) is merely
indicative of the well-known fact that Plato derived his knowledge and
wisdom from the Egyptians in the first place. However, as this present book is
fundamentally concerned with the question of explaining Plato's 'Atlantis', it is
entirely apposite that such references should also be used to explain some of
his own background philosophy.

A sixth area of reference is de Santillana and von Dechend's book
Hamlet's Mill, which deals with the history and development of astronomical
myth from ancient times. The reason for including references in this area
will become apparent when we look at the whole question of astronomical

associations and cycles, as well as that of the appearance of humankind on Earth, long before even the Atlanteans.

Three other areas of reference need to be mentioned, although they are not pursued in any real detail in this current work. First of all, possibly the most widely known (but still least understood) of the generally available historical references to Atlantis and its peoples are to be found in the Hindu epic, the *Mahabharata*, and also in the *Puranas*. Ancient Indian myths are not well understood simply because particular references to actual prehistory recorded in them are widely interspersed among even more obscure sacred allegory and metaphor. These elements are woven together so subtly that only someone very familiar with Sanskrit, the language of these ancient texts, and Brahmanic esotericism, or otherwise with esoteric philosophy across many cultures, could begin to perceive the different threads. However, as this field alone would require a book of its own, I have made no attempt to deal with associated details here. Nevertheless, several usefully relevant quotations have been added from the works of the well-known Vedic scholar, Dr David Frawley.

Ignatius Donelly

One should perhaps not conclude without mentioning Ignatius Donnelly (1831–1901), the grandfather of all modern authors on the subject of Atlantis. Although written off by scholars in general as merely a remarkable enthusiast, who used all sorts of information to support his own preconception as to the existence of a mid-Atlantean island, his own scholarship was (at least in part) quite considerable and carried much rational conviction. Donnelly was really one of the first to draw attention to the many trans-Atlantic and trans-Pacific correspondences to the native geology, plants and anthropology of the Americas, many of which, even today, remain unexplained by science. He was also the forerunner of those in the mid to late 20th century – a full century later – who pushed hitherto recalcitrant scientists to an eventual, grudging acceptance of the idea that trans-oceanic travel by prehistoric man was not only a distinct probability, but also a demonstrable fact.

The other reason for mentioning Donnelly is that he was one of the few to accept Plato's description of his Atlantean island as facing the Pillars of Herakles from the nearby west. However, his interpretation of Plato's directions led him to look principally *due* west to the Azores, whereas, as will be seen in later chapters of this book, there are good and logical reasons for looking southwestwards as well. To be fair, however, Donnelly did this, although curiously without paying the area as much attention as it deserved.

Regrettably also, Donnelly was yet another who assumed that all the Greek gods must have been, in origin, Atlantean kings. While this misguided assumption served well at the time to heighten the drama of Donnelly's story, in retrospect it did him no favours at all, lessening the impact of the rest of his scholarship. Had he concentrated solely on building up the scientific and rational logic of his study, Donnelly's subsequent place in history as an enlightened amateur might well gleam rather more brightly than it actually does.

Edgar Cayce

Finally, mention and acknowledgment is also due to Edgar Cayce (1877–1945), 'the sleeping prophet', because some at least of his predictions about Atlantis reappearing off Bimini appear to have come true – although much further careful excavation and research will be necessary before this is proved beyond all contention. However, this present book is more particularly about Plato's Atlantean island – not the original and much larger continental landmass off Florida and around the Gulf of Mexico, with which it is all too frequently confused. Whilst that southern Atlantean continent mentioned by Cayce is touched on here, it is really only to put Atlantean civilization and culture (and its humankind) in its proper global perspective.

J. S. Gordon

INTRODUCTION

Why yet another book on Atlantis? Hasn't the subject by now been exhausted? Well, actually, no it hasn't. To come straight to the point, there are several reasons why this book is very different to any others on the same subject. Here are just some of them:

- It considers the subject from the standpoint of Plato's own time and culture;

- It takes into account the rational science in ancient esoteric philosophy;

- It takes into account the connection between geological cataclysms and astronomical cycles;

- It takes into account the progressive psycho-spiritual evolution of human consciousness;

- It considers the anthropological background to Atlantis;

- It considers the question of Atlantean belief and religious culture;

- It suggests what happened to Atlantean civilization and culture *after* Plato's cataclysm.

But is this book likely to be any more believable than any of the others? After all, most of them seem to take what Plato said with a large pinch of salt.

Fair comment, perhaps. It is certainly one of those strange curiosities of modern life that many scholars, scientists and intelligent lay people alike, although fascinated by his story of Atlantis and its destruction, generally refuse to believe that it could have been located where Plato himself placed it. This is despite the commonly overlooked fact that several other ancient traditions appear to support his account. So what lies behind this contradiction? And in any case why should the idea of a highly sophisticated prehistoric civilization and culture continue to have any general appeal in our own day and age?

Prejudice and the Deliberate Distortion of Tradition

In his misguided efforts to support early Christian evangelism at any cost, the theologian Euhemerus (lived c316BC) tried to bury ancient local 'pagan' mystic traditions by claiming that they were no more than the products of half-remembered historical events and personalities. Thus deprived of their original religious and philosophical significance, these traditions were then progressively forgotten by subsequent generations over the following centuries. This process of explaining away mythic and mystic lore that is not to one's doctrinal liking is hence known as 'euhemerism'. Rather depressingly, however, generations of scholars have followed suit over the centuries, applying the same distortive technique to other ancient traditions around the world, so obscuring and fragmenting even further the original sacred truths and philosophical perspectives of our ancient ancestors. One example of this, which will be touched on later, is the way in which mainstream archaeology has treated the biblical narrative of the Old Testament. But there are many other examples.

Where even more obscure sacred or ancient historical traditions are concerned, modern science has used the same technique, in conjunction with technologically derived data, to belittle them either as outright errors and lies, or as the poorly remembered products of the supposedly unsophisticated pre-modern mind, or merely as superstitious fantasies. This however, is exactly what has happened with the subject of Atlantis, despite the fact – as we shall see – that it was actually known of many thousands of years before even Plato's time.

It is said that more books and articles have been written on the subject of Atlantis than on anything else except the Bible itself. Whether or not that is true, this literary extravaganza has been augmented in recent decades by television documentaries and feature films, almost all seeking to relocate Plato's island, often by thousands of miles, to all four points of the compass. This has often been done in conjunction with a sideways focus upon the purely fantastical aspects of Atlantean magical science and its associated 'powers' – which have themselves led in all sorts of even more bizarre directions.

It is therefore with a certain amount of hesitation that I have allowed myself to be drawn into adding to this field of commentary. That I have done so is purely because so many modern theories completely fail to address broadly what Atlantis was, undoubtedly, all about in both anthropological and cultural terms. Moreover, many openly fail to report with accuracy what was said on the subject by the Ancients themselves.

This book is therefore aimed at proving – contrary to modern scientific opinion – that Plato's Atlantean island could have existed (and probably did exist) in the northeastern Atlantic, roughly facing the 'Pillars of Herakles', west of the modern Strait of Gibraltar. However, I also seek to explain that there is a purely esoteric aspect to Plato's story which is important in its own right. But even on the purely physical side, this book goes much further than looking at the subject of Atlantis alone, in purely geographical and geological terms. Nevertheless, these contexts are also carefully considered, and my survey touches on several radically new ideas not generally discussed before in books on this topic.

Some of the ancillary material will of course be familiar to those who have already read widely about Atlantis. However, its orientation and focus is also very different to what might otherwise have been expected. This is because I come from a rather different tradition and school of thought to that of modern mainstream science, although I am fairly familiar with the latter. But, having said as much, let us jump straight into the fires of controversy.

The Dating of Humankind

Modern scientific and scholarly orthodoxy currently believe that our species, *Homo sapiens sapiens*, has existed for only the last 180,000 years or so. Ten years ago it was believed to be only 120,000 years. Two decades before that it was merely 80,000 years. A century earlier, in the infancy of archaeology as a science, it was under 20,000 years. However, it has also (quietly) been recognized that pretty well the same human type as Cro-Magnon Man (the name given to an early archaeological type of *Homo sapiens sapiens*, named after the French site where it was found) existed at least 1.5 million years ago, at the very beginning of the Quaternary Age. This human was significantly taller than we today are, with a 15–20 per cent larger brain. Yet Darwinian natural selection theory asks us to believe that the (supposedly unguided) evolutionary drive in nature produced appreciably bigger and better human physiques and brains than ours over 1.5 million years ago, then inexplicably waited around another 1.5 million years (until *c*10,000 years ago) before humankind in general began to realize that communal urban life and its associated forms of culture might perhaps be a good idea.

Straight common sense should tell us that if Nature produced superior versions of ourselves over 1.5 million years ago (at least), it must have done so for good reason – namely for the purposes of evolutionary necessity and/or for its own self-expression. After all, humankind is an integral part of Nature. It is not detached from it, either objectively or subjectively. Quite clearly, however, it is the *subjective* development of human (and all other) intelligence which, through functional necessity, precedes corresponding 'evolutionary' changes in the external form. That is another important point to remember in placing

Atlantean civilization and culture in its proper historical and psychological context, as we shall see in later chapters. It also calls into question the very basis of modern Darwinian theory.

If human beings were, on average, much taller 1.5 million years ago and with much larger brains, it follows quite logically that the intelligence which evolved that better physique and brain had actually developed or evolved long before. Bearing in mind just how slowly such major evolutionary changes supposedly take place, it immediately lends credence to the research findings of Michael Cremo and Richard Thompson in their groundbreaking classics *Forbidden Archaeology* and *The Hidden History of the Human Race*.

Their work, as we shall see in greater detail later on, clearly and rationally demonstrates why and how proper scientific research and discovery has – without openly acknowledging the fact – already confirmed that intelligently and culturally creative *Homo sapiens* is actually *many millions* of years old. This being so, it follows in parallel that the traditions of a highly sophisticated Atlantean civilization and culture, existing merely 12,000 years ago by Plato's reckoning, can no longer be brushed aside as merely conjectural nonsense. However, I shall be providing further circumstantial evidence to support my case from sources much older and further afield than just Plato.

Darwinian and Archaeological Theory

As we shall also see (and as is becoming more generally recognized by main-stream science), Darwinian theory is extensively flawed. It therefore really cannot be relied upon to answer in serious depth any anthropological questions relating to ancient prehistory when its own foundations are so scarce and makeshift. But nor can general archaeological and palaeontological theory either, for they have largely hitched their wagons to the Darwinian star. They have consequently produced, by mere inference and auto-suggestion, a pro-posed structure of prehistory which is now trundling precariously close to the edge of a huge precipice with its axles rapidly wearing out.

Curiously, mainstream archaeology once endeavoured to support itself on suspect wheels borrowed largely from biblical tradition. Notwithstanding its original erroneous belief in the Old Testament as historical evidence of purely Israelite/Jewish (rather than generally borrowed) tradition, archaeology has come around within the last 50 years or so to a sensible recognition of the fact that there is no proof at all that any of the Israelite Patriarchs existed or that events such as the Exodus from Egypt ever took place. However, this has not stopped some archaeologists from unjustifiably *assuming* that such tribal figures 'must' have existed and that such events 'must' have occurred at some point in time, rather than seeing them as the archetypal myths and esoteric religious metaphors which rather more careful consideration would immediately suggest them to be.

It is not altogether surprising that 19th-century science welcomed Darwin's theories with such open arms. The prevalent Western alternative at the time was an anthropocentrically literal Creation Theory. This saw a supreme Deity as responsible for the omniverse, within the wilds of which our own microscopically tiny planet had been singled out for His special interest and treatment, creating life upon it, and human life in particular, for no apparent reason other than to have humankind engage in His worship. Added to the fact that this Deity seemed to possess all sorts of unedifyingly human emotional qualities, Western Christian theology was completely unable to rationalize or adequately paper over the self-evident cracks and holes in its own logic. So it is unsurprising that it was unable to put up much of a struggle against Darwinian theory – other than to keep on insisting upon following biblical statements with blind faith.

The actual efficacy of biblical theology of this type is best seen in the fact that many 20th-century theologians, apparently even within the Vatican, have widely adopted neo-Darwinian concepts and quietly adjusted their own interpretations of the Bible in consequence, so as not to be totally out of step with rational science. The main bastions of Creation Theory are today to be found, unsurprisingly, within the evangelical Christian churches, which discourage their adherents from questioning the objective truth of *anything* in their scriptures, or from taking the latter anything other than literally.

Blind Literalism in Science

However, this particular infection has begun to spread to the world of modern (Western) science, which also has its literalists, or 'fundamentalists'. Modern orthodox scientific 'rationalism' just as short-sightedly hypothesizes that our world and its parent universe are the continuing products of mere chance. This is notwithstanding the fact – as established but as yet unexplained even by Quantum Theory – that it is actually based upon a foundation of *consistent* order and scientifically demonstrable *law*. For mere rationalists, however, the fact that this somehow induces matter (with absolute and unerringly accurate regularity) to emerge in systematically recurrent and *intelligently* predictable forms from an indefinable background of universal cosmic chaos, remains an irritating puzzle.

Whilst utterly rejecting the facile tenets of modern Creationism, I take the view that the phenomenon of reliably consistent Creation is philosophically and logically impossible without causal intelligence lying behind it. Hence my belief, by simple deduction – and shared with the Ancients and many other thinking people today – that the universe and all forms within it must be systematically generated and driven by the principle of mind: in fact, by a hierarchically organized spectrum of *Universal Mind*.

Within this continuum, a majority of intelligent and semi-intelligent beings are self-evidently able to exist and generate local phenomenal influences without the need (to our limited range of perceptions at least) for objectively visible physical forms. This view is the result of careful analysis, as I will later demonstrate.

It naturally follows from this view, and from the fact that wholly inert matter cannot logically give rise to organic life and consciousness (or function), that there can be no such thing as 'dead' or 'inorganic' matter in the universe. As the Ancients themselves stated, there is no such thing as a void or vacuum. *Kosmos* itself is an infinite and eternal *plenum* containing the 'One Universal Life'. Matter and Life itself are thus one and the same principle, alternating in polarized aspect with each other (just like $E=mc^2$) according to the nature and purpose of the Intelligence within whose field of existence they lie; for as the Ancients perceived, each world system is contained by a hierarchically organized consciousness which they classified as that of the creative 'Demiurge'.

Magic and the Quantum World

Through the convertibility of energy and force, we come not only to the issue of how evolution and consciousness themselves operate, but also to that of Atlantean magic and technology, as also mentioned in several of the ancient traditions. However, to attempt to deal with that subject in any detail would be a complete distraction from the main thrust of this book, so while there is a chapter on the subject (*see* Chapter 17), not much will be said here other than to suggest that magic is essentially no more than knowledge of how Nature works from the unseen side. It is thus concerned with knowledge of how to follow Nature's own serial manipulations – something which modern science has itself been doing for decades anyway, without actually acknowledging the fact. Today's chemists, engineers and doctors are but yesterday's 'magicians'.

Modern quantum science has already come to the conclusion that all forms are merely varying vibrations of light substance and that the mere attention of an observer can have a definitely positive or negative influence on an experiment. So, there can surely no longer be an issue over the suggestion that the focussed mind is capable of influencing and even manipulating matter at a distance – even within the field of objective Nature. The only outstanding issue is the *extent* to which this is possible and under what conditions. But even here it becomes logically self-evident that just as the directing mind is extraneous to the matter it directs, the mind and its directing intelligence – whether human or otherwise – must themselves be, *in origin*, extraneous to the body. However, this is precisely what the Ancients themselves said and it coincides with what some moderns suggest in terms of the body being merely a hologram.

Nature as an Intelligent Organism

Now, why mention all this in a book on Atlantis? Well, because it helps to explain why and how the Earth is itself an organism and why Nature on our planet does indeed possess a creatively purposeful intelligence. In fact, as we shall see in subsequent chapters, it possesses a whole spectrum of intelligence and semi-intelligence, with a *modus operandi* which works consistently, coherently and logically through all its various 'kingdoms' in tandem. Inevitably, it does so to promote and maintain its own evolutionary existence and development in due cycle – *and that partly through cataclysm*. Consequently, neither Atlantis nor its ancient peoples can be considered in isolation, or as other than part of a geologically and anthropologically logical sequence leading up to our modern 'historical' era of the last 5,000 to 6,000 years and its assorted cultures and civilizations.

The Intention of this Book

The essential aim of this present book is to open up and consider on a much broader front than hitherto *what* Atlantis might have been as a human civilization and culture and *why* historically it should have existed in the first place. It is intended to be of general interest to all intelligent lay people, and I also hope that it will be of serious interest to the more open-minded scholars and scientists of orthodox persuasion – irrespective of any immediately negative reaction on seeing the name 'Atlantis' yet again. However, this latter hope may be somewhat of a forlorn one, particularly as the first chapters recurrently criticize some areas of mainstream scholarship and science for their consistently insensate materialism and the prejudiced blind alleys of false assumption up which it has so persistently led them.

Bearing in mind the criticism of some areas of modern scientific and scholarly orthodoxy in the following chapters, I ought to state very clearly that I am not in any way anti-science or anti-scholarship; in fact, quite the reverse. However, I am unequivocally against 'scientism'. This is the wilfully blind type of scientific and scholarly prejudice which attempts to emasculate or even obliterate alternative or 'maverick' ideas at birth, purely on the grounds that only academically qualified scientists and scholars can understand such matters, or that anybody following a path of thought other than the orthodox one – itself based upon literalism and scientific materialism – is lacking in appropriately intelligent or rational objectivity.

These days, high standards of information and public debate are much more generally available than they were a century ago. Consequently, through the medium of literature, radio and television, as well as the Internet, the general public is much better informed (and consequently often more sceptical) of mainline orthodoxy. Because of that, I feel reasonably confident that I can rely upon the natural intelligence of my readers (from whatever background) to decide for themselves whether my reasoned arguments for specific alternatives to current orthodoxy carry sufficient weight for them to adjust their own perspectives.

It is noteworthy that most commentators on the subject of Atlantis like to be seen to stick entirely to what is very obviously in line with mainstream orthodoxy and thus less vulnerable to attack by scientists and scholars. However, my feeling is that to do so again would merely result in yet another predictably unoriginal book on the same subject. If we are going to have some discussion, let us at least have a bold new perspective and something original to discuss – and there is plenty here that is both original and worthy of reasoned discussion.

The Association of Ancient Myth and Philosophy

Rather than concentrating purely upon geography, geology and archaeology, as most other writers concerned with Atlantis seem to do, this book perhaps unusually takes into account a wider range of analytical considerations in the field of ancient myth generally, as well as in the field of 'old', philosophic science. 'Myth' itself however is merely the ancient technique of expressing primal esoteric philosophy and knowledge in metaphor and allegory – some of it of a clearly 'scientific' nature, even if modern orthodoxy refuses to consider such a possibility. As Dr Jeremy Naydler recently commented on the subject of modern orthodoxy:

> The assumption, of course, is that only modern scientific knowledge is 'true knowledge'. During the 19th and 20th centuries, it was argued that in ... ancient cultures, where the guardians of learning were priests, knowledge remained at a primitive level because of the stranglehold of superstition, magic and uncritically held beliefs that supposedly characterised pre-Greek societies. The reason why there was no 'true knowledge' was that it was totally inhibited by their religious outlook and theocratic power structures. The implication here is that a religious structure such as that of ancient Egypt is necessarily an ignorant one.[1]

The sort of modern unthinking prejudice described here blinds many to the fact that some 'old' scientific knowledge, although dressed up in 'myth', appears to be more accurate than current 'knowledge' – many areas of which are based upon speculative assumption dressed up as supposed fact and given the impressive name 'paradigm'. Several aspects of popularly accepted modern scientific orthodoxy are thus treated here as target material to show precisely where current, so-called 'Atlantean' theories come unstuck through modern scientific misinterpretation itself.

It is perhaps also worthwhile remarking in passing upon the further, completely back-to-front presumption that it was superstition which gave rise originally to myth. This again derives from the entirely false assumption by modern scientists and scholars that nearly all pre-Aristotelian thought must essentially have been intellectually incapable of true scientific objectivity and rationality. This attitude also takes no account of the fact that general superstition abounds today, resulting from constant degradation and distortions of truth in all areas of life. In fact, our own highly technological age quite certainly generates far more such distortion (curiously, even amongst some scholars and scientists) than existed five or six thousand years ago, by virtue of the limitations of the merely written word to convey truth. For example, it is highly debatable whether the proliferation of material on the Internet on balance enlightens or confuses.

The Issue of Psycho-Spiritual Existence

In these pages I have treated with complete seriousness and objectivity the ancient view of humans in their inner nature as psycho-spiritual or even semi-divine beings, rather than as merely evolved pithecoids. That is because, without understanding the associated principles, it is impossible to understand either the true nature of the human type or its origins. Whereas modern (Western) science has, in my view, rather arrogantly adopted the stance that any sort of divinity or spirituality in the field of Creation is 'unnecessary', I have deployed a range of literary forces here to show where and how such an arbitrary view arose in the first place and was then able to gain its present wholly counterfeit currency.

Nevertheless, I simultaneously reject the involvement in our world scheme of the purely *personalized* (or anthropomorphic) Universal Deity posited (in various forms) by Judaism, Christianity, Islam and other religions. This is on the grounds that their theologians have no more proved their point than modern scientists have theirs. My approach here thus follows in the well-beaten tracks of the Ancients. It does so by endeavouring to explain the logical correlations between spirit/energy and matter which in turn support the idea

THE RISE AND FALL OF ATLANTIS

of an intelligently rational structure and dynamic behind the processes of Creation and Evolution, as self-evidently apparent all around us today.

It is not my intention that this work be drawn into the field of merely superstitious fancy or fantasy. That is a cul-de-sac resulting from lazy ignorance and fear. Such ignorance existed in the medieval and even Renaissance eras because theologians and philosophers were, in the main, unable to understand the Ancient Wisdom Tradition in any real breadth and depth. That is unsurprising, since in most cases these thinkers had access only to a relatively small part of it. In addition, they were also frequently too conditioned by their religious background to pursue what they did know of ancient wisdom on its own terms. Not only did they rightly fear ignorant religious persecution, but they also simply did not know how to deal with the real knowledge which they encountered when their philosophical and theological enquiries took them to the shadowy borderlands of an even greater mystery. This mystery – which is now of such universal interest in this 21st century – is that of consciousness.

Consciousness and Science

It is widely acknowledged that the next great frontier of discovery facing science is that of consciousness itself. However, consciousness provides the key to the whole process of evolution, with evolution in turn providing the retrospective key to the human types and cultures of the (even prehistoric) past.[2] So, the reader will be unsurprised that this subject too is treated here as of genuine auxiliary importance to the issue of Atlantean culture and civilization.

In addition to that, however, the already clear implications (via scientific experiment and the consequently evolved quantum doctrine of non-locality) are that this foundational sensory faculty of consciousness is actually somehow extraneous to the body. But this immediately forces reconsideration of the issue of alternative states of psycho-spiritual being and their effects, for good or evil, upon the external world. The problem for science will not go away. That is why in this book it has been attacked head-on by considering it in conjunction with the evolutionary process itself, as part and parcel of the issue surrounding pre-historic (and particularly Atlantean) civilization and culture.

To approach the subject of Atlantis from as unusual a standpoint as that adopted in the following few chapters of course runs many risks. That is more particularly so as some of the suggestions made there in the associated scientific field are so radical as to suggest the complete overthrow of significant areas of present Western scientific and scholarly orthodoxy. This is even though the alternatives still need to be finally confirmed by cross-correlation or measurement and formal experimentation. However, I make no apology for this when so much of modern scientific theory, particularly in the fields of astrophysics and anthropology, is itself based upon a range of – frequently illogical and unproven – speculative assumptions, some of which are described later on.

So, whilst I hope that this book will appeal to those who are interested in exploring the rationally radical and interdisciplinary answers to the questions 'Why?' and 'How?' Atlantis and its civilization arose, it will probably have significantly less appeal to those still gravitationally mired in the status quo of general modern orthodoxy. It is also doubtful that it will have any great appeal to those interested in conspiracy theories, in supposed Atlantean super-technology (including 'death-rays' and the like), or in merely finding some supposedly new location for Atlantis which nobody else has yet thought of.

PART ONE

·

PLATO AND HIS STORY

Chapter One

•

THE CULTURAL BACKGROUND OF PLATO'S TIME

'Mythology, meaning proper poetic fable, has been of great assistance, but it can help no further. The golden island of Kronos, the tree-girt island of Calypso, remain unlocatable notwithstanding the efforts of Homeric scholars ... Some data in Homer look like exact geography, as Circe's island with its temple of Feronia, or the Land of the Listrygones, which should be the Bay of Bonifacio. But most elements from past myth, like Charybdis or the Planktai, are illusionistic. They throw the whole geography into a cocked hat.' [1]

It would be fair to suggest that Plato's story of Atlantis has caused not only widespread fascination in our present era, but also widespread confusion. That is because the actual details in the narrative are so utterly fantastic in terms of scale that they are pretty well unbelievable, even from the viewpoint of our own sophisticated civilization's technological and engineering capabilities. That fact – added to the concept that the original island was supposedly refashioned by a titan god (Poseidon) – has induced scholars and scientists alike to discount the likelihood of Atlantis *per se* having ever really existed. So they have instead focussed entirely on the basic central ideas of there having apparently been a horrendous (possibly prehistoric) cataclysm and a sophisticated prehistoric society supposedly destroyed by it. Consequently, however, everything else in Plato's narrative has been treated by most commentators as mere 'window dressing', thereby missing the point that there is an important kernel of esoteric knowledge carefully concealed within it.

It is because of this simplistic approach, plus a complete failure to perceive and grasp the actual nature of ancient esoteric metaphor and allegory, that the real story has become so distorted. It is also the reason for the story having become increasingly more 'mythic' to modern perception as time has passed – even though the Ancients' use of symbolic language is well known. However, in order to understand the story and its background properly, we must first of all understand the nature of the times in which Plato (*c*427–*c*347BC) himself was living and writing. We can then perhaps begin to separate fact from apparent 'fiction', on the basis of a properly argued rationale.

Why should Plato have mixed up an esoteric allegory with the story of a historical continent and its people? Well, Plato was an acknowledged initiate in the sacred Mystery School tradition of Greece. As well as this, he would have been sworn to secrecy regarding his sacred knowledge by his priestly tutors in Egypt, where he is known to have spent an extended period during his formative student years. So conjecture might lead us to suppose that Plato may well have used a deliberate ploy

Figure 1. An ancient Greek bust of the philosopher Plato

to convey sacred knowledge to a wider public in safely guarded terms. There does not appear to be any other logical answer, as the story itself stands alone and unique within two dialogues – the *Timaeus* and *Critias*[2] – whose subject can only be construed as educational philosophy. But what reasons would have had led him to do so?

The Beginnings of European Interest in Egyptian Religious Culture

Some 250 years before Plato's day, in the early 7th century BC, we come across the so-called first of the Greek philosophers, Thales of Miletus, visiting Egypt for the first time.[3] This was a period when the days of Egypt's greatest glory were past, and its ancient social and religious culture was under intense pressure due to foreign invasion plus shifting political and economic realities in the region that were forcing Egypt to look outward to the Mediterranean. The opening up of unrestricted trade with other Mediterranean countries made Egypt more open to outside influences than ever before.

Having learned a little of the science behind the Egyptian philosophy of life, Thales returned to Greece and began propagating his understanding of the ideas which he had come across. The first and foremost of these concerned the universal 'waters' (or rather 'aethers') of Space, from which he had been told that all things were generated by emanation. However, Thales – by his own admission unable fully to understand and thus correctly transmit the

Egyptian system of thought – proposed to his disciple Pythagoras (c582–507BC) that he should go to Egypt himself and learn at first hand.

Pythagoras, whose intelligence and intellect were held in great awe by his peers, is said to have spent over 20 years amongst the Egyptians, first of all gaining full access to their School of the Mysteries and then learning of Egyptian science and philosophy in detail, at first hand. But he was not alone in going there. Other contemporaries like Anaximander also went and spent time under the tuition of the Egyptian priests of Sais and Heliopolis. They were then followed by a veritable procession of all the best-known Greek philosophers of the next 300 to 400 years, including Plato[4] – though excluding Aristotle.

The Decay of the Egyptian Mysteries

As already indicated, the public practice of the Egyptian Mysteries was in a considerable state of decay by this time. Although due in part to other cultural influences derived from earlier foreign invasions, it was also more seriously degenerate because of the internal corruption of the Egyptians' own basic esoteric philosophy of life. This decline had taken place progressively over some 1,500 years, initially through a growth of materialistic opportunism in the higher echelons of Egyptian society, in the search for greater international influence and wealth creation.

That in turn led to the appearance of nepotism and family-based social divisions in Egyptian society where none had existed before. It also resulted in a liberalization in the hitherto strict performance of religious ritual, leading to a progressively widespread loss of self-discipline amongst the lesser priesthood and a resultant 'leakage' of fragments of esoteric knowledge which, through ignorance, were taken out of context. There then occurred a 'professionaliza-tion' of the priesthood which progressively led to the appearance of theo-logical literalism and the blind pursuit of ritual for its own sake, without the understanding that underlay it – as occurs so extensively in every religion. The consequent spread of spiritual ignorance plus a loss of faith and knowledge in the lower orders of the priesthood eventually resulted in the appearance of a fear of death amongst an increasingly cosmopolitan population. This was an entirely new phenomenon in Egypt. Amongst the indigenous Egyptians there had previously been no such fear, due to Egypt practising a doctrine of 'progressive livingness' (completely misinterpreted by modern Egyptology), involving a scheme of reincarnation.

It may well have been such trends that prompted senior Egyptian priests to welcome intelligent and spiritually motivated Greeks (and probably others too) into their halls of learning to pass on their knowledge of Egyptian philosophy and way of life. Some 500 years earlier, the idea of foreigners having direct access to Egyptian sacred knowledge would almost certainly have been out of the question.

It is a fascinating coincidence – *if* it is a coincidence – that at the same time that the Egyptian Mysteries were being opened up to such thinkers as Thales and Pythagoras, Gautama Buddha (*c*566–*c*486BC) appeared on the scene in Nepal and northern India in an effort both to restructure Brahmanism and also to open it up to participation by laypeople in general. In addition, a more 'public' form of Chinese philosophy was being taught by Laozi (or Lao-Tse, *c*6th century BC) who appeared almost simultaneously, pushing the 'Dragon Mysteries' of ancient Chinese philosophy progressively into the background. In Central America, it seems that the pre-Maya, Mysteries-orientated Olmec civilization quite suddenly and inexplicably came to an end at around the same period. (The archaeologists who claim that the Olmec culture ended *c*400BC are indulging in pure guesswork, starting from an assumption that the Americas were only colonized from *c*20,000 years ago – something which has already been shown as completely wrong.)

The fact that all of this happened two-thirds of the way through the zodiacal cycle of Aries is also interesting. That is because it appears to be a general and esoterically logical rule in each zodiacal cycle (and in the cycle of every religion) that such a moment sees the appearance of a 'renaissance' and 'reformation' of the culture of the time. Such has happened within recent history in the Christian tradition, and it is taking place in Islamic culture right at this very moment, two-thirds of the way through its own main cycle of existence. However, during the zodiacal age of Aries – which traditionally commences the great 25,920-year cycle of precession – such change had special significance because it would have indicated a planet-wide 'reshuffle' of human consciousness.

The Greek Mystery Schools

At and before the time of Thales and Pythagoras, some two centuries or so after the writing of the *Iliad* and *Odyssey* by Homer (8th century BC), the religion of Greece devolved around its own Mysteries. However, these Mysteries had undoubtedly already been in existence for at least a thousand years, probably considerably longer – it is worth noting that the Greek historian Herodotus (*c*484–*c*425BC) claimed they were derived from the ancient Egyptians.[5] Although modern scholarship seems to imagine that the various Greek Mysteries were unconnected – which again merely shows a complete lack of insight into the ancient way of thought – these Mysteries were essentially (and sequentially) threefold in nature, as follows:

1. The Eleusinian Mysteries

Open to literally all people – men, women and children – except murderers, the Eleusinian Mysteries were themselves twofold, being divided into the 'Lesser Mysteries' and the 'Greater Mysteries'. The ceremonial rituals of the former were held annually, whilst those of the latter took place only every five years. In essence the Eleusinian Mysteries dealt generally and through symbolism with the underlying nature of Creation. Hence they expressed in mystical terms the cyclical appearance and function of all Creation's various powers and forces – represented in the guise of major and minor 'gods', 'nymphs', 'demigods', 'heroes', and so on. As a result, the population was raised from early childhood with a core understanding of Nature and its seasonal cycles (symbolized by Demeter and Persephone/Kore) as not just a chaotic state, but as something operating under intelligent and hierarchically directed rule, according to certain inherent and inviolable laws.

2. The Orphic Mysteries

Centred around the mythic figure of Orpheus, the demigod hero-minstrel whose lyre-playing and singing charmed the gods and Nature itself, the esotericism within this particular Mystery tradition was focussed on the experiential development of the psycho-spiritual individuality in man – the Ego. Thus, through the sweet and bitter extremes of human experience, the faculty of psycho-spiritual discrimination was developed, enabling the individual to distinguish between the qualities and forms of the lower spiritual world (then referred to as 'Earth') inhabited by souls and those of the 'Underworld' (of objective human existence) inhabited by mere 'shades'. Many ancient cultures followed the same concept of a triple world scheme involving a Heaven-world, an Earth-world and an Underworld, inhabited respectively by a host of divine souls, spiritual souls and terrestrial souls. This scheme has been serially misconstrued by both mediaeval and modern scholars, who have all failed to recognize that the 'underworld' is in fact this phenomenally objective (but actually illusory) world in which we ourselves live, the physical body-form being the lowest 'shade', which is itself informed and animated by the human terrestrial soul.

In this tradition, Orpheus symbolizes the individual human spirit which engineers the whole process of evolution through intelligent control and discipline of the lower nature, thereby leading to gradual spiritual liberation of the lesser soul nature. Euridyce, the 'wife' of Orpheus, in fact represents the individual's terrestrial soul, which is borne off (esoterically, and as a matter of due cycle) to the 'Underworld' (as part of the cycle of reincarnation), from where she has to be recovered by Orpheus (the Orphic intelligence following her and then leading her back to the surface of 'Earth'). He, in the story, of course looks back towards the Underworld to see if she is following him and thereby condemns her to another cycle of existence there. In short, the story has to do with the whole principle and process of reincarnation and personal karma (a Sanskrit term meaning the 'universal law of cause and effect'). I have explained things here in a manner which I hope will clarify the overall concept for the average reader.

3. *The Dionysian Mysteries*

Centred around the figure of Dionysos, another mythic demigod-metaphor, these Mysteries were focussed on the progressive self-realization of the highest divinity in human nature. The Dionysian Mysteries were thus originally considered the most sacred of all. However, they were completely misunderstood by Romans, medievals and modern scholars alike, few of whom were able to perceive the inner truths concealed by the esoteric metaphors of the vine, the phallus and the Bacchic frenzy of the elemental Maenads, the female followers of Dionysos. Instead, they have mistakenly regarded these metaphors merely as literal evidence of licentious orgy. Whilst there is little doubt that this is indeed the degenerate form into which the ritualistic meetings fell in later Roman times, it certainly did not coincide with the original approach, which was fastidiously ascetic.

Corruption of the Greek Mysteries

The Greek Mysteries too had already begun to decline and corrupt by the time of Thales and Pythagoras. That is almost certainly why they went looking elsewhere for esoteric inspiration. Originally, the gods, demigods and heroes had been treated by all with due respect as esoteric metaphors – representations of natural forces and universal truths. Within the vast Greek pantheon, ranging from minor water spirits and tree spirits and other *genii loci* ('spirits of place') through demigods and up to the great elemental deities of Mount Olympus and beyond, was concealed the whole mystery of humanity's own sacred progression, the gradual spiritual evolution towards self-realized godhood. Now, however, these metaphorical beings began to take on a literal, even personal connotation in the mind of the Greek priesthood and public. The very same thing had by then already happened with Egyptian religion.

However, this happens in every religious belief system, in every zodiacal cycle, and we can see its unfortunate replication in the 'fundamentalist' and 'evangelical' trends in Judaic, Christian and Islamic religion today. No longer were the divinities of the Mysteries treated with reverence and respect as universal *principles* and expressions of universal Truth. Instead they were treated either with contempt as objects of mere superstition, or with fear and grovelling obeisance as actual divine personages, to be cajoled and placated on account of their arbitrary moods and whims or otherwise because of a desire for 'divine approval'.

The wholly allegorical stories of the gods' and demigods' adventures consequently began to take on quasi-historical dimensions, with the result that a sort of ancient 'political correctness' began to inform public attitudes (as we will see below in the case of Socrates). Not surprisingly, all the real spiritual light within the Greek Mysteries gradually departed as this infection took hold, and in consequence there occurred among the Greeks as a whole a natural drift away from what had previously been the automatic acceptance of dignified religious observance.

Latterly, in the time of Aristotle (384–322BC) and thereafter, the gods and demigods increasingly became figures of fun and ridicule for their supposedly amoral antics. The growing disbelief in them was not just because Greek philosophical thought was 'growing up', as many modern scholars assume, but rather because increasingly little understanding and practice remained of the purely esoteric side of Greek religion. The disintegration of the public practice of the Greek Mysteries followed on quite quickly as younger generations of Athenian intellectuals decided that they did not wish to be associated with the merely mythic figures of comedy and subversively antisocial behaviour with which – through scholarly misinterpretation – we are familiar today.

The Tragedy of Socrates

In Plato's time, this degree of open degeneracy had clearly not yet been reached. Philosophers had still to be very careful not to breach openly the religious mores of the time. Whilst thinkers of Thales' and Pythagoras' time might in retrospect be seen as the initiators of a sort of 'renaissance' of true esoteric philosophy, they tended to keep their own thoughts and those of their followers within their own 'schools', well apart from the rest of Greek society, in order to avoid the inevitable conflict that would arise from lay citizens taking the side of one belief system or another.

Imagine, then, the crisis that occurred during Plato's own young manhood (c410BC) when his teacher, Socrates, made no attempt whatsoever either to conceal his philosophical thoughts, or to relate them to the civic gods – a prudent move that most thinkers were careful to follow, whatever their private views. Socrates questioned the basis of literally everything in life. In addition, he did so whilst holding firm to the idea that every person's own *daimon* (his semi-divine spirit, or higher Self) was his sole teacher and guide.

This viewpoint, denying as it did the power and role of the gods, thoroughly scandalized the politically correct nature of Athenian society, and public opinion ultimately forced the Archons (the political governors of Athens) to put Socrates on trial for heresy and sedition (since his views were deemed likely to undermine Athenian society at large). He was found guilty and condemned to end his own life by drinking poisonous hemlock. Although appalled in retrospect at what they had done to such a brilliant and highly spiritual man, the Archons were discredited among the Athenian intelligentsia and effectively had to draw a line under any such future action against philosophers. The tragedy of Socrates thus had a silver lining, for it ultimately allowed far greater free-thinking among Athenian philosophers.

Plato's Technique

However, in the short term, any attempt by Plato to follow Socrates by openly discussing matters pertaining to sacred knowledge, ran the high risk of being treated in the same way. It should be appreciated that Greek 'rational' or discursive philosophy and its open form of discussion were, at this time, in their very early stages of development. However, in his writings and teaching in his own school, the Academy, Plato opened up all sorts of avenues of *public* interest and debate which no philosopher before him – excepting Socrates, the great maverick – had openly dared approach. As already mentioned, all preceding philosophers had tended to keep their ideas and disciples largely segregated as a group from mainstream society.

This is similar to the pattern followed generally by the *gurus* (spiritual teachers) of India and the Far East, where their disciples are taught in secluded retreats, or *ashrams* – a word (Sanskrit *ashrama*) perhaps related to the Greek word for a sacred grove, *asra*. In fact, there is at least a hint that the name Pythagoras was only an adopted one, perhaps – in view of his time in the East – borrowed from the Sanskrit title *pitar-guru*, meaning 'father-teacher' and used by disciples of spiritual masters.(In similar fashion, 'Plato' is also an assumed name, probably meaning 'broad shouldered' – a nickname acquired during his youthful training as a wrestler. His real name was Aristocles.)

It is interesting to note that, in Plato's story, the Egyptian priests, who were described as having talked to his ancestor, Solon, expressed the view that the Greeks – even a century or so earlier – tended to be rather shallow in their fascination with mere intellectual novelty. The various forms of 'philosophical' dialectic later pursued by the Greeks, involving clever argument for the sake of it ('sophistry'), confirm this tendency and it is interesting to note that it was even absorbed by the much later Jewish intellectuals of Alexandria in their pursuit of Aristotelian philosophy.

It was a combination of this peculiarly aggressive Greek approach to philosophy and the growing influence of Greek culture generally which led to the complete and utter corruption of the Egyptian spiritual culture. This was already halfway complete by the time of Alexander the Great, who conquered Egypt in 332BC. From the time of Alexander's death, Egypt was under the rule of a Greek dynasty, the Ptolemies, who ruled from a new and thoroughly Hellenic capital, Alexandria, until they in turn were overthrown by the Romans. It was under the ignorance and exploitation of Roman rule that Egypt's traditional religious culture finally died.

Notwithstanding what modern scholarship has to say on the subject of our civilization owing its foundations to the Greeks, there can be little doubt that this is actually an unconscious *criticism*. The Greeks of the later Classical era – other than those pursuing the Ancient Wisdom tradition through the use of sacred metaphor and allegory, in the manner of Pythagoras and Plato – again tended to use intellectual dialectic in an analytically destructive manner. It was precisely that approach that opened the door to a fixation with empirical literalism and speculative intellectualism in the style of Aristotle. That in turn then led to the politically based (but outwardly philosophical) anti-heretical dogma of the later, Christianized, Romans and then to the even later re-liberalization of thought during the European Reformation and Renaissance. (The intervening medieval period was characterized as an oasis of light amidst an ocean of orthodoxy.) This in turn gave rise to the modern, technologically based so-called 'Age of Enlightenment'.

Jeremy Naydler deals with this very question of modern scholasticism's inability to understand, or even contemplate, the real nature of ancient mysticism as having a scientific basis or even a clear rationale to it.

> For several centuries a fundamental assumption of modern Western culture has been that the way to attain to reliable knowledge is through science rather than through religious or mystical experience, and that science was a product of Greek, not Egyptian civilization ... In this paradigm [Francis Bacon's method of dry, Aristotelian empiricism] scientific knowledge is purged of personal opinion, feeling or value judgement ... Its objectivity is thus guaranteed, whereas the insights, visions or revelations of religious or mystical experience are viewed as irredeemably subjective, impossible to verify or repeat by third parties, and thus unreliable sources of knowledge.
>
> The second part of the assumption, that it was the Greeks who invented the one and only reliable method of attaining knowledge called science, began to take root considerably later – during the 18th century, when William Warburton and others first argued that the Egyptians were unable to think scientifically or philosophically ... But slowly the view took hold that it was the Greeks who laid the foundation of the scientific pursuit of knowledge and that the cultures of Mesopotamia and Egypt that existed before that of Greece were 'pre-scientific' and 'pre-philosophical'.[6]

Plato as the Cornerstone of Philosophical Change

As we have seen, Plato – despite being an avowed Pythagorean – was clearly an initiate of the true and ancient Mystery tradition, who saw his role as a positive propagator of the *rational basis* – in modern terms – of that tradition. But as the Roman historian Ammianus Marcellinus (4th century AD) tells us, Plato acquired 'his glorious wisdom' from the Egyptians.[7] It was thus Plato, I might suggest, who first brought to general public awareness the science and art of psychology and who also brought Greek philosophy into the modern era. Despite the fact that his Academy in Athens produced the metaphysically myopic Aristotle and his own followers, the 'peripatetics' – who moved philosophy fundamentally away from its spiritual focus and thereby created the foundations of materialistic science – there can be no doubt that Plato's greatest achievement was the intellectually systematic clarity and force of his own presentation. It was this which made possible a necessarily complete break from the by then moribund Mysteries of Greek tradition.

It was as a direct consequence of this right-angled turn by Plato, away from the then current conventional, blind pursuit of the Mystery rituals and traditions, that Aristotle and his school of 'peripatetic' philosophers were able progressively to move even further away from reliance on such religious ceremonials. That is even though these ceremonies were already in terminal decline anyway – just as Christianity largely is today. Other modern parallels could also be drawn with Freemasonry, generally treated by most of its adherents as almost entirely concerned with fellowship and philanthropy. Today, its rituals tend to be seen as existing mainly for the purposes of 'social bonding' as a community or cultural fraternity, rather than for reasons of spiritual education in the Mystery tradition from which these rituals derive.

Aristotle

The extent of the Mystery Schools' decline is apparent in the fact that, whilst the Hermetic (Egyptian mystery) and Platonic traditions clearly acknowledged the heliocentric nature of the solar system, Aristotle's seemingly did not (the same is also said of the famous Graeco-Egyptian geographer Ptolemy of Alexandria [cAD85–c165], but this is based upon a clear misinterpretation of his ideas). However, as we can see from studying Plato's writings, his whole philosophy is rationally scientific (or scientifically rational), even though much of it – for example dealing with the nature of creation and the soul – is still treated by modern science with deep suspicion. But then modern science and scholarship tend to follow the Aristotelian method of employing inductive (and thus almost entirely speculative) empiricism rather than using philosophically deductive logic.

Perhaps it was because of Aristotle's complete failure to grasp intuitively deduced truths, such as those related to astronomy, that Plato felt himself compelled to deliver the allegorical side of his story of Atlantis in such public terms. It is clear from Aristotle's writings that he certainly failed to perceive that there was far more to Plato's story than a merely fictional tale. One suspects that Plato's comment on one occasion when Aristotle was away from the Academy that 'the Mind is not here today', reflects a degree of wryly ironic humour, the nickname perhaps hinting at a degree of arrogance on Aristotle's part rather than an accolade.

Atlantis as Allegory

Whatever Plato's reasons for dressing up aspects of his knowledge in metaphor and allegory, it is quite clear that the traditions of Atlantis as a historical civilization and culture were by then widely familiar to the Greek public. After all, some 300 years earlier Homer had spoken of the 'Atlantes' as an ancient people of northwest Africa in his *Iliad* and *Odyssey* – revered epics that were used as basic educational texts throughout the Classical Greek and Roman periods. So the idea of the Atlantes being an ancient people of (north-)west Africa could hardly have been anything other than mainstream public knowledge by Plato's time. But Homer also deals in all sorts of other esoteric traditions – all having an astronomical basis – by retailing them as mythic stories. These were almost certainly widely understood in their true sacred context amongst the initiated of Plato's time.

For example, the story of Jason and the Argonauts is *all* astronomical metaphor and spiritual allegory. In it, Jason starts off with 49 (a deeply esoteric 7 times 7) companions in his ship, the *Argo*. However, the name *Argo* derives from the ancient Egyptian concept of the *Akhu*, an ancient word meaning a hierarchy of 'fallen' divine spirits. The 'ship' has to be steered between a great marine vortex (Scylla) and a cattle-eating demon (Charybdis) who lives in a glass-sided cave, each being metaphorical aspects of the entrance to our local universe. The twins who guide the ship through the most perilous waters are Castor and Pollux, synonymous with the two stars of the same name which lie close to that point in the Milky Way, through the plane of which our solar system cyclically passes in its own great orbital path – and so on.

Ancient Astronomical and Astrophysical Knowledge

Long before Homer, the Greeks seem to have inherited an extensive knowledge of astronomy, which is to be found concealed in the stories associated with the Greek Mysteries. One such story is that associated with Sisyphus, husband of the missing Merope, youngest of the Pleiades – seven sisters who represent the group of seven stars referred to by the same name. In the tale, Sisyphus is condemned by the gods to spend his life in eternity rolling a great rock up a hill, only to have it roll back down to the bottom every time he reached the summit.

This allegory is in fact a straightforward depiction of the angled orbital movement of the Earth (Sisyphus's rock) around the Sun. However, it is also a recognition of this being a general principle in celestial nature (on the basis of the great esoteric principle of 'as above, so below'); for entire solar systems were undoubtedly held to orbit at an angle around parent stars in the same way. Hence, for example, the phenomenon known to us as the 'precession of the equinoxes' (its cycle being known to the Ancients as the 'Great Year of the Pleiades').[8]

Figure 2. The legendary Sisyphus rolling a rock up a hill, from an ancient Greek vase

There will be many who would question whether Plato could have been able to formulate any clear idea of the solar system's constitution and movement in Space. Such objections would of course be on the grounds that astronomical technology and knowledge was not sufficiently developed at that time. Yet, despite the modern misconception that Hipparchus 'discovered' the precession of the equinoxes in 127BC[9], it is clear that not only was the heliocentric nature of the solar system well understood by then (and had already been known for many thousands of years) but also that the 25,920 year cycle of precession was just as well recognized – and used in astronomical calculations.

Herodotus, who visited Egypt before Plato in the mid 5th century BC, was told by the priests of Sais that their astronomical records covered at least the previous two cycles of precession. Their very specific statement to him that 'four times within this period, the Sun changed his usual position, twice rising where he normally sets and twice setting where he normally rises'[10] is a clear indicator that the precessionary cycle is what is being described. Furthermore, it also indicates that precession is not quite the phenomenon based upon a mere planetary 'wobble' that modern science believes it to be.

Rather interestingly, another Hipparchus – not the supposed (and much later) 'discoverer' of precession – is mentioned in the *Timaeus* and *Critias* as being aware that the Assyrians possessed highly detailed astronomical knowledge and supporting data going back over 720,000 years.[11] Diodorus Siculus (1st century AD) also mentions something along the same lines in his historical writings, in relation to the Chaldeans' astronomical observations going back 473,000 years.[12]

The modern suggestion then, that precession could not have been known of until the 2nd century BC, appears rather to lack support from the Ancients themselves. These same details also call into question modern anthropological orthodoxy which, c720,000 years BC, still has humankind running around in skins as a mere cave-dwelling 'hunter-gatherer'; but it would be something of a distraction to pursue that issue any further just at this point.

The Background to the Story

Plato was the son of a noble and highly respected Athenian family and thus perhaps unlikely to be dealt with in the same manner as Socrates if he were to make his views known to the broader Athenian public. However, he evidently decided that some degree of discretion was called for in the shorter term, in relation to the promulgation of his philosophical ideas and ideals, probably on behalf of his followers as much as himself. He seems to have decided that whilst the development of 'scientific philosophy' by debate and its subsequent spreading had to continue (amongst those willing to listen), it should be couched in terms which the 'politically correct' masses just would not understand, even though they were already familiar with the general outlines of the story of Atlantis. That they were indeed familiar with it is evident in the fact that, even in Plato's time, during the feast of the Little Panathenaia, the ceremonial *peplos*, or veil, which was carried around the city of Athens and draped around Athena's statue was decorated with scenes of 'the great war between the Athenians and the Atlanteans.'[13]

De Santillana and von Dechend also remark about Plato and his technique:

> Plato knew ... that the language of myth is, in principle, as ruthlessly generalizing as up-to-date 'tech talk'. The manner in which Plato uses it, the phenomena which he prefers to express in the mythical idiom, reveal his thorough understanding. There is no other technique apparently, than myth, which succeeds in telling structure. The 'trick' is, you begin by describing the reverse of what is known as reality, claiming that 'once upon a time' things were thus and so, and worked out in a very strange manner.[14]

It is perhaps unsurprising in the face of this that the merely *enlarged* description of 'Atlantis' came to be conceived by Plato and eventually emerged in an immediately semi-recognizable form, with the names of its central characters having been devised to represent particular functions or characteristics in Nature. This was of course a literary technique as common in ancient times as it was during the era of Shakespeare, himself a well-known user of other ancient stories in his plays. However, the central part of Plato's tale also contained – in metaphorical and allegorical form – ancient *scientific* knowledge which, at the time, was still held to be sacred and not for general public dissemination. What exactly was that scientific knowledge? In the following chapter we will begin to answer that by reminding ourselves of the story of Atlantis itself, following Plato's own narrative.

Chapter Two

·

THE INTERPRETATION OF PLATO'S 'MYTH'

'The order of Number and Time was a total order preserving all, of which all were members, gods and men and animals, trees and crystals and even absurd errant stars, all subject to law and measure. This is what Plato knew, who could still speak the language of archaic myth.'[1]

The Story of Atlantis

Plato begins his account (and immediately lends it respectability) with his famous ancestor Solon, an Athenian archon, or governor, and one of the seven sages of ancient Athens. Solon is in Egypt, where he encourages one of the priests of Sais to tell him about the island of Atlantis as it was in his day (c600BC), some 9,000 years after the cataclysm. The priest describes it thus:

> In comparison to what there then was, there are remaining in small islets only the bones of the wasted body, as they may be called, all the richer and softer parts of the soil having fallen away and the mere skeleton of the country being left.[2]

The priest of Sais also describes the origins and geography of the original, pre-cataclysmic island:

> On the side towards the sea and in the centre of the whole island, there was a plain which is said to have been the fairest of all plains and very fertile. Near the plain again and also in the centre of the island, at a distance of about fifty *stadia*, there was a mountain, not very high on any side. In this mountain there dwelt one of the Earth-born primeval men of that country, whose name was Evenor, and he had a wife named Leucippe and they had an only daughter who was named Cleito.[3]

The Titan god Poseidon then fell in love with Cleito and

> broke the ground and enclosed the hill on which she dwelt all round, making alternate zones of sea and land, larger and smaller, encircling one another; there were two of land and three of water which he turned as with a lathe out of the

centre of the island, equidistant every way, so that no man could get to the island, for ships and voyages were not yet heard of … He also begat and brought up five pairs of male children, dividing the island of Atlantis into ten portions. He gave to the first born of the eldest pair his mother's dwelling and the surrounding allotment, which was the largest and the best, and made him king over the rest. The others he made princes and gave them rule over many men and a large territory. And he named them all. The eldest, who was king, he named Atlas and from him the whole island and the ocean received the name of Atlantic.[4]

A First Explanation

There are several main points of interest here. First of all let us take a look at the symbolism associated with the god Poseidon (figure 3) because, as we shall see, this is crucial to the interpretation of the overall story in both a metaphysical and an astronomical sense.

In Greek myth, the younger generation of gods (the Olympians), led by Zeus, overthrew the older generation (the Titans) led by Zeus's father, Kronos. After this conflict – the original 'Battle of the Titans' – Zeus appointed Poseidon to command Ocean, the waters that lay between the heavenly world of Olympus and the underworld, the domain granted by Zeus to their brother Hades. But this story of the three Titan brothers becoming rulers of adjoining 'kingdoms' is actually an ancient esoteric metaphor (within an esoteric allegory) for three *kosmic* states of being or consciousness. (Note that 'Kosmos' means the totality of the subjective and objective universes, whereas 'cosmos' is merely the objective part.) In order to understand this in its proper context, however, we need to see a graphic model by way of reference (figure 3).

In this diagrammatic model we see seven kosmic states of consciousness. All ancient philosophical systems insisted that every scheme of being had an internally sevenfold structure. This is of primary importance in our understanding of the Ancients' esoteric metaphors and allegories. As we can see, it involves two triple groups of states, plus one intermediate state. However, the lowest of the seven states contains within itself another sevenfold system in microcosm, the lowest sub-state of which then follows suit according to the same concentrically repetitive principle. This is also implicit in the 'divine Tetraktys' of Pythagoras which contains further implicit triangles between the various points – and so on into infinity. Hence the ancient idea that 'the point is everywhere and nowhere at the same time' (figure 4).

According to the Ancients, following the principle 'As above, so below', the whole universe was concentrically organized – as Ptolemy indicates in his *Tetrabiblos*. Hence our *solar* world, the lowest of the seven kosmic states (which in turn contains the sevenfold planetary world scheme), was the 'underworld'.

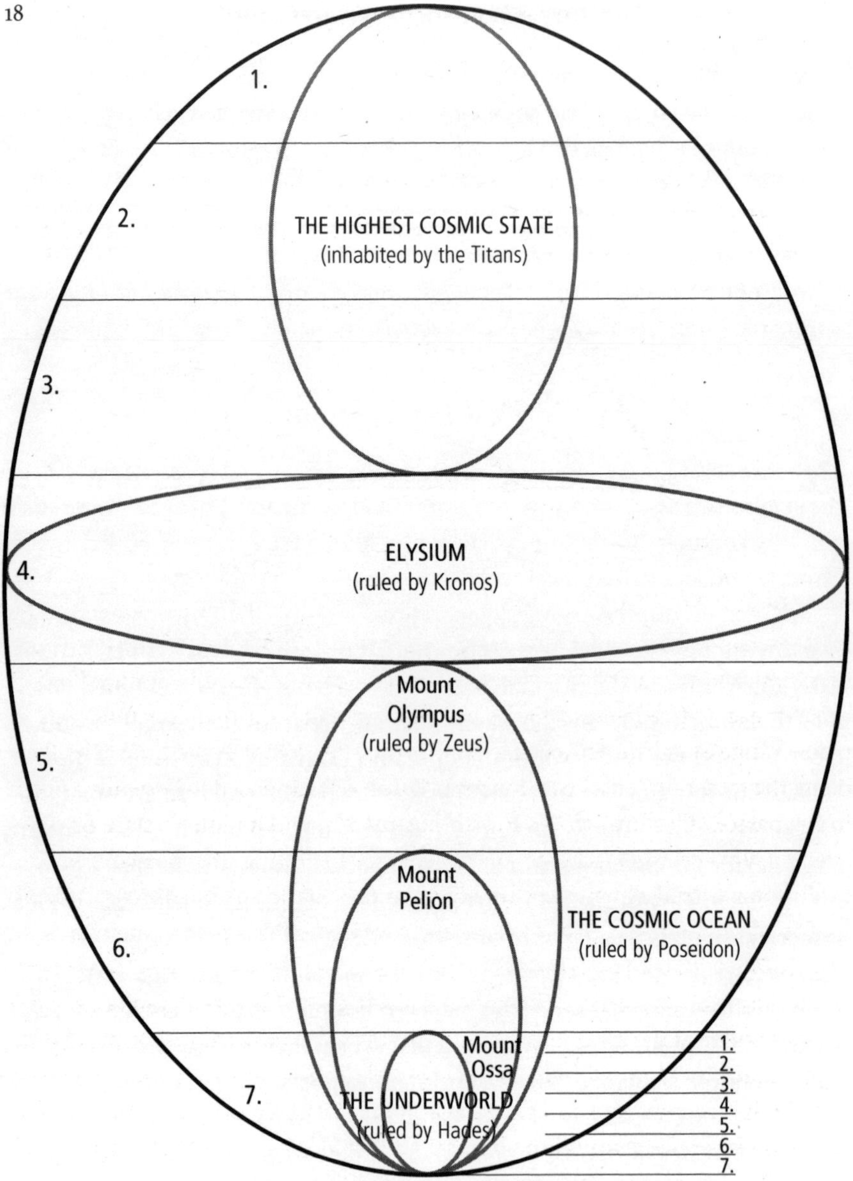

Figure 3. The ancient Greek view of the sevenfold kosmos

The sevenfold kosmic system was seen as the overall field of consciousness of an absolutely inconceivable duality of Being – Gaia enfolded by Ouranos. In the Greek scheme, the female Gaia and male Ouranos were represented as the first gods, the 'parents' of the Titans and 'grandparents' of the Olympians. Modern scholars have misinterpreted both names. Gaia means that portion of kosmic Space (not Earth) contained by Ouranos (i.e. Aura-Nous, the enfolding Mind-emanation of the Logos principle). In one sense, one could say that

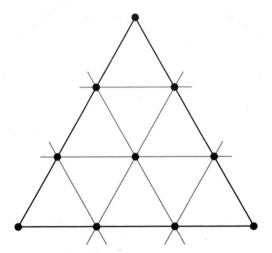

Figure 4. The sacred tetraktys *of Pythagoras*

Gaia means matter and Ouranos means Mind. Within this system, certain hierarchically organized functions – akin to those possessed by humankind – existed, each of the seven planes or states comprising that function plus a whole range of sub-functions. Hence Kronos, the god of cyclic time as well as being the father of Zeus, Poseidon and Hades, was supposed to lie gently asleep in his palace (Elysium) in the fourth kosmic state. (The fourth state or sub-state in any celestial scheme or organism (including the human) is the evolutionary 'bridge' between the higher and lower triads of consciousness – spirit and matter respectively – in the scheme. It 'sets the tone' in a manner corresponding with the fact (recognized by musicians) that *Fa* is the predominant musical note of our own planetary Nature.) At the same time, Zeus became the supreme ruler of the lower three kosmic worlds. Zeus's kingdom – represented symbolically by Mount Olympus – was peopled by Titans, gods and demigods at its higher reaches and by nymphs, satyrs and various other psychic exotica on its lower slopes. Around the base of Olympus lay the great circular sea or river called Ocean and below them both lay Hades' Underworld.

Macrocosm and Microcosm

The sevenfold kosmic system being the super-macrocosm of the sevenfold human organism, Zeus symbolically represents the highest aspect of the kosmic mind (akin to the human spiritual Ego), whilst Poseidon represents the field of kosmic desire and Hades the chthonic field of the kosmic body form. Hence it was that Zeus was depicted in the Greek Mysteries as forever becoming amorously involved with goddesses, nymphs and even human women – all symbolic of the mind's constantly flitting range of interest – whilst his 'thunderbolts' were merely a metaphor for the power of the kosmic will-force.

In like manner, the divine brothers Prometheus (another Titan god) and his less intelligent brother Epimetheus were symbolic of the higher and lower aspects of the kosmic mind (intelligent organization and indiscriminate memory respectively). The story of Prometheus (signifying the principle of Imagination) bringing the 'celestial fire' (of the mind principle) to mankind down in the Underworld and then being suspended by Zeus in eternity between two great hills, is a straight allegory of the dynamically evolving relationship between our very own highest and lowest human natures, in terms of consciousness. Correspondingly, the story of the slower-witted Epimetheus (signifying Memory) and his wife Pandora – who, through curiosity, released all the worst karmic vices into the human world – is yet another allegory associated with the cycle of evolutionary unfolding of human consciousness.

Metaphorical Waters

Poseidon was one of the less talked about gods of the Greek Mysteries. That is mainly because – like the Egyptian river god Hapi – he remained largely concealed from view during the generally peaceful, rolling existence of his watery medium. He only became 'visible' during inclement weather – hence the power-association of the oceans and seas and rivers with 'currents' of passion. Greek myth had six 'rivers' flowing down from Ocean into the Underworld, these being directly associated with the six lower sub-states of Hades (the name of the god is commonly used as a synonym for his domain). The four lowest of these (corresponding with the elements of fire, air, water and earth) involved the 'involutionary cycle' of descending Nature spirits – the Salamanders, Sylphs, Undines and Gnomes – which were held to give form to the lower world order. These rivers were the Styx, Kokytos, Phlegethon and Acheron, all of which were said to converge in a great marsh at the very centre of Hades. The fifth and sixth rivers, descending from Ocean into the higher parts of Hades, were Eridanus and Lethe.

These sacred rivers were together symbolic of the cycle of solar reincarnation – corresponding, on a higher turn of the evolutionary spiral, to the cycle of human reincarnation. This involved divine and semi-divine spirits,[5] descending into the solar netherworld of planetary existence and subsequently returning to their (lesser) Olympian home, before being forced back into the cycle. So, as we can see, there was an indirect relationship between Poseidon and the Underworld – the latter, as already mentioned, being an esoteric metaphor for the purely *objective* celestial universe.

Looking once again at Plato's story, we find Poseidon becoming enamoured of a female 'mortal' who lives, with her parents, on an 'island'. But that island is a local island *universe* – in other words, it is a solar system, or at least a prospective one, within which local Creation may be made to take place. But before this can happen, it has to be wrought from its primordially amorphous, pristine state into something rather more complex and this is precisely what Poseidon – the force of kosmic desire and will – does, by creating alternate 'rings' of land and sea around it. However, these too, it is suggested, are esoteric metaphors related to progressively advanced fields of being and consciousness.

The Occupants of the 'Island'

The original occupant of the island, Evenor, does not have a Greek-sounding name, and is referred to as 'Earth-born' and 'primeval' (as well as being one of many). Why such an odd description? Well, first of all, the ancients in general perceived three 'heavens' associated with our immediately local solar universe. As we saw earlier, 'Earth' referred to the central 'heaven' between the divine heaven world of the lesser Titans) and the Underworld, the latter however being synonymous with our own objective physical world state. Thus 'Earth' was the 'lesser' or 'intermediate heaven' – what we might today call the 'spirit world' – as opposed to its higher, divine counterpart.

Secondly, the fact that the almost Arthurian-sounding Evenor was 'primeval' implies that he represented one of the earliest hierarchies of spirits within that state. Thirdly, the fact that he lived 'in a mountain' which lay right at the very centre of the 'island' is interesting, because the Ancients quite frequently used mountains symbolically to represent a transition between one state of being and another. The Greeks had Olympus, Ossa and Pelion, for example, whilst the Egyptians also had a sacred mountain, or tumulus, which was itself a metaphor associated with the god Atum-Ra and his female consort, Hathor. She, the Egyptian equivalent of the Greek Demeter, is shown in various papyri as a cow goddess emerging from it, whilst the spirits of humankind hid inside it.

Linguistic Clues

One has to be rather careful in dealing with the significance of ancient names because their original provenance and pronunciation have largely been lost in the mists of time. Natural distortions of pronunciation (compounded by different written scripts) occur between different (and often distant) cultures over even relatively short periods of time. In addition, even in ancient times, words, names and ideas travelled widely between cultures along trade routes and mutated somewhat, even as they do today. However, one thing we can be sure of is that the Ancients considered names to be of great significance.

So, when we take a closer look at the three names in this part of the Atlantis story, certain ideas become apparent. To begin with, the name of Evenor's wife – anglicized in translation as 'Leucippe' – appears to be derived from two roots, the first of which means 'light', as in the Greek *leukos*, the Latin *lux* and the ancient Celtic god-name Lugos (the 'Shining One', later becoming Llew in Welsh and Lugh in Irish). The second element I believe to derive from the same root as 'sepher' and 'cipher', meaning 'number'. Hence the overall name would signify something like 'the divine hierarchies of Light', all such hierarchies in the ancient magical tradition, being known by a sequence of numbers, according to their respective functions.

The name 'Evenor', correspondingly, also appears to be the intended product of a multiple foreign stem, for example Af-en-aur or A-vin-ur, the prefix 'A-' meaning 'from' and the suffix '-or' (or '-ur') being a common ancient word meaning 'primordial', as in the 'Ur-Shu' (ancient beings of light) of the Egyptians. Alternatively, it could derive from 'aur' meaning 'encircling', as with 'aura' and the Greek god 'Ouranos' (i.e. 'Aura-Nous'). The 'vin' or 'ven' appears to have definite northwestern European overtones, as in the Nordic 'Vinland', and the Anglo-Saxon 'fen', which appears to imply an association with landlocked waterways – which seems very apposite in connection with the later hydrological re-engineering of the geography of the island undertaken by Poseidon.

However, there are other possibilities. The Indo-European root *win-* (light) (related to the root *vid/wid-*, knowledge, enlightenment, truth) is seen in Irish god Finn, the god of omniscience, whose followers, the Feinn or Fenians, seemingly represented the various aspects of Universal Knowledge. One can consequently see possible associations here too with the idea of containment. Whilst all this may perhaps seem obscure, it is elsewhere confirmed in the name *Ven-did-ad*, given to one of the holy books of ancient Persia, which means 'primordial Truth'.

The Creation Myth Background

The combined parental product then appears somewhat akin to the Greek traditions of Creation. In this the creative kosmic breath (the biblical Divine Spirit that moves over the waters) and fertilizes the 'ocean' of dormant matter. According to the Greek Creation myth, Ouranos (Aura-Nous, the encircling mind) then enfolds Gaia (again, the 'Earth', but really meaning a portion of Space) within his embrace and thus forces her to conceive or regenerate the various Titan gods.

In Plato's story, the 'child' of Evenor and Leucippe's union is called 'Cleito',

which although itself sounding rather more Greek, implies a second generation spiritual hierarchy. Poseidon, king of the Underworld 'waters' (in other
words, of our portion of space in general) then becomes infatuated with
Cleito. This, however, is a common ancient method of symbolizing the attraction of higher (kosmic) intelligences to the lower states of celestial being and
consciousness, into which aspects of themselves thus temporarily 'fall'. (This is
paralleled by the fallen biblical 'Elohim' who in Genesis 'came in unto the
daughters of men', or the Greek gods depicted as lusting after both nymphs
and human women.)

The Meaning of Cleito

When we look closely at the name 'Cleito', or more accurately Kleito, we find
that there appears to have been no such female name in general use by the
Greeks, although 'kleit-' is found prefixed in some Greek male names and
appears to be the root of the word for a 'hill'. However, if we adjust the anglicized spelling to conform with ancient esoteric nomenclature (the ll of the
Celtic Welsh language, for example, being pronounced 'cl' or 'tl'), we can derive
from it the compound 'Llha-Itu'. Now 'Llha' (or 'Lha') is a common name in
the ancient world for a creator spirit whilst 'Itu' – being the plural of 'Iti' (as in
the Vedic 'Ad-iti' and the Polynesian 'Tah-iti') – meant 'the higher heaven
world' in many cultures around the world. This was frequently represented as
being located on top of a hill or mountain – like Olympus.

Tah-iti, however, appears originally to have been 'Tau-iti'. 'Tau' or 'Tao' is of
course 'the Way' in the Chinese tradition – the dualistic origin and end of the
solar cycle of existence. However, it actually derives, we suggest, from 'Taur-us',
meaning the zodiacal bull – of which Poseidon is himself the symbol. Hence
also in the Greek tradition we have the 'Minotaur' which is itself derived from
'Men-a-taur', meaning the 'mind-from-the-bull', or a 'spark' of kosmic intelligence which originates in and has 'fallen' from the zodiacal constellation of
Taurus into a lower world system and cycle of existence. This is a concept on
which we shall enlarge in subsequent chapters in relation to Atlantean
humankind.

The Imposition of Kosmic Will

The overall implication then is that Cleito (or Lha-itu) is the representative
hierarchy of divine creator spirits in the lower solar universe, upon which
kosmic desire (represented by Poseidon) imposes its will. Hence this hierarchy
is symbolically depicted as the 'bride' of the greater kosmic intelligence. As we
shall see in a later chapter, the Ancients believed there to be a direct correlation

between the circumpolar constellation Ursa Major (the 'leg' of the zodiacal Bull, bitten or torn off by the kosmic Crocodile,[6] Draco), the Pleiades (the 'Seven Sisters') and our own solar system. This is central to ancient cosmological esotericism all over the world and, as we shall also see later on, it was directly associated by the Ancients with the appearance of Man, the divine spirit, specifically within our own solar system.

One of the ancient techniques of esoterically depicting the unfolding of universal principles of function, or otherwise of states of consciousness and associated states of being, was to provide a family sequence. This, for example, is done in the ancient Greek tradition, where Ouranos and Gaia produce six pairs of Titan children – each pair being male and female – thereby arriving at an overall sevenfold structure. Within this we then find that one pair of Titan gods – Kronos and Rhea – give rise to a lesser (solar) scheme via their own six children (three males: Zeus, Poseidon, Hades; and three females: Hera, Demeter, Hestia).

In Plato's story of Atlantis, when we add to the primal trio the five alternating strips of 'land' and 'water' which Poseidon is described as carving out of the 'island', we have, I suggest, the following structure, each strip of land of water actually representing the various universal elements:

1. Evenor and Leucippe – representing the divine solar-to-kosmic state of being

2. Cleito – representing the semi-divine solar state of being

3. Water – Aether

4. Land – Fire

5. Water – Air

6. Land – Water

7. Water – Earth

The Universal Sevenfold Principle

As we shall see again in slightly different contexts, we have in this a sevenfold structure and dynamic, which, as we have already noted, is without exception the foundational basis of all ancient esoteric and cosmological systems, wherever in the world we find them. The essential idea inherent in it is the same as that involving the seven colours within the spectrum of white light and also the seven notes in the octave of the harmonic scale. In other words, the octave generates the *hebdomad* or sevenfold structure and dynamic out of the lower aspect of itself and then, at the end of the cycle of existence, withdraws them back into itself. As we shall see in further detail in the next chapter, this is the nature of the soul principle.

As we have already suggested, the 'fall' from the kosmic state which is represented by the desire of Poseidon for Cleito must sequentially be into the lower, solar universe state of the kosmic Underworld. So, if Evenor, Leucippe and Cleito live in a 'mountain'[7] right at the very centre of the solar *state*, what are we being told? The implication is that this original 'island' is in fact a dual metaphor – on the one hand symbolizing the solar state as a whole and on the other the objective solar system itself. So, in the latter instance, the 'mountain' at the very centre of the 'island' would be actually no less than the Sun at the centre of our solar system.

Thus the implied meaning is that kosmic desire (Poseidon) unites itself with one of the foundational solar hierarchies and thus forces it to generate out of itself a series of five *dual* states of being and consciousness.

The 'Children' of Poseidon and Cleito

Thus it is that Poseidon begets upon Cleito 'five pairs of male children', who – Poseidon dividing the land between them all – are just as clearly symbolic of the driving influences within the dual (centrifugally outgoing and centripetally inward-drawing) aspects of the five universal elements (aether, fire, air, water and earth). If we continue to treat this as a dual allegory, however, we could also speculate that the five pairs of 'brothers' are perhaps also intended to act as the counterparts of the ten planets (counting the Sun as a planet, as astrologers do) within our solar system (*see* figure 5).

This of course works only on the basis that the Ancients were fully aware of all the planets and their respective movements within our system, which is, however, a possibility that modern scholarship and science would at present reject, claiming that Neptune and Pluto were unknown before modern times. However, as we have already suggested that there are clear indications that the Ancients did indeed know of all the planets, we shall proceed on that basis, whilst also taking into consideration the parallel of their representing the dual aspects of the elements.

Atlas, First King of Atlantis

The first son of Poseidon and Cleito is named Atlas and made king over all Atlantis. For his own use he is given the central part of the island, which is 'the largest and the best'. This is not altogether surprising because Plato's Atlas is a synonym for the principle of light. This sheds light on the other Greek myth featuring Atlas, where he appears as a god – the Titan brother of Prometheus

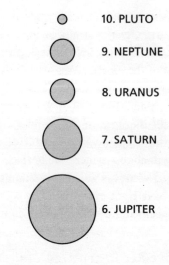

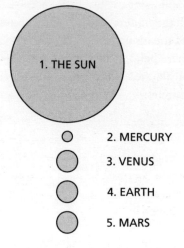

Figure 5. The ten-planet sequence. There is a direct relationship here with the chakras, or energy centres, in humankind, with Mars representing the spine base chakra, the Sun the heart chakra, Jupiter the throat, Saturn the top of the spine, and so on.

and Epimetheus – who is condemned to stand in the far West of the world and bear the heavens on his shoulders. (Actually, there is reason to believe that Atlas also bears an astronomical correspondence with the constellation of Orion). Esoterically, Atlas is the Sun, holding the heavens and underworld (the kosmic mental and physical states) apart. Given that the central part of the 'island' bears a striking resemblance to the Sun at the centre of our solar system, which is supposed to be the source of the principle of light, we can immediately see the correspondence.

Meanwhile, the twin brother of Atlas is rather interestingly given the outer-most ring of territory, metaphorically located in the vicinity of the 'Pillars of Herakles' (traditionally regarded as the 'gate' to Hades). This, however, is directly reminiscent of the esoteric allegory behind the story of the two bibli-cal brothers Esau (who was 'red and hairy' like the Sun) and Jacob (who was 'smooth', like the 'crystal sphere' that was believed to surround the solar system). It also recalls the story of the two Aztec gods Nanahuatzin and Tec-ciztecatl (the latter having a 'pock-marked 'face', just like the Sun), who are described as having to choose which one of them was going to jump into the central solar fire and who was going to remain on the perimeter. In Plato's story, however, we have eight other planetary 'sons', beside these two, whose 'kingdoms' are unspecified. But the narrative continues as follows:

The Massive Reconstruction of the Atlantean Island

Plato tells us that 'Atlas had a numerous and honourable family and his eldest son handed on to his eldest for many generations.'[8] In other words, there were many solar cycles following the original 'Creation'. Plato follows this, however, with a litany of all the minerals, plants and animals which contributed to the amazing wealth of the island (the solar system) – not altogether surprisingly, because what is here being talked about is the appearance, from a germinal spiritual state, of all these kingdoms, sub-kingdoms and species in solar Nature. Plato continues:

> All these things they received from the earth [the spiritual state] and they employed themselves in constructing their temples and palaces and harbours and docks; and they arranged the whole country in the following manner. First of all they bridged over the zones of sea which surrounded the ancient metropolis and made a passage into and out of the royal palace;[9] and then they began to build the palace in the habitation of the god and of their ancestors.
>
> ...
>
> And beginning from the sea, they dug a canal 300 feet in width and 100 feet in depth and 50 *stadia* in length [that is, nearly 6 miles (10 km); 1 Athenian *stadion*, or stade = 606 ft (185 m)] in length, which they carried through to the outermost zone making a passage from the sea up to this, which became a harbour and leaving an opening sufficient to enable the largest vessels to find ingress. More-over, they divided the zones of land which parted the zones of sea, constructing bridges of such width ... and roofed them over; and there was a way underneath for the ships, for the banks of the zones were raised considerably above the water.
>
> ...
>
> The palaces in the centre of the citadel were constructed in this wise: in the centre was a holy temple dedicated to Cleito and Poseidon, which remained inaccessible,

and was surrounded by an enclosure of gold; this was the spot in which they originally begat the race of the ten princes and thither they annually brought the fruits
of the earth in their season from all the ten portions.[10]

Plato's Solar and Planetary Metaphor

We see from this description that the central 'temple' remained inaccessible in
perpetuity (for what good reason?) and was surrounded by an enclosure of
'gold' – in other words, by the solar photosphere. As we shall see in Chapter 5,
esoteric philosophy holds that the Sun and planets were originally one
nebuloid mass, before they separated – hence 'here they originally begat the
race of the *ten princes*', that is, the planets.

Additionally, of course, it was here that all the 'fruits of the earth' were
brought 'in due season' because at the end of each cycle, the expended or
radiated matter from the planets is (again, according to esoteric philosophy)
recycled back to the Sun, the central 'furnace'. These materials are described as
being used for the subsequent construction of the entirely metaphorical
'temples, palaces, harbours and docks'.

We turn next to the central, 300-ft-wide 'canal' and the raised 'embank-
ments' around the 'zones', plus the 'roofing' over of the 'bridges'. What is all this
about? In order to understand it, one must first conceptualize what takes place
when all the planets within the solar system are orbiting around each other,
whilst the solar system itself is sailing through space on its own cyclical
passage. Figure 6 describes the solar equivalent to the Earth's atmospheric
belts.

Whilst this can only provide a vague parallel, what we see involves the
following correspondences, just to take three examples.

1. The central plain is the solar equatorial plane – what astrophysicists today
   call the 'interplanetary magnetic field' – whilst the 'Hill of Evenor/Cleito' is
   the Sun.

2. Because of the Sun's forward motion through Space, and the angled elliptical orbits of the planets around it, the resultant effect is that the central
   'plain' or solar horizon becomes ringed by 'mountain chains', symbolic of
   their upper orbital path.

3. The 300-ft-wide and 100-ft-deep canal from the outer 'sea' to the innermost
   landmass appears then to correspond with the 'bow wave' opening in the
   solar field caused by its forward passage through the 'ocean' of space. This
   opening passes 'under' the angled orbits of the various planets as they
   themselves pass around that side of the Sun.

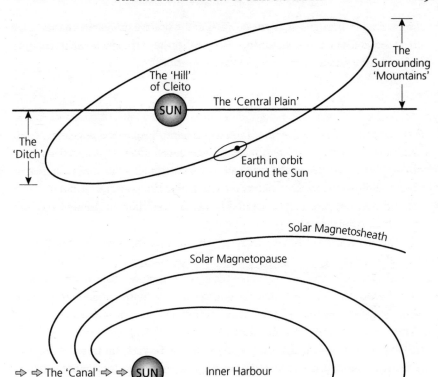

Figure 6. Plato's description of his 'island' is in reality a metaphor for the movements of the heavenly bodies in our solar system.

Plato's description continues:

> Crossing the outer harbours, which were three in number, you would come to a wall which began at the sea and went all around; this was everywhere distant 50 *stadia* from the largest zone and harbour and enclosed the whole, meeting at the mouth of the channel towards the sea ... The whole country was described as being very lofty and precipitous on the side of the sea, but the country immediately about and surrounding the city was a level plain, itself surrounded by mountains which descended towards the sea; it was smooth and even but of an oblong shape, extending in one direction 3,000 *stadia* and going up the country

from the sea through the centre of the island 2,000 *stadia* [i.e. 10,000 stadia in perimeter]. The whole region of the island lies towards the south and is sheltered from the north.

...

I will now describe the plain ... It was rectangular and for the most part straight and oblong [a curious mixture indeed!] and what it wanted of the straight line followed the line of the circular [probably meaning ellipsoidal] ditch. The depth and width and length of this ditch were incredible and gave the impression that such a work, in addition to so many other works, could hardly have been wrought by the hand of man ... It was excavated to the depth of 100 feet and its breadth was 1 *stadion* everywhere; it was carried around the whole of the plain and was 10,000 *stadia* in length.[11]

The Inconsistencies of the Story

Now why would any architect or engineer – no matter how much of a genius – want to build a sea wall which not only encircled the harbours (at a distance of over half a mile) but also the island as a whole?[12] And why would a gigantic ditch, 100 ft deep and 600 ft wide (30.5 x 183 m) be built around the plain as well? Given the effort involved, not even an antediluvian Isambard Kingdom Brunel would have conceived of such unnecessary civil engineering monstrosities. Neither statement makes any sense – if taken literally rather than symbolically. However, it does make sense if the 'ditch' is seen merely as a metaphor for the lower end of the orbital path of each planet relative to the solar horizon.

The Atlantean 'sea wall' on its own is extraordinary enough, but, encircling the whole island it would have been an impossible undertaking. That is because of the necessity of using a progressive sequence of giant coffer dams extending several thousand miles in length, out at sea, in order to build seriously immense concrete walls capable of withstanding the most powerful oceanic currents. However, nowhere in his description does Plato mention anything about the amazing technology needed to carry out any of the phenomenal building or civil and marine engineering projects he describes. In fact, the whole tenor of his description of Poseidonian culture is quite clearly *non*-technological.

Numerological Significances

Quite apart from this, Plato's constant allusion to specific numbers is very noticeable and would be highly unusual in any merely descriptive, as opposed to technical, narrative. But given that Plato is purporting to record his childhood memories of listening to his grandfather Solon, such detail seems even more unusual. However, as the Neoplatonist philosopher Proclus (cAD410– 458) remarks,

> Plato, for the sake of concealment, employed mathematical names as veils for the truth of things, in the same manner as theologists [sic] employed fables and the Pythagoreans symbols. For it is possible in images to survey paradigms and through the former to pass to the latter.[13]

The Ancients, however, also used number to define esoteric potencies. For example, thousands indicated the hierarchical potencies of the spiritual realm or 'fourth heaven', whilst millions alluded to the divine powers of the 'seventh heaven'. The numbers six and ten were of great importance in an astrological as well as a numerological sense. That is because the whole system functioned around the powers of the Decan gods, which, as described in the *Hermetica*, are responsible for literally generating the rotational activity of the celestial bodies of our local universe.

The number six, on the other hand, represented the dualistically operating nature and power of the Aeonic gods (the Greek form of the Indo-Tibetan demiurgic hierarchy, the 'Ahi'), such as we find in the '*saros*' and '*naros*' system of computation of the Chaldeans and Babylonians. Thus, for example, 6 x 6 x 10 = 360, i.e. a full circle, or cycle of celestial revolution whether of a planet or a local universe. (The saros was 3,600 years.)

We find the very same numbers re-appearing later on in Plato's narrative. For example:

> As regards their manpower, it was ordained that each allotment (of which there were ten) should furnish one man as leader of all the men in the plain who were fit to bear arms; and the size of the allotments was 60,000 ... Each such leader should provide for war the sixth part of a war chariot's equipment, so as to make up 10,000 chariots in all. Such then were the military dispositions of the royal city.[14]

This rather interestingly brings to mind the fact that the biblical Exodus from Egypt (another wholly allegorical account) supposedly involved 600,000 'departing' Israelite men, before even considering women and children. Just as unbelievably, these are then described as spending the next 40 (4 x 10) years in the 'wilderness' of Sinai. But the term 'Israelites' is merely another esoteric metaphor for humankind's 'fallen' yet 'returning' spirit, the Asur-el.

The Occupants of Atlantis

> Each of the ten kings, in his own division and his own city, had the absolute control of the citizens ... The relations of the governments to one another were regulated by the injunctions of Poseidon as the law had handed them down ... There were ten bulls who had the range of the temple of Poseidon.[15]

Here we find the idea that each of the ten planets or the dualistic (involution-ary and evolutionary) five elements was (and is) run according to universal law. It is interesting to note that the ancient pre-Hispanic Guanche people of the Canary Islands (*see* Chapter 15) also maintained a system of ten kings, with one supreme over all the rest.

Man As a 'Divine Bull'

The other concept of there being ten Poseidonian bulls is a curious one, again clearly related to the zodiacal constellation of Taurus and to bull worship. However, as we suggest in later chapters, even the idea of bull worship has been seriously misunderstood by scholars as supposedly deriving from the erro-neous conception that human civilization only commenced during the Age of Taurus, some 4,000–6,000 years ago.

Bull worship is in fact linked to two other related ancient concepts: first, that the divine spirits of humankind had fallen en masse, from an original celestial state amongst the stars of the Milky Way, into the sphere of 'fixed stars' – and thus the constellation of Taurus; secondly, that when thus 'fallen', humankind eventually became fully spiritually Self-aware of its own highest aspect – as a 'divine spark' of kosmic will-force. As ancient Egyptian texts describe it, the 'Inner Man' automatically became the 'bull of his mother' (the 'mother' being the 'Oversoul' of planet Earth). However, this only happened at that point when, through spiritual individualization, it had already left behind both the human and spiritual kingdoms in its onward evolutionary progress.[16] The human spirit had thereby become a semi-divine and thus fully fledged 'planetary spirit' – what the Vedic traditions of India refer to as a *dhyan chohan.*

Hence the mentioning of 'ten bulls' is, I suggest, actually a reference to these guardian spirits of the ten planets, whereas the ten princes or kings who ruled over the ten areas of landmass appear to refer to other hierarchical groups of divine intelligences. The fact that the ten bulls had free 'range of the temple of Poseidon' makes it quite clear that this is another esoteric allegory because, as in Freemasonry, the 'temple' is a metaphor for the overshadowing 'soul' principle. But more of that later.

The tradition of humankind's innermost or divine nature being (esoterically) that of a bull was widespread throughout the ancient world. For example, in the non-biblical book of Enoch, Noah is described as having been a bull before becoming a man; in the Babylonian epic of Gilgamesh, Enkidu is described as half-bull, half-man, as is also the Greek Minotaur; and the god Merodach (Marduk) in the Chaldeo-Babylonian tradition is the 'Bull of Light'. The bull – by virtue of its relationship to the zodiacal constellation of Taurus – was absolutely central to Hindu, Egyptian, Cretan, Iberian, Assyrian, Mithraic and Celtic traditions, as well as many others including, in the form of the buffalo, those of the Americas.

As we shall see in the next few chapters, the idea of man having been born a 'bull' (esoterically) ties in fundamentally with the astrological basis of *all* ancient religion. It also acts as the foundation of *all* ancient beliefs regarding the nature of humanity's divine origin and essential spirituality. However, because that is tied in with all sorts of other astronomical and astrological issues, I shall leave it to one side just for the moment in order to conclude our comments regarding the metaphor and allegory in Plato's tale.

The Extent of Ancient Psychology

If what we have suggested so far is true, then it is clear that the Ancients had an extensive knowledge of astronomy,[17] although fundamentally based upon evolutionary spiritual issues and not merely seasonal or climatic ones likely to affect crops, and so on, as modern anthropologists assume. In fact, they must have possessed an astronomical knowledge extending far beyond that of modern science which, despite its technology, still has no clue as to the *principles* behind the origin and structure of our local universe.

One might ask why the Ancients could not have just made their knowledge on such issues public? Would it not have helped to improve the general intellectual quality of their culture? What was the point of keeping such things secret in the first place? The answer to these questions lies in the fact that the Ancients regarded knowledge not in our modern utilitarian fashion, as something merely to be exploited for gain, but literally as progressive access into the very Mind of Deity. They were not so much concerned with 'knowledge as power', but rather that 'a fragment or area of knowledge *was* a Power'.

By virtue of this perception, there were all sorts of accompanying powers with which individuals would come into contact once a particular area of knowledge was made known to them. By coming into conscious contact with such powers, the individual could automatically – by sympathetic association – *contain* them and thus take on something of their nature. However, if lacking in self-discipline and self-control, the person would to some degree be over-come by the powers. This would lead to the derangement of his subjective nature, resulting in madness, so endangering both himself and also the community at large.

This might strike the reader, to begin with, as somewhat far-fetched. However, it is based upon an ancient perception that there is a fundamental unity of existence in the universe and that *a* consciousness is derived from what we might call 'intelligently controlled isolation' – which is almost a definition of 'self'. Paradoxically perhaps, intelligence is based upon the principle of 'self' – but 'self' can develop into either 'self-discipline', thereby leading to intelligence (which is fundamentally ascetic or self-denying and altruistic in nature), or it can develop into mere 'self-ishness' with a consequent drift into either incoherent self-indulgence or the blanket pursuit of self-centred power.

It logically follows that any spiritually orientated culture, concerned to develop and maintain a harmonically coherent intelligence, would seek to make deeper levels of knowledge progressively (but slowly) available to all, according to each person's own desire for such. However, this would have been on the understanding that everyone who sought greater enlightenment would also submit to a progressive test of their self-discipline, as well as their altruism. This then is the basis of the ancient system of initiations into the 'Mysteries' – admissions into progressively deeper, wider and more inclusive areas of conscious awareness and understanding, through a process of educational training and examination of a much broader and more thorough type than usually found today.

The Evolution of Human Intelligence in General

The opening up of greater areas of knowledge to general public awareness of course carries the danger that such knowledge, in the absence of the disciplines provided by acknowledged social ritual and its associated controls, is like an over-excited wild horse. This area of social psychology was well recognized in ancient times and it lies behind the biblical allegory in the biblical Book of Revelation, where it talks of 'the Beast' cyclically being allowed free rein in human society for a given period before it is eventually brought back under control.

The 'Beast' is the personification of *subjectively* rampant elemental Nature in humankind. This, like the Dionysian Korybantes or Maenads, wreaks karmic havoc wherever there is no conscious acknowledgement of the guiding power of a higher divine intelligence in humankind, or, consequently, the self-conduct to match. Thus in the Greek tradition, the demigod Dionysus was presented in allegorical terms as a great benefactor of humankind – but he would destroy any human being who did not acknowledge him and pay him due obeisance.

The progressive opening up of human consciousness which we have already described as commencing around the time of the Buddha, Pythagoras and Lao-Tse, is indicative of a natural phase of *apparent* corruption and eventual regeneration which takes place not only during each astrological Age, but also within each greater sidereal cycle involving several 'Great Sidereal Years' (1 sidereal year = 25,920 Earth years). These great changes see the widespread, root-and-branch destruction of old systems of culture and civilization in order to make way for the new ones that will eventually spring up to replace them. However, remnants of the old system inevitably tend to persist for some considerable time afterwards, to baffle and fascinate historians and antiquarians.

At least one tradition suggests that the demise of Plato's Atlantean island (and much of the *real* ancient Greek culture co-existent with it) was actually the result of *two* such astrological cycles coinciding, thus causing a much greater degree of destruction than would otherwise occur with the single cycle. But more of that later. There is also an accompanying suggestion of some degree of intelligent intention and purpose behind the way in which these changes work. However, that is something on which I shall also touch much more specifically in the next few chapters. To begin with I will now move on to discuss the issue of consciousness itself and the way in which it was represented by the Ancients.

PART TWO

·

PLANET EARTH

Chapter Three

·

THE GENESIS OF INTELLIGENCE

'The number seven unfolds an equal number of ideas and even more in the case of incorporeal things which are perceptible only by the intellect; and its nature extends also over every visible essence, reaching to both Heaven and Earth, which are the boundaries of everything. For what portion of all the things on Earth is there which is not fond of seven, being subdued [only] by an affection and longing for the seventh?'[1]

Knowledge derived from mere human experience is very variable. The body of current knowledge of our planet, for example, is very largely based upon an intellectual paradigm structure, which involves a central set of opinions founded upon a mixture of partial perceptions and interpretations, plus a whole range of assumptions. It is also covered by many different scientific disciplines and sub-disciplines, each rather jealously guarded by its own specialized hierarchy from the world of academia. It is only very recently – really since James Lovelock suggested in 1988 that the Earth is a sort of self-balancing organism (*see* below) – that any true interdisciplinary approach has begun to emerge. Yet, a quarter of a century later, that sense is still in its very formative stages and lacks any sort of genuinely universal coherence.

In the Introduction to this book, I pointed out that the Ancients held to the view that – there actually being no such thing as 'dead' matter – the universe and every celestial body within it had to be a multi-aspectual and multi-functional organism. It follows, however, that if Earth is indeed an organism, geology alone cannot begin to answer all the queries as to how and why it functions. But no more can zoology, botany, anthropology, climatology or any other science. It can only be done by commencing the other way around – with a general, overall appreciation of the fact that there is a systematic linkage of intercommunicating *sentience* between not only all the kingdoms of Nature, but also all the elements (including the climatic functions) as well.

Only once we, as interested enquirers, have established that clear perception in our minds, does it become possible to start looking into each scientific discipline with sensible perspective. We can then more effectively establish how, where and why each discipline fits into the bigger, overall picture. That applies to cataclysms and anthropology as much as it does to nanotechnology and even quantum science.

Why mention all this in a book on Atlantis? Well, as I have indicated, the subtitle to this book should perhaps give the clue. In order to have any real chance of knowing what the true Atlantis and its prehistoric culture (and cataclysms were all about, we surely have to commence by understanding something of the philosophy of the Ancients concerning the evolution of our world and those aspects of its functional unity which have been passed down to us within the last 5,000 or so years of recorded history. That is because our own ancient, inherited culture – according to tradition – was derived, at least in part, from the Atlanteans. The other reasons for this approach will become much more apparent in the last three chapters on Atlantean religion, magic and technology.

To begin with it needs to be said that whilst there are fundamental differences of approach to the world of knowledge between the Ancients and present-day scientists and scholars, they are all still talking about the same things. This chapter concerns itself with explaining some of those differences of approach and showing how and why, for the Ancients, *philosophy and science were one and the same* – as opposed to the artificially divorced and frequently antagonistic couple which we know today.

As we shall see, the major area of difference lies in terms of interpretation and presentation. That is because the Ancients saw Universal Nature as an infinitely interactive organism within which the sub-organism of our own planet (and the sub-sub-organism of our own species) had a particular range of functions to fulfil. As we shall also see, our approach in this chapter and the next also provides the foundational rationale for answering the hotly debated question as to whether modern human beings were derived from Darwinian evolutionism or biblical creationism – or neither. This is fundamental not only to the issue of Atlantean anthropology, but also to the whole question of ancient humanity's relationship with the other kingdoms of Nature.

The Intellectual Attitudes of Academia

Modern (Western) scientists and philosophers are curiously divided concerning the universe and the consistent laws and order found throughout it wherever one looks. They refuse on principle to entertain the idea of a suprahuman (divine) creative and organizing Intelligence; yet they are forced to admit that the universe functions like a great Mind. One of the latest to admit this (albeit obliquely) is the British Astronomer Royal, Sir Martin (now Lord) Rees, who is also professor of astronomy at Cambridge University. In a recent (2004) television documentary entitled *What We Don't Know About the Universe* he asked: 'Could we ourselves be involved in some sort of great computer simulation?' and 'Could what we think is the universe be some sort of vault of heaven rather than the real thing?'[2]

Of course, computers are machines created by the minds of humankind. So, when it is observed that the universe appears to scientists to behave like a computer, it is a clear indication that it is actually behaving like a mind – or at least, like that part of the multi-functional mind principle which we humans use to organize and replicate data. From the philosophical viewpoint, however, this 'computerized aspect' of the universe is only representative of the merely repetitive and organizational 'lower mind' principle. The 'higher mind' involves discriminative reason and ethical perceptions which are completely beyond the range of the merely reactive or instinctual logic and function that characterize even the most sophisticated computers. It is thus associated with 'self-conscious intelligence'. But, quite logically, some of the celestial orders of being are said to contain both. Hence it is that humankind is said to be the microcosm of the macrocosm of the kosmos. This functional difference of the lower and higher mind was depicted by the ancient Egyptians in symbolic metaphor in the form of the Sphinx at Giza, involving a lion's body with a human head.

But computers use hierarchically organized systems for their operation – which implies that a 'computerized' universe too must have its variously operative component groups. These must also be organized by function, in a manner remarkably similar to ancient descriptions of the functionally distinctive legions of angels and Nature spirits.

Previewing the evolving modern scientific mind some years before the above admission by the Astronomer Royal, the scientific journalist Richard Milton pointed out that:

> In the baffling new world of modern physics, scientists find themselves observing and examining a cosmos that has become less and less like a clockwork machine and more like an intelligence. Whether the intelligence is that of ourselves, the observers, or that of the world we examine, is not yet clear and may perhaps never become clear. But it would surely be absurd to bestow intelligent characteristics upon the behaviour of nuclear particles yet fail to accord such characteristics to living structures.[3]

Anthony Flew, the internationally renowned emeritus professor of philosophy at Reading University in England, is yet another whose views appear to be re-orientating themselves in the same direction as that of the Ancients. In recent years, despite having been an avowed and lifelong atheist, he has admitted that the most recent scientific discoveries clearly indicate the existence of an organizing intelligence at work throughout the universe, although he continues to deny this an equality with the religious idea of God. Furthermore, like Richard Milton, Flew has stated quite unequivocally that the Darwinian theory of evolution just does not work – specifically because the idea that the first living matter evolved out of dead matter and then evolved by mere chance into complex organisms is, in terms of purely rational logic, 'simply out of the question'. As professors Hoyle and Wickramsinghe have pointed out:

> Biochemical systems are exceedingly complex. So much so that the chance of their being formed through random shufflings of simple organic molecules is exceedingly minute, to a point indeed where it is insensibly different from zero.[4]

Intelligence in Nature

There is an equally curious division in our own present-day public perception of the Earth. On the one hand, there is an increasingly general acceptance of the mineral, plant and animal kingdoms having an as yet unspecified form of positively interactive relationship with one another. This combines to make of them a sort of ecologically coordinated and finely tuned multiple organism, with its own inherent checks and balances. On the other hand, this perception has not yet fully extended to seeing humankind, and not at all to seeing climatic elements, as part of the organism. Yet, at the quantum level of existence, at least, both are also fundamentally part of Nature on Earth.

In 1988 Professor James Lovelock, a Fellow of Britain's prestigious Royal Society, put forward the then apparently revolutionary idea that every part of the Earth, including its rocks, oceans and atmosphere, as well as all organic entities, was a part of one great living and intelligent organism.[5] This idea is now part and parcel of everyday social conviction, even amongst politicians, and even industrial and commercial concerns pay it lip service (while remaining more interested in pure profit than in the philosophy of wholism). Yet the idea itself has curiously never been openly pursued to its logical conclusions – involving the necessary recognition that the Earth's (to us) *invisible* elements are also part of this same organism. They too must somehow possess a faculty of sentient consciousness, along with all the rest, for the whole to work together.

The atmospheric elements have both characteristic form and considerable force, irrespective of the fact that their forms are far less apparent and more short-lived than those of the mineral, plant and animal kingdoms. But clouds and storms, for example, have definite life cycles and their tendencies are definitely (at least to some extent) predictable by climatologists, even though scientific knowledge in these fields is still only in its relatively early stages.[6] Even seas and lakes have their corresponding characteristics.

It follows from simple logic that the creation of any phenomenal form or function in Nature must require a causal *noumenon* (which roughly translates as an innate guiding spirit), involving, at some level, both awareness and intent – something materialistic science refuses to acknowledge. From the very fact that all matter is living, it also naturally follows that any active phenomenon must be the product, or by-product, of some or other form and degree of intelligence, or semi-intelligence, or combinations of both. Hence, as ancient philosophy had it, in universal Nature there is always the 'driver' and the 'driven'. Thus everything in Nature must logically have its discarnate 'architects and builders' just as much as it has bodily form – whether we are consciously aware of the fact or not.

It may seem strange to think along these lines, but anyone with personal experience of them knows that the manifesting forces within Nature sometimes seem to give their forms a strange (sometimes beautiful, sometimes deadly) percipient individuality and independence of their own. This, however, is *not* just the result of pure imagination, even though that cannot yet be 'scientifically' proved (other than statistically, by the common experience of educated and objectively intelligent people).

Given that we are trying to understand the question of Atlantis within the wider context of *world* history, our starting point in this book has to be therefore that the Earth in its entirety is indeed a living, breathing organism with an intelligently (albeit instinctively) coordinated sense of its own existence and purpose. Furthermore, bearing in mind that there is a general, ordered coherence and balance throughout Nature, it is logical that there has to be an overall principle of coordinated, *governing intelligence* central to and inherent in it. Otherwise there would be no evolutionary order and consistency – merely random chaos.[7]

However, the fact that some sort of directing intelligence has to be central to the way in which Nature operates on our planet (let alone in the wider celestial system) presents a huge problem to much of modern science and scholarship. That is because they function on the assumption that only human beings possess the principle of a rational, directing intelligence and that humankind is the highest intelligence on Earth. Why do they believe this? Because they assume that (a) the human species – the fourth kingdom in Nature – is the pinnacle of evolution; and (b) that only what can be seen and measured must be all that exists, even though this is flatly denied by quantum physics – and straight logic.

Where then lies this supra-human intelligence and how does it function? And what form or forms does it take?

The Drawbacks of Assumption

We live in an age where the concept of space travel beyond the Moon has become commonly accepted as a rational possibility. This fact plus UFO sightings and crop circle phenomena have led to a belief in some quarters at least – amongst conspiracy theorists – that the Earth and its natural kingdoms are in fact being manipulated in some extraordinary sort of interstellar genetic experiment which has been in progress since at least Atlantean times. But this wild speculation pays no attention to the whys, hows and wherefores of the *subjectively* multiple interactive connections between Earth's various kingdoms of Nature in their very own right.

The central problem is also compounded by those who follow biblical 'creationism' in purely literal terms – without actually understanding (or often wanting to understand) the process by which it might *perhaps* be able to operate within the laws of Nature. By virtue of their belief in the Bible, the Quran and so on as the literal 'Word of God' – in support of which claim, however, no argument has ever been offered (except the threat of blind force) – those who regard themselves as 'fundamentalist' in their literal beliefs are happy to accept in blind faith the rather varied and inconsistent biblical translations or interpretations of medieval scholars, rather than use their own powers of reason and common sense. For many of these literalists, using reason to question biblical 'authority' is next to blasphemy. For them, blind faith is itself a sort of spiritual testament or proof of their religious commitment. Yet true faith is actually based upon intelligent Reason – in the philosophical sense of insight into that which is, rather than that which is only mentally explained. It is *never* blind.

As yet, modern science is incapable of cross-examining Nature subjectively in any depth, its 'behavioural' science still being exceptionally crude and extremely limited. The simple reason for this is that it has painted itself into a corner by (a) assuming (without using basic logic) that there is such a thing as 'dead matter' and (b) insisting that brain and mind are the same thing. Thus, notwithstanding general acceptance of the Gaia hypothesis, science continues to insist that consciousness and intelligence cannot exist apart from the *objectively* physical form.

But laboratory testing plus straightforward logic and empirical reasoning by the more intuitive scientific intellects of our day are fortunately beginning to see through this veil of self-induced blindness. In this they have been partly aided by reference to the philosophical thought of the Ancients – who, from their written texts, had clearly considered the same issues untold thousands of years ago. For example:

> The Kosmos also … has sense and thought; but its sense and thought are of a kind peculiar to itself, not like the sense and thought of man, nor varying like his, but mightier and less diversified. The sense and thought of the Kosmos are occupied solely in making all things and dissolving them again into itself … There is nothing in which the Kosmos does not generate Life; and it is both the place in which Life is contained and the maker of Life … For the kosmic Life-breath, working without intermission, conveys into bodies a succession of qualities and therewith makes the universe one mass of Life.[8]

And elsewhere:

> The Kosmos also is ever-existent; but it exists in process of becoming. It is ever-becoming in that the qualities and magnitudes of things are ever coming into being … thus the universe is composed of a part that is material and a part that is incorporeal and inasmuch as its body is made with soul in it, the universe is a living creature.[9]

And again:

> But Life is the union of body and soul. Death then is not the destruction of the things which have been brought together, but the dissolution of their union … The Kosmos assumes all forms; it does not contain the forms as things placed in it, but the Kosmos itself changes.[10]

Energy and Spirit

As we can see from the above quotes from the works of the Egyptian priest-philosophers, as written down in the *Hermetica*, the Ancients openly confirmed their opinion that there was no such thing as dead matter in the universe, despite modern orthodoxy's completely illogical view that there is, or could be. The Ancients also saw that the whole of phenomenal existence involved a fundamental unity of Being, founded on the principle that there was but One Life in the omniverse. Hence everything – down to the smallest conceivable particle of matter – interactively shared in its Life-force and faculty.

Whereas today's science calls the active aspect of this by the name 'energy' and indiscriminately regards it as inanimate and thus purely (and homogeneously) *quantitative*, and therefore measurable, the Ancients called it 'spirit' and saw it in quite different terms as both living and *qualitative* – in other words, diverse in functional type and evolutionary capacity. Thus, from this

viewpoint, there is as much of a spectrum of spirit-being as there is a scientifically provable electro-magnetic spectrum behind the phenomenon of Matter.
In fact, bluntly put, the two must be synonymous.

This is of fundamental importance because it provides the operating
foundation of the principle of consciousness and also of the distinction
between 'being' and 'beings'. Thus a 'being' would thereby be defined as an
intelligently (or semi-intelligently) coordinated group of energies (or 'spirits')
with a 'common sense'. The fact that modern science dismisses spirit as an
abstraction or as unnecessary to its own hypotheses shows just how inade-
quately it has considered the whole issue – and why it has itself wound up with
such an absurdly materialistic view of life and Nature in general.

It follows logically from this that, just as there is a spectrum of celestial
forms – planets, comets, solar systems, nebulae, and so on (all necessarily
informed and conditioned by relative degrees of intelligence) – so there must
be a qualitative spectrum of accompanying and hierarchically organized
spirit-matter and spirit-entities to match. This is following the ancient tradition of terrestrial, spiritual and divine causation. The assumption by modern
science that matter is to be found in exactly the same qualitative state throughout our solar system – even though subject to the same universal laws – is
completely unjustified.[11] This was something recognized by the philosopher-
scientists of ancient Indo-Persia and Egypt as a fundamental fact of life. It
was also written down in their sacred texts in allegorical format to show the
principle of the naturally sequential progression (in consciousness) from one
state or sub-state of matter and being to another.

Intelligence in Creation

The Ancients held to the view that the principle of sensory intelligence (in
relative degree) was fundamental to *all* existence; hence the capacity of all
spirit-matter to respond so readily (and with due relativity) to the principle of
interactive Order – and consistently systematic Order at that – generated by
a Mind.[12] Hence also they would immediately have understood the general
principle behind Einstein's equation $E=mc^2$, involving the interconvertibility,
or relativity, of spirit and matter. Nevertheless, the Ancients would have added
to it the principle of a hierarchical *quality of light* as a mathematically calculable variable.[13]

In addition to that, they would have related it to both the microcosmic
quantum world of particle physics *and* the macrocosmic world of metaphysics – with which modern science has yet to come to terms. In other
words, in their view higher and lower forms of life, despite all having different
capacities, all necessarily function according to the same universal laws.

However, modern science will never understand these laws as long as it attempts to draw inference from merely technological measurement – which is again purely quantitative in nature and function.

The Ancients, furthermore, saw in the way that spirit functioned instinctive tendencies towards, on the one hand, constancy and balance and, on the other, change. Thus it was that they incorporated into their philosophy the idea of hierarchically ordered groups of spirit-beings. The purpose of these beings in Universal Nature was to pursue the expression of these same principles (of constancy/balance and of change), some of them in cycles of incarnation, whether in a kosmic, solar or terrestrial environment; hence the associated distinction which they made between divine, spiritual and terrestrial spirits and souls.

Hence also the distinction which they made between the 'angelic' hierarchies of Nature spirits (called *devas* in the Indian tradition and *neteru* by the ancient Egyptians) on the one hand, and 'Man' on the other. That is because Man – using the term generically to mean a self-conscious spirit – was seen as the initiator of all change (and thus also of all evolutionary instinct) in the universe. However, more of this in a moment when we come to deal with the issue of the distinction between humankind and animal in Lemurian times.

Spirit and Soul

Similarly to the way in which it dismisses spirit, modern Western science relegates the principle of 'soul' to the realms of superstitious fantasy – but again without actually understanding what it is rejecting. The 'soul' principle was as fundamental to the ancient system of philosophico-scientific thought as 'spirit'. That is for the simple reason that the soul was seen as a *group* of spirits with a coherently unified consciousness, plus a common sense of identity and purpose. At the same time, these soul entities were also composed of sub-groups, each having characteristically different functional instincts and capacities. Hence, following John Donne's poetic dictum that 'No man is an island unto himself', the consciousness of *every* individual entity, without exception, is itself necessarily part and parcel of a *group* consciousness. Thus it is that, for example, our consciousness is distinguished from the Atlantean and, in turn, the Atlantean consciousness from its predecessor, the Lemurian.

The soul-being was thus always regarded as possessing *a* consciousness and *a* sense of function, both instinctively and telepathically connected to the larger hierarchical group of which it formed part. Hence the principle of Universal Consciousness – of which *all* individual and group consciousnesses form part, by virtue of all souls being functional microcosms of the One Universal Soul.

It follows quite logically from this that each such soul consciousness necessarily contains within itself an again hierarchically organized spectrum of lesser group consciousnesses. From this we can deduce (as did the Ancients) that the terrestrial is contained within the spiritual which in turn is contained within the divine. This is in parallel to the fact that the terrestrial planet is contained within the solar system, which is in turn contained by the kosmic scheme of the nebula, or group of solar systems; and so on. It is as a direct consequence of this principle that a sevenfold spectrum of lesser *states* of being and consciousness is generated within each greater soul-field.

Thus it is also that the *involutionary*[14] impulsion to generate form always works from up to down whilst the *evolutionary* impulse correspondingly always works from down to up. This is something which our modern science at present completely fails to grasp, because it – albeit self-confessedly – fails to grasp the real nature of consciousness itself.

Rather interestingly, the English biologist Rupert Sheldrake has (perhaps unknowingly) stumbled upon the factual existence of the soul and its relationship with the nature of group consciousness. This is contained within his concept of *morphogenesis* (evolutionary change in the external appearance or body form), which he describes in his book *A New Science of Life* – and others. This adaptive change works as a result of what he calls 'morphic resonance' within and through 'fields' of consciousness.

Sheldrake's concept involves the idea that the subjective recognition by one entity in the animal kingdom of a useful change to previous practice leads to an automatic telepathic transmission of that same understanding to other groups (even overseas) within the same species, which then instinctively follow the same lead. Quite how this works Sheldrake has not yet explained in terms satisfactory to 'orthodox' science and it also fails to address certain important issues concerning group and individual consciousnesses. Nevertheless, Sheldrake's timely research is important and continues to attract widespread attention from scientists and the public alike.

However, one might draw certain inferences from his ideas, along the following lines.

The Nature and Form of the Soul

The form taken by the soul has bothered Western theologians for the last 2,000 years. Yet it is an important issue which we should deal with to some degree before moving on because it is currently open to so much misinterpretation. As we shall see, it is fundamental to the whole evolutionary process. Briefly then, the soul-body – like its microcosmic counterpart, the cell in an organic body – was regarded as a spheroidal or ovoid-shaped aura (or field) of light, of some or other quality and size, reflecting its terrestrial, solar or kosmic nature.

However, that same auric field was said to possess a definite peripheral 'membrane' and it is within and from this (just like the 'brane' of the quantum physicist's 'string' entity) that its intelligence and consciousness supposedly operate – by resonance and self-emanation. One can thus immediately see the connection with Sheldrake's concept. It should perhaps be added that, according to ancient tradition, this membrane is contained and kept in a coherent state by the focussed projection of a Mind (the Greek 'Nous') from a higher sub-state of being – again, whether of a terrestrial, solar or kosmic nature.[15] The Egyptian *Hermetica* confirms this same idea in relation to the Macrocosm as follows, although the principle works generally at all levels of being on the by now well-known basis of 'as above, so below':

> The Kosmos then has been made immortal by the Father, who is eternal. The Father took that part of matter which was subject to His will and made it into a body and gave it bulk and fashioned it into a sphere ... Moreover, the Father implanted within this sphere the qualities of all kinds of living creatures and shut them up in it, as in a cave ... And He enveloped the whole body with a wrapping of immortality that the matter might not seek to break away from the composite structure of the universe and so resolve into its primal disorder.'[16]

Interestingly, the same principle is also to be found in the very first verses of the biblical Book of Genesis where the Elohim, or Creator-Spirits, separate the 'waters' (of Space) above from the 'waters' of Space below and create a 'firmament' between them which they turn into a heaven world, from which all cycles of Creation then emanate. Similarly, it is to be found in the Mazdean tradition, where Zeroana Akerne – the 'Boundless Circle of Unknown Time' – radiates dark light from itself, which then mutates into the solar 'god' Ormazd[17]. He then gives rise to the operational duality of light and darkness in the forms of Ahura-Mazda and Ahriman. It appears in Egypt in the form of the great 'crystal sphere' of the world-soul created by the god Ptah (synonymous with the Indo-Tibetan 'Buddha') and also in the Greek, in the form of the Titan god Ouranos (Aura-Nous – the enfolding sphere of Mind).

Modern 'String Theory'

It is interesting to note that modern quantum science (albeit as yet unconsciously) finds itself in almost complete accord with this same concept. However, scientists in this field have not yet fully understood what their intuitions have already perceived in very vague outline. Consequently, they still conceive of and express their concept of a multitude of planes interacting with each other in the form of an essentially compressed, three-dimensional model, even though they talk of there being up to ten or twelve dimensions.

However, their description of the 'string' as a perpetually vibrating 'organism' in a state of relative tension is very close to a perfect description of the traditional form taken by the soul entity as a general principle in Nature. But more of that in the next chapter.

Soul As a Universal Principle

We might mention in passing the Ogdoad, or equal eight-sided geometrical figure, which is used to represent the eightfold, demiurgic 'demi-deity' which we today call 'the soul' principle; for that is precisely what the sphere of consciousness is and was always seen to be. Plato himself confirmed as much in his many writings. To him and to ancient philosophy in general, the soul was no abstraction. It manifested itself (again, as a sphere of light) in that aurically enfolding 'presence' which we (in our anthropocentric way) call 'the guardian angel'. Thus it was held to be responsible not only for guarding and guiding each sacred place or individual human being during their life, but also for literally providing the source of the very life, consciousness and function *of all organisms*. Hence *all* organic forms would appear to be but the marionette offspring of their parent soul – which is their true 'self'. Rather appropriately, Plutarch says on the same issue:

> They who imagine the mind to be part of the soul err no less than they who make the soul a part of the body; for the mind is as far superior to the soul as the soul is better and diviner than the body. The combination of the soul with the mind makes the Logos, or reasoning faculty ... The soul being moulded and formed by the mind and itself moulding and forming the body, by encompassing it on every side, receives from it impression and form.[18]

It is interesting to note that representation of the soul's maternally self-sacrificial role in Universal Nature is found in many traditions, even today. For example, one of the best-known (although least-understood) Rosicrucian symbols is that of the mother pelican tearing open her breast to feed her seven offspring from her own blood.[19] But in the case of each human being, it is the true maternal principle, which constantly gives of its nature throughout the person's life, to ensure its continuity of existence and its faculty of consciousness.

In today's age, when science is still puzzling over what consciousness actually is, or might be, we should perhaps remember that the Ancients were already very clear about it. To them the body was a mortal aggregate and the merely temporary 'vehicle' of the soul's partial emanation, whilst the soul (as the conglomerate vehicle of spirit) was immortal and maintained its faculty of consciousness throughout eternity.[20] It was also accordingly seen as the source of all knowledge and functionary capacity in Nature as a whole. Its unity of consciousness is of course what provides it with its sense of identity, or 'self-hood' in relation to human experience – something which is still in the process of evolving in the Animal kingdom generally and, to an even slower extent, in the Plant and Mineral kingdoms.

According to ancient tradition, it is because of the combination of this sense of self-hood and the fact that spirit is able (under certain conditions) to move between one soul organism and another, that Man is able to experience his own higher and lower selves as different qualitative potencies of conscious-ness. It is also the very basis of the functional evolutionary process in Nature, which has already produced kingdoms of Nature more evolved than the human. However, we shall consider this in more detail in the next chapter when we take a look at the practical function of the soul principle in Creation as a prelude to what we shall later have to say about Atlantean consciousness.

Chapter Four

·

GODS, ANGELS AND MAN

'Man is a being of divine nature; he is comparable not to the other living creatures upon Earth, but to the gods in heaven. Nay, if we are to speak the truth without fear, he who is indeed a man is even above the gods of heaven, or at any rate he equals them in power. None of the gods of heaven will ever quit heaven and pass its boundary and come down to Earth; but Man ascends even to heaven and measures it. And, what is more than all besides, he mounts to heaven without quitting the Earth. To so vast a distance can he put forth his power.'[1]

In the previous chapter, we began by trying to understand the nature of consciousness and we ended by dealing with the nature of its organism – the soul principle – as seen by the Ancients. In this chapter, we shall go a step further by looking at the distinctions – again, as seen by the Ancients – between the divine parentage of Man and the actual agents of Creation, the angels or, as they are termed in Indo-Persian tradition, *devas*. These are the superior and inferior 'Nature spirits' (the Egyptian '*neteru*') who were also said to be the first mentors and tutors of early humankind, long before even Atlantean humans ever existed.

For some people, the very idea of considering the issue of angels, devas and Nature spirits within a scientific or rational context would make no sense. But that is because they view the subject merely as fantasy, or superstition. However, the way in which Nature operates *subliminally* is not at all well understood by rational science for the simple reason that it is really not concerned even to look in that direction. The suggestion that the organized forms and instinctual tendencies of the plant and even mineral kingdoms are the result of intelligent manipulation – as clearly described, with examples, in the book *The Secret Life of Plants* (*see* Bibliography) – has yet to make a general impact.

The Distinction Between Humankind and Angels

Later in the book I shall look at the subject of the first appearance of self-conscious humankind and its evolutionary development through the Lemurian
and Atlantean races. This is so that the latter can be seen in their proper
anthropological context. However, it needs to be remembered from the outset
that each such race is to be regarded as but the objective and temporary expression of a sequentially unfolding *world* consciousness. In this – as humankind
is part of Nature – the functional purpose of Man and Angel (like man and
animal) were always seen as complementarily different.

The ancient philosophical systems, in distinguishing the hierarchies of
angelic or deva spirits from those of Man-spirits, saw the associated principles
as twin expressions of the One Consciousness of an Intelligence (Logos) which
contained our whole local universe within its Mind. This is fundamental. As
far as they were concerned, the angelic hierarchies were there to maintain the
status quo and balance of harmonic Order in the universe. They were thus the
agents of kosmic or divine *Memory* – hence the fact that they had no sense of
choice or alternative. Their whole instinct was to go on and on creatively
repeating the status quo and thus instinctively maintaining the principle of
Order under Law.[2]

Humankind, on the other hand, it is suggested, was seen as the agent of
divine or kosmic *Imagination*. Man's whole instinct was therefore towards
reorganization of the status quo in line with a yet greater potential of divine or
kosmic Self-expression. So, just as in our own consciousness, where memory
and imagination necessarily work hand in hand, Angel and Man (the spirit)
were seen as working together within the consciousness of the Macrocosm to
generate the forms of self-expression required by its own guiding Intelligence.

Man as an Evolving 'Divine Spark'

Quite apart from understanding the essential nature of what we today call
'General Relativity Theory' (*see* Chapter 2), the Ancients also distinguished
Man (the spirit) from the rest of Nature by reference to the fact that the *modus
operandi* of his *inner* perceptual consciousness involved a progression through
a series of critical points of individualization, or greater self-realization. Thus
the lesser spirit, or 'spark', which had fallen into the terrestrial world scheme
had to arrive by its own evolutionary efforts at a definite point of *spiritual* self-
consciousness.

The 'spark' which had fallen into the world of solar consciousness correspondingly had to arrive at a point of *divine* self-consciousness. But this had
to be done by first reorganizing and then transcending the self-limiting

consciousness of the angelic kingdoms – the fields of mere celestial memory – into which Man, the spirit, had 'fallen'. Only then could it progress to fields of yet subtler light.[3]

The Egyptians, for example, represented this progression symbolically by the head (that is, the consciousness) of the initiate Nefer-Tem (*see* figure 7), shown emerging from the lotus flower (itself symbolic of the spiritual plane of existence in several ancient cultures). This was then later to become the fully emergent 'spiritual babe'. In the Egyptians' view, this achievement of a critically balanced duality of spirit and matter enabled Man to be and do certain things which even the other higher spirits could not. Man was thus pivotal in the evolutionary process.

Figure 7. The initiate Nefer-Tem

Cycles and the Operative 'Zeitgeist'

Notwithstanding this, however, the whole process of Nature's unfolding and subsequent evolutionary development was seen by the Ancients as being subject to cycles. Those same cycles were viewed as the expressions of the unfolding memories of the Logos of the system, taking the form of the sequential manifestations or movements of different groups of Nature spirits within the kosmic, solar and terrestrial environments. Consequently, Man was seen as being unable to make his escape from one cycle of existence (or state of being) to another – except subjectively and at the critical points of transition between one celestial cycle (or state of being) and another – hence the importance of astrology.

It was for this reason also that each new cycle was seen as producing its own 'zeitgeist'. But that is something which I shall look at in more definite terms in a later chapter, when I deal with the evolutionary process resulting in the appearance of self-consciousness humanity in pre-Atlantean (that is, Lemurian) times.

We use the expression 'zeitgeist' to mean the influential 'Spirit of the Age', from its literal meaning in German, although the modern interpretation of that expression gives it the flavour of no more than some sort of unspoken communal human perception of, or instinctive urge towards, cultural change. The Ancients would have laughed at the idea. The suggestion that humankind, alone and unaided, with all its self-concerns and schisms, should suddenly come up with regular and extremely powerful accelerations of cultural development and organization (for good or bad), such as found historically in Egypt, Greece, Rome, Renaissance Europe or even communist Russia, would have been treated as absurd.

To them, the 'Spirit of the Age'[4] was an 'avatar' – a very real and very highly evolved (albeit usually discarnate) Intelligence whose divinely appointed task it was to ensure that its ideals and aims were infused into human consciousness. These otherwise had to be met in overall Nature *according to due cycle*, in accordance with the greater Plan of (spiritual) evolution in Nature. Such cyclical infusions of 'Zeitgeist Purpose' could be either constructive or destructive, according to the relevant point reached in the overall cycle – just as we see in seasonal Nature all around us.

Consequently, as far as the Ancients were concerned, every major and minor cycle had its guiding spirit whose inspirational ideas were always (where appropriate) channelled through the most dependably reliable and far-thinking human minds of the era in question. Through them it was then disseminated amongst human society generally.[5] It follows logically that this relates not only to cultural development but also to a sympathetically accompanying physiological change. But the counterpart of these infusions is that Nature provides a subsequently long period of assimilation and testing, followed by a 'ripening' (or relative perfecting). There is then an inevitable degeneracy in the *outer* forms it produces, before the necessary sub-cycle of their destruction takes place. It is for this reason that human culture is distinctly 'seasonal'.

As we shall see, this same principle applied in the case of the Atlanteans and their predecessors – as well as to ourselves; for Nature is ruthlessly versatile in generating and producing its requirements and then, in due cycle, getting rid of what excess or dross it does not need for the future. Hence it is that whole races ultimately pass away, as well as whole civilizations and cultures. However, humankind itself continues onwards through constant evolutionary adaptation *of its consciousness*, under natural Law.

The Sevenfold Scheme: 'Blueprint' of Creation

This highlights the fact that, if our planetary Nature is indeed guided by Intelligence and functions according to the principles of interactive Order and Law, there must by definition be a guiding plan or archetypal blueprint behind humankind's very existence and future evolution. Humankind is part of Nature and our planetary Nature undoubtedly fulfils a quite specific role in solar Nature, even if we do not yet know what it might be. However, as we shall see – and as was outlined in the quotation from the Neoplatonist Philo of Alexandria at the beginning of the last chapter – the Ancients perceived the structure and dynamics of Universal Nature in terms of a very logical (and self-repeating) *sevenfold* scheme, within the field of a sequentially unified Consciousness.

What was that sevenfold scheme and how were the soul and spirit involved in it? And how does it apply in relation to the evolutionary development of the human race? In order to understand this and the background to the appearance (and eventual disappearance) of Atlantis and its humankind in general, we perhaps need to spend an extended moment or two carefully considering these issues and certain other ancillary aspects of ancient thought in a little more detail before moving on. When we have done so Atlantis will dawn even more brightly than previously imagined.

To begin with, it was mentioned earlier on that the Ancients saw the universe as a concentrically organized sequence of fields of consciousness, this being to them a universal principle. Figure 8 (page 56) may help to illustrate this and the point which I am about to make, for it graphically depicts the higher and lower triplicities of conscious being *within any system* – whether kosmic, solar or terrestrial – interacting with each other through the medium of an intervening state contiguous with them all.

Because of three of the spheres being in counter-revolution to the large sphere enclosing them all, resistance and thus friction occurs between them. Hence 'sparks' fall from the greater soul-sphere of being into the lesser ones. In the case of humankind within the planetary sphere, the unfolding in an eventually sevenfold progression follows exactly the same principle; but, as we shall see, it works out objectively as the progressive consciousness of a *sequence of races*.

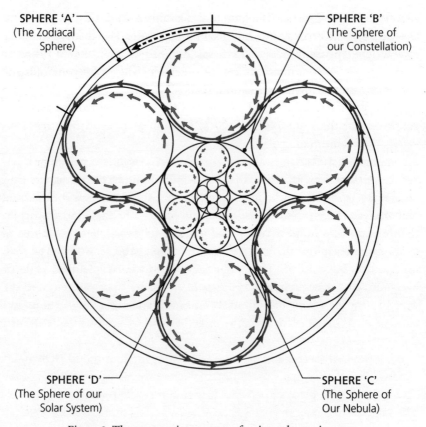

Figure 8. The concentric structure of universal consciousness

The Multiple Nature of Humankind and the Seven Races

In order to understand where and why Atlantean humanity should have appeared in the first place, we need first of all to explain the concentrically and self-consistently repetitive sevenfold structure and internal dynamic of our local solar universe (and thus of humankind's own appearance and evolution), as seen by the Ancients. But to do this properly and effectively, we (like science) need some form of model to provide a focus of comparative reference. We also need to resort to some very fundamental metaphysics in order to explain how the Ancients saw consciousness unfolding and then evolving. However, to keep it simple, we shall combine the modern idea of a series of states or 'planes' of consciousness with the kabbalistic 'Tree of Life' structure as shown in figures 9a and 9b. As drawn, both are fundamentally of a sevenfold nature, corresponding with every other structure in Nature, but *dualistically* so in Man.

Figure 9b shows the kabbalistic 'tree' of *sefirot* (singular *sefira*), or archetypal emanations of Deity, superimposed upon the structure of the seven planes of being and consciousness within our local solar universe. To this are also added the names of those states/planes as provided by Vedic thought and echoed in the modern Theosophical system. In addition, above and beyond the seven purely solar planes, is the triple *kosmic* continuation (as Ain, Ain-Soph and Ain-Soph-Aur, the highest levels of the kabbalistic 'tree') of the greater system within which the solar scheme forms merely the seventh and lowest part. This confirms that the systems interconnect through a concentrically repetitive system of organization.

Figure 9a on the other hand shows the parallel correspondence of the inter-active spiritual and objective world schemes from which we can see the sequential cycle of the unfolding global consciousness of the various races of humankind. The First Race was almost completely spiritual in nature, whilst the consciousness of the Second Race (the Hyperborean) emerged from that field of influence into the lower planes of being, with the preliminary mass influence of the Mind principle (Manas). That, subsequently tinged with the mass Desire (Kama) principle, then produced the sense of group motivation which led to the differentiation of species from archetypes. The Third Race

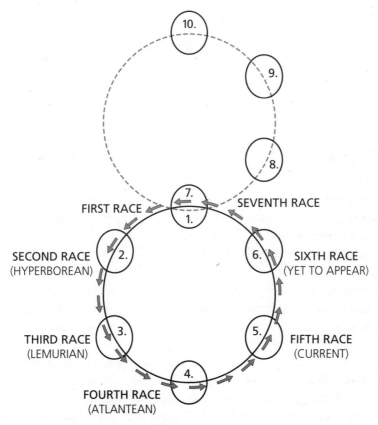

Figure 9a. The evolving intelligence of humankind (see also figure 9b)

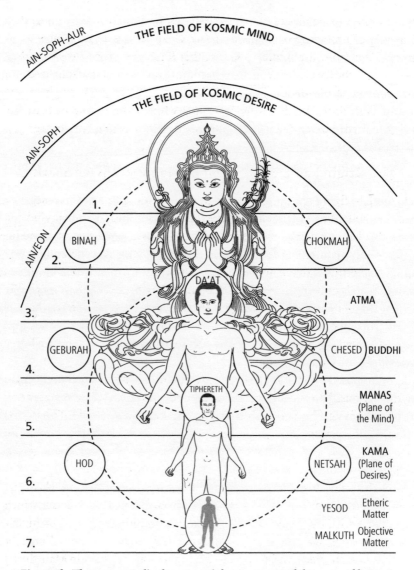

Figure 9b. The correspondingly sequential appearance of the races of human-kind (see also figure 9a)

(the Lemurian) then further developed the mass Desire principle, and its consciousness thereafter became 'grounded' in the world of as yet ethereal physical matter (corresponding to the *sefira* of Yesod on the kabbalistic tree). Although by now active in physically objective substance, the consciousness was still largely ephemeral, or 'Yesodic'.

The Fourth Race (the Atlantean), corresponding to the kabbalistic *sefira* of Malkuth, became fully grounded in its 'Malkuthic', dense body consciousness, with the three principles of Mind, Desire and physical Form fully integrated. The cycle of unfolding or 'involution' (*see* Chapter 3, note 14) is now completed. Thus from the middle point of this Race, the process of 'evolution' commences, the Desire principle now becoming increasingly personalized and dominant in each individual and each local group. Correspondingly, in the present Fifth Race, it is the Mind principle which is becoming increasingly individualized and dominant in the integrated personality and the local group.

The Origin and Development of Man the 'Divine Spark'

Returning to figure 9b, the two outer 'pillars' represent the positive-negative duality of unfolding potentiality in the *mass* consciousness of humankind as a whole, the left one being 'involutionary' and the right one being of a general 'evolutionary' nature. The central 'pillar' then represents the coherently evolving and upwards-striving intelligence within. It is from within the outer (kosmic) levels of being, however, that Man the 'divine spark' is said originally to have been emanated as the triple agent (divine, spiritual and psychic) of kosmic Imagination. Man then 'falls' down into the lower solar worlds and their associated states of consciousness before being forced into an even lower cycle of objective manifestation.

Superimposed upon both the depicted structures in figure 9b, consequently, are the various figures of Man, the lowest and smallest of these representing the purely physical human body form, within its auric soul-field. The second represents the developing consciousness of the human being, triple in nature (physical, psychic and mental) and overshadowed by the lesser 'divine spark', known to us as the 'Spiritual Ego'.

Kabbalistically this stage represents the *sefira* of Tiphereth, which in the kabbalistic tradition is associated with creativity and beauty. It is this which provides us with our sense of self-consciousness and creativity. The higher centre known as 'Da'at' and either depicted as a circle with dotted lines or omitted altogether, is representative of the higher Divine Spark in Man, the all powerful and frequently destructive demigod which the Greeks referred to as 'Dionys(i)os'. This name may be derived from the Sanskrit compound 'Dhyani-dhyaus', meaning a 'contemplative solar god'.

The fourth and largest of the human figures represents the (also still evolving) multiple Divine Man (or 'Buddha'), whose being ultimately comprises all the seven planes of consciousness of the purely solar universe and then begins to extend beyond it into truly 'kosmic' states. Within the system, however, the 'Buddha nature' is that of the Demi-Urge, who emanates the whole sevenfold system from within his own consciousness (in response to a yet greater kosmic Purpose) and then withdraws it back into himself at the end of each cycle of manifestation.[6] As we can see, his general 'organism' is primarily focussed around three emanating centres – those known in the kabbalistic system as Kether, Da'at and Tiphereth (respectively paralleling the Crown, Heart and Spine-Base *chakras* (energy centres) in the purely human organism). His emanating centre then becomes that known to kabbalists as 'Ain-Soph-Aur' – 'Ain' being the same as the Greek 'Aeon' or god of cyclic Duration. Thus Ain-Soph-Aur is the *kosmic* counterpart of the radiant Spiritual Ego, the latter being the lesser 'divine spark' overshadowing and motivating each human being.

However, Ain-Soph-Aur is also sevenfold, the aeonic force-centres representing the influences of seven great groups of kosmic Intelligences (Aeons) which themselves give rise to seven succeeding cycles of Duration. It is the sequential development of these various centres of force which was said to be the causal factor behind *all* evolutionary development on our planet and also within the solar system as a whole – in both the individual and the group (or species) – and all the incidental problems of adjustment arising out of it.

Whilst we are not concerned here with the many ancillary philosophical issues arising out of such associations, the fact of these emanating centres representing groups of 'sparks' of creative intelligence (of some or other evolutionary degree) is important. For it is from these same centres of consciousness (*laya* centres in the Vedic tradition) that the successively outward impulse towards objective Creation takes place. It is also back to them that the whole evolutionary process is directed. Consequently, we can perhaps understand the ancient principle that the objective human being was and is merely the lowest (and very partial) expression of the overshadowing Divinity which is his own real Self. However, the latter is itself merely a centre in the consciousness of a yet greater Being, whose essential nature is beyond our remotest conceptualization.

The four main emanating centres – Kether, Da'at, Tiphereth and Yesod-Malkuth – are thus central to the appearance of the seven Races of Man, a concept which is completely foreign to modern anthropology, although it finds echoes in the ancient tradition of the Gold, Silver, Bronze and Iron Races of Greek mythology. Here, the Atlantean ('Iron') Race consciousness inherited by today's humankind is represented symbolically by the fourth and smallest human form, shown at the lowest part of the unfolding evolutionary cycle.

That cycle, it should be noted, involves the gradual materialization (from a primordially ethereal state) of the many forms of our world system, with a consequently increasing *reduction* in physical size. This, however, is paralleled by an increasingly focussed *expansion* of the differentiated sensory faculties and percipient consciousness found in the various kingdoms of Nature. This principle will be found of fundamental importance when we come to deal with the evolutionary development of consciousness and the consequent reduction in physical size (from their progenitors) of the Lemurian and Atlantean races. However, we shall leave that issue to one side just for the moment.

Duality and Triplicity in Creation

What ancient philosophy tells us (as must also have been apparent to the Atlanteans) is that – whenever expressing itself as the duality of 'spirit' and 'matter' – the creative intelligence in question (the divine being or Logos) always manifests itself phenomenally as a simultaneously matching higher and lower pair of triplicities, or trinities. This is simpler to understand if we remember that we are here considering the principle of divine consciousness (and divine memory in particular) *in parallel to our own*. To the Logos and the Divine Man in each of us therefore, the coherent nature of spirit represents the field of certainty whereas the incoherent nature of matter represents the field of uncertainty, or ignorance. Thus the higher (spiritual) trinity involves: the Will-to-Be, the Will-to-Know and the Will-to-Create, whereas the lower trinity (of expression in elemental matter) involves the Desire-to-Be, the Desire-to-Know and the Desire-to-Create.[7] The higher and lower expression of this original creative Impulse thus produces a sixfold manifestation of differentiated force within the fields of solar and terrestrial light which comprise the consciousness of the Logos. These, however, have to be brought together and their differences resolved by the coordinating influence of a superior hierarchy of beings representing the purposeful nature of kosmic imagination – thereby also completing the sevenfold nature of Man as both Macrocosm (the Logos) and microcosm (the human being). That union then generates (a) idealized or archetypal forms (which are in fact mere holograms), and (b) the phenomenon of cyclic *Duration*.

The latter was the basis of the Vedic *yuga* and the Chaldean *sar*, or *saros*, units dealing with the cyclic measurement of Time (or, rather, of Duration).[8] The dual triplicity is also the source of the ancient glyph known sometimes as the 'Star of David', or 'Seal of Solomon', which was taken from the Chaldeo-Babylonian tradition, but is undoubtedly far older even than that. The Chaldeans and Sumerians appear to have derived their philosophy, at least in part, from that of the prehistoric Brahmans (followers of Brahma) of ancient northwestern India, whose own sacred traditions are said to go back several hundred thousand years, to Atlantean times.

Something of the same principle is to be found in the Scandinavian tradition; for here the sacred ash, the metaphorical embodiment of the Tree of Life, or structure of world-being, is called Yggdrasul, which, separated into its component parts is *ygg* (egg), *dra* (three) and *sul* (soul). In other words, the

Tree of Life comprises three concentrically organized soul-worlds (the kosmic, solar and terrestrial, or divine, spiritual and mundane) to which they gave the names As-gard (Heaven), Mid-gard (Earth) and Nifl-heim (the Underworld), each of which was itself triple in nature.

The result of what is described here is as already depicted graphically in figure 8 (*see* page 56). In other words, the Ancients esoterically described objective Creation as a dualistic (solar and terrestrial) triplicity of spirit-impulses. These, although moving in opposite directions, are yet contained within a single celestial sphere of divine (or kosmic) consciousness. The inter-action of these two triplicities then gave rise in turn to a secondary, internal manifestation of localized consciousness – represented by the smaller sphere at the centre of the figure.

The 'Double'

This smaller sphere was known to the Egyptians as 'the double' principle and was seen as a *reflection in microcosm* of the consciousness of the surrounding outermost sphere. The whole glyph thus contains eight spheres, the eighth and largest incorporating the other seven internally. This principle is again the basis not only of light itself, but also of the harmonic scale in music (involving the octave) – and much else in Nature generally.

The 'double' was also known as the 'shadow'. That is because it represented a darker or denser quality of light by comparison with the others, because of the intermingling of all their various qualities with it. It was thus the 'archeos' from which emanated the various archetypes and prototypes within the various kingdoms of Nature.[9]

Light as the Initiator of Cycles

Meanwhile, it was also clear to the Ancients that Universal Being evidently had its active and passive (or objective and subjective) aspects. These were appar-ent in the phenomena of light and darkness respectively, indicating to them that cyclic existence involved only some of the Universal Life taking a trans-itionally phenomenal form. In other words, it was seen as passing from causal darkness to light and then back again to the same darkness. However, what we undiscriminatingly call 'darkness', is actually nothing but the more subtle light of a higher (or lower) dimension or state of being, which thus acts as the originating source of all cycles of phenomenal existence in the objective world order visible to human beings in general.

Correspondingly, to the more evolved solar spirits, the light of merely terrestrial Nature (our 'sunlight', so called) appeared grey and gloomy – hence the Underworld land of Hades and of the 'shades' described in Greek myth (which scholars have, in the main completely misunderstood). It logically followed from this that all incarnating spirits necessarily took an ethereal form comprising a body of light substance of some or other quality – only some of which would again be apparent to our limited human visual faculty. It is this 'entombment' of the spirit in light-matter of a lower order which, for example, is symbolically depicted in the funereal wrappings of Ptah and Osiris (as well as the human mummy) in ancient Egypt, as described in my earlier books. Interestingly, the Egyptians called those higher adept spirits or demi-gods who were able to manifest on Earth in spheres of light, by the name 'Ur-shu' (or 'Aur-shu'), *shu* literally meaning light.

Light and Aether

Furthermore, it follows quite logically that the so-called 'speed' of light is itself a complete misnomer, because again it is based upon a false assumption. Light *per se* is a mere effect in local matter and does not move from one place to another any more than seawater does when an ocean current passes through it. As scientific experiment has already long ago proved, the atoms and molecules of water – these being fundamentally 'etheric' or of the nature of 'quantum fluid' – merely stay in the same place and rotate upon their axes in response to a current of energy passing through them.

Well, according to the Ancients, the universe is likewise composed of inter-stellar 'aether' – which they metaphorically referred to as 'the waters' (of Space).[10] Thus, when currents of energy (including 'subtle celestial influences') pass through this, atoms *of a nature sympathetic to that particular energy* vibrate and rotate in response. In doing so, they discharge their own energy, thereby radiating particular qualities of sound into the depths of 'dark' light, which is then, in turn, caused to differentiate into a local light spectrum. So, the basic assumption by science that the speed of light is universally constant, has to be a fallacy.

Correspondingly, the speed at which the atom or its macrocosmic counter-part, the soul, *vibrates*, is quite another matter and it is highly variable. Thus, when it is taken into consideration that the 'soul' body is itself an atom on a much larger scale than the scientist's quantum version, it becomes more obvious why bodies not only have different textures, but also why they em-anate light and sound of different qualities, some more aesthetically pleasing than others. It is also the reason why the Ancients depicted the highly evolved individual or entities of the angelic world as enfolded by an ovoid aura of light. However, as light has mass, it is again evident that such a phenomenon is itself due to the spirit-being in question being able to generate energy. It does so in such a way and at such a potency that it causes the latent matter of the local environment to glow, thereby giving the visual impression of radiant light.

The very same principle was evidently recognized by the Ancients who were firmly of the opinion that what we call 'sunlight' was not *directly* produced by the Sun. With that in mind, it is interesting to note here that the Sun at the centre of our solar system has been shown by the solar satellite SOHO to emanate sound. The reason why it should do so is not yet apparent to modern science, purely because it does not yet understand the inherently different nature of the laws of occult science – close as these occasionally seem to our own science of physics.

The Concept of Man as a 'God'

The further distinction between Man (the spirit) and the rest of Nature was that Man was seen as 'an evolving god' – albeit a temporarily 'fallen' one. Hence my mention in Chapter 11 of the *kumaras* (the Kimmerioi, or Cimmerians, of Homer's *Odyssey*) as 'Man-gods', relatively speaking. They – like the Chaldeo-Babylonian primordial figure of 'Oannes' – are said to have appeared amongst Lemurian humankind (in due cycle) and taught them all the sciences and arts and crafts. However, as this idea of 'gods' has been serially misunderstood – and often ridiculed – by both scholars and scientists alike, it too needs to be briefly explained in the correct context, as follows.

As already explained, Man the *divine* spirit was seen as the expression and agent of the imagination of an extra-cosmic Intelligence, which the Egyptians called 'Amun'[11] (actually Amn, as the second vowel is silent) and which the Greeks called 'Logos'. All the rest of Nature, however, was regarded as the expression of His memory – which was thus, in turn, the expression of His generalized field of autonomic consciousness. This field of memory-consciousness was held to be contained within – and thus ensouled by – the spheroidal field of limitation of a great cosmic Thought, all lesser memories within that field of thought constituting in toto the status quo 'Law'.

All such 'memories', however, are themselves living entities. They thus took the essentially spheroidal form of 'souls'. These involved those coherently organized *groups* of 'Nature spirits' known to us today as 'angels' or '*devas*' in their higher ranks, and 'elemental' nature spirits – such as the sylphs, salamanders, elves, fairies and dwarfs – in their lower ranks. Man (the spirit), however, being of the nature of divine Imagination, had to 'fall' into this morass of groups and thereby begin the task of reorganizing them according to a new 'plan'. This reorganizational instinct then is the very basis of what we call 'evolution', of which Man himself was held to be the sole initiator, on behalf of his parent 'Logos'.

The Fall of the 'Divine Sparks'

Initially projected into the field of kosmic Memory (the 'Celestial Oversoul') as one great mass impulse, this great surging stream of kosmic Imagination (the originating 'Dark Light of God') was held to have contained literally billions of spirits – the 'divine sparks' of Man. These in their singular entirety were known to ancient philosophy as 'Adam Kadmon' and otherwise cryptically referred to as 'the Word'.[12] This creative surge of 'Dark Light' then became refracted by the mass field of kosmic Memory which constituted the Celestial Oversoul enveloping the field of future world Creation. It was thus made to diversify, as it 'fell' deeper and deeper into it, just as light and sound refract into those seven groups which we today know respectively as the colour spectrum and the harmonic scale.

As a consequence of the fundamental impulse behind Creation always involving the Will-to-Be, the Will-to-Know and the Will-to-Create (*see* above), the manifesting groups of 'divine sparks' then instinctively subdivided into fraternally organized trios, in line with this trinity of willed being. It is this trio of differentiated 'sparks' that the Ancient Wisdom tradition thus regards as constituting the evolving inner nature of each *individual* human being.

It was the *lowest* of these, however, which then became the subject of the well-known Hermetic concept of human evolution 'first as a stone, then as a plant, then as a beast and finally as Man', which is parallelled in Sufi wisdom by 'In the stone (the) god sleeps; in the plant he dreams; in the beast he stirs and in man he awakes'. Thus, in order to bring about a fundamental change in elemental Nature to a higher evolutionary order, the *lowest* 'spark' has to incarnate progressively in all of Nature's lesser states of objective being – the mineral, plant and animal – and (as we do today) ultimately in humankind. Whilst this may appear Darwinian, the actual process and sequence of development is, however, quite different because it occurs through the agency of the soul nature.

The Process of Soul Evolution

Now, because the falling hierarchies of divine Man were as (triply) diverse as were the hierarchically organized groups of Nature spirits, it effectively meant that each 'spark' of kosmic Imagination was forced at the outset to take residence within a local 'memory-soul' group of Nature spirits. Thus each fallen 'divine spark' became a radiant (sevenfold) being of light, contained by an ethereally spheroidal soul-body of consciousness.[13] This it then had to learn to adapt, control and finally bring around to its new evolutionary sense of purpose.

Having done this, it then (through incarnation and the associated process of experience) had to reunite with its two fellow 'sparks' of divine Will in their own more evolved soul-bodies. This was necessary in order to regenerate themselves as a unity. Hence we have the concept of the 'Three-in-One' found in so many world religions, plus that of the building of the three 'temples' in Freemasonry. With this achievement and the associated unity of the Will-to-Be, the Will-to-Know and the Will-to-Create, the reintegrated entity thereby became a lesser god, a full expression or reflection (at its own level of being) of the extra-cosmic Intelligence which gave it birth in the first place.

This same evolutionary process was held by the Ancients to take place by incessant reincarnation of the 'divine spark' in Man, so that it developed increasingly greater powers of self-control over its lesser soul and elemental aspects. As we shall see, that process was regarded as having commenced properly in Lemurian times – long before Atlantis even existed – and is even today clearly seen to be still continuing, with some considerable distance yet to go.

The Evolution of Human Consciousness

It is fundamentally important to realize that 'evolution' *per se* has to do with the development of natural intelligence – which is itself a progressive spiritual faculty. Intelligence, Mind and Consciousness are *not* the same thing. They are three distinctively different principles. Intelligence forces change in the field of Consciousness by using the principle of Mind to induce the soul nature to adapt to it. This thereby generates an increasingly wider sense of interest, purpose and personal responsibility in the soul entity.

Evolution (so-called) of the physically objective form is merely an effect resulting from the soul nature's own subjective self-reorganization producing morphologically sympathetic changes in matter. Now, bearing this in mind, we can infer the sequential unfolding of an increasing *intelligence* in humankind which has led to the following progressive development in humanity's *objective* consciousness since the middle of the Lemurian Race – the first, as we shall later see, in which a truly human type of consciousness first appeared:

1. Late Lemurian humankind (3rd Race)   – self-consciousness

2. Early Atlantean humankind (4th Race)   – family consciousness

3. Late Atlantean humankind (4th Race)   – tribal consciousness

4. Early 5th Race humankind   – cultural consciousness

5. Late 5th Race humankind   – nationalistic consciousness

6. Early 6th Race humankind   – internationalistic consciousness

7. Late 6th Race humankind   – one-humanity consciousness

The essence of the progression being described here is that of an inclusive expansion. Thus within the framework of the triple soul consciousness just described, there appears in parallel – in humankind's objective behaviour – a *simultaneously* triple and actively *progressive* foundation of functional awareness, namely:

1. Intuitive consciousness

2. Sense of self-consciousness

3. Instinctive consciousness

An individual may thus, for example be self-consciously grounded in his sense of cultural identity, which, however, he expresses in an instinctively tribal manner. At the same time, the individual is intuitively aware of belonging to a sense of national consciousness or national identity, although this may have little immediate personal impact upon him as an individual. The individual's overall behaviour patterns in society will stem from this tripartite consciousness and the proportionate balance (or imbalance) within it. But this is itself continually changing.

Thus this same individual will eventually progress (in this lifetime or another) to a less parochially nationalistic sense of identity, with the cultural sense dropping in importance to become part of his instinctive nature. The hitherto strong tribal sense will then diminish in parallel, whilst his intuitive nature will simultaneously start to develop an internationalistic sense and range of interest. What we can perhaps see from this is that the evolutionary sequence follows a naturally widening, outwardly *spiralling* progression.

Young Souls and Old Souls

Because the sense of consciousness is the synthesized or unitary sense of the soul, as described earlier, we sometimes find that an individual – because of his behaviour patterns – is referred to as 'a young soul' or 'an old soul'. A young soul, for example, might still be personally grounded in a tribal sense of identity whilst living within a society (or even a family) largely geared to a sophisticated sense of cultural identity. That individual could thus feel 'socially alienated'. An older soul, on the other hand, might be personally grounded in a sense of internationalistic consciousness which is already moving in the direction of a 'one-humanity' consciousness and, for similar reasons, might feel himself to be alienated from the general views of the society in which he lives. Evolution is by no means straightforward.

Western society today is a colourful mixture of tribal, cultural and national consciousnesses, all mixed up together, reflecting the varied age of the millions of souls at present in incarnation. The preponderance at present, however, still instinctively tends towards a mixture of tribal and cultural consciousness – which is why Western society tends to be so competitive; hence the urge to 'belong' to a particular social or political grouping being the cause of so much 'gang' mentality on the one hand and social 'one-upmanship' on the other.

In parts of the Middle and Far East plus Africa, the evolutionary issue is a quite different one. The general tendency (at present) still involves an (extended) family consciousness, which is itself essentially tribal in nature. Consequently, in some places, whilst a sense of definite cultural identity is clearly apparent, this is as yet far stronger than the slowly and as yet only intuitively developing sense of national identity.[14]

Now, because the Ancient Wisdom tradition has it that the appearance and disappearance of whole civilizations and their cultures occur as a result of the constantly changing sequence of soul groups coming into incarnation, we can perhaps see why the present riotous mix on our planet is purely temporary. Thousands, indeed hundreds of thousands of years ago, in Atlantean times, civilizations with a national and even international consciousness were far more generally preponderant than they are even today, even though humanity as a whole was far less *intellectually* evolved. But they, in due cycle, necessarily disappeared as each succeeding new cycle required at least some correspondingly new growth from scratch, just as occurs in the plant kingdom. Our own world civilization and culture will thus eventually disappear for the same reasons, to give way to a completely new major cycle of evolutionary development.

The Fallacy of Racial 'Superiority'

A parallel evolutionary achievement is to be seen on a much smaller scale in our own human consciousness, by the working out of an originally imaginative idea into a realization. Hence the idea – although poorly and misleadingly phrased – that 'Man (the microcosm) is made in the image of God (the Macrocosm)'.[15] The same process is thus continually taking place on a quantum scale *within* the organism of 'man the microcosm'.

Where the mass is concerned, it logically follows that the process of 'Self-realization' of humankind in general is necessarily a gradual process; hence its merely objective, external expression (in terms of human anthropological development) cannot possibly be the sole determinant of supposed evolutionary achievement.

For its own evolutionary purposes, the superior 'Divine Spark' may decide that the lesser 'divine spark' within its sub-group should incarnate in an anthropologically less evolved body in order to round out and fulfil an aspect of a yet greater and more inclusive range of experience for that particular racial type. It also gives the clue – as we shall see in a later chapter – as to the apparent paradox of why less evolved consciousnesses can be found manifesting in racially *more* evolved bodies. For that reason alone, if no other, the idea of supposed 'racial superiority' falls flat on its face.

The true evolutionary determinant is the *quality of consciousness* manifesting within the individual and the social group as a result of the quality of intelligence behind it. The understanding of this is absolutely fundamental to understanding the Ancient Wisdom tradition in general and the evolutionary progression from Lemurian to Atlantean to present times in particular. That is because, as we shall see in later chapters, the vast majority of today's human *consciousness* is still basically Atlantean in nature.

Chapter Five

·

LIGHT AND THE PHILOSOPHY
OF CREATION

'As to Void, which most people think to be a thing of great importance, I hold that no such thing as void exists or can have existed in the past, or ever will exist. For all the several parts of the kosmos are wholly filled with bodies of various qualities and forms, each having its own shape and magnitude; and thus the kosmos is whole and complete … For matter, having no quality or form of its own to make it visible, is in itself wholly invisible and for that reason, many people think that it is like Space and has the properties of Space. It is only by reason of the shapes derived from those ideal forms in the likeness of which we see it carved, so to speak, that men suppose it to be visible; but in reality, matter in itself is ever invisible.'[1]

Modern science (following in the wake of the Ancient Wisdom tradition) has shown us that matter and energy are relative and that their appearance in the form of light is but one expression of energy in the electromagnetic spectrum. It has also shown us that information can readily be transmitted by way of pulses of light energy. In fact, it would be true to say that it now sees light itself as a definite agency of information, if not an actual record in itself.

However, *all* phenomenal forms in Nature – including the mineral kingdom and the body of the Earth as a whole – are essentially composed of temporarily crystallized shapes arising out of vibrating patterns caused by episodic (pulsed) light interference – as with the laser-induced hologram. This light is constantly being 'programmed' into forms in Nature or otherwise shed (as radiance) at some or other rate of loss, thereby producing a visual perception to our eyesight, which is recoverable by that faculty which we know as 'the mind's eye'. So it is no longer science fiction to suggest that light itself is the foundational expression not only of all form and function, but also of all phenomenal memory and Intelligence. But is not that the essential nature of ancient Pantheism?

This is something which we shall deal with later, when we come to the issue of Atlantean religion. Nevertheless, it is important to consider it briefly here, in relation to the way in which Nature creates and adapts her own techniques and forms of self-expression (including the human body) throughout the field of living matter.

The Qualitative Nature of Light

The one thing about light which our science does not tell us – because it is not even aware of it itself – is (as we have already suggested) that it is *qualitative*. In other words, light has its own differential spectrum which extends far beyond the issue of mere colour – and which also extends far beyond the range of our so-called 'sunlight'. The Ancient Wisdom tradition had it that, whilst it was Sound which was the true creative agent in the kosmos, it was light that matter (local 'spirit') generated out of itself to produce all forms in response.

It follows, therefore, that light was the *medium* of Creation in which all primordial beings (that is, spirits) necessarily first appeared. However, it was the interaction of different qualities of light-substance (different because magnetically polarised) that enabled those same spirit-beings to maintain fields of continuity of consciousness. This is of fundamental importance in the consideration of both anthropology and also general evolutionary theory, even if our modern science is as yet unaware of the fact. It is also central to the phenomenal appearance of self-consciously illumined humanity in pre-Atlantean times, many millions of years ago, as we shall see in a later chapter.

Thus it is that the divine Pymander (the kosmic Mind) is made to say in the Egyptian *Hermetica*:

> Now fix your thought upon the light … and learn to know it … And when I raised my head again, I saw in my mind that the Light consisted of innumerable Powers and had come to be an ordered world, but a world without bounds.[2]

As the Ancients realized, not all parts of the (macrocosmic) spectrum of light are accessible to our purely human vision. Other, subtler areas of it could only be perceptually accessed by the use of a much higher quality of consciousness involving our psycho-spiritual nature. However, this again brings into consideration the idea of successively different and hierarchically organized states of consciousness. But more of that again later, within the context of general evolutionary development on our planet.

Now, if all the forms of our planetary Life – comprising all the states of being and the various forms in the various kingdoms of Nature – are (and always were) composed of a spectrum of light substance particular to it, then our whole planetary entity has to be seen, in essence, as a (spheroidal) body of interactive light, of varying density and quality. Furthermore, it has to be seen as a web-like spectrum of existence and living function which must extend (in a variety of dimensions) from the outermost limits of the planetary atmosphere to the innermost limits of the planetary core.[3]

The question then arises as to what motivates and guides the constant transitions of form and force taking place (evidently as *different* qualities of light) not only *within* each kingdom of Nature but also *between* the various kingdoms and states of matter. We need to know this in order to understand how the evolutionary process itself works and, ultimately, how humankind came to be what it is today. This should then enable us to understand the phenomenal nature of Atlantean humankind in its proper place, in the sequence of evolution.

In order to arrive by a process of logical deduction at the answer to this issue, we need first of all to work backwards from the nature of creation of our solar system as a whole. The formation of our planetary world as an organism in its own right will thereby make far more sense and we shall then see how the various kingdoms of Nature and the various races of mankind fit sequentially into the overall picture.

The Orthodox View of Planetary Creation

However, before we go any further in this direction, let us remind ourselves of the current orthodoxy as regards the origin and constitution of our planetary Life, as put forward by present-day scientific opinion.

The planets in general are believed to have evolved out of a disc of gas and dust enveloping the 'primitive Sun', this disc being seen as extremely hot and having itself been generated by the so-called 'Big Bang' of modern astrophysical theory. As the disk cooled, so various solid minerals and other solid compounds condensed out of it, the natural gravity (whatever that might be) of the larger masses pulling in others and thus growing by accretion. Thereafter, the immature planets started to grow even bigger as a result of collisions between them, creating 'shotgun marriages'. At this stage, so we are told, our planet was probably a mass of assorted silicon compounds, iron and magnesium oxides and a host of other natural chemical elements in smaller amounts, the iron apparently comprising as much as a third of the overall mass.

Next, as natural, radioactive heat was generated from the condensing core whilst the outer casing was cooling (so trapping the radioactivity and heat), this caused the iron to melt. The molten iron then somehow 'fell' towards the centre of the globe, thereby releasing a vast amount of gravitational energy, which also converted to heat, so raising the inner core temperature to some 2,000 degrees centigrade. Some of the molten iron then solidified whilst the remainder remained in a molten state surrounding it, this also being the causal source of the 'magma ocean' – the lithosphere on which the continental crust has subsequently floated.

This orthodoxy, however, is full of assumptions – some of them very highly speculative indeed and hugely open to question. Not least of these is the hypothetical 'Big Bang' paradigm itself. The truth of the matter is that modern science just *does not know* the answer to how our planet actually commenced its existence and hardly knows where it can find a substantive base to start its own speculations from in the first place. 'Big Bang', as a paradigm theory, is not only a merely movable feast, but is also as full of 'holes' as a kitchen colander. But let us take a corresponding look at the distinctively different concept derived from ancient occult philosophy, in this case the Egyptian *Hermetica*.

The Ancient View of Celestial Creation

The Aeon is the power of God; and the work of the Aeon is the kosmos, which never came into being but is ever coming into being by the action of the Aeon ... The kosmos is encompassed by the Aeon. The Aeon imposes order on matter, putting immortality and duration into matter ... The kosmos is thus dependent on the Aeon, as the Aeon is dependent on God. The Aeon's source of Being is God and that of the kosmos is the Aeon.[4]

As we have already seen, the philosophical method of the Ancients proceeded by deduction from the basis of universal principles, from the Macrocosm to the microcosm – the 'as above, so below' principle. Hence their view that all forms in Nature (including species) are the result of intelligent or semi-intelligent *ensoulment* by the Mind of a more evolved spirit. This causes them to generate light and thereby release (in due cycle) a progressive sequence of instinctive knowledge and functional capacity. But the same process is repetitively infinite.

In relation to our local universe, the originating spirit (what the Greeks of the later centuries BC called 'the Logos' and the Egyptians and Freemasons called the 'Great Architect of the Universe') was held to use a technique of mental projection, almost exactly as we humans ourselves do when generating an idea. However, this was done in order to harness a *lesser* group of divine spirits (that group being known as an 'Aeon', or demiurgic 'world-soul') to 'capture' an area of Space plus all the matter contained within it, in order thereby to set in motion a dynamic cycle of existence. The Aeon thus becomes the deific overlord of this local universe.[5]

The next stage also follows the same sequence as the human mind – which is itself, of course, merely the microcosm of the Macrocosm and thus behaves in precisely the same way. By a process of applied concentration, the superior

Intelligence forces the captive soul-group into a state of tension. This causes it not only to expand and contract in rhythm, but also to rotate on its own axis. That in turn forces the mass of trapped matter first of all to vibrate, thereby causing it to condense into a nebuloid plasmic cloud of ethereal light, which becomes progressively denser until it begins to generate its own epicyclic motions.

It is interesting to note that this principle was well known in ancient times because, as *The Secret Doctrine* tells us:

> Almost five centuries BC, Leucippus, the instructor of Democritus, maintained that Space was filled eternally with atoms actuated by a ceaseless motion, the latter generating in time, when these atoms aggregated, rotary motion ... Epicurus and Lucretius taught the same, only adding to the lateral motion of the atoms the idea of affinity.[6]

As the Greeks had all their knowledge from the Egyptians and Babylonians, this clearly scientific philosophy is self-evidently far older still. It is interesting to note, in passing, however, the correspondence between this 'ceaseless motion' and that of the modern quantum physicist's 'string theory', as well as the 'background microwave noise' attributed to the supposed aftermath of modern Big Bang theory by its adherents.

The Nebula and the Celestial Disc

What happens next is much more clearly recognized by orthodox science, because this axial rotation – through the principle of centrifugal force – then induces the nebuloid cloud of plasma to flatten out into a disc shape. As the process of axial rotation, plus that of a fluctuating concentration continues, the disc starts to separate into a series of still highly ethereal rings (somewhat like the Cassini Rings around Saturn) within which local vortices of force gradually appear. These vortices then (like the theoretical 'black holes' of modern astrophysics) suck the surrounding nebulous matter in towards them, producing an apparently homogeneous mass of orbiting plasmic 'planetesimals'.

It is only now, however, that these planetesimals begin to collide with each other, within their own rings, as modern science suggests. Nevertheless, as they are all still in an ethereal state, these 'collisions' do not result in gigantic 'bangs', but rather electro-magnetically glutinous assimilations of the smaller planetesimals by the larger ones. As a result of this continuing process, the largest planetesimals eventually evolve into full 'planets' – still, to begin with, in a massively ethereal state (*each* with its own 'rings') which has yet to condense into a fully physical body following a rather later sequence, which we shall describe in a moment or two. However, it is interesting to note what *The Secret Doctrine* has to say on this issue too, as follows.

Having evolved from cosmic Space and before the final formation of the primaries and the annulation of the planetary nebula, the Sun (we are taught) drew into the depths of its mass all the cosmic vitality he could, threatening to engulf his weaker 'brothers' before the Law of Attraction and Repulsion was finally adjusted; after which he began feeding on 'the Mother's refuse and sweat' – in other words, on those portions of Ether (the breath of the Universal Soul) of which science is as yet absolutely ignorant.[7]

The Real Nature of the Sun and 'Sunlight'

The Sun meanwhile – or rather the visible photosphere – is itself to be seen as but the densest accretion of the nebuloid solar cloud at the very centre of the system. This is where the maximum centrifugal force is generated by the expansion and contraction of the consciousness of the peripheral parent soul group, the Aeon. Consequently, at this point the solar surface *appears* to 'boil' (or to be in a state of perpetual incandescence) with huge jets of electro-magnetic plasma cyclically being ejected from it.[8]

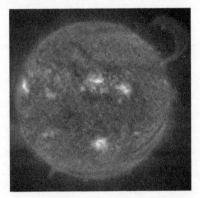

These plasma jets are due, I might suggest, to the Aeonic Oversoul achieving intense points of concentration every 11 years – hence the solar sunspot cycle. The latter is induced, I also suggest, by the field of the solar system turning once on its own axis every 22 years – hence the considerable importance of the mathematical figure π (pi, 22 divided by the universal kosmic number 7) in calculating the various aspects of a circle – or rather, of a solar *cycle*. But what was the ancient view?

Figure 10. The perpetually 'boiling' surface of the Sun

> Philolaus says that the Sun receives its fiery and radiant nature from above, from the aetherial fire [i.e. projected inwards by the Aeon] and transmits the beams to us through certain pores; so that, according to him, the Sun is triple, one sun being the aetherial fire, the second that which is transmitted from it to the glassy thing under it which is called Sun and the third that which is transmitted from the Sun in this sense to us.[9]

Not surprisingly, in the light of this, the Ancients took the view that the objectively visual Sun was *not* the actual source of light on our planet; nor did it provide much of the direct heat necessary for life on Earth. On the face of it, this might seem absurd. But there is a definite rationale to the idea.

To begin with, it is known that the Sun periodically emits great bursts of electro-magnetically charged plasma into the solar system as well as a constant stream of charged particles called the 'solar wind'. But this is not 'light' *per se*. Nor is it the 'real' Sun, for the latter energy source, according to ancient tradition, lies concealed far behind the merely outer surface, the curtain of plasma which science refers to as the 'fourth state of matter'.[10]

As Blavatsky tells us from her ancient sources:

> Surya [the objective Sun] in its visible reflection, exhibits the first or lowest state of the seventh and highest state of the Universal Presence ... The real substance of the concealed Sun is a nucleus of Mother substance. It is the heart and the matrix of all the living and existing forces in our solar universe. It is the kernel from which proceed to spread on their cyclic journeys all the Powers that set in action the atoms in their functional duties and the focus within which they again meet in their seventh essence every eleventh year [a reference to the 11-year sunspot cycle].[11]

It is of course known that light is a radiant *effect*, produced by an inertial body of resistance in response to an incoming electrical charge at a certain voltage. By simple deduction, therefore, there is adequate reason to suppose that it might be the Earth's own captive atmospheric inertia which responds to incoming solar energy (which again, however, is not light *per se*) by generating light *out of itself*. If this is indeed so, the visually apparent Sun could only be regarded as something of an illusion – which is precisely what the Ancients said about it in the first place.

As modern science regards the Earth and all the other planets in the solar system as having been thrown off by the primordial Sun, only to cool later into solid geological bodies, what we have just suggested obviously throws down the gauntlet of challenge in a very fundamental manner. However, in order to understand the nature of the Earth – and of its various kingdoms of Nature – we need first to understand, in at least general terms, the nature of the solar system and thereby of the Sun itself, at its centre. Here, therefore, we should perhaps mention the associated Greek tradition, as outlined in Thomas Taylor's *Hymns and Initiations*.

The Real Nature of the Solar System

According to the Orphic theology, each of the planets is fixed in a luminous ethereal sphere ... and is analogous to the sphere of the fixed stars. In consequence of this analogy, each of the planetary spheres contains a multitude of 'gods', who are the satellites of the leading divinity of the sphere and subsist comfortably to his characteristics. This doctrine, which I have elsewhere observed, is one of the grand keys to the mythology and theology of the Ancients.[12]

The same idea is found in the Vedic tradition of India, for the *Vishnu Purana* says:

> Intellect [Mahat] … the unmanifested gross elements inclusive, formed an egg … and the Lord of the Universe himself abided in it, in the character of Brahma. In that egg, O Brahman, were the continents and seas and mountains, the planets and divisions of the universe, the gods, the demons and mankind [i.e. the archetypal seed-essences of all those phenomenal forms and entities].[13]

Working from the same fundamental principles as already described, the Ancients described the solar system as being contained within a gigantic 'crystal sphere', that sphere (of consciousness) itself being held intact by the vastly powerful Intelligence of the Aeon. Hence it was that the latter otherwise became esoterically known as the 'Ring-Pass-Not'. That same group Intelligence was then regarded (in both India and Egypt at least) as that of a hierarchy of what are called 'Dhyani Buddhas'. The Aeon and the Dhyani Buddha (plus the Tibetan Ahi) are thus to be regarded as one and the same. In fact, we might go so far as to suggest that the Buddha figure (or its Egyptian equivalent, Ptah) would almost certainly have been at the centre of Atlantean religion as well.

Creative Generation from Isolation

In the biblical texts of the Chaldeo-Babylonians, these great Intelligences were known as the El, or Eloi, the lowest of the *kosmic* Intelligences, or Kosmocratores ('Kosmos-Rulers') – hence the subsequent 'Elo(i)him' of the Hebrews who merely borrowed the name from that source. It is also the source of the 'al-*Illah*' (or 'Allah') of the Muslim faith (which also borrowed the name) and the rather unspecific God of the Christians, as well as of the rather more specific Ouranos ('Aura-Nous') the Titan and supreme father-god of the Greek Mysteries. He, we may recall, also enfolded a portion of Space (Gaia) within his embrace and forced it to conceive out of itself all the creative powers and elemental forces of the future phenomenal universe.[14]

As long as this 'sphere of thought' (or consciousness) remained in a state of concentrated tension, so the Ancients held, just so long would the solar system remain in a state of coherence, with the Sun at its centre providing a steady stream of centrifugal energy – and atomic life. However, the Sun itself was regarded as a merely temporary phenomenon resulting from the (piezo-electric) 'squeezing' or cyclical re-tensioning of this same 'crystal sphere' containing the solar system (*see* figure 11 in relation to the same principle as regards Earth).

That in turn was seen as due to natural fluctuations of concentration in the consciousness of the great Intelligences who inhabited it. In other words, the Sun is indeed an emanating energy centre. However, it is only an electro-magnetic *effect* in Time and Space, responding to the unseen energies emanating from the Aeonic, parent 'Oversoul', which aurically contains the whole solar scheme within the field of its consciousness.

This concept of 'crystal spheres' or fields of restraining influence surrounding our planet and our solar system can to some extent be proved by reference to the characteristic activities of the Sun. For example, it is already recognized by science that the upper and lower hemispheres of the Sun rotate in opposite directions. The cause of the phenomenon is already known in physics (the 'coreolis effect') and it is only possible if there exists a perfectly balanced

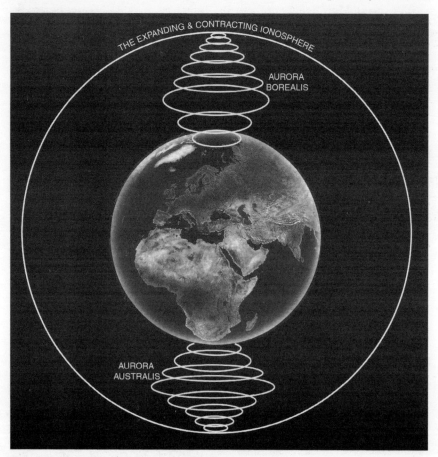

Figure 11. The piezo-electric 'squeezing' of the ionosphere and the consequent torsion effect on the Earth (not to scale)

vertical pressure on a sphere (from above and below) from a surrounding field of influence. In other words, it is due to containment by a spheroidally shaped energy field which itself fluctuates in radial tension (*see again* figure 11) in response to energies emanating from its parent Oversoul.

Now, whereas modern (atheistic) science would see this spheroidal field (and others) in purely atomistic or mechanistic terms, the Ancients saw it as possessing rational Intelligence. Modern science believes that the Sun's energy is finite and that once expended it will turn into a 'red giant' before exploding. Esoteric philosophy, however, says not only that the actual source of energy is not the physical Sun at all, but also that when that source is withdrawn by an act of Will on the part of the Aeon (at the end of the greater solar cycle) the Sun itself will disappear from view *in an instant*. Thereafter, the already vacant planets will be left slowly to disintegrate in the darkness, into the chaos of their constituent matter.

Solar and Terrestrial Spirits

Modern Western scientific orthodoxy likes to believe that anything to do with the subject of 'spirits' necessarily treats of mere superstition (which it holds itself proudly above). However, we have already seen that the Gaia perception of the Earth as an organism makes of this but blind prejudice. Thus proper research into this area of knowledge is unavoidable and needs to go far beyond the limited self-interest of mere 'spiritualism'.

It surely follows, therefore, that we (as did the Ancients) need to consider the *functional* reality of the various groups of entities which make up the evolutionary field of phenomenal existence, *whether immediately visible to us or not*. This the ancient Egyptians, for example, did in their temple art by putting the heads of animals and birds on human bodies in order to depict the functional nature or identity of a hierarchy of spirit-powers (not 'gods') in Nature.[15]

So, with regard to the issue of the various 'spirit genera' that the ancient tradition regarded as inhabiting our solar and planetary system, we might advance the following suggestion based upon ancient tradition.

As descibed in the last chapter, the impulse behind any form of intelligent self-expression – whether in the macrocosm or the microcosm – has to be seen as involving the three primary aspects of all willed action. As we saw, this trinity has been commonly recognized since the most ancient times as:

1. The Will-to-Be

2. The Will-to-Know

3. The Will-to-Create

We find it in Christianity as the Trinity of Father-Son-Holy Spirit; in ancient Greece it was Ouranos-Gaia-Eros; in Chaldeo-Babylonia it was Anu-Ea-Bel (or Anu-Nua-Bel); in Hinduism, Shiva-Vishnu-Brahma; and so on.

But these are just a few examples. The Trinitarian doctrine was actually fundamental to all ancient world religions – Islam and Judaism being the sole exceptions.[16] However, it needs to be borne in mind that it is a universally self-repeating principle, which applies pantheistically to *all* forms of existence. It is thus the source of *all* structure. But we perhaps need to explain this in a little more detail, as follows.

The resultant effect of this trinity of kosmic Will being projected into the elemental ocean of kosmos within the spherical field of intended Creation was that it created an also triple reflection. Hence there initially existed two such trinities, comprising the volitional nature within the duality which came to be known as Spirit and Matter. But as this was effectively a sterile state of balance, which could progress no further on its own, the higher expansionary drive projected a further impulse – poetically referred to as a 'fall of the creative Divine Sparks'. This sought to bring about a rapprochement between the two by bridging their respective fields of consciousness. It was this that then enabled a process of evolutionary transition to take place, along the lines already described earlier on.

As a consequence of this rapprochement, the overall field of kosmic self-expression became sevenfold, this thereby becoming the universal principle behind *all* Creation, at whatever level of existence. However, within our own planetary system it was deemed to have given rise to the following groups of entities and their associated consciousnesses:

1. Archangels/Dhyani-Buddhas (representing the solar system's Will-to-Be)

2. Semi-divine Man (the Spirit) – representing the kosmic Imagination, or 'Will-to-Know' which has 'fallen' into the lower, solar world scheme

3. Solar Nature Spirits – 'Angels'/'Devas' (representing the Will-to-Create within the system)

4. The self-sacrificing 'divine sparks' of kosmic Mind actually involved in the process of cycles of destruction and regeneration – and thus of (re)incarnation

5. Terrestrial nature spirits

6. Terrestrial elemental groups (expressing the principles of fire, air, water and earth)

7. Undifferentiated elemental essences (i.e. homogeneous quantum substances)

Of these, the higher three are conscious *solar* beings whilst the lower three are *terrestrial* entities. The middle (fourth) group of 'sparks' in this sevenfold system are those entities whose progressive influence lies in engineering increasingly more complex and sophisticated body-forms in objective Nature. This, through constant cycles of reincarnation, literally binds the internal structure and dynamic of all forms within the system together. Their existence on any planet is fundamental to its active Nature. They otherwise have a most interesting correspondence not only with the development of the *chakra* system, but also with carbon and the Earth's carbon cycle, which is known by scientists to be fundamentally important to the appearance and disappearance of species. As science knows, all organisms on Earth are carbon-based, although science does not know why this should be so.

The Issue of Man's 'Celestial Origins'

All ancient traditions, without exception, had it that Man (the spirit) was 'born in the stars' but, although it is acknowledged by science today that we are 'made of star dust', the ancient idea is taken as pure fancy, based upon mere superstition. Not, however, as far as the philosophers of old were concerned; and as this book is based upon the idea that there appears to be more than a germ of factual truth in the old traditions, we had better spend a moment considering what they actually said before moving on.

First of all, I have already made the point that the omniverse is merely the objective expression of the kosmic Mind of a Being beyond all conception – something which modern astrophysical science is itself beginning to wonder about, as I mentioned in the last two chapters. Thus on this basis, all the galaxies in the cosmos have to be seen not just as whirling masses of kosmic dust, manifesting as great clouds of light and colour. Rather should they be seen as the objective manifestation of separate kosmic ideas – the Universal Memory – within which Universal Consciousness is manifesting in its many and varied potentials.

Within each galaxy there is a varied hierarchy of celestial forms, as follows:

1. The rotating galaxy itself

2. Revolving zodiacs within the galaxy

3. Zodiacal constellations

4. Nebulae

5. Solar systems

6. Planetary systems

7. Man (the septenary microcosm of the Macrocosm)

The scientific author Peter Russell makes the following rather interesting suggestion about the make-up of the galaxy, from the somewhat parallel viewpoint of a more open-minded physicist:

> If we liken an entire galaxy to a single atom, then what astronomers are observing is reminiscent of the way in which atoms collect together to form simple molecules, which in turn group to form complex macromolecules. If thousands of macromolecules can build up a living cell, could the numerous (galactic) super-clusters be integrated into a single system? Could the Universe as a whole become a living system?[17]

From the esoteric viewpoint, as each such celestial form must necessarily be a relative manifestation of the overall range of Universal Consciousness inherent in its parent galaxy, so it logically follows that each must have an associated spectrum of consciousness. Along with this there must also be associated hierarchies of spirit-beings, collectively representing that same spectrum. Thus the range and quality of consciousness (which, as we have already seen, is ever sevenfold in nature) must necessarily reduce the further one travels down the progressively less evolved sequence of celestial systems and kingdoms of Nature. This again is the basis of the process of 'involution', the unfolding process or supposedly mythic 'fall from Grace' that necessarily precedes the process of evolution, or gradual 're-liberation'.

As consciousness is itself the source of all motive power in the omniverse – which thereby produces all the variables of celestial motion – it also follows that self-consciousness (of man as macrocosm or microcosm) involves both the creation of forms for self-expression and the destruction of those forms in the process of realization. Consequently, where consciousness is concerned, there is a constant cycle of going forth and returning, rather like the activity of a hive of bees.[18] So there is a constant cycle of dualistic interchange taking place and it is this which, in practical terms, leads to the whole process of evolutionary development, through reincarnation.

Now, as each hierarchy of spirit-beings is itself the expression of that one energetic life, it follows quite logically that some of them will be drawn into the process of that same dualistic interchange. In other words, some will 'fall' from one higher field of consciousness into a lower one in order that a kosmic thought or purpose can be naturally passed on 'downwards' within the overall system. In the same way, but in reverse, it follows quite logically that where a process of partial realization takes place, some spirit-entities will pass on 'upwards' within the overall celestial scheme.

The Kosmic 'Gods'

As we have already described, the ancient traditions saw each such celestial system as contained by its own Oversoul, comprising a group of spirits of a particular order, or range of orders, whose purpose was dedicated either towards manifestation of the status quo or to its progressive destruction – by evolutionary adjustment. Within each sevenfold galactic organization, the nebulae (seen as groups of seven stars) were seen as the intermediate heavenly fields into which the greater sense of Kosmic Purpose 'fell' (from the Milky Way), there to serve as a sort of 'staging post' for the whole process of kosmic involutionary-evolutionary interchange.

In the case of our own local system, the nebula in question was regarded as the Pleiades. Hence it was here, so ancient tradition had it, that the great primordial kosmic spirits – who were the actual progenitors of humankind – 'fell' and thereby metaphorically 'died' to celestial existence. Hence also this state became known as 'Meru', from the word for 'death'. Thus the myth (or rather allegory) of 'Merope' in the ancient Greek story, mentioned earlier, of the seventh Pleiades sister who married the demi-mortal 'Sisyphus' and then mysteriously disappeared.[19] Hence also the widespread use amongst the Ancients (and in many languages today) of the root 'mer' or 'mor', signifying death – originally, however, the temporary 'death' of the divine sparks which 'fell' into this lesser state of being from a yet greater one.

The Divine 'Watchers'

In the ancient Egyptian tradition, it became the celestial land of 'Pe', home of the 'Watchers of Pe', celestial spirits who observed all that was going on down in the lesser planetary world systems, including our own. Down from this celestial state, into the lower solar worlds, they then projected great cycles of involutionary and evolutionary influence.

That same downward radiant influence, however, took the form of the massed spirits of divine Man (the Egyptian 'Akhu'), which thereby themselves 'fell'. Thus it is *our* activities which the 'Watchers of Pe' overlook, for we – according to the Ancients – are their progeny. Hence it is we who therefore manifest Kosmic Purpose on their behalf, within the purely local celestial continuum . Such is said to be our responsibility.[20]

From all this it should become clear that the Ancients were utterly certain as to their own origins having been celestial ones. Everything that we come across in esoteric traditions the world over, even today, carries the echoes of that same conviction having been based upon philosophical deduction combined with psycho-spiritual experience, rather than mere superstition. Furthermore, all such traditions in one form of depiction or another, also describe the concept of humankind's spirit and soul having progressively 'fallen' from a high celestial-spiritual state into the solar-planetary sphere of existence which we inhabit today. We shall deal with this in greater detail in later chapters when we come to the issue of the first appearance of self-conscious humankind in Lemurian times – at the same time showing how modern Creationism has managed so absurdly to distort the original esoteric tradition.

The 'Underworld' Continuum

As already described, any such 'fall' in those ancient traditions automatically and necessarily involved an unfolding triplicity of consciousness involving the Will-to-Be, the Will-to-Know and the Will-to-Create. Thus in the ancient tradition, the higher three spirit genera within our solar world scheme were associated with the following sub-states of spirit-matter and its associated consciousness:

1. **Az/As/Ad** – The primordial state of the kosmic Underworld – hence the primordial figures known in Chaldeo-Babylonian tradition (borrowed by the Hebrews) as 'Ad-am'; in Greek and Canaanite tradition as 'Ad-onis'; and in the Egyptian tradition as 'As-r' and 'As-t' (or 'Osiris' and 'Isis', to give their Greek forms)

2. **Man-as** – The 'spark' of Mind – hence the '*monas*' of Pythagoras and the 'monad' of Leibnitz, as also the 'Manes' in ancient Egypt.

3. **Aether** – The extra-terrestrial or higher solar equivalent to the purely terrestrial 'ether'.

As the solar and planetary world states represent the kosmic Underworld duality of spirit and matter, the falling trinity of solar 'sparks' were seen as giving rise to their own 'organic' triple reflection in purely planetary matter. This evolving lower trinity then in turn gave rise to the appearance of the Mineral, Plant and Animal kingdoms as their forms of objective self-expression. However, contrary to Darwinism, esoteric philosophy has it that this trio came into being *simultaneously*, in a primordially ethereal state of light substance. This thereafter, over hundreds of millions of years, gradually densified in part into the solid forms with which we are familiar today.

Man, the 'Fallen' Spirit

As already indicated, the spirit-Man (or divine '*monas*') fell *en masse* into the Oversoul of our solar scheme. However, tradition had it that some of these beings then fell yet further – by an act of self-sacrifice – into the lesser field of light comprising the Oversoul of our planet, which is an intermediate state of being and consciousness between the solar and planetary worlds. Hence, metaphysically, it was regarded as the fourth of the seven states within our immediate overall system (*see* figures 9b and 11) – humankind correspondingly comprising the fourth kingdom in Nature.

The fourth principle was thus the source of the dualistic state of consciousness within which the interaction and *raison d'être* of the higher and lower triads took place and became understood. It thus gave rise to the reflective fourth state (of seven) within which the archetypal 'web' of manifesting existence came into being within the local system. It consequently became the transitional source of a sense of *knowing* – which we today call the 'Ego' (perhaps derived from the ancient Egyptian word Akhu, meaning 'fallen' spirits) – hence its particular association with humankind.

From this same intermediate state, these lesser spirits, or Akhu, (of which there were traditionally seven groups) were seen to project their influence telepathically downwards from the Ak-as(a) into which they had fallen into the compound planetary atmosphere.[21] In so doing, they sowed and then nurtured the seed of a gradually coordinated evolutionary instinct in the mineral, plant and animal kingdoms[22] – eventually resulting in the necessary segregation of the consciousness of animal-man from that of the animal kingdom. That was then followed by the later appearance of fully self-conscious humanity itself, within the Fourth Race – the Atlantean.

There is one thing which perhaps needs to be further clarified. The *three* successive 'falls' of Man (the spirit), as described above, are what gave rise in turn to the appearance of the sixth, fifth and (finally) the fourth kingdoms of our planetary Nature. *All* of these kingdoms exist together (even if we are unaware of the fact) and all of them together comprise the evolving nature of Man. Hence humankind is but one partial expression of Man in general.

Further explanation concerning all this will be provided in greater detail in Chapters 10 to 12, where we shall also deal with the actual nature of pre-Atlantean civilization and culture. In the meantime, let us move on to consider the issue of the Earth as a celestially dependent organism within which humankind and all the other kingdoms come to exist.

Chapter Six

•

OUR PLANETARY NATURE

'We accept a vast range of systems as living organisms, from bacteria to blue whales, but when it comes to the whole planet we might baulk a little. It is, however, worth reminding ourselves that four hundred years ago no one realized that there were organisms within us and around us, so small that they could not be seen with the naked eye. Only with the development of the microscope did people begin to surmise that there were living organisms that minute. Today we are viewing life from the other direction, through the 'macroscope' of the Earthview; and we are beginning to surmise that something as vast as our planet might also be a living organism.'[1]

In trying to understand the nature of our own planet's physical structure and magnetic characteristics, geologists – through a mixture of technological measurement and assumption – have arrived at the notion that the Earth's core must be composed of either solid, or near solid, iron, this being the source of the planet's magnetism. To some extent, this is also due to the perception of the Sun as a ball of flaming gaseous plasma with a gigantic temperature, its incandescence supposedly providing the direct light that illumines our atmosphere. As we have already seen, however, this appears to be an illusion.

Our planet, on the other hand, unlike the Sun, is (by now) a relatively solid body. But, in one sense it mimics the solar system by having not only a central 'generator', but also an outer 'crystal' shell (the electro-magnetically charged ionosphere), which necessarily expands and contracts (*see again* figure 11, page 78) – in response to the photoelectric energies emanating from the Sun. As we shall see in a moment, this in turn produces a parallel response in the Earth's core – hence the phenomenon of gravity. The inference is, however, that the Earth's core is not solid or near solid metal after all. It remains instead, one might suggest, the highly energized and concentrated ball of electro-magnetic plasma it was from the outset, now concealed by the planetary mantle but undoubtedly rotating upon its own axis and itself capable of responsively cyclical expansion and contraction.[2]

J.W. Keely, the extraordinary American electro-mechanical engineer and inventor, had the clearest of sympathetic presentiments about this when, in the 19th century, he wrote:

> As regards planetary volume, we would ask in a scientific point of view, how can the immense difference of volume in the planets exist without disorganising the harmonious action that has always characterized them? I can only answer this question properly by entering into a progressive analysis, starting on the rotating etheric centres that were fixed by the Creator with their attractive or accumulative power ... We will imagine that, after an accumulation of a planet of any diameter, say 20,000 miles, more or less, for the size has nothing to do with the problem, there should be a displacement of all the material, with the exception of a crust 5,000 miles thick, leaving an intervening void between this crust and a centre of the size of an ordinary billiard ball, it would then require a force as great to move this small central mass as it would to move the shell of 5,000 miles thickness. Moreover, this small central mass would carry the load of this crust forever, keeping it equidistant; and there could be no opposing power, however great, that could bring them together. The imagination staggers in contemplating the immense load which bears upon this point of centre, where weight ceases ... This is what we understand by a neutral centre.'[3]

It is interesting to note that the latest research news from the Lamont Doherty Earth Observatory in New York (*see* their website) confirms that the core of the Earth appears to be rotating far faster than the rest of the planet. Why should it do this and how could it do this unless it were composed of something other than what present orthodoxy suggests? It is the emergent energies from this neutral *plasmic* core, I further suggest, which provides the basis of that phenomenon known to us as 'gravity', whilst the correspondingly influential force generated by the ionosphere produces its counterpart – levity. The latter, however, is a force not yet recognized as such by our present-day science, which merely believes that some gases are naturally lighter than others, without ascribing any other rationale. The associated rationale as seen by esoteric philosophy, however, is as follows.

The nature of gravity and levity might be defined from one viewpoint as the negatively charged products of the energies emanating from both the core and ionosphere, *when returning to them,*[4] with the planet's lower atmosphere being the 'zone of interaction'. This is why gravity is called 'the weak force' and levity is not even recognized as such. However, both of them fluctuate according to the voltage, or electrical pressure, in the outer field, the ionosphere – the electricity in each, however, being of different quality. But what medium actually connects or correlates these energies, since they certainly do not function in a vacuum?[5]

The Planetary 'Aether'

The short answer to that is the 'aether' of early Hermetic science – called the 'astral light' by 19th-century Hermeticists and now known to modern science as the 'quantum fluid'. That is at least in relation to the version found on Earth, which might perhaps be regarded as the terrestrial equivalent of the astrophysicist's 'Dark Matter' of Space. Only this too appears to have its own qualitative spectrum of existence. Thus the characteristic 'quantum fluid' of our planet would be quite different in quality to that of say Mars – which would necessarily result in any human or animal physical body leaving the Earth's atmosphere finding that its bodily coherence would begin to be affected. It has already been discovered that astronauts suffer in this way from extended space flights.

This 'astral light' or 'quantum fluid' is itself said to be the homogeneous substratum of all the Earth's gases, liquids and minerals. Like the 'Dark Matter' of Space (which is said to hold the celestial bodies of the galaxies in thrall), it holds the various forms of planetary matter together. It is their very essence and thus both their source and their nemesis, a literal reservoir of Life-force, which both gives life and takes it away – all in due season. Extending from the Earth's very core to its outermost atmosphere, it is also that which actually responds to incoming solar energies, transmuting them into phenomenal 'sunlight' – and 'moonlight'.

It is otherwise that medium to which the animal and plant kingdoms' instincts react when volcanic or earthquake activity is imminent. They are naturally very sensitive to changes in the 'astral light' which is otherwise also the source of all telepathic transmissions and of the so-called 'sixth sense' – as well as of electricity and electro-magnetism in general. Modern humans – because of the use of their mind and imagination – actually de-sensitize themselves to this planetary medium, whereas the aboriginal native and the countryman do not need to intellectualize their experience and, because of this, they thus avoid the problem.

Although often thought of as 'spiritual' in nature, this fluid medium is in fact a merely psychic substratum of existence, within which the mass of elemental essence, plus the terrestrial elemental groups and nature spirits are said to permanently exist. The intermediate fourth group which we have already mentioned – the evolving 'sparks' (carbon atoms being the lowest of these) – then circulate downwards and backwards through this 'astral light', into and out of organic body forms, from and to the uppermost atmosphere (the junction of the stratosphere and the ionosphere).

The Aether as the Source of Magic and Astrology

As we shall see later on, it is the knowledge of this so-called 'aether' or 'quantum fluid' and its various denizens and sympathetically related properties which was the source of all 'magic' in ancient times, although the modern concept of both 'magic' and the 'supernatural' is merely a creation of superstitious ignorance. All associated faculty on the part of the ancient philosopher-magus, on the other hand, was based upon actual knowledge of the nature of universal sympathetic association, and of the forces of attraction and repulsion, plus an understanding of how either to bring them together or separate them. Such knowledge was therefore fundamentally 'scientific', no matter how distasteful modern scientists might find that suggestion.[6]

It is also this same ethereally plasmic medium which was recognized as responding (through sympathetic vibration to another octave of being) to the emanating energies of the planets and stars – hence the true nature of astrology, which traditionally had its doctrinal genesis in ancient Atlantean times. In the lower register, the medium is regarded as the 'playground' of greater and less evolved entities – *devas* and 'elemental' nature spirits – said to be the actual builders of the various phenomenal forms in our planetary Nature, as well as being the manipulators of climate. As we shall see later on, it appears to have been the ill-advised attempt at manipulating these same entities, and the occult forces they contained, which hastened the end of Atlantean civilization.

The Question of Proof

One might ask how can all this be proven? The short answer to that is it cannot – at least not at present in a manner that would satisfy current scientific parameters. The problem is that modern science sets artificial parameters by virtue of its arbitrary segmentation of Nature into different scientific specializations. It then tries to understand these through the use of almost entirely speculative and intellectually based 'models'. The moment one does this, however, it becomes impossible to see things in their true perspective. An intellectual model is just a separative paradigm.

The approach of ancient esoteric philosophy, however, was always to consider the whole of Universal Nature as being a living 'unity in diversity', composed of intelligent and semi-intelligent forces. Thus, instead of trying to build different empirical 'models' in the hope of their inductively confirming different 'laws of Nature', the true esotericist is an interdisciplinary observer who sees *by deduction from fundamental principles* the same essential function in different fields, irrespective of their seemingly different outer appearances.

This is the so-called 'Platonic' method. But it necessitates the following of a coherent and interdisciplinary philosophy.

The fundamental problem, therefore, is not that Western science (as presently structured) cannot see but rather that it *will* not see. It will not see for the simple reason that to do so will inevitably result in its having to completely re-jig its present structures of thought, with consequent reshuffling of priorities and reductions in prestige – and this the 'Establishment' refuses to contemplate. When it eventually accepts, however, that philosophy and science are actually inseparable – as is already becoming increasingly obvious to the more far-sighted scientists of our time – the problem will automatically resolve itself. But that, seemingly, lies some way ahead in the future.

Notwithstanding this, there lies hope in the field of quantum physics, which itself wanders irrevocably into the field of metaphysics, without actually being aware of so doing. One of the effects of this has been to confirm to science in general, via what has become known as 'string theory', that Space is chock-full of dimensions – although its idea of 'dimensions' – that these are all 'tightly curled up in the folded fabric of the cosmos'[7] – remains curiously materialistic and distinctly at odds with true metaphysical philosophy. The author of *The Elegant Universe* further goes on to say that

> According to string theory, if we could examine these particles with even greater precision … we would find that each is not point-like, but instead consists of a tiny one-dimensional loop. Like an infinitely thin rubber band, each particle contains a vibrating, oscillating, dancing filament that physicists … have named a string … Particle properties in string theory are the manifestation of one and the same physical feature – the resonant patterns of vibration (the music so to speak) of fundamental loops of string … hence all matter and all forces are unified under the same rubric of microscopic string oscillations – the 'notes' that 'strings' can play.[8]

Quantum physicists have thus unconsciously stumbled upon the primary characteristics of both the soul and the atom itself, these actually being one and the same principle in macrocosm and microcosm respectively. The so-called 'string-filament' is in fact the two-dimensional membrane of the soul/atom principle,[9] the 'tympanum' upon which the vibratory 'music of the spheres' plays, thereby confirming the ancient tradition that the manifest universe is created (and maintained in existence) by sound.

It is also worth reminding ourselves that ancient philosophy often graphically depicted the soul principle as the 'serpent of knowledge' biting its own tail. Thus the kosmos as a whole was seen as being full of these ever-in-motion serpentine entities, as groups of spirits. Hence the waves of the 'ocean' of Space – which are only ever induced to mutate into the spheroidal soul/atom principle as a result of their response to the projection of a Mind which seeks to contain them and force them to discharge their latent instinctive faculty.

As regards the 'tightly curled up dimensions' contained within each 'string', we might suggest that these are the very same *in potential* as the electron fields already accepted by science as composing the outer field of the atom. As we know, there are three such electron fields, thus again conforming with the tetraktys principle described in Chapter 2. However, each is itself composed of a concentric series of potential sub-fields, each again based upon the number seven. It is consequently unsurprising to find that the composition of the larger 'atom' of our planetary world sphere is based upon the very same principle, both internally and externally.

The Sevenfold Key to Earth's Nature

From what has already been suggested, it can be seen that the various internal geological layers of the planet involve (or are) the functional expression of a sequence of energy transmission as between the ionosphere and the planetary core, with the outer crust and lower atmosphere being the critical crossover point and state. It is consequently within this latter state that we find the *objective* kingdoms of Nature, held in an ecological balance which is recognized by science as of a very finely tuned nature. The Earth's biosphere, however, itself appears to be dually sevenfold, made up as follows:

1. Magnetosheath
2. Magnetopause
3. Radiation belts
4. Ionosphere
5. Stratosphere
6. Mesosphere/Troposphere
7. Lower atmosphere – the Plant, Animal and Human kingdoms
   (+ the Elements)

---

1. Outer geological crust – the Mineral kingdom
2. Lithosphere
3. Asthenosphere
4. Transition zone
5. Lower mantle
6. Outer core
7. Inner core

What has all this got to do with Atlantis? The answer is once more that of sympathetic association. As we have already seen, the Ancients saw the universe as being driven by the raw electrical power of the Life-spirit, but directed by the principle of Mind – that is to say, the *conscious* Mind. Thus Matter in any lesser state is forced by subjective force majeure (in greater or lesser degree) to respond to the focussed energies of a higher state of consciousness, as well as being more directly manipulated by the sheer physical power of a greater electrical Life-force.

This duality of objective and subjective force is to be found on Earth in (a) the alternating electrical energies passing between the ionosphere and the planetary core (b) the alternating subjective energies which humanity in general not only passes back and forth, but also applies technologically, acting thereby as a largely unconscious evolutionary transformer (of the Mineral kingdom in particular) as it does so.

The Duality of Universal and Terrestrial Consciousness

As we have also already seen, in the ancient world philosophy, it was believed that there were but two primary aspects of Universal Consciousness, each generating characteristic forces in Nature. One was that of Universal Memory, constantly repeating itself ad infinitum and represented by the hierarchies of solar Nature spirits (the angelic or *deva* hierarchies) and supporting sub-hierarchies of planetary nature spirits. The other was that of Divine Imagination, the source of all evolutionary Change, finding its focus and expression in the self-conscious faculty of humankind. The former generates, enfolds and nourishes, whilst the latter liberates. The former is said to have no sense of choice and can only instinctively follow 'the Law'. Humankind, however, has the sense of choice and is thus the architect of all true change in Nature, whether that Nature be terrestrial, solar or kosmic.

As in our own human mind, Memory prevails over the Imagination most of the time, but the latter can be used and adapted to change our attitudes and ways of doing things, if we employ sufficient will-force. This is all but another expression of the ancient adage 'As above, so below.' Thus *all* evolution is actually driven by Man – progressively from within the fourth, fifth and sixth kingdoms of Nature, as further explained in a moment – sometimes in tandem with instinctive Nature, but also sometimes in apparently direct conflict with it.

The Cosmic Sevenfold Sequence

But if there is a sequential transition of energetic influence in the greater cosmos, how does it work? The answer to that – as seen by the Ancients – was both astronomically and astrologically, these being seen as but the objective and subjective aspects of one and the same science. As far as they were concerned, the very same principle of a hierarchically organized system involving the planets rotating axially and orbitally around the Sun as a greater centre of kosmic force, had to apply in the wider kosmos too. Consequently, they might themselves be said to have conceived of the following sevenfold progression:

1. Our Galaxy orbiting around a superior galaxy in Space

2. Our Zodiac orbiting within the Galaxy

3. Our zodiacal constellation orbiting within the Zodiac

4. Our nebula orbiting within its parent constellation

5. Our solar system orbiting within the nebula

6. Our planet orbiting within the solar system

7. Our soul 'orbiting' within the planetary biosphere

Each of these was subject to axial rotation (even the human soul-body) and some sort of intelligent orbital instinct within its parent system. Consequently, as far as ancient astrology was concerned, the location of each such soul-sphere relative to (a) its parent soul-sphere (b) its parent soul-sphere's centrifugal focus, and (c) other celestial spheres, involved a predictably changing sequence of influences which necessarily had some greater or lesser effect upon the various kingdoms in Nature – including the fourth, the human.

The Celestial Origin of Man the Semi-divine Spirit

As we saw in the last chapter, many of the ancient beliefs had Man originally born (as a spirit) within the Pleiades nebula, part of the constellation of Taurus. This is the source of countless ancient religious traditions being founded upon the cult of the bull. For example, the Berber people of northwest Africa (and the Arabs too) believed that in the Pleiades lay 'the seat of immortality' and the 'centre of our universe', whilst the Maya regarded themselves as 'children of the Pleiades'.[10] In the *Ruba'iyat* of Omar Khayyam, the Pleiades are referred to as 'the begetters of everything'.[11] Even in the traditions of Freemasonry we find echoes of the same idea in the symbolism of the two pillars (one being 'broken', like the angled pole of the Earth) between and on the far side of which lies a ladder, at the top of the latter being a group of seven stars.

As explained above, it was also seemingly held that our own star was in fact Merope, the 'missing sister' of the Pleiades.[12] Hence again the idea that the celestial heaven world was called 'Meru' (for example in Hinduism and Buddhism), from the element *mer, mor* meaning 'death' – in the metaphorical sense of falling from a higher state to a lower one (as we saw earlier). Thus Man – born as a pure spirit which had fallen from 'Celestial Grace' into an 'Underworld' state which had buried his divine consciousness in the elemental materials of objective, terrestrial Nature – was eventually destined to rise back above his lowly human state to that (within the sixth kingdom of Nature) of a fully self-conscious and self-individualized god, or Buddha (Ptah in Egypt) – the 'bull of his mother', as the Egyptian sacred texts had it. But there are yet further implicit celestial relationships here that the Ancients recognized.

Perhaps most apposite is the fact that the cycle known simply to us as the 'precession of the equinoxes' was known in ancient times as 'the Great Year of the Pleiades', which clearly indicates a relationship between them and our Earth. Bearing in mind also that the Pleiades were held to be symbolically representative of the sky goddess Net (or Neith) in ancient Egypt, the idea has further support. Net's primary function was represented as the 'clothing of the dead'.[13] However, the 'dead' was itself an esoteric metaphor for the 'divine sparks' of Kosmic Mind which, as we also saw in the last chapter, had fallen from a higher state of being into the field of solar substance/light. So, we can again see the sequential rationale which the Ancients applied in their philosophy of a concentrically organized 'fall from Grace'.

The concentric celestial system into the depths of which the 'Divine Spark' of Man had thus fallen was apparently organized as follows, remembering that this is based upon each lesser system's internal orbit being set at an angle to its parent's poles. Hence, supposedly, our 'local' celestial system came to be organized in this manner:

4. The pole of the Pleiades relative to the pole of its mother constellation (Taurus)

5. The pole of our solar system relative to the pole of the Pleiades system

6. The (magnetic) pole of Earth, relative to the Sun's vertical pole[14]

7. The human pole (i.e. its uprightness) relative to the planetary pole

Precession and the Equinoctial Pole

Consequently, we may suggest, just as our Earth moves orbitally at an angle around the Sun, so our solar system moves forward in Space also at an angle relative to the direction of travel and the pole of the celestial soul-sphere which contains the Pleiades nebula system (*see* figure 12). And so on, concentrically

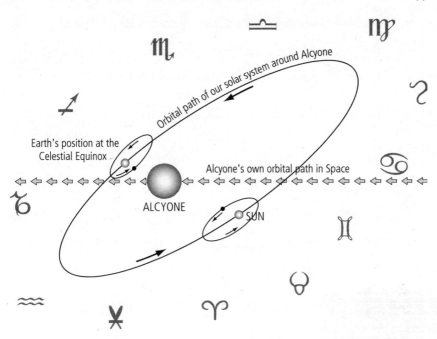

Figure 12. The suggested reason for the importance of the Earth's spring equinox

upwards. But the vertical pole of the Pleiades-centred system was seemingly held to be the star Polaris in the constellation of Ursa Minor. Correspondingly, so it would appear, the vertical pole to the system (i.e. Taurus) containing the Pleiades system itself was to be found as a blank point immediately adjacent to the neck and behind the head of the constellation Draco. This is now known to us as the 'equinoctial pole' – the central pole relative to that greater celestial cycle known to us as the 'obliquity of the equinoctial pole'. The fully reasoned outline of why that should be so is given in my previous book *Khemmea*.

It is because of these relativities, one might suggest, that the cycle of so-called 'precession' of the equinoxes takes place every 25,920 years, whilst that associated with our as yet limited perception of the greater solar orbit around the equinoctial pole takes some 82,000 (just short of 7 x 12,000) years.[15] But the immediate importance of these cycles to the Ancients – certainly as far as our Earth's humanity is concerned – lay in relation to certain phenomenal effects which they generate on our planet, producing results of sympathetic association which are to be found embedded in its geology, botany, zoology and anthropology. Some of these have already been noted by modern science and are outlined in further detail in the next chapter, although the reasons for them are not as yet understood.

The Reasons for Earth's Magnetic Reversals

Perhaps the most notable of these phenomena in terms of modern concerns is that involving magnetic reversal of the Earth's poles – which has led some to believe that the Earth must occasionally 'flip over backwards'. However, when we take into consideration the idea of each celestial system orbiting within a yet greater celestial system, the most probable reason for such phenomena quickly becomes apparent. The critical factor, it is suggested, is the equatorial plane of each system, through which each lesser system has to pass in its orbit. That plane is an electrical one, with its own consequent voltage and electrical resistance.

Consequently, when our planet – every 183 days – passes diagonally through the equivalent plane in our solar system (known as the 'Interplanetary Magnetic Field') the ionosphere reacts slightly (twice), this electrical jolt being noted by astrophysicists as a sort of 'wobble'. However, when our whole solar system passes orbitally through the equivalent field of a yet greater system, with its own far more powerful solar centre and equally more powerful equatorial electrical field, the 'wobble', it is suggested, becomes something far, far greater still.

The Earth's magnetic field is forced to act as an electrical alternator every time it passes through this field and, as it does so, we suggest, its polarity reverses in response. However, this takes some considerable time to complete – with inevitably wandering poles and with cataclysmic events taking place in the climate and geology of Earth as it struggles to accommodate the new energies and forces. That is why this issue is of central importance in relation to the cyclically operative destruction or regeneration of Earth's various landmasses. However, we shall deal with these effects more fully in our next chapter when we shall also be looking more closely at the issue of plate tectonics and associated modern theories. For it is in relation to these that we shall later come to the issue of the cataclysms affecting Atlantis itself and its predecessor, Lemuria.

The Wandering Poles of the Earth

Before we finally move on to the next chapter, it might be useful to look at this particular issue, where the straight line of modern orthodoxy has successfully managed to obscure another fact. This has an important esoteric association with the sevenfold structure of the universe – and also with the nature of cataclysms affecting our planet.

Figure 13a shows us the axial distinction between the Earth's 'true' pole and its magnetic pole. However, as already indicated, following the ancient viewpoint would result in a perception that the poles are actually some way *above* the Earth's surface. Now when one otherwise takes into consideration the principle of the ionosphere expanding and contracting according to the solar system's location in the greater overall cycle, it follows quite logically that the actual pole would change its position relative to ground level – it would be either higher or lower. But that in turn would change the effects at ground level itself, thereby altering the palaeomagnetic pattern in a historically serpentine sequence, rather like a figure eight on its side – which in mathematics means Infinity (∞).

But there is something else to be taken into consideration. It is known that the cyclically maximum disparity between true north and magnetic north is 24.4°. However, when one considers the actual travel of a geographical point from and back to true north during that maximum deflection, it is actually 48.8°. So what? Well, there is an esoteric numerological association.

The actual range of travel is *just within* an arc of 49° and 49 = 7 x 7. So what is actually happening is that every point on (and within) the Earth is actually subject to an equivalent cycle which has to be seen as a correspondence to the 7 x 7 sub-planes or sub-strata of consciousness within a sevenfold system. In other words, the whole Earth organism is subject to a major involutionary-evolutionary cycle during the time that it takes for the polar axis to 'fall' to its furthest point away from the vertical (i.e. at 'true' north) and then to return to it (*see again* figure 13a).

It is quite clear that the Ancients were aware of this rise and fall between the extreme points reached by magnetic north as a general principle because it is, so I suggest, allegorically depicted in the wall picture (*see* figure 13b) of the

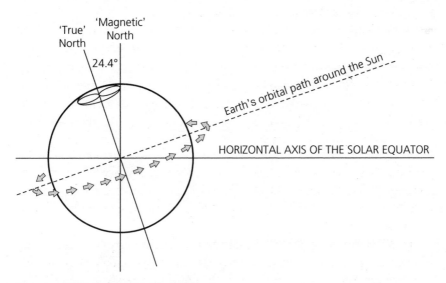

Figure 13a. The full polar angle of deflection

Figure 13b. The raising of the Djed Pillar at Abydos

'raising of the Djed Pillar' found at the temple of Osiris at Abydos in central-southern Egypt.[16] Osiris was known as the god of the Underworld and what we see here is effectively the major Underworld orbital cycle which our planet follows.

But there is one final thing to be considered in relation to this matter. It is not just the transition at the beginning or end of the cycle which results in electro-magnetic variations producing geological crises. The transitions between the sevenfold sub-states would appear also to result in intermediate points or periods of stress. Thus cataclysms of major and minor degree would tend to be ever present. Now, what we know of the major cataclysm of roughly 12,000 years ago, which appears to coincide with the end of the last great Ice Age and the destruction of Plato's island, is that it took place roughly one-seventh of the way through the overall 82,000-year cycle of obliquity of the ecliptic pole – about 11,700 years ago. In view of this it is perhaps unsurprising that we find the following concise statement in the *Hermetica*:

> Destiny generates the beginning of things; Necessity compels the results to follow.
> And in the train of Destiny and Necessity goes Order, that is the interweaving of
> events and their arrangement in temporal succession. There is nothing that is not
> arranged in order; it is by order above all else that the kosmos itself is borne upon
> its course; nay the kosmos consists solely of order.[17]

Chapter Seven

·

DARWINISM AND THE CHANGING
FACE OF OUR PLANET

'Whole areas of the western scientific model fit into this category; theories that seem as solid as rock and indeed are the foundations of much of western thinking. Yet, in reality, they are at best unsubstantiated and at worst, no more than superstitions. Among these flat-Earth superstitions, Darwinism stands out as being central.' [1]

In endeavouring to understand the forces that might have given rise to the Atlantean cataclysm, we need to understand something about the nature of the fabric or mantle of the Earth, which sometimes seems to change shape with dramatic rapidity. Modern science has, as yet, no really clear idea of how the Earth's crust actually formed and is thus unable to hazard any sort of logical guess as to what the Earth might have looked like in its early and formative years. Quite apart from this, because of the recent fresh assault of modern Creationism upon its more self-evident areas of self-contradiction and missing information, the world of geological science is itself again in somewhat of a ferment.

Science has assumed that our planet was originally an incandescent ball of flaming gases thrown off by the Sun. This then supposedly cooled gradually over several billion years amidst a largely methane atmosphere and seas within which intense electrical activity caused the gradual differentiation of natural elements. So the theory goes, that then resulted in the formation of an atmosphere plus the Mineral kingdom. The latter subsequently went through a prolonged cycle of several hundred million years of volcanic, metamorphic and sedimentary activity, before settling down sufficiently to allow the appearance of the first plants, followed much later by the first animals and last of all by humankind.

The Decreasing Size of Earth and its Organisms

There are all sorts of question marks over this current theory, not least relating to the suggestion that either the Sun or the primordial Earth were actually balls of superheated gases in the first place, rather than spheroidal masses of hyperactive electrical plasma, as outlined in the last chapter. Notwithstanding this, it seems fairly certain that the Earth in its formative period was gigantically larger than it is now, the so-called 'cooling' process naturally resulting in its considerable shrinkage.

In fact it might be more accurate to describe this process as the internal segregation of its various atmospheric belts and future geological strata from the originally homogeneous and nebulous mass of electrified matter within which a form of generalized consciousness or sentience was later to manifest. But even the later 'physical' Earth would have been much larger in circumference than it is now because everything about it and on it would have remained, for a very long time, in a far more light and 'plastic' state than today.

Modern science already acknowledges the fact that some elements of the Plant and Animal kingdom in ancient times, tens of millions of years ago, were hugely larger than they are today. Examples of these involve millipedes some 6 ft 6 in (2 m) and insects 2 ft (60 cm) in length, as well as dinosaurs 200 ft (60 m) in length, plus trees and even tree ferns well over 300 ft (90 m) in height.[2]

So the fact of natural shrinkage of virtually the whole 'Gaia' organism over the last several hundred million years is conclusively not in question. What has not yet been acknowledged, however, is that the Earth itself must correspondingly have been gigantically bigger in those days. In addition, however, we face the thorny issue of humankind's existence at that same time, despite this being completely contrary to modern anthropological theory, the suggested mistaken assumptions of which will become apparent in this and the following chapters.

Whilst this may provide something of a background setting for what I am about to suggest regarding the Earth's geological genesis and subsequent development, I shall need to bring into my argument a number of references to chronological correspondences in order to establish a logical sequence of events that will bring a clear perspective to this line of thought. What I am going to say has already been quite extensively outlined in Blavatsky's work *The Secret Doctrine*, to which I will refer several times as I explain the rising and disappearance of the various continents, plus the appearance and disappearance of their associated peoples, civilizations and cultures, according to the most ancient traditions.

The Ancient Mystery School Records

Blavatsky's work was based upon ancient historical records which had been maintained by an esoteric school in the Far East, said to have had its own origins in the 'Mystery Schools' of an antiquity which was reputedly many millions of years old. Whilst such an idea may be pooh-poohed by the field of orthodox science, these records – as we shall see – have occasionally identified matters which only much later, 20th-century scientific research has been able to confirm through the use of highly advanced technology. Some of them are also known to have identified sequences of prehistoric cataclysms, plus the births and deaths of hundreds of great civilizations and cultures, by reference to astronomical cycles and personal observation, in a manner inevitably far wider and more detailed in scope than even Cremo and Thompson's work.

That, however, is because the Mystery Schools were concerned with understanding the detailed sequence of evolutionary development of our planet and its various kingdoms of Nature in the round, primarily from a *subjective* or spiritual angle, whilst also recording the *objective* phenomena resulting from the changes that took place. As we shall see, the structure and dynamics of these sequences were viewed as particularly concerned, yet again, with the number seven.

Time, Cycles and the Cause of Change

The first thing to take into consideration in approaching this subject is obviously Time itself, although perhaps seen from a rather different angle to what we are familiar with today. As I have already described, the universe is clearly driven by cycles of an astronomically (and thus astrologically) based nature, as suggested in figure 14 (*see* page 103).

However, the same principle necessarily applies to every single form within it – whether it be a celestial body or the forms of a particular kingdom of Nature, or even of a particular species – rather than by Darwinian 'natural selection'. All takes place according to previsioned Purpose.[3] Thus both the ancient Lemurian and Atlantean civilizations and cultures are themselves to be seen fundamentally as products of a particular prehistoric cycle (or cycles) of greater and lesser magnitude.

The whole issue of what Time actually might be is still hotly debated by physicists, who still see it in purely materialistic terms. In fact, however, historical Time is merely the visually apparent effect of the phenomenal stage reached by the lesser cycle's natural unfolding within the greater environmental continuum. Time *per se* is only the registration by the sensory consciousness of a repetitive lesser cycle of activity, or duration, by reference to the conditioning induced by celestial phenomena.

The second main thing to remind ourselves of is the fact that the objective universe and all its forms are clearly driven by Intelligence – which necessitates the pre-existence of Consciousness. This, being essentially a vibration, is wave-driven. However, it is literally intelligence which vitalizes the wave and which thus maintains, moves and causes change throughout the universe. Consequently, phenomenal effects or changes in historical or prehistorical time on Earth cannot be divorced from subjective causes that may be only partially self-evident from their objective effects. So, when we talk about the appearance or disappearance of a celestial body, or of a species in Nature, or even about major cataclysms, we *have* to take into consideration the associated causal factor of an accompanying (or, rather, a preceding) change in consciousness *in its soul nature* – relative to the greater soul nature (the Oversoul) of which it forms part.

Morphogenesis and the Factor of Consciousness

As the spectrum of Universal Consciousness contains within itself an infinite number of lesser group-consciousnesses – rather like a Russian *matreoshka* doll – so we must bear in mind that all these will also have their own greater and lesser cycles of both unfolding and evolutionary development, in due sequence. Perhaps unsurprisingly, these greater and lesser cycles must occasionally converge or conflict with one another, their influences thereby causing periodically great changes of either direction or priority – or velocity. The same principle applies in physics with the cyclically interactive correlations of waves and carrier waves, where one is released by and yet later rejoins the other. But this applies just as much in terms of consciousness as well. As shown in figure 14, there is a direct equivalent to this in the astrological association of the precessionary zodiacal cycle with the greater vibratory cycle of which it, in turn, forms a lesser part. Here yet again we find the number seven consistently fundamental to the natural progression of the cycle.

On this same basis, our own planet has to be seen primarily as a sphere of celestial consciousness of a particular quality, even if we do not yet know what that quality might be. That same consciousness, however, must necessarily be responsive on the one hand to the pan-solar consciousness of which it forms part, whilst also containing within itself a spectrum of lesser, hierarchically organized and dynamically interactive sub-consciousnesses. The expression of the latter as physical phenomena we refer to as 'the kingdoms of Nature', the cycles of each of these also being unavoidably interconnected by at least the very nature of the shared materials of the (subjective and objective) elemental forms which they develop and use.

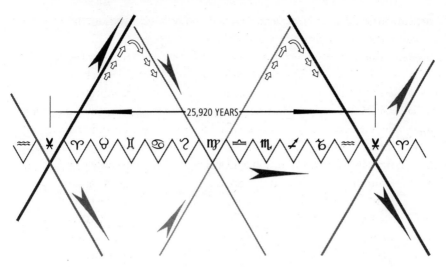

Figure 14. The correlation of the zodiacal cycle with the greater evolutionary life wave

It follows that this vibratory interconnectedness between the various king-doms of Nature within the field of shared soul-consciousness must result in a critical change of evolutionary faculty in one resulting in an outward adapta-tion of its form of self-expression. This must in turn have a demonstrable effect upon the external environment shared with other species, thereby resulting in necessary adaptations of *their* consciousness. That then leads to eventual changes in *their* forms. As I have already suggested, this appears to coincide with what the biologist Rupert Sheldrake sees as the simultaneously operative morphogenetic changes which periodically take place in species across the world. This occurs, so he tells us, through an unseen and as yet unmeasured telepathic resonance, even though the various members of those species may sometimes be oceans apart.

So what we see and experience in Nature all around us is a cyclically driven process of constant and variable change, of both a subjective and objective type, although the latter is what we tend to focus on because of its immediate effects upon us. Notwithstanding this, it is the cytoplasmic soul-organism which is the true container of consciousness, as we have already seen; and it is the unfolding emanation of the potencies contained within this field which gives rise to sub-species (including the very cells of the bodies of plants, animals and humans). But it also orders their very existence and function, as well as their eventual demise, or rather, their withdrawal from *phenomenal* activity or existence.

Bearing this in mind, it is interesting to hear what (despite their somewhat different approach) the well-known astrophysicists Hoyle and Wickramsinghe[4] have to say on the subject, in response to popular Darwinian theory – and unconsciously in support of what I have just suggested:

> Most of the biochemical complexity of life was present already at the time the oldest surface rocks of the Earth were formed. Thus we have no clue, even from evidence which penetrates very far back in time, as to how the information standard of life was set up in the first place and so the [Darwinian] evolutionary theory lacks a proper foundation.[5]

However, they then take the issue even further:

> As soon as we turn from a terrestrially limited theory to a cosmic point of view, all the difficulties mentioned above are either overcome or are mitigated in some degree. The Earth becomes a part of a vastly wider system, the universe itself, and it is the wider system which supplies the informational standard … Life had already evolved to a high information standard long before the Earth was even born. We received life with the fundamental biochemical problems already solved.[6]

The Evolutionary Sequence

Therefore, when we consider the phenomenal appearance of our planetary Life, or of a species or racial type, it must follow that what we are considering is the sequential materialization of a group (that is, soul) consciousness and a group memory which comprises (in germinal essence) all the kingdoms of Nature, except the human, from the outset. It cannot logically be a case of the Mineral kingdom alone appearing first, followed by the Plant kingdom and then the Animal kingdom, by a process of extension or emanation of one from the other.[7] All of these, together with the far less coherent forces of the elements, are part and parcel of the one Gaia organism; but they all take on different forms, each containing something of the other.

Thus it is that the Plant kingdom is made up of more sophisticated forms than the Mineral kingdom, whilst borrowing matter from it and also from the Elements. On a higher turn of the evolutionary spiral, the Animal kingdom has a substantially more evolved range of consciousness than the Plant. Yet its forms and functions are made up of materials, structures and even tiny organic entities taken from both the Plant and Mineral kingdoms, plus the Elements.[8]

The Sequence of Unfolding

Now, in the Ancient Wisdom tradition, there is a definite sequence of unfolding in the *objectively phenomenal* states of existence. This – in line with the Elements – was fivefold, the Aether, or fifth Element, being in a sense foundationally common to all of them. But why, one might ask, are there not seven elements, in line with apparently everything else in Nature? The answer is that there *are* indeed seven. However, the first two are 'meta-physical' and thus comprise Matter in its respectively dormant and germinal essences. According to the ancient philosophical system of thought, this is Matter in its 'pregenetic' state – comprising the ever-unmanifest 'points of Life' (monads) which project a proportion of themselves into the field of Creation by a process of self-emanation. Thus what we call the fifth state (the Aether) is really the third state, but also the first *phenomenal* state.[9] It is the first and most primordial state of emanation and is thus entirely homogeneous in nature.

The fourth state is that of alchemical Fire – and of transition. Bearing in mind that the whole evolutionary process involves the transmutation of the lower *intelligence* into the higher, it is the combined *essence* of the three lowest states which must pass through this purifying crucible before it can drop its lesser form altogether, so as to merge into the higher aetheric state of being. The same principle applies with humankind. The best of our physical, psychic and mental attributes must be combined and synthesized into one *before* they can pass through the very real initiatory fire which stands before the gate of access into the world of spiritual consciousness. It thus follows that *any* system which is sevenfold in nature is one in which this alchemical transition of consciousness is taking place. In the case of our planetary Life, humankind itself is the fourth kingdom in Nature and *is* thus the crucible of transition.

So, when we come to consider the general densification of our planetary Life as a whole, it naturally follows that it must do so in a progressive, fivefold sequence of states – of both consciousness and material form. That fivefold sequence, however – as we have elsewhere indicated – is necessarily part of a greater overall system of evolutionary development, in conformity with all structures in our world system. Hence the process of *phenomenal* unfolding continues to occur in fivefold sub-sequences through each of the sevenfold states – and through each sequence of sub-states.

Thus, for example, the watery state goes through five sub-sequences of progressive densification in conjunction with the other states of matter – hence the fact that, following full materialization of our planetary existence, we now have five aspects of the liquid state – solid (ice), liquid itself, vaporous (the invisibly evaporating and condensing vapours), steam (vapour electrified when under high pressure), and ozone. However, the principle remains the same for the other elements – of Aether, Fire, Air and Earth – as well, even if such gradations are not yet recognized (or even noticed) by our science.

Even in the rabbinical tradition (ultimately derived from the Babylonian Mysteries) there is a teaching which says that there are to be seven successive renewals of the planet and that each will last 7,000 years – an esoteric metaphor for the seven 'Round' periods of planetary development, the numerological value of a thousand representing a complete spiritual cycle in the Ancient Wisdom traditions of antiquity. Correspondingly, in the Mayan tradition, there exists the idea of the seven solar renewals. Anyway, from the *objectively* phenomenal viewpoint only (that is, excluding the first two meta-physical or unmanifest states), that sequence of our planet's unfolding from a primordially spiritual state must have been as follows:

1. The cloudily nebulous state – corresponding with the aetheric state

2. The apparently fiery (although still purely ethereal) plasmic state of primordial radiance (i.e. light)

3. The airy state – involving the variable unfolding of the gases

4. The liquid state – involving the variable unfolding of both water and magma

5. The dense state – involving processes of mineral sedimentation and differentiation

Each of these follows an internal sequence of separation and densification in which the various kingdoms of Nature and the Elements became gradually more objectively distinct from each other, whilst still sharing the matter of which their objective forms are made. Thus in terms of the way esoteric philosophy sees the progression of unfolding forms resulting from an unfolding mass consciousness, we have the following in the lower register (this should be read according to the numbering – that is, downwards and then upwards in a sort of sinoidal curve, representing the fall (involution) into matter followed by the emergence (evolution) from it). *See* upper part of the opposite page.

Genesis from an Ethereal Origin

Hoyle and Wickramsinghe's own theory of evolutionary development involves what they call 'genes from Space', which 'ride around the galaxy on the pressure of light waves from the stars':

> Genes are to be regarded as cosmic. They arrive at the earth as DNA or RNA, either as fully fledged cells, or as viruses, viroids or simply as separated fragments of genetic material. The genes are ready to function when they arrive ... The problem for terrestrial biology is not therefore to originate the genes, but to assemble them into whatever functioning biosystems the environment of the Earth will permit.[10]

1. Ethereal matter and its inchoate elemental consciousness – resulting in (a) atomic mass, (b) light and (c) electricity (this is the '4th state of matter')

2. Gaseous matter and its disparate elemental consciousness, resulting in (a) fluid motion, (b) temperature variability and (c) inertia

3. Liquid matter and its variable elemental consciousness – resulting in (a) condensation, (b) evaporation and (c) precipitation

7. The human form and its consciousness (involving the Intuitive sense)

6. The animal form and its consciousness resulting in the functions of movement and sight

5. The plant form and its consciousness (the senses of Touch and Taste)

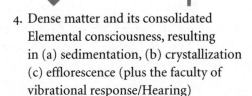

4. Dense matter and its consolidated Elemental consciousness, resulting in (a) sedimentation, (b) crystallization (c) efflorescence (plus the faculty of vibrational response/Hearing)

The central problem with this theory is that it has no immediately obvious origin in intelligent first causes, nor does it attempt to look at the way in which the principles of Mind and Consciousness might interact with the processes which they describe, because it simply avoids these issues altogether. This appears strange in view of Hoyle and Wickramsinghe's own other observation that:

> The revulsion which biologists feel to the thought that Purpose might have a place in the structure of biology is therefore revulsion to the concept that biology might have a connection to an intelligence higher than our own. This fits the way most people think.[11]

Ancient esoteric philosophy, however, takes the view that the whole process of genetic unfolding is merely an effect of life and matter metamorphosing from one state to another as a result of the interaction between Mind and

Consciousness which, in so doing, produce different phenomenal forms. In relation to this issue Blavatsky has this to say by way of example:

> But we would call hydrogen and oxygen (which instils the 'fire of Life' into the 'Mother' by incubation) in the pre-genetic and even pre-geological ages, the spirit, the noumenon of that which becomes in its grossest form oxygen, hydrogen and nitrogen on Earth, nitrogen being of no divine origin but merely an Earth-born cement to unite other gases and fluids and serve as a sponge to carry in itself the breath of Life – pure air. Before these gases and fluids become what they are in our atmosphere, they are interstellar ether – still earlier, on a deeper plane, something else.[12]

The Logical Sequence of Unfolding on Earth

The essence of what is being described here then, is fourfold. Firstly, the appearance of the solid Mineral kingdom-based planet had to have been preceded by a sequence of other progressively more ethereal states of being,[13] comprising the various Elemental kingdoms of Nature. Second, the densification of the Mineral kingdom (and the other by then distinct forms of the Plant and Animal kingdoms) must itself have followed a similar progressive sequence. Third, this sequence must logically be sevenfold. Fourth, *all* the states must co-exist and interrelate not only at the end of the cycle of unfolding, but also at the beginning and all the way through it. However, these same principles must also apply in terms of the unfolding of consciousness through the various human races – of which the Atlantean is but one.

The inevitable conclusion one must draw from all this is that, if matter is indeed homogeneous in its essence (that subliminal essence being as yet unrecognized by science), then every molecular aggregation is merely the result of an atomic conditioning of Life-substance in response to the sensed need to perform a particular function. But since a response to a sensed function involves some degree of consciousness (and intelligence), it follows quite logically that it is consciousness that actually generates a state of being in which larger-scale entities will then normally function, like fish in the sea, or birds in the air. In other words, the essence of matter contained by our planetary organism is induced by the consciousness of that organism to generate a range and spectrum of faculty in response to its own unified sense of a yet higher need.

Thus it is that matter is induced by a Sun to evolve into atoms. These, however, once projected into the ionosphere of our planet, become conditioned by the latter and so generate by their molecular activity the many states and sub-states of the five Elements. However, only some of these become phenomenally objective. That is to say, some become the more tenuous sub-stance of humankind's own *subjective* states of consciousness. Hence it becomes rationally possible for a more evolved organism or intelligence to descend (or 'fall') into progressively lower states of being and consciousness which in turn have their own parallel dimensions of objective form.

The Background Cycle

With this in mind, we can perhaps understand rather better the ancient meta-physical concept of a more evolved spirit becoming involved with a less evolved group of spirits. The same applies with the parallel of a more evolved *group* of spirits (i.e. a soul) having to pass back and forth, in due cycle, through elemental matter of progressively lower quality in order to fulfil its own higher function. For example, the human soul itself is said to do this daily in the waking-sleeping cycle.

In the ancient Egyptian system, the same principle is allegorically depicted in the passage of the 'Boat of Ra' through the Duat each day. However, when the progressive appearance within our world of the various kingdoms of Nature in the mass is considered, it follows that the various states of planetary matter must naturally unfold alongside them (i.e. all of them, together) and thus condition their subjective and objective appearances. Inevitably, there-fore, as the cycle develops, the forms must become more complex and also more densely packed, or objectively 'physical'.

As the unfolding of the various kingdoms' forms had only reached their maximum point of potentially final self-expression by the *commencement* of the fourth major cyclic stage of sequential planetary unfolding and densifica-tion (Blavatsky calls each such stage a 'Round'[14]), we may perhaps suggest that it is only at this same point that we can start to consider the Earth as a fully coherent entity. It is also only now that the various truly geological layers can begin to be 'laid down'. Consequently, this had to be accompanied by a final densification of the ethereally 'plastic' state achieved by the end of the *third* main stage of unfolding, which I have just described. But why should it be that the current scientific orthodoxy has the beginning of sedimentary deposition commencing at 570 million years ago, whereas the tradition of which Blavatsky spoke puts it very firmly at only 320 million years?

The First Sedimentations

The short answer to that must be that present scientific dating techniques fail to take into consideration the greater, progressive cycles of which eventual physical sedimentation is the last – and forms only a relatively small part. In other words, the forms generated by Nature during the preceding third major cycle (Blavatsky's 'Third Round') would themselves have undergone a prolonged period of densification of their already well-established forms long before the process of sedimentation actually commenced. However, those same densified Third Round forms (of the Mineral, Plant and Animal kingdoms) would themselves then have become the first (or amongst the first) to become 'stratified' in the present Round. As *The Secret Doctrine* says:

> The astral prototypes of the mineral, vegetable and animal kingdoms up to man have taken that time [300 million years] to evolve, re-forming out of the cast-off materials of the preceding Round which, though very dense and physical in their own cycle, were relatively ethereal as compared with the materiality of our present, middle Round. At the expiration of these 300 years, nature on the way to the physical and material, down the arc of decent, begins with mankind and works downwards, hardening or materialising forms as it proceeds. Thus the [first] fossils found in strata ... belong in reality to forms of the preceding Round.[15]

Now, there is no way in which this concept of a preceding 'Round' cycle can be proved, despite the background metaphysical logic. However, modern science with all its technological wizardry is seemingly in no better position to hold court on the subject. As Richard Milton tells us in relation to the supposed age of our planet, where he draws our attention to current scientific dating methods:

> Science has proposed many methods of geochronometry – measuring the Earth's age – all of which are subject to some uncertainties ... But of these many methods, only one technique – that of the radioactive decay of uranium and similar elements – yield an age for the Earth of billions of years. And it is this one method that has been enthusiastically promoted by Darwinists and uniformitarian geologists, while all other methods have been neglected. So successful has this promotional campaign been that today almost everyone, including scientists working in other fields, has been led to believe that radioactive dating is the only method of geochronometry worth considering and that it is well nigh unassailable because of the universal constancy of radioactive decay. In fact, none of these widely held beliefs is supported by the evidence.[16]

And again in relation to what is known as the 'geological column'[17] (*see* figure 15):

> It turns out that what has been dated by radioactive decay methods is not the sedimentary rocks or fossils themselves but the isolated intrusion into them of igneous or primary rocks, usually as volcanic material. This has been a rare and purely fortuitous process and one that is unreliable – so rare and so unreliable

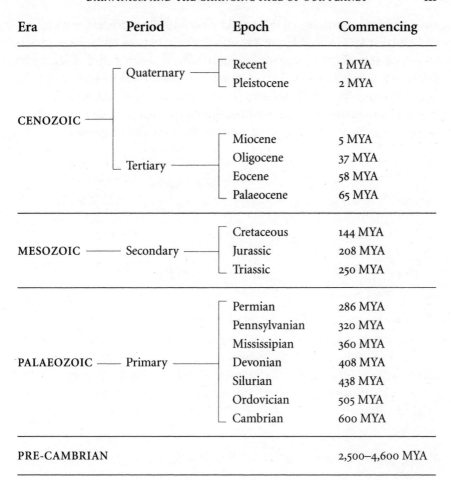

Era	Period	Epoch	Commencing
CENOZOIC	Quaternary	Recent	1 MYA
		Pleistocene	2 MYA
	Tertiary	Miocene	5 MYA
		Oligocene	37 MYA
		Eocene	58 MYA
		Palaeocene	65 MYA
MESOZOIC	Secondary	Cretaceous	144 MYA
		Jurassic	208 MYA
		Triassic	250 MYA
PALAEOZOIC	Primary	Permian	286 MYA
		Pennsylvanian	320 MYA
		Mississipian	360 MYA
		Devonian	408 MYA
		Silurian	438 MYA
		Ordovician	505 MYA
		Cambrian	600 MYA
PRE-CAMBRIAN			2,500–4,600 MYA

Figure 15. The modern 'geological column'. Figures shown are rounded up to the nearest million years (MYA = Million Years Ago).

that the Institute of Geological Sciences thinks it unlikely ever to replace or even rival fossils as a method of dating. Nor is this all, for the method depends in turn on a further chain of inference. For the geological column of von Eysinga is nowhere to be found in Nature. It is an imaginary structure that has been synthesized from comparing a stratum of rock in one part of the world with a similar looking stratum in another part of the world.[18]

As Milton points out elsewhere, the founders of the radiocarbon dating method, when developing the technique back in the 1960s, assumed that the influx of cosmic rays was constant and that the amount of carbon 14 in the Earth's atmosphere could not possibly have varied since humankind first appeared. Yet subsequent research has confirmed that the rate of decay appears to be anything up to 25 per cent less than the natural production rate, thereby making a complete nonsense of the whole idea. The other point to be taken into consideration (which current scientific orthodoxy does not) is that the amount of cosmic dust absorbed into the Earth's atmosphere via the North Pole might be said to vary quite substantially according to astronomical cycles, rather than remaining more or less the same as currently assumed to be the case. The current absorption rate is (very roughly) about 20 million tonnes per year.

However, as our solar system and Earth pass through particular areas of Space within our little local universe during the galactic round, this amount could expand or diminish very considerably. That in turn would result in the geological record being correspondingly altered in parallel to it – as well as resulting in considerable changes in the climate.

Milton completes his demolition of both Darwinism and the current geochronological methods with the following further comment:

> Darwinists needed time and lots of it; uniformitarians had the geological theory that demonstrated great antiquity. Geologists needed a firm foundation for the relative dating and correlation of the many sediments piled one on another in the past – the many strata of the geological column; Darwinists were able to supply the key to the stratigraphical succession of the rocks by comparative anatomy of the fossils contained in those strata, interpreted along evolutionist lines. Thus an unusual academic interdependence sprang up between the two sciences that continues to this day … Fossils were used to date rocks; rocks were used to date fossils … No other scientific discipline would be permitted even to consider such procedures, but when palaeontologists date rocks by means of fossils, they do so with the authority of Charles Darwin himself.[19]

The Geological Record and the Ancients

It is all very well demolishing the current scientific paradigm theory. But is there anything to replace it with? There is indeed, but it again comes from the very different angle of the ancient Mystery Tradition records. These, as we shall now see, envisage the various geological stratifications known to science as being rather younger.

In *The Secret Doctrine*, Blavatsky gives an alternative to the orthodox modern geological column set out above (*see* figure 15). She tells us that 'as it is certain on occult data that the time which has elapsed since the first sedimentary deposits is 320 million years,'[20] we can infer the following rough approximations (MYA = Million Years Ago):

PRIMORDIAL	Laurentian ⎤ Cambrian ⎬ Silurian ⎦	lasted 171,200,000 years (commencing 320 MYA)
PRIMARY	Devonian ⎤ Coal ⎬ Permian ⎦	lasted 103,040,000 years (commencing 150 MYA)
SECONDARY	Triassic ⎤ Jurassic ⎬ Cretaceous ⎦	lasted 36,800,000 years (commencing 46 MYA)
TERTIARY	Eocene ⎤ Miocene ⎬ Pliocene ⎦	lasted 7,360,000 years (commencing 9 MYA)
QUATERNARY	Palaeolithic ⎤ Neolithic ⎬ Historical ⎦	the current geological age (commencing 1.6 MYA)

In view of the modern palaeontological view that birds evolved from the reptile kingdom at some time during the Secondary Era, it is interesting to note *The Secret Doctrine*'s own observation. This, whilst agreeing with the central proposition, states that this evolutionary variation actually took place during the still ethereal 'Third Round', long before even the Primordial Era which commenced this, the present fourth evolutionary 'Round' on this planet. It is otherwise interesting to note that the latest palaeontological research suggests that many more of the dinosaurs were actually still feathered in the early stages of the current planetary cycle than has hitherto been supposed.

The Issue of Progressive Sedimentation

Richard Milton slams the door shut, on the following grounds, on any counter-argument by modern science in support of the suggestion that sedimentation is due more to the effects of cataclysms of one sort or another than to anything else:

> There is one final observation that can be made about all the sediments of the geological column in relation to present day processes and it is the greatest anomaly of all. Today, there are no known fossiliferous rocks forming anywhere

in the world. There is no shortage of organic remains, no lack of quiet sedimentary marine environments. Indeed, there are the bones and shells of millions of creatures available on land and sea. But nowhere are these becoming slowly buried in sediments and lithified. They are simply being eroded by wind, tide, weather and predators.[21]

Given what has already just been said, there is not a great deal of point in arguing the difference between the sedimentary cycles advocated by science and the ancient tradition.[22] Therefore I will now go on to look at some other issues where the ancient traditions clearly diverge with those of modern orthodoxy, starting with the concepts of continental drift and plate tectonic theory. As we shall see, this leads directly to the rationale of how and why the great continent of Atlantis once existed and then disappeared – in the very same place.

Chapter Eight

•

CATACLYSMS AND CONTINENTAL DRIFT

'It is very difficult to find examples of non-living systems which both possess the nineteen critical sub-systems and are self-regulating. Gaia appears to satisfy both criteria. Its self-organising nature has already been clearly demonstrated in Lovelock's work on the bio-system's ability to maintain planetary homeostasis.' [1]

Modern scientific theory has it that the Earth's crust originally formed in such a manner that all the currently visible landmasses above the oceans consisted of one great continental mass, which science has named 'Pangaea' ('All Earth'). This idea is based upon the more than questionable proposition that the outlines of all the continents can be fitted together rather like a jigsaw puzzle. Furthermore, so the theory goes, this great super-continent (for some wholly inexplicable reason) eventually started to split up into several different continents, each on its own bit of supporting 'plate' which then began in snail-like fashion to slide around the globe's surface, supported by the volcanic magma of the lithosphere.

This is the theory of 'continental drift', first proposed by Dr Alfred Wegener in 1915 in his book *The Origins of Continents and Oceans* and itself left to drift for several decades amidst deep and sustained opposition. Then, in the 1960s, somebody came up with the idea of moving 'tectonic plates', which duly gave Wegener's theory scientific credibility and recognition. According to the theory as developed, once the Earth's crustal plates began to split and drift, they then began to collide with each other, thereby either creating earthquake zones (like the modern San Andreas Fault) or forcing one continental plate to move over the top of another and slide over it down the other side, in doing so pushing up high mountain chains out of its own mass, all apparently without affecting its own overall coherence. Richard Milton has this observation to make on the theory:

One can be sure that continents cannot really simply wander aimlessly over the surface of the Earth; exceedingly strong forces must be applied to cause them to move through the powerful ocean crust. In fact, when they do move, it is only under a force sufficient to fracture and plastically deform massive rocks of extremely high strength, a process that cannot occur uniformly but only in sudden, explosion-like processes … The central problem with continental drift, or plate tectonics, and the factor that delayed its acceptance for decades, is that no-one so far has proposed a satisfactory mechanism to drive the process.[2]

It is worthwhile remembering that plate tectonics is but a paradigm concept. In other words, one that provides an operative framework that reasonably answers all queries thrown at it, thereby confirming the apparent viability of the theory itself. Notwithstanding this, plate tectonics has never been confirmed beyond all doubt as the true answer to why the geology of the planet behaves as it does. It is just a case of the fact that, hitherto, nobody has been able to come up with a more workable idea, notwithstanding the fact that

> many geologists rationalise that the geology of the continents is so different from that of the ocean floor that it was formed independently of plate movements of the oceanic crust, having been produced or affected by plate movements that were related to now-destroyed former oceanic crusts. The present oceanic crust is not the first one, nor is the present continental crust the product of only non-plate tectonic processes.[3]

The Rationale of the Theory

It is highly important to note that the latter operative part of this whole theory of continental drift aided by plate tectonics had its genesis in the mid-late 20th century by way of a conceptual answer to the assumption on the part of scientists that the Earth did not have sufficient 'organic' energy of its own to generate the force needed to lift high mountain chains like the Himalayas and Andes by itself. But, as Richard Milton helpfully tells us:

> It has been calculated that the amount of heat generated by mantle convection great enough to cause continental drift would be between 1,000 and 10 billion times greater than the rate of radiogenic heat generated in the crust as a whole, which currents … are impossible because either they would melt the Earth in a very short time, or one would observe an enormously greater heat flux from the Earth than is actually observed.[4]

The assumption that the Earth did not have enough 'organic' energy to generate these phenomena by any other means was in turn based upon the prior assumption that the Earth's core passively consists of solid or near solid iron, as we saw in the previous chapter, where we pointed out its illogicality. We also made the alternative suggestion that it is in fact composed of an electro-magnetic plasma that is highly sensitive and reactive (in terms of expansion and contraction, plus associated heat generation) to changes in the also electro-magnetically charged ionosphere.

As we shall later see, geologists have also used this theory of inadequate force to support their own contention that no such prehistoric continent as Atlantis (or Lemuria) could have existed. But their own concept is wide open to question. First of all, we have seen that the Earth *does* have enough energy of its own to create great mountain ranges. Secondly, the idea that one continental plate could slide over another keeping the coastal outlines of both intact, is altogether ludicrous. Thirdly, it is self-evident that dozens of acres of new landmass are being created each year through volcanic action – for example, in Hawaii and Iceland. Fourthly, it is known that both large and small portions of the Earth's crust keep rising and/or sinking and otherwise fragmenting all the time, thereby making the idea of landmass continuity absolutely impossible. Fifthly, it is clear that the gigantic oceanic trenches (several miles deep) which are supposedly formed by one continental plate diving under another, are in fact due to natural rotational collapse of the crust next to a fault line.

The suggestion that the substance of the Earth's core is closely related to solar plasma and also reactive to electro-magnetic fluctuations in the ionosphere should already have been recognized as a result of other observations by geologists and other scientists. That is, because it has been known for some years that there are all sorts of correlations between the geological record on the one hand and changes in the Earth's dipolar field on the other. The fact that cycles are involved in this is also apparent, although nobody seems to have drawn the self-evident conclusion that astronomy and/or astrophysics must therefore have an input. The authors of *The Geology of the Atlantic Ocean* make the following rather interesting statement:

> Changes in the dipolar field with periods of about 10,000 years have been recognized in the geological record. But few fluctuations produced polarity reversals. Frequency of reversals in the geological record commonly have been put at five per million years. However, it has been reported that ... only about half of all reversals are noted because of their short durations and ... reversals are due to infrequent reaction of the dipole field with the smaller and more rapidly fluctuating non-dipolar field, where the latter acts as a sort of trigger. In addition, ... changes in frequency of magnetic reversals occur at times of tectonic change, further indicating a coupling between the core and the upper mantle.[5]

These authors then make a further interesting observation in relation to the widening hole in the Earth's ozone layer, where they say:

> At the time that the Earth's dipolar magnetic field is absent during polarity reversal, the Earth's surface is not shielded against cosmic rays. Greater influx of cosmic rays then may produce mutations of species.[6]

This is undoubtedly a cyclically operative factor of which Darwin himself could not have been aware. Bearing in mind that scientists today have already publicly indicated that another polarity reversal is anticipated in the near future, at a time when global warming appears to be accelerating, we should perhaps take a little more notice of what the Ancients had to say about astronomical cycles.

The Earth's Major Fault Lines

Scientists have also otherwise assumed that the major oceanic fault lines in the Earth's crust stay in the same location, when this is quite clearly not the case. For example, the Grand Canyon in Colorado is but one example of such an ancient fault line which has subsequently been pushed up above the Earth's surface. But there are many others scattered all over the various continents.

It is as a result of variations of the plate tectonics theory that we have the more recent crustal displacement theories which have in turn led to suggestions, for example, that the continent of Atlantis now lies under the south polar icepack, having somehow 'wandered' down there from an original location in the mid-South Atlantic. However, this interestingly imaginative concept does not work, when the bastions of plate tectonic theory are themselves shown to be unsound.

Figure 16 shows the gigantic geological fault line that extends all the way from the South Atlantic up to and past Iceland. It has been named the Mid-Atlantic Ridge and is a clear example of what we have been discussing.

Discovered in the mid 19th century by the exploration ship *Challenger*, the Mid-Atlantic Ridge was immediately held to be a confirmation of the existence of the 'lost continent' of Atlantis. In the aftermath of the discovery, Ignatius Donnelly wrote a hugely popular book *Atlantis, the Antediluvian Continent*, and for decades there was absolute certainty on the part of many scholars and scientists, plus the lay public, that Atlantis had indeed been rediscovered.

The idea was also supported by H.P. Blavatsky in *The Secret Doctrine* (1888). She confirmed from her own oriental sources the tradition that the Mid-Atlantic Ridge was the central range of mountains of the original ancient continent which had, however, begun to split up around 850,000 years ago[7] as the result of a complete polar shift which had taken place at that time. Given

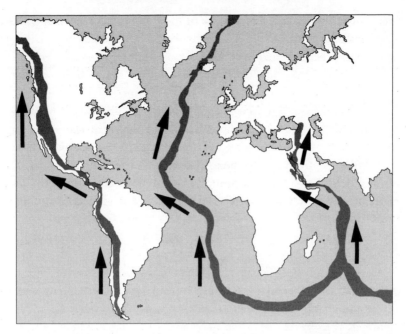

Figure 16. Volcanic ranges and fault lines, including the great Mid-Atlantic Ridge

the disbelief in some quarters about Blavatsky's oriental sources, it is worthwhile underlining the fact that this polar reversal was not even known of by scientists until confirmed by them in the mid to late 20th century, well over half a century later. So, yet again, the reliability of Blavatsky's sources is unimpeachably confirmed by our own modern science – which in turn, one must say, increases the very probable reliability of her material in other fields from the same sources.

However, mainstream science has historically been unwilling to give any possible credibility to the idea of sophisticated, prehistoric civilizations and cultures, which might then threaten the whole structure of merely nascent Darwinian thought. So it vigorously rejected the idea of a prehistoric Atlantean continent out of hand once it had come up with its own theories of plate tectonics and continental drift. Yet, if we look at the configuration of the Mid-Atlantic Ridge in figure 16, something else becomes apparent to the open-minded eye – something which, yet again, has clearly astrophysical connotations.

Astrophysics and Terrestrial Torsion Effects

As we can see, there is a gigantic kink in the Mid-Atlantic Ridge right on the Equator at the same latitudes that western Africa extends westward into the Atlantic and the northeastern corner of South America appears to lean eastward into the Atlantic. Proponents of the theory of continental drift say that this is circumstantial evidence of the two continents having once been joined together, because their Atlantic extremities fit together so well. On this basis, they say, the Mid-Atlantic Ridge is a fault line at which the submarine crusts of the two continents are pulling apart, supposedly at the tiny rate of 1 inch (2.5 cm) per year. But there is an alternative possibility that needs to be considered of at least equal validity with the one just described.

In Chapter 2 we suggested that our solar system is, twice in each greater cycle, dragged in orbit through the electro-magnetic belt of the greater celestial system of which it forms part. Hence, at the mid-point (or celestial equinox) of the last cycle, the electro-magnetic field of the Earth would have been put under huge pressure by the vastly superior voltage which it thus encountered. That same electro-magnetic pressure on the Earth would have been at its greatest at the poles, where its downward force upon the ionosphere and biosphere and the geological body itself, would have created immense electrical vortices. That in turn would have generated huge geo-magnetic forces twisting in opposite directions at the Equator. That same phenomenon has already been noted by scientists in relation to the Sun, for the lower hemisphere of the Sun spins in the opposite direction to the northern hemisphere. On Earth, the Trade Winds still do the same on either side of the Equator.

This ancient and temporary downward pressure would have taken place not at the magnetic poles of the Earth but rather at the geographical poles – which are set at the same vertical angle as the Sun's poles. So, when we look carefully at the geographical map (*see again* figure 16), we find that this same geological twisting has taken place elsewhere in parallel formation. The results are evident in the configuration of not only the Mid-Atlantic Ridge, but also the Mid-Oceanic Ridge (in the Indian Ocean) and the East Pacific Ridge involving the Andes mountain chain. This can be no mere coincidence. It must have resulted from the same phenomenon, involving huge geological torque action on the planet as a whole.

For those who find the principle behind this idea extraordinary, we might here mention that it has a real degree of support from geologists themselves – although not originally intended by them in quite the same context. For example, Dr Maurice Ewing of the Lamont Docherty Marine Observatory observed:

> The opposite effect of tension is compression, which results in a folding of the Earth's surface. The mountain systems of the continents, such as the Rockies and the Andes, were probably caused by such a folding.[8]

Counter-Rotation of the Earth's Crust

What then appears to have taken place – as the result of a vastly powerful intra-cosmic transit and consequently huge tension generated in the ionosphere at the poles – is that our Earth's northern tropics (as a whole) rotated towards the west, whilst the southern tropics rotated towards the east. As a direct result, a gigantic kink formed in the original mountain range (which has subsequently become known as the sub-oceanic 'Mid-Atlantic Ridge'). In addition, the intense, compressive geological strain put on the then extant continental land-masses caused them to become extensively dislocated and even partially shattered. The same pressure in what is now the Gulf of Mexico and Caribbean Basin would have caused the original landmass to fragment, leaving the skeletal mass of islands and island chains (such as Cuba, Haiti, the Leeward and Windward Islands, and so on) which are still visible today.

Rather interestingly, by way of confirmation of what has just been sug-gested, the main lateral fractures in the East Pacific and Atlantic Ridges also occur right on the Equator. These fractures are known respectively as the Gala-pagos Fracture Zone and the Romanche Fracture Zone. Although the westwards kink in the Mid-Oceanic Ridge (in the Indian Ocean) also occurs right on the Equator, in matching fashion, the corresponding fracture (the Owen Fracture Zone) lies very slightly further to the north. However, the recurring pattern of correspondence is undeniable.

A further interesting and related issue is that during the 1990s, the US Navy's ocean bed research teams discovered that the lateral ridges in the ocean bed to either side of the main north–south ridges, themselves expressions of major crustal displacement, seemed to recur at regular cycles of around 41,000 years. This cycle (as outlined in my book *Khemmea*) coincides with that of exactly half the orbit of our immediate celestial system around the Equinoctial Pole; and so it is yet further indicated that our geological phenomena on Earth are directly related to the planet's position, in astronomical terms, within the much greater system of which it forms part. Rather interestingly, the last major crustal displacement has been confirmed by the same source as having occurred approximately 12,000 years ago – which provides an extraordinarily close fit with the reported date of the cataclysmic submersion of Plato's island, some 11,500 years ago.

The Egyptian Festival of Zep Tepi

This is of even greater significance when considered in relation to the fact that the same period coincided with the cyclical Egyptian festival called 'Zep Tepi' ('The First Time'), which celebrated that part of the Great Sidereal Year (the roughly 26,000 year cycle associated with the precession of the equinoxes) at which 'the gods' were supposed to return. I have again dealt with this in some detail in my previous book *Khemmea*;[9] suffice it to say here that the point in the greater celestial cycle is equivalent (although not in magnitude) to the point in our Earth's orbit around the Sun which we call the winter solstice. As our planet approaches that point in its elliptical orbit, it begins to decelerate quite markedly until during the period three days before and after the solstice, it appears to remain at a virtual standstill ('solstice' literally means 'Sun standstill'). Thereafter, the Earth accelerates away again, back to its normal orbital speed.

Just imagine the effects upon the planets within our solar scheme of the whole solar system decelerating like this around its own parent star and then subsequently accelerating away again. It would be immediately reminiscent of the tradition found in the Old Testament story of the battle of Jericho, when the Hebrew god Yahweh is supposed to have been induced to bring the Sun, Moon and stars to a standstill.[10] So, what appears to be a relatively minor (almost indistinguishable) effect upon our planetary Nature in the terrestrial cycle would become a supercharged effect in the greater cycle because of the hugely greater compressive forces of the Sun and Moon acting upon our immediate system.

We can thus safely surmise that a very considerable increase in the number and size of annual earthquakes and tidal waves would be inevitable over the extended period of time immediately preceding and succeeding the celestial solstice. On the mere basis of the mathematical ratio between the two cycles, that same period would be about 500 years – that is, 250 years before and after the same solstitial point. It is interesting to note that we already appear to be just within that 250-year period before the next celestial turning point.

With that in mind, it is also very worthy of note that scientists have recently remarked upon the fact that the Earth's orbital spin is already slowing down. It would seem therefore that we have already entered that part of the overall cycle which inevitably results in an increase in worldwide cataclysms and volcanic activity. Within this, 'global warming' would appear to be just one more characteristic of natural cyclic change.

The Power and Suddenness of Cataclysms

Now although Nature, in the main, works slowly and progressively to produce its effects, resulting in gradual coastal erosion and submersion, for example, it does also produce terrifying cataclysms of varying types and force. One of the most devastating characteristics of many of these is the speed and power with which they eventually discharge their accumulated energies. This is notwithstanding the fact that the latter may have been building up for months or years, or perhaps even decades. Such frequently results in the sudden, dramatic appearance or disappearance of huge landmasses above or below oceanic sea level, many of these over the last 2,000 to 3,000 years being known to history – and even very recent history.

For example, in the 19th century, Brasseur de Bourbourg translated a part of the Mayan *Codex Troano* which very specifically spoke of a great cataclysm exactly 8,060 years before the Mayan author's own time (further details of this will be given in a later chapter). This cataclysm, it said, resulted in a vast coastal landmass in Central America suddenly sinking into the ocean, killing a staggering 64 million people. That is the equivalent of the whole population of Great Britain, or 20 per cent of the population of the United States.

There is reason to believe that this event may have coincided with far wider ranging planetary cataclysms occurring around the time of the submersion of Plato's Atlantean island. Even modern archaeological theory is of the opinion that the population of the Andean city of Tihuanaco suddenly and for no as yet immediately obvious reason, deserted it and the adjacent region of modern Bolivia about 12,000 years ago. Was it perhaps because of this part of South America having been suddenly elevated far above its original height, relative to sea level?

In Jamaica, in 1692, an area of some 1,000 acres (400 ha) of coastal land suddenly disappeared beneath the waves. Six decades later, in Lisbon, some 60,000 people were killed when a large part of the coastal area incorporating the city's docks disappeared within the space of some 5 to 6 minutes on 1 November 1755. The landmass in question was subsequently found to have sunk to a depth of over 500 feet below sea level. Both calamities occurred during massive earthquakes.

Alexander von Humboldt, the great 19th-century explorer, confirmed that an area extending from the Baltic to the West Indies and from Canada to Algiers had been affected by the huge earthquake activity of the 18th century. The hugely destructive effects throughout Southeast Asia of the eruption and immediate self-destruction of the volcanic island of Krakatoa in 1882 have been widely documented. More recently still, the great Japanese earthquake of 1923, measuring 8.3 on the Richter Scale, killed around 150,000 people and set off multiple firestorms. A repeat of this disaster is currently expected, with the expectation that at least half of the city of Tokyo itself may well disappear into the ocean. The 2004 earthquake in the Indian Ocean off the coast of Sumatra, registering a massive 9.0 on the Richter Scale, is now known to have killed over 300,000 people through the huge tsunamis it triggered, which literally obliterated whole communities and areas of coastline around the Indian Ocean.

Correspondingly, however, there are many examples of completely new landmasses having just as suddenly appeared, or of existing landmasses having suddenly been elevated. Several hundred acres comprising what is now part of the southeast coast of New Zealand's North Island suddenly appeared in the late 19th century and have subsequently been taken over and urbanized. Various volcanic islands have just as suddenly appeared all around the world – most notably in Iceland during recent decades. As this is being written (late 2005), a recent volcano in the Sandwich Islands is generating dozens of acres of new land every year.

Quite apart from suddenly rising landmasses, there is also progressive annual movement. For example, the Andes are known currently to be rising at the rate of about 1 ft (30 cm) per year. However, that is equivalent to 1,000 ft (305 m) per millennium, or in excess of two miles (3.7 km) over the 12,000 years since Plato's Atlantean island is supposed to have disappeared.

In the face of this, what is so extraordinary about the possibility of a landmass rising several hundred feet above sea level during a cataclysm and then continuing upwards progressively thereafter? Similarly, what is so extraordinary about the possibility of a landmass suddenly disappearing several hundred feet under the ocean surface in a cataclysm and then continuing to sink by thousands of feet thereafter?

The Factor of Giant Sub-Oceanic Landslides

One other submarine phenomenon, which has been confirmed within the last 15 years or so, is the fact that the ocean beds are subject to massive landslides, often up to 20 miles in length. The effects of these are clearly visible on the Marie Tharp bathyspheric map of the North Atlantic ocean floor (*see* figure 17). Here we can otherwise see in graphic detail where large and small areas of the ocean floor have literally collapsed, leaving escarpments and sunken valleys and plains often many miles deep. These, however, are to be found all over every ocean floor, right across the planet.

It is worth pointing out in relation to all this that in order for a landslide to be 10–20 miles in length, it would necessitate the collapse of that geological mass from a height of at least 4–5 miles (6.5–8 km). This in turn confirms that island landmasses such as those in the Azores and Canarias could disappear due to earthquakes, leaving no apparent trace, even on the sea bed. The same progressively applies to even large continental landmasses.

In *The Secret Doctrine*, Blavatsky described (although not just from her oriental sources) a great primordial continent which existed some 20+ million years ago. However, it was not the 'Pangaea' of modern geology. As we shall see in greater detail in Chapter 10, this giant continent – which she called 'Lemuria' – covered the major part of the Pacific and Indian Oceans, extending in a great

Figure 17. Detail of 'World Ocean Floor Panorama' by Bruce Heezen and Marie Tharp. (Copyright Marie Tharp 1997/2003. Reproduced by permission of Marie Tharp, Oceanographic Cartographer, One Washington Ave., South Nyack, New York 10960.)

horseshoe shape around South Africa, up the Atlantic, through Scandinavia and across Siberia. Blavatsky makes it clear that the later gigantic continent of Atlantis was merely the western part of Lemuria, which had fragmented so violently and extensively through submarine volcanic activity as well as earthquakes, that most of it disappeared under the sea. Such 'valleys of vulcanism'[11] have been recognized by scientists only during the last 10 or 15 years.

The Distinction Between Earthquake and Volcanic Effects

It would appear from Blavatsky's description that many violent earthquake phenomena are due to the Earth's core energies receding, producing a devastating 'rippling' effect in the Earth's crust, whilst many volcanic phenomena appear, correspondingly, to be due to the expansion of those core energies. The receding energies cause the crust to cool and shrink (thus pulling together in violent contraction) whilst the expanding energies force the magma to boil, which causes volcanoes to erupt and landmasses or ocean beds to rise, because the crust has cooled and is not capable in the shorter term of liberating expansion. Consequently, the crust's resistance provides the inertial restraint which leads to the underlying magma generating such enormous upward force.

At present, the measuring of geological activity makes little or no distinction between what must involve expansion and contraction of the Earth's crust as a whole or in part, because it is seemingly unaware of the real mechanics and dynamics behind earthquakes and volcanic activity. However, if this is so, one is forced to ask how geologists can be so certain that the continent of Atlantis did not exist.

The 'Black Smokers' of the Mid-Atlantic Ridge

Among recently discovered marine phenomena are the hydro-thermal vents, or so-called 'black smokers', in the Mid-Atlantic Ridge. Scientists have again seized on this discovery (which has been the subject of frequent television documentaries) to dispute the idea that the Mid-Atlantic Ridge was the mountainous spine of Atlantis. These 'black smokers' are vertical mineral-chemical extrusions from the ocean bed, several metres in height, which emit intensely hot gases (over 300°C) and around which strange, heat-loving polyp growths occur in abundance, despite the apparently complete lack of light available to them. The existence of these 'smokers' has been taken to suggest that the Earth's crust has cracked open in these areas – as the two continental plates supposedly move apart – thereby allowing the super-heated gases to well up from the magma below. So the idea goes, this forces the continental plates increasingly further apart through the creation of new geological mass.

Here again we have an assumption, also based upon the theory of tectonic plates; and, once again, it does not stand up to close scrutiny. Volcanoes generate new landmasses and earthquakes either raise seabeds above sea level or cause landmasses to submerge, both gradually and dramatically. However, mere faults do none of these, otherwise we would have magma continually pouring into view all over the Earth's surface, above and below sea level.

Exploring a Counter-Theory

We return again, therefore, to the idea that the Mid-Atlantic Ridge was indeed the main mountain range which formed the spine of an ancient mid-Atlantic continent; and I would answer the doubts of modern science by putting forward the following proposition.

Just consider for a moment the suggestion that an original continent as a whole (either quickly or gradually and progressively) eventually sank below the ocean surface. The first thing that would have happened as a result of massive earthquake activity is that the whole geological mass would have been multiply fractured, particularly in the area of any mountain range where faults are quite normally to be found all over the place. This would have seriously destabilized and fragmented the existing rock structure and formations. The by now submarine tops of the mountains would then have become subject to the tremendous forces of erosion generated by the immensely powerful oceanic currents and storms, these inevitably resulting in serious crumbling and erosion of their higher peaks and slopes. That in turn would have led to their progressive collapse, resulting in large and small submarine landslides and the rough levelling (at much lower levels) of what had previously been high mountain slopes and valleys.

However, the severe erosion would also have led to the magma channels under the central part of the ridge/chain correspondingly becoming much closer to the surface of the new ocean bed (*see* figure 18). Consequently, the upward geological fissures would have provided far less resistance to the natural escape of magma gases, which would otherwise provide the pressure that forces magma up through volcanic cones. As a consequence, I suggest, the naturally easy escape of these gases has resulted in the formation of mineral-rich mini-cones (the 'smokers') and at the same time helped to reduce the extent of potential volcanic activity in the area generally. However, where any severe geological obstruction occurs – for example the island of Iceland – real volcanoes reappear in abundance.

It seems quite clear that our planet possesses several major magma 'arteries' and 'veins' (not all of them perceptible), together with immense underground cavities which periodically fill and then empty, thus making of Gaia a

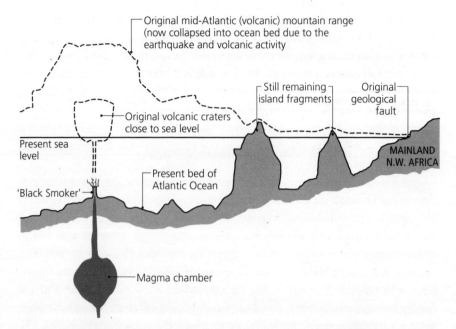

Figure 18. The creation of the hydro-thermal vents, or so-called 'black smokers', in the Mid-Atlantic Ridge

genuinely organic entity, with a very distinct biology of its own, which our present humanity is only just beginning to understand. However, as we shall see in a later chapter, it appears that some sections of Atlantean society chose to ignore this and the associated danger signs which ultimately led to the cataclysmic destruction of their civilization and culture over a prolonged period of time.

Asteroid and Comet Collisions

In concluding this chapter, let us look at two other modern scientific theories which have steadily gained in popularity over recent years: asteroid or comet collision with our Earth; and polar deglaciation resulting from erosion of the polar ozone layer supposedly through human technology. As we shall see, both theories are based upon various unwarranted assumptions – notwithstanding the (interestingly sevenfold) segmentation and crash into Jupiter of the Shoemaker-Levy comet only a few years ago, and the fact that the polar ice is indeed steadily melting whilst the 'ozone hole' is steadily increasing.

The foundation of the theory of comet/asteroid impact is that there are a few places on the Earth's surface (and thousands on the Moon and other planets) where there exist almost perfectly rounded craters, often of great size and depth, and often surrounded by tektites – variously dark green to black, glassy masses of previously molten mineral matter – in great profusion. Enormous mathematical time and effort has gone into proving trajectories, and so on, for the asteroids or comets that are supposed to have made these craters. But nobody has ever found any actual asteroid fragments other than, it is claimed, the tektites – which are just as commonly found spewing forth from volcanoes. Volcanoes also produce perfectly rounded craters plus their 'dead' forms, calderas, which are also frequently surrounded by tektites as a matter of course.

It is also a scientifically observable fact that the perfect circle is a phenomenon found throughout Nature in the form of certain flowers which have stems just like the upward-flowing magma arteries in a volcano. So it seems far more likely that all these 'asteroid craters' – on the Moon and other celestial bodies in our solar system as well as the Earth – are in fact calderas, the result of historic volcanic activity. But why should major calderas automatically be interpreted as due to asteroidal impact? Ancient traditions suggest that the Moon was once a fertile planet, so these calderas could well have formed during that time, *before* the Moon lost its atmosphere and thus 'died'.

The Disappearance of the Dinosaurs

The theory of asteroid/comet impact has been allied to the supposedly sudden disappearance of the majority of dinosaurs, some 60 million years ago, or so we are told by modern science. The suggestion is that whilst many were destroyed outright by the immediate cataclysm and its associated tidal waves and shockwaves, the rest failed to survive partly because the widespread destruction of vegetation removed the food and water sources for these creatures, with their huge appetites, and partly also because there remained no tree vegetation to shade and protect them from the Sun. Another variation of the theory suggests that the impact caused such huge amounts of dust to hang around the upper atmosphere that the sun's heat and light were significantly *obscured* for long enough to cause falls in temperature that were disastrous *per se* for the dinosaurs (which, unlike modern reptiles, were warm-blooded), as well as limiting the vegetation and prey on which they lived.

The curious thing is that many large carnivorous and vegetarian dinosaurs appear to have continued living for tens of millions of years after this cataclysm – which should have given them plenty of time to rebuild their species. Now the largest remaining land animals we see are only much smaller-scale elephants and rhinoceroses. The suggested reason for this phenomenon will, however, be dealt with later on.

Ice Ages and Cycles Generally

One of the things which we keep hearing about from geologists and anthropologists is that the last great Ice Age affecting the northern hemisphere came to an end about 12,000 years ago, which again coincides strikingly with Plato's dating for the cataclysmic disappearance of Poseidonis. This era also supposedly heralded the emergence of humankind from our 'hunter-gatherer' past into the dawn of urban civilization and culture. Yet, when we look more closely at what scientists are telling us, it becomes apparent that this great Ice Age, which supposedly lasted for nearly 2 million years, involved a mass of well over 30 minor Ice Ages (the figure is still very imprecise), with the climate becoming correspondingly much warmer than it is today during the intervals.

To anyone familiar with the ancient teaching that our world operates according to cycles, it is immediately clear that what has been noted by scientists (so far in very approximate terms) looks as though it involves a multiplicity of sub-cycles within a greater cycle. The unavoidable inference is that our planetary climate is actually based upon astronomical factors – and not just those associated with the Sun and Moon.

The sub-cycles that we are here considering are almost certainly those of the 25,920-year 'precession of the equinoxes'. This – as I have pointed out in my last two books – seems to have nothing whatsoever to do with a 'wobble' in the Earth's axis, but is rather the result of our solar system's own orbit around a parent star. Seen from the Earth, this phenomenon creates the visual illusion of *reversing* through the Zodiac. During these cycles, the Earth is subject to prolonged celestial seasons of about 6,480 years, which have a dramatic effect upon both the climate in different parts of the world and also upon the many and varied cultures and civilizations which exist at the time.

The Problem of Global Warming

Connected with this same issue is the theory that 'global warming' – leading to the rapid deglaciation of the polar icecaps – is being caused by excessive GHGs ('greenhouse gases' such as CO_2 and methane) from human sources trapping heat from the Sun and causing a significant rise in the temperature of the Earth. Now, there is little doubt – despite the theory of human-generated 'greenhouse gases' – that there is taking place a definite widening of the 'ozone hole' at each pole and that this is clearly contributing to (if not being the fundamental cause of) the polar deglaciation and also the melting of glaciers. However, ancient texts indicate that this deglaciation is in fact cyclical and the implication, therefore, is that it has little or nothing to do with modern technology. It should be added that science itself has confirmed that periodic deglaciations have taken place throughout this geological era. This then is fact whilst the GHG theory as yet remains just that – a theory.

It has to be said that the GHG cause is based upon purely circumstantial evidence and takes no account of other potential factors; nor does it take into account the Earth's amazing organic capacity to neutralize imbalances in its various kingdoms of Nature, within its own due cycles. Consequently, it would appear that the current (and quite natural) global warming will be unstoppable, defying humankind's attempts to avoid the inevitably devastating effects. Thus worldwide submersion of low-lying lands will be unavoidable, even in economically wealthy countries, as the direct result of progressive oceanic expansion and rising sea levels.

There is no scientific doubt that the polar icecaps have melted and reformed many, many times over and that this has always affected human society (plus animal and plant species), often catastrophically. As the priests of Egypt told the Greek historian Herodotus, the Earth suffers regularly from alternating and prolonged periods of severe rainfall and *ekpyrosis*, – the latter actually meaning solar radiation from above.[12] These cyclic periods each last several thousand years and so it is not altogether surprising that the geographical pattern of human civilization and community development alters radically in response. In North Africa, during the earlier part of the current precessionary cycle, it resulted in the whole Sahara Desert becoming for several thousand years a grassy savannah, criss-crossed by rivers and lakes, of which modern desert oases are merely the scattered remnants. Many of these ancient rivers and lakes can be seen quite clearly on Charles Hapgood's reconstituted Piri Re'is map (*see* figure 19). In the mid-1960s Hapgood, Professor of the History of Science at Keene State College of the University of New Hampshire, wrote a remarkable book called *Maps of the Ancient Sea Kings* in which he described the amazing results derived from cartographic research he and his students had carried out in relation to an ancient map once in the possession of a 16th-century Turkish admiral, Piri Re'is. This map (and others also researched) clearly showed a variety of Atlantic islands which no longer exist, as well as showing that the coastline of the Americas had undergone radical change; that the Sahara Desert, at the time of the map's origin, had been covered with rivers and lakes; that the polar regions had been cartographically surveyed when no ice cap existed and that, contrary to the belief of modern science, spherical trigonometry had evidently been in use in ancient times.

So, it is becoming increasingly apparent that the Earth as an organism is itself driven by astronomically-based cycles, which result in various phenomena, including:

- The relatively sudden onset of Ice Ages

- The relatively sudden deglaciation of the polar icecaps, leading to an increase in equatorial sea levels of some 300 feet

- The relatively sudden dying out of large masses of temperate species incapable of adaptation to sudden and prolonged climatic change

- The sudden and unexplained quitting of highly sophisticated urbanized environments and the fragmentation or disappearance of associated cultures

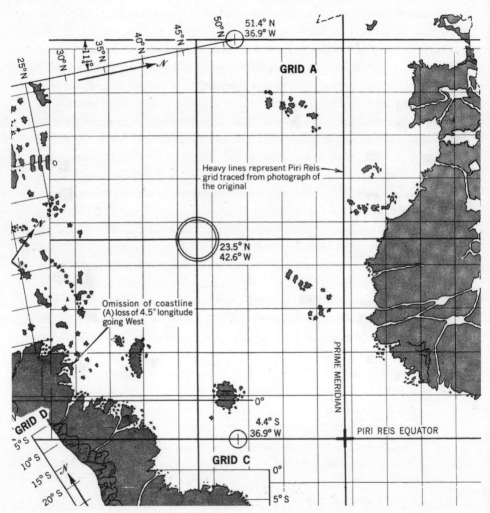

Figure 19. Part of Charles Hapgood's reconstruction of the Piri Re'is map, clearly showing rivers and lakes in what is now the Sahara (right), as well as the interior of the Iberian peninsula

These astronomical cycles are clearly of huge importance. For example, we have already mentioned the 25,920-year cycle of precession, believed to be the source of the prolonged rainfall and *ekpyrosis* described by the Egyptian priests to Solon. In addition, the perigee and apogee of the cycles of the giant star Sirius appear to result in brief but very severe climatic change. Taking place at 730-year intervals, these generate brief periods of intense cold on Earth. The last one occurred in the early 17th century, when winters became so severe that in 1607 the tidal River Thames in London froze over. Similarly, geologists have recorded that in the late 9th century, *c*870, Europe suffered from a sudden 'mini-Ice Age'.

I would therefore again suggest – against a background of logic – that human civilization and culture must be affected in as great a degree by the fluctuations of these great cycles and consequent climatic depredations as must the Animal and Plant kingdoms. However, humankind has much greater mobility and much greater powers of adaptation. Consequently, even though human civilizations may be destroyed, people can and do take fragments of their culture with them, to re-seed them elsewhere. So cultures adapt to circumstances – and that particularly includes spiritual cultures. Thus, when we find ancient Chaldean and Egyptian cultures suddenly springing apparently 'ready-made' into existence without any apparently visible learning curve, it is unsurprising that many regard this as circumstantial proof of a cultural legacy which has been merely resuscitated and expanded.

In the next chapter we shall take a rather more detailed look at the appearance of new landmasses in ancient times; for the world's geography was then completely and utterly different to what it is now. We shall then see how our modern landmasses compare in location, shape and size to the old ones, thereby approaching the issue of the actual location of Plato's Atlantis against a background of due logic and reason.

PART THREE

·

HUMANITY

Chapter Nine

•

THE ORIGINS OF HUMANKIND

'In 1979, researchers at the Laetoli, Tanzania, site in East Africa discovered footprints in volcanic ash deposits over 3.6 million years old. Mary Leakey and others said the prints were indistinguishable from those of modern humans ... It seems permissible therefore to consider a possibility ... that creatures with anatomically modern human bodies to match their anatomically modern feet existed some 3.6 million years ago.' [1]

'In the decades following the publication of Darwin's The Origin of Species, *many scientists found incised and broken bones indicating a human presence in the Pliocene, Miocene and earlier periods. Opponents suggested that the marks and breaks observed on the fossil bones were caused by the action of carnivores, sharks or geological pressure. But supporters of the discoveries offered impressive counter-arguments ... Nonetheless, reports of incised bones and broken bones indicating a human presence in the Pliocene and earlier are absent from the currently accepted stock of evidence.'* [2]

'The objections made to the existence of humans in the Pliocene and Miocene periods seem habitually to be more related to theoretical considerations than to direct observation.' [3]

In this chapter we shall begin to look at the historical and anthropological origins of humankind. However, before actually moving on to deal with the Lemurians and Atlanteans in turn, we should first of all perhaps spend a brief moment or two looking again at the patent failings of Darwinian theory. Firstly because Darwinism provides the current general orthodoxy on the development of humankind; and secondly because I argue that the earliest humankind existed over tens of millions of years ago at a period where not even the earliest anthropoids are considered (by today's anthropological 'establishment') to have existed. As we shall see, modern Creationism – involving the 'special creation' of humans as distinct from the animals – does not even begin to figure in this scheme either.

To begin with, it is generally accepted, even by esotericists, that relatively minor mutational changes in the body forms of species do undoubtedly occur as a result of environmental pressures or incentives. However, Darwinian theory goes much further in *assuming* that this principle must apply across the board to complete transformations of one family species or genus into another, even though this has no fundamental justification and has also never been proved. Hence the idea, still current, that somewhere there exist 'missing links' between the Plant and Animal kingdoms on the one hand and the Animal kingdom and the Human on the other. This does not take into consideration, of course, any such transformation between the Mineral and Plant kingdoms, although esoteric philosophy maintains that the Life principle is just as much to be found in the Mineral kingdom as in any other kingdom of Nature, despite taking different forms.[4]

It follows quite logically that the whole process of 'evolution' *per se* must involve dissimulation into experimental prototypes from an archetype, or a series of archetypes, as a result of some factor or factors imposing upon that archetype the sense that there is some necessity for change, or merely for self-expression. The biologist Dr Rupert Sheldrake appears to follow this principle in his theory of morphogenetic mutation, following on from the subjective telepathy enjoyed and employed by each species. However, despite his having shown quite conclusively that such telepathic faculty exists – a fact already so well known amongst native peoples all over the world as to cause no conjecture – his scientific peer group in the main refuses to accept it. This is usually on the wholly prejudiced and unscientific basis that such a faculty is either impossible or imaginary, notwithstanding the acknowledged existence of radio, television and other 'telepathic' wave-forms.

Darwinian theory proposes that the incentive to 'evolutionary' dissimilarity derives entirely from physically environmental factors. Esoteric philosophy, on the other hand, holds to the view that the causal factor is predominantly, if not entirely, *subjective*. However, it does not derive from the individual or group in the objective species at all, but rather from its parent *soul* – for this is the true archetype and 'missing link' that, by definition, will never itself take physical form. It remains the watching parent *in absentia*. Hence esoteric philosophy holds there to be an overall instinctive sense of a greater Purpose in Nature, perennially emanating from a variety of 'group-souls', to which *all* genera subjectively subscribe and within which they *all* participate in their own way.[5]

Notwithstanding this, there remain fundamental distinctions between groups and species. As Richard Milton tells us:

> In the animal world, the most striking thing about species today is their discontinuity. The living world consists mostly of gaps between species; gaps that remain

unbridgeable even in the imagination. The fossil record indicates clearly that the living world also consisted of gaps in every past age, from the most recent to the most remote. Yet Darwinists believe that whilst the present consists of gaps, the past was a perfect continuity of evolving species – even though this continuity is not recorded in the rocks.[6]

And again:

The gaps in the fossil record are reflected in the living world where many major animal and plant groups are high and dry with no discernible predecessors. The development of the entire order of mammals is missing from the fossil record, from its supposed shrewlike ancestor of the late Cretaceous until modern times.[7]

Twentieth-century ecological science has shown beyond any reasonable shadow of doubt that there is a subtle and often critical balance throughout Nature that involves the functional inter-relationships of 'eco-systems'. However, this principle clearly operates in an intelligently cooperative manner, even though there is – according to scientists – no 'intelligence' *per se* in the plant, insect, lower animals and bird species. There is, we are told, mere instinct, instinct itself meaning 'lack of self-awareness in function'. Yet there appears to be no given scientific reason why or how instinct itself should have evolved so intelligently. Nor has any even semi-rational idea yet been suggested as to why and how, for example, some creatures should have evolved to lay eggs and others to produce mammalian placentae. All is put down to 'natural selection' as though this answers everything – when in fact it generates more questions than answers.

There is one further and crucially important point to bear in mind in relation to the supposed process of trans-species evolution. It is that there appears to be an in-built point beyond which any species is unable to mutate in response to circumstances – which implies that this point is as much subjective as it is objective, perhaps more so. On this general issue, Richard Milton has this to say:

The natural limit on the amount of variation that can be induced in a species is merely the expression of the fact that nowhere in the animal or plant kingdoms is there a species that is capable of the infinite biological plasticity demanded by evolution theory, capable of unlimited adaptation to different environments and different modes of life. Living organisms are systems with limited potential for change, in which variation of one characteristic reacts on other characteristics, usually with unfavourable results.[8]

The fact is – as Milton confirms – that *any* organism artificially forced to the point of being threatened with going beyond its natural limits of experiential faculty, experiences a sort of 'subjective breakdown'. It thereafter begins to go backwards, its natural extroversion and resilience of character much weakened. As gardeners know, this 'reversion to type' occurs routinely in the plant kingdom, and it is also well known amongst both animals and humans. I shall refer to it again later in dealing with the issue of new human races appearing historically in line with a process known to esoteric philosophy and commented upon as early as 1891 by H.P. Blavatsky in *The Secret Doctrine*.

What Came First?

Returning to the question of archetypes and prototypes, it follows quite logically that, if the orthodox idea of evolution were actually true, then at some time a plant must somehow have given birth to or emanated directly from itself the first primordial animal organism. That genus must then have developed a diversity of functional experience (and instinct) which eventually enabled it first of all to develop a characteristic form and then to diversify into different species and sub-species. But *why* would it have done so in the first place? And where is the proof? Anthropology has no answer to these questions any more than it has to its own suggestion that the first cellular organisms just *happened* to materialize out of the first combination of gases produced by the supposedly all-encompassing volcanic activities of the early Earth state.

But then what impulse or incentive gave rise to the appearance of organic life itself? And from what? The response of science is only silence. However, when one queries such gaps in scientific knowledge or thought, one is told that these questions are for philosophers, not for scientists. Yet scientists make what is actually a philosophical assumption and then deny any responsibility for it. As I have suggested before, by seeking to deny philosophy its rightful lead in the field of true science, modern (at least Western) science has merely put out its own eyes and is thus reduced merely to feeling its way forward like one blind from birth, making up inductively speculative theories about the world as it goes along.

The Counter-Theory of Hoyle and Wickramsinghe

Professors Fred Hoyle and Chandra Wickramsinghe also pointed out the patent failings of Darwinist theory specifically by reference to the fossil record:

> The prognosis for Darwinism is now very poor. We can only explain the absence of intermediate insect forms in the fossil record either by supposing the different insect orders to be of separate origin or by arguing that the divergences from the common stock … took place with extreme rapidity. Only the second of these possibilities is consistent with Darwinism, yet rapid evolution is just what Darwinism cannot achieve.[9]

They then go on to add with damning clarity:

> What we are actually given in Darwin's books are very many changes of adaptation by already adapted species ... The key issue, namely that origins from scratch cannot be explained in the same way, is not dealt with at all.[10]

Hoyle and Wickramsinghe's own theory of the basis of evolution on Earth is a fascinatingly original one. As mentioned earlier, it basically suggests that new (already formed) 'genes from Space' are 'constantly riding around the galaxy on the pressure of light waves from the stars'. These genes, according to the theory, are constantly being absorbed into the Earth's atmosphere and it is because of these acting like computer software upgrades that no obviously intermediate forms, or 'missing links', are produced between species as they would be if in accordance with Darwinist theory. As regards the implicit underlying issue of there being some sort of intermediate hierarchy or hierarchies of being (that is, solar and/or terrestrial Nature spirits) involved in the direction of intelligent purpose behind this, Hoyle and Wickramsinghe have this to say:

> While many are willing and some are anxious to postulate an ultimately surpassing intellect (God), few are happy with the thought of intervening at levels between ourselves and God. Yet surely there must be such intelligences. It would be ridiculous to suppose otherwise.[11]

And they conclude by adding humorously:

> The mathematician may prefer to think in terms of a sequence that never attains its limit, in which case God is an ideal element that exists in the abstract but which is never reached in practice.[12]

Hoyle and Wickramsinghe's concept is actually, in certain respects, quite close to the way ancient esoteric tradition saw the whole process. This (along with the implicit potential associations with astrology) is probably why Darwinists reacted so strongly against it when it first appeared. Taken in conjunction with Hoyle and Wickramsinghe's 'Steady State Theory', however, it comes even closer to the ancient way of thinking. Nevertheless, there are two things they do not tackle, namely (a) primal origin, and (b) the direct relationship between genetic inheritance and light. These are central to the philosophy of the soul principle and without them the whole core of the overall concept is missing.

The Archaeological Inheritance

In the first few chapters of this book, we outlined the rationale of the archetypal soul principle as derived by reason from the metaphysical philosophy of the Ancient Wisdom tradition. In this chapter, having further sidelined

Darwinian theory for its solid want of reason, we shall continue with our consideration of the alternative perspective – that self-conscious humankind has been around for many millions of years and that its own ancient *objective* prototype was the ancestor of *all* the mammals from a historical past of several hundred million years ago.

In Chapter 4, I first outlined the full extent of the giant Lemurian super-continent, as described by H. P. Blavatsky from the ancient historical traditions of her oriental sources, which she referred to as 'the Ancient (Esoteric) Com-mentary'. I also explained that the original giant continent of Atlantis was actually one of the fragments of Lemuria, rather than an originally separate continental landmass. In this chapter, I am going to explore in rather greater detail the various traditions found around the world concerning these two vast continents and their peoples. In doing so, however, I shall continue to give particular attention to the works of Cremo and Thompson on the one hand and Blavatsky on the other, because these are the only extant books which (with sound reasoning) have shown archaeological orthodoxy to be based upon a string of false assumptions.

Cremo and Thompson's work lay in the field of sifting, re-examining and re-designating existing archaeological data from the past 150 years, thereby allowing much of importance that had been put to one side and forgotten (because of uncertainty at the time) to be properly reconsidered, in context. The net effect of their work has been to demonstrate quite conclusively, from the incontrovertible evidence of human artefacts and fossil bones found under deep geological layers, that, in their own words, 'anatomically modern humans have coexisted with other primates for tens of millions of years'.[13] But more of that below.

What I propose to do in the remainder of this chapter, then, is to compare modern archaeological and anthropological orthodoxy with what these authors (and others) have told us from their own quite different research angles. By doing so, we shall at least be able to see where the various similari-ties and differences of time and interpretation lie. That will then enable us to establish the different perspectives clearly.

The Sequencing of Human Types

To begin with, let us take a look at the modern orthodox view of human origins, as succinctly outlined by Cremo and Thompson:

According to modern views, the first apelike beings appeared in the Oligocene period, which began about 38 million years ago. The first apes thought to be on the line to humans appeared in the Miocene, which extends from 5–25 million years ago. These include Dryopithecus. Then came the Pliocene period. During the Pliocene, the first hominids or erect-walking humanlike primates are said to appear in the fossil record. The earliest known hominid is Australopithecus ... and is dated back as far as 4 million years. This near human, say scientists, stood between 4–5 feet tall.[14]

The orthodoxy continues by suggesting that a branch of *Australopithecus* somehow evolved into *Homo habilis* about 3 million years ago, and then into the first species of *Homo erectus* about 1.6 million years ago – the latter supposedly being 5–6 ft (1.5–1.8 m) tall, but not very hirsute.[15] Thereafter, some 300–400,000 years ago, according to the orthodox view, there appeared *Homo sapiens* in the form of still hirsute Neanderthal man (*Homo sapiens neanderthalensis*, or just *Homo neanderthalensis*), later to be succeeded within the last 200,000 years by the bodily hairless Cro-Magnon man, or modern human type (*Homo sapiens sapiens*). However, it is (quietly) acknowledged that counterparts of Cro-Magnon man (commonly some 6 ft 6 in [2 m] or more in height and with a brain capacity 15–20 per cent larger than our own) also existed at the beginning of the Quaternary period, some 1.6 million years ago. So what price scientific consistency?

The Peabody Museum at Harvard University has the faithfully reconstructed body and facial features of an example of Cro-Magnon man, taken from actual bones (*see* figure 20). However, it would not be unfair to suggest that with modern clothes such an individual would hardly attract a second glance if he passed by us in the street today.[16]

Figure 20. Ancient human types. Left: Neanderthal man, or Homo sapiens neanderthalensis. *Right: Cro-Magnon man, or* Homo sapiens sapiens. *By courtesy of the Peabody Museum of Archaeology & Ethnology at Harvard University.*

So, if such human types existed over 1.5 million years ago, how can anthropologists in all seriousness avoid the implications that the various forms of Neanderthal man, not to mention the Australopithicenes, were not evolutionary developments, but rather mere degenerates? With that in mind, let us now, by comparison, look at the analytical system which Blavatsky derived from the ancient records she referred to as 'the Ancient Commentary'.

Races, 'Root Races' and Sub-Races

Because so much of what we are going to say involves world cataclysms and their effects upon the various races of humanity, let me first be clear as to what I mean by the word 'race'. It is certainly not a mere question of 'ethnicity' or physical ethnology in the modern sense. As we saw in a previous chapter, the whole process of Nature is involved with an unfolding of *world consciousness* and faculty, the consciousness of the human race being just one part of that. Consequently, we may infer that here again – as with everything else – a repetitive but evolutionary sevenfold cycle is almost certainly involved. In other words (as Blavatsky outlines), there have to be seven major Race periods, which she calls 'Root Race' cycles. Each of these comprises seven sub-race periods, each of which in turn comprise seven sub-sub-race periods, and so on – all of these, however, being directly related to a variety of astronomical cycles. The sequential dynamic which Blavatsky describes is thus as follows:

- 1 Root Race (e.g. the Lemurian or Atlantean) comprises seven Sub-Races

- 1 Sub-Race comprises seven Branch Races

- 1 Branch Race comprises seven Family Races

- 1 Family Race comprises seven Family Branch Races

- 1 Family Branch Race comprises seven Continental Races

- 1 Continental Race comprises seven Nations[17]

It should thus become gradually obvious from this that whilst ethnological evolution of the human race is a valid scientific study, the present-day lay fascination with 'race' in the sense merely of 'ethnic' groups is a complete red herring – and often a pernicious one – compared to serious consideration of the place in society of particular cultural groups.

The time-spans associated with each of these greater and lesser races described by Blavatsky varies, for the simple reason that the cycle of unfolding depends upon the quality of the associated consciousness. Consequently, the relatively crude and undiscriminating consciousness of the earlier races and genera progressively gives way to the far subtler and more quickly-moving consciousnesses of the later ones. However, in conjunction with this, there has to be taken into consideration the fact of intermittent, or rather cyclical, *degeneracy* in the historic racial types and sub-types, coexistent with those still in the forefront of the evolutionary drive.

The expression in form of the previous cycle's evolutionary development (of consciousness) thus takes a great deal of time to process. Consequently, the early periods in each cycle are far longer in duration than the later ones.[18] This is clear from figure 15 (*see* page 111), which shows the geological periods acknowledged by modern orthodox opinion (however, Blavatsky's geological periods, taken from the Ancient Commentary, are rather shorter, for reasons already described in Chapter 7). But what about the various back-dating techniques available to us? Are these able to identify precisely when, in historical terms, these various anthropological groups appeared and also how they fitted into the overall scheme of Creation?

The Basic Dating Technique

The first and most logical technique used by geologists and archaeologists was that of geological strata dating. This was carried out on the basis that the various layers of the Earth's crust were visually discernible and that their relative age could be calculated on the basis of roughly known rates of sedimentation and general deposition. On the face of it, this seemed sensible. However, the given rate of sedimentation was based upon the supposedly *current* rate of deposition, it being assumed that this rate has always been roughly the same —something that cannot actually be proved and is, from several angles, wide open to question. But even the current rate of deposition hardly supports the present scientific orthodoxy in the field of geochronology. As Richard Milton rather pointedly confirms:

> Throughout widely changing climatic conditions, advancing and retreating oceans, droughts and Ice Ages, the rate of sedimentation appears to remain amazingly constant regardless – throughout the thousands of millions of years that are said to have elapsed. The presumed rate of deposition itself is about the thickness of a human hair in a year ... But it is worth pausing in passing to note that such a slow rate would be incapable of burying and fossilizing entire forests, dinosaurs, or even a medium-sized tadpole.[19]

Deposition is based upon the rate at which cosmic dust, having passed into our system via the North Polar region, actually settles and creates a definable type of rock, the age of which can then be calculated. However, the dust is subject to the vagaries of the high- and low-level winds of our atmosphere, much of it in any case falling into the oceans and seas. So the deposition could by no means prove regular. But, in addition to all this, no account seems to have been taken of the fact that such dust – being matter – is at least partially reconverted (after deposition) into energy by the Earth's natural processes. It is thus a contributor to the planet's own radiation, the rate of which undoubtedly fluctuates too. So, the present system of scientific dating *cannot* be regarded as even nearly reliable.

In addition to this, we must also take into consideration the fact – as described earlier – that geologists have failed to account for the Earth's own progressively cyclic materialization. Thus the earliest sedimentary strata (the Pre-Cambrian) have to be considered as having actually formed into a somewhat plastic state during a previous greater planetary cycle, only becoming 'hardened' into a recognizable geology in the earliest part of this present greater cycle. Unfortunately, however, our modern science does not yet even recognize the existence of such cycles. But then even – as we saw in Chapters 2 and 3 – the more modern and more sophisticated dating techniques based upon radiometric and other technology can hardly be relied upon without extensive qualification either.

The Problem with Modern Identification and Dating Techniques

The associated matter of designating plant and animal species accurately is initially complicated by the fact that cyclical cataclysms never manage to wipe out all members of the outgoing race or genus. Many continue side by side with the new race or genus, often for millions of years, and only gradually die out by attrition or absorption. Consequently, the finding of their remains and artefacts in the sedimentary deposits of our world by field scientists is entirely dependent upon chance. Frequently, whatever is found leads research opinion up completely blind alleys of speculatively historical reasoning. As Cremo and Thompson also confirm,

> The drawbacks of palaeoanthropological facts are not limited to excavations of objects. Similar drawbacks are also found in modern chemical or radiometric dating studies. For example, a carbon 14 date might seem to involve a straightforward procedure that reliably yields a number – the age of an object. But actual dating studies often turn out to involve complex considerations regarding the identity of samples, and their history and possible contamination. They may involve the rejection of some preliminary calculated dates and the acceptance of others on the basis of complex arguments that are seldom explicitly published. Here also the facts can be complex, incomplete, and largely inaccessible …

Since the information conveyed by palaeoanthropological reports tends to be incomplete and since even the simplest palaeoanthropological facts tend to involve complex, unresolvable issues, it is difficult to arrive at solid conclusions about reality in this field.[20]

The latter statement is also true of both radiocarbon dating and dendrochronological dating. The former depends entirely upon having pure and uncontaminated samples (which in reality is exceptionally difficult to achieve) and it also takes no consideration of the possibility that the rate of radiation may well fluctuate quite markedly in conjunction with different planetary and solar cycles. Radiation dating inevitably becomes less and less reliable the further one goes back in historical time.

Dendrochronology, or tree-ring dating, works entirely on the assumption that there is a reasonable regularity of response to climatic change by different trees, even perhaps in entirely different locations and environments. However, these environments themselves change dramatically over millions or even only tens of thousands of years. Consequently, it is pretty well impossible for scientists (without depending upon a raft of assumptions) to ascertain the local micro-climates of the time and thus state quite accurately what reflects a macro-climate and what only a micro-climate – and the consequent effect upon tree rings.

Similarly, ice core sample dating cannot be relied upon for equivalent reasons. It is based upon the idea that because seeds, pollen and small organisms can be found in increasingly deep layers of ice, by producing a corresponding analysis of the associated snowfall which gave rise to the ice, it becomes possible to date one against the other. But this assumes that the snowfall is reasonably regular and that one annual layer can thus be relatively easily distinguished from another. However, knowledge in this area is as yet very limited. It was not so long ago believed that the last Ice Age extended solidly from 100,000 years ago to about 10,000 years ago. Now it is reckoned that this whole era comprised a mass of mini-Ice Ages (nobody can be sure quite how many) interspersed by periods of semi-tropical climate, while many northern parts were not affected by glaciation at all. In addition, those areas with the deepest ice-sheets are those with the least snowfalls. How exactly does this paradox come about? Science has as yet no answer.

By way of proving that the current dating techniques are even less reliable than strata dating, we show below some of the data mentioned by Cremo and Thompson confirming the nature of human artefacts found by archaeologists and others, and their age as confirmed by stratification itself. However, with regard to the oldest finds, I would suggest that one needs to take into consideration the fact that because the theory of plate tectonics has taken such a hold, geological science does not as yet recognize the Earth's capacity for recycling the planetary crust by subsidence and rotation. Geology accepts that mountains fold, concertina-fashion, but not that they actually rotate, whereas rotation is a basic force in Nature, as any structural engineer will confirm. Consequently, some of the oldest artefacts (if they survive the associated crushing motion) will inevitably be found under literally miles of rock, even where that rock has subsequently been reformed into a mountain. Thus designated ages of hundreds of millions of years may perhaps turn out to be only tens of millions of years instead.

Examples of anomalous archaeological discoveries dated by reference to sedimentary layers (MYA = million years ago).[21]

2800 MYA	Grooved metallic spheres found in Ottosdalin, South Africa (1960s)
600 MYA	A metal vase found in Dorchester, Massachusetts, USA (1852)
510 MYA	A fossilized shoeprint, found in Utah (1968)
360 MYA	An iron nail found in a stone in Brewster, California, USA (1844)
320 MYA	A gold thread found in a stone, N.E. England (1844)
312 MYA	An iron cup found in Oklahoma (1912)
260 MYA	A gold chain found in Morrisonville, Illinois (1891)
260 MYA	A block wall, found under a coal deposit in Oklahoma (1928)
33–55 MYA	A human skeleton found in California (1855)

It is thus clear that literally none of the present methods of scientific dating can actually be unequivocally relied upon to support what modern orthodoxy is saying about the supposed climatic and other ages which the kingdoms of Nature on our planet have experienced[22] – any more than it can be relied upon to confirm just how old the human race actually is. That being so, where do we go from here? Well, one alternative at least lies with consideration of the Ancient Wisdom tradition, at least to see what alternative perspective it offers.

One might counter in response that one cannot rely upon Blavatsky's prehistoric insights or dates on the grounds that she offers no even semi-scientific technique to back them up. There is merely the suggestion that they are the product of the consciously retrospective perceptions of countless generations of highly qualified adept seers, whose own self-imposed rules have necessitated the ruthless cross-checking and cross-confirmation of such insights over millennia by literally all their peers before being generally accepted. But so what?

It is true that the use of consciousness in a retrospective manner (using particular techniques of meditative regression) is neither understood by nor acceptable to modern science. However, the fact remains that it is well understood in certain oriental traditions. There it has been practised for untold thousands of years and, in relation to it, the practice of accurate memorization has always been rigidly enforced.[23] The same applied to the ancient Druids who, as the Romans and others recorded, committed to memory all their lore, from sacred rites and myths to the entire canon of laws, during a *20-year* training. Their memorization capacity, like that of their Eastern counterparts, must have been stupendous. Being unwritten, however, only a tiny fragment of (ancient) Druid lore survives. Unfortunately, in the West, such accuracy of memorization has become a mere theatrical novelty.

Such retrospective research is said to involve the process of using sound and light in a *subjective* manner – sound to access the correct field of knowledge and light to manifest it within the consciousness itself. The fact – as I have already described in Chapter 3 – that light provides a historical record of all that takes place in our world, means that the complete history of our planetary Life must be available for examination, by at least those who understand the *scientific* laws involved and have access to the appropriate technique. But, in addition to this, there is a well-established tradition that actual written records have also been maintained by certain closed esoteric groups in the Far East, covering a period of many millions of years.

So, taking all these various factors into account, and notwithstanding any passing criticisms, I propose here to continue with the timetable provided by the ancient records as being possibly rather more reliable than the modern one. That in turn would appear to suggest that the Lemurian (Third Race) commenced its existence about 45–50 million years ago (at the beginning of the Secondary or Mesozoic period), with the first appearance of self-conscious humankind taking place about 18 million years ago. The Atlantean (Fourth Race) type would then have first appeared about 9–10 million years ago at the beginning of the Tertiary or Cenozoic period. Clearly, however, the continents on which both these Races lived had themselves come into existence at an earlier date, the Atlantean Fourth Race continent having been – as already suggested – merely a fragment of the original Lemurian super-continent. But that is something which I shall pursue in the next chapter.

Chapter Ten

·

LEMURIA AND THE EARLY THIRD RACE OF HUMANKIND

'The Vedas speak of periodic renovations of humanity, with the power of the gods passed on to new peoples who return culture to its spiritual roots. The Vedic people appear as a spiritual reform of an older humanity, marking a new Age.' [1]

In this chapter we shall be looking at the first (pre-Atlantean) emergence of humankind from the 'animal' kingdom – but from the viewpoint of an Ancient Wisdom tradition, which runs quite counter to what Darwinian theory has to say on the subject. As we shall see, that tradition has its own definite sense of a completely natural evolutionary process which, although it appears to have elements of Creation theory in it, explains *why* the process works as it does (which Creation theory does not) and also what evolution *really* involves.

This chapter also looks at the issue of the continental landmasses on which tradition and speculation have placed the various prehistoric Races of humankind. These landmasses do *not* coincide with modern geological orthodoxy because – according to the Ancients – our planet's geological mantle has always been in a constant process of mutation, a fact that plate tectonic theory could not begin to assimilate or agree with. Consequently, very few indeed of the original landmasses or seabeds still exist today.

The approach I shall take in dealing with these issues necessarily involves the extensive use of descriptive quotations from H.P. Blavatsky's *The Secret Doctrine*. As I have explained, Blavatsky stated that her work was an exposition from an age-old 'Ancient Commentary' possessed and maintained by a society of Adept teachers (known as 'Mahatmas') based somewhere on the borders of northern India and Tibet. Although some have suggested that these teachers were a figment of Blavatsky's own imagination, their existence has been well known and even documented in Middle and Far Eastern sources from the most ancient times. As the respected Vedic scholar Dr David Frawley remarks:

> There is a class of human beings, perhaps very small in number, who have always looked over humanity. These are the great gurus, avatars and spiritual teachers. In ancient times they had a much greater role in developing and shaping human culture. As humanity declined from the ancient ages of light, they gradually withdrew into seclusion. Today, they still exist, though they may be hard to find ... The prime area they relate to is the Himalayas ... Whilst many occult teachings glorify such masters and may put a cloak of illusion or mystery about them, there is still a core of truth about them which we cannot ignore.[2]

This chapter will not only introduce us to the great planetary cataclysms, of which fragmented mention has otherwise passed down to us via the various sacred books of present and past world religions, it will also offer a reasoned description of how and why our kindred, the anthropoid apes, came to exist. Rather than seeing them as the ancestors of humankind, as Darwinists insist, we will have a better understanding of the equally ancient tradition that they are in fact merely degenerate forms from Nature's (and humankind's) past. However, let us turn first of all to the issue of where the ancient landmasses of our planet are supposed originally to have existed.

The Location of Lemuria

With regard to the second great continental landmass of our world, *The Secret Doctrine* tells us:

> Lemuria, as we have called the continent of the Third Race, was ... a gigantic land. It covered the whole area of space from the foot of the Himalayas, which separated it from the inland sea rolling its waves over what is now Tibet, Mongolia and the great desert of Schamo [Gobi]; from Chittagong westward to Hardwar and eastward to Assam. From thence it stretched south across what is known to us as southern India, Ceylon and Sumatra, then embracing on its way, as we go south, Madagascar on its right hand and Australia and Tasmania on its left, it ran down to within a few degrees of the Antarctic Circle; when from Australia – an inland region on the mother continent in those ages – it extended far into the Pacific Ocean, not only beyond Rapa-nui [Easter Island].'[3]

She continues a little later:

> It must be noted that the Lemuria which served as the cradle of the Third [Lemurian] Race not only embraced a vast area in the Pacific and Indian Oceans,

but extended in the shape of a horse-shoe past Madagascar, around South Africa (then a mere fragment in the process of formation), through the Atlantic, up to Norway.[4]

Blavatsky adds by way of clarification:

No more striking confirmation of our position could be given than the fact that the elevated ridge in the Atlantic basin, 9,000 feet in height, which runs for some 2,000–3,000 miles southwards from a point near the British Islands, first slopes towards South America, then shifts almost at right angles to proceed in a south-easterly line towards the African coast, whence it runs southwards to Tristan d'Acuna [sic]. This ridge is a remnant of an Atlantean continent and could it be traced further, would establish the reality of a submarine horse-shoe junction with a former continent in the Indian Ocean.[5]

Verification of Blavatsky's Prediction

At the time that *The Secret Doctrine* was written (1889), the full southward extent of the Mid-Atlantic Ridge was not known, nor was there any even slight indication from the scientific research by then carried out that it might extend all the way around South Africa into the Indian Ocean as Blavatsky described. The full extent of the ridge only became apparent well over half a century later, when scientific technology allowed a much more thorough examination of the ocean beds. This resulted in the production of the Heezen-Tharp bathyspheric map of the world's sea and ocean beds, part of which is shown in figure 17 (*see* page 125). This confirmed beyond any shadow of doubt the 'horse-shoe shape' mentioned by Blavatsky, which can clearly be seen in figure 16, showing the location of the various oceanic ridges of the Atlantic and Indian Oceans (*see* page 119).

One is thus unavoidably drawn to the conclusion that Blavatsky's statements, obtained from her obscure oriental sources, must have been based upon factual knowledge, even though modern science may not be able to understand quite how such knowledge could have been obtained in the depths of prehistory. However, Blavatsky's source information seems to go back even further, because she continues her description with a comment on the very origin of Lemuria, which must have been well over 50 million years ago. Part of this is cited below. First though, one might also observe here that Blavatsky's description makes it clear that the current theory of 'continental drift' cannot hold good. The idea that Australia, Madagascar and India were part of the same continental landmass (the intervening parts of which are today merely submerged), cannot be reconciled with modern science's concept that each forms part of a separate 'tectonic plate'.

The First Great Continent and its Associated Race

Blavatsky's narrative continues as follows:

> The first continent which came into existence capped over the whole North Pole
> like one unbroken crust and remains so to this day … During the Second [Root]
> Race, more land emerged from under the waters as a continuation of the 'head'
> from the 'neck'. Beginning on both hemispheres, on the line above the most
> northern part of Spitzbergen, on Mercator's projection, on our [i.e. the Euro-
> pean] side, it may have included on the American side the localities that are now
> occupied by Baffin's Bay and the neighbouring islands and promontories. There
> it hardly reached southward the 70th degree of latitude; here it formed the horse-
> shoe continent of which the Commentary speaks; of the two ends of which one
> included Greenland, with a prolongation which crossed the 50th degree a little
> south-west and the other Kamschattka, the two ends being united by what is now
> the northern fringe of the coasts of eastern and western Siberia. This broke
> asunder and disappeared.[6]

The Second (Root) Race is not a subject which I propose to deal with in any
depth, but since it has just been mentioned, I might add here in passing yet a
further reference from Blavatsky. This may help to give some background to
the evolutionary appearance of the later Third (Lemurian) Race when we
come to deal with it.

Concerning the First Root Race, *The Secret Doctrine* makes it clear that it
was an entirely passive, psycho-spiritual group of what could only be called
basic (although giant sized), ethereal 'soul-organisms'. This description is best
understood in the sense of giant cytoplasmic entities which were macrocos-
mically comparable to single cell organisms like the amoeba. Here then is the
key to why the cell, as an organism, acts as the archetypal foundation of all
organic life on our planet and also why scientists have only found evidence of
merely single celled organisms in existence when the first sedimentary
deposits were being laid down.

Perhaps unsurprisingly, Blavatsky describes the Second Race as a mere
mutation of the First Race. Of the Second Race itself, she says that much later,
following a process of diversification from the original, psycho-spiritual
archetype just described, it 'was composed of the most heterogeneous gigantic semi-human monsters, the first attempts of material Nature at building
human bodies'. Of the landmass on which these creatures lived, she says:

> The ever blooming lands of the second continent (Greenland among others) were
> transformed in order from Edens with their eternal Spring into hyperborean
> Hades. This transformation was due to the displacement of the great waters of

the globe, to oceans changing their beds; and the bulk of the Second Race perished in this.[7]

To give some indication of just how crude were Nature's first attempts at producing proto-humanoid body forms, the Ancient Commentary tells us that during the only slightly later period, just after the great cataclysms,

> there were four-armed human creatures in those early days of the male-females [hermaphrodites] of the Third Race; with one head, yet three eyes.[8]

These 'three-eyed men' were of course the progenitors of the much later Lemurian Cyclopes giants, who are recorded in Greek 'myth' – the 'third eye' being in the middle of the forehead, between the eyebrows.

The Sudden Mass Disppearance of the Dinosaurs

Bearing in mind that the 'oceanic displacement' catastrophe, which devastated the Second Race, seems to have coincided with the appearance of the Third Race, and that the latter is thought to have emerged 45–50 million years ago, it seems not impossible that the same cataclysm may also have been the one that resulted in the wholesale destruction of the mass of the dinosaurs.[9] Modern science currently puts the destruction of the dinosaurs at about 60–65 million years ago but it seems somewhat likely to have been rather more recent.

Current scientific theory has no real idea as to how or why this cataclysm might have occurred and, as indicated in the previous chapter, has consequently adopted the 'asteroid theory'. This supposes that a gigantic lump of cosmic rock, the size of Manhattan, hit the Earth somewhere in the Gulf of Mexico, thereby unleashing a huge tidal wave which swept away all in its path. The destruction apparently extended not just to the dinosaurs, but also to a vast proportion of marine life in general. It is interesting to note that this purely hypothetical speculation has now 'evolved', in a very Darwinian fashion, into the popular modern orthodoxy.

In practical terms, however, it seems more likely that at this time the Earth's weather systems first started to operate powerfully in distinct seasonal cycles. The main reason behind this must have been that the axial rotation of the planet was itself slowing down in conjunction with the process of increasing planetary densification. The principle is well understood in basic physics as a fundamental characteristic of inertial drag. But one of the side effects must have been to make the huge bodies of the dinosaurs also rather heavier, resulting in far greater pressure on their hearts and blood circulation systems. That would certainly have resulted in large-scale deaths as the atmosphere itself grew heavier.

The First Volcanic and Earthquake Activity

What must also have happened is that the planet's plasmic core first began to react to containment by the newly formed and rapidly hardening crust. This would have resulted in crustal stress coincident with the expansion of core energies, duly followed by the generation of the magma lithosphere just under the crust. There would only then have followed the progressive appearance of volcanic and earthquake activity and the consequent emergence of newly formed landmasses out of the superheated magma which had hitherto been building up under the already existing oceanic crust.

It is interesting to note what Blavatsky had to say on the issue of the polar regions a few million years on:

> The occult teaching shows the [now] polar regions as the earliest of the seven cradles of humanity and as the tomb of the bulk of the mankind of that region during the Third Race when the gigantic continent of Lemuria began separating into smaller continents. This was due ... to a decrease of velocity in the Earth's rotation.[10]

However, the Ancient Commentary that Blavatsky credits as her source tells us that the Third Race was only at about the middle point of its cycle of development when

> The axle of the Wheel tilted ... People [for the first time] knew snow, ice and frost, and men, plants and animals were dwarfed in their growth. Those that did not perish remained as half-grown babes in size and intellect.[11]

The 'axle of the Wheel' appears to be a reference to the astronomical position of Ursa Minor as seen from Earth. That in turn indicates a distinct change affecting the Earth's poles and a severely worsened climatic environment. However, the specific point of interest in the last quotation is that the dramatic change in the climatic conditions resulting from this was what led to the mass death of the larger humanoids, animals and plants. This is presumably a reference to another mass extinction of dinosaurs; but it serves to provide another reason for the dramatic reduction in size of all species, not only at that time but also again later.

The Progressive Continental Break-up

Writing of the era of the rather later, post-mid-Lemurian cataclysm, Blavatsky writes elsewhere:

> In the epoch we are treating of, the continent of Lemuria had already broken asunder in many places and formed new separate continents. There was nevertheless neither Africa, nor the Americas, still less Europe in those days; nor was

there much of present Russia/India, for the cis-Himalayan regions were covered with seas and beyond this stretched the lotus leaves [peninsulas] of Sveta Dwipa, the continent now called Greenland, eastern and western Siberia, etc.[12]

It is also interesting to note – given Blavatsky's suggestion that Africa did not even exist in mid-late Lemurian times – what Cremo and Thompson have to say on the popular modern orthodoxy that humankind 'came out of Africa':

> One need not suppose that either Africa or Asia was a centre of evolution. There is, as shown in preceding chapters, voluminous evidence – much [of it] found by professional scientists – suggesting that humans of the modern type have lived on various continents, including South America, for tens of millions of years.[13]

Blavatsky herself adds, concerning the progressive destruction of Lemuria during the later Atlantean period:

> The immense continent [of Lemuria] which had once reigned supreme over the Indian, Atlantic and Pacific Oceans, now consisted of huge islands which were gradually disappearing, one after the other, until the final convulsion engulfed the last remains of it. Easter Island, for instance, belongs to the earliest civilization of the Third Race. Submerged with the rest, a volcanic and sudden uplifting of the ocean floor raised the small relic of the archaic ages, untouched, with its volcanoes and statues, during the Champlain epoch of northern polar submersion, as a standing witness to the existence of Lemuria [whilst, in addition,] a large bit of California belonged to it.[14]

The Causes of the Later Planetary Cataclysms

With regard to the characteristics and reasons for the major cataclysms which destroyed the Lemurian and Atlantean civilizations, we are told:

> The cataclysm which destroyed the huge continent of which Australia is the largest relic, was due to a series of subterranean convulsions and the breaking asunder of the ocean floor [whereas] that which put an end to its successor, the fourth continent [Atlantis] was brought on by successive disturbances in the axial rotation.[15]

The huge twist in the three oceanic ridges, described in Chapter 8, thus appears to coincide with the mid-Fourth Race cataclysm. By way of explanation, Blavatsky adds elsewhere from the Commentary:

> When the Wheel [here meaning the Zodiac] runs at the usual rate, its poles agree [conform vertically] with its equator; when it runs slower and it tilts in every

direction, there is a great disturbance on the face of the Earth. The waters flow towards the ends [i.e. the poles] and new lands arise in the middle belt [the tropics], whilst those at the ends are subject to *pralayas* [periods of dormancy] by submersion.[16]

The Changing Axial Movement of Our Planet

Basic physics would confirm that, at a certain rate of axial velocity above what now prevails, an increasing amount of the world's oceanic water would flow towards the Equator. The Moon would then condition this in both northern and southern latitudes by its cycle, thereby creating predictable tidal cycles and surges. In parallel to this, the deceleration of the axial spin beyond a certain point would cause the worldwide ocean levels to re-equilibrate. This would thereby allow large amounts of seawater to move back towards the poles, inevitably causing the northern lands to become flooded over. The question then arises, what exactly causes the Earth's axial spin to alter so radically?

Well the only logical answer is again an astronomical (or astrophysical) one, resulting from the position of our solar system relative to (a) its own greater cycle (b) other star systems and their greater electro-magnetic force-fields. In the same way that our Earth's axial velocity actually slows down as it approaches both winter and summer solstice points – at perihelion and aphelion – and then accelerates away again once the solstice is passed (*see again* figure 12, page 95), so it would appear that our solar system as a whole does precisely the same thing. That would then account for the various phenomena described.

The Earliest 'Human' Types

Bizarre though it might appear to us today, the late Second Race and early Third Race types were supposedly androgyne to begin with and then hermaphrodite, all being only semi-human, self-reproductively egg-laying creatures of gigantic size, in conformity with the then stage of development of the animal kingdom as a whole. In the very early Third Race era, it must be remembered, all the animals and proto-humanoids still had semi-ethereal body forms, with a cartilaginous structure but with no solid bones as such. However, the Ancient Commentary elsewhere makes it clear that, although vertebrate animals (that is, reptiles) were the first to develop a skeletal structure, the later Lemurian proto-human was the first mammalian species to appear – during the mid-Third Race period – having previously been an entirely asexual entity.

Interestingly, in unconscious support of this, we find the 19th-century French anthropologist de Quatrefages making the following unequivocal statement:

> Man can be shown to have lived in the mid-Tertiary period and in a geological age where there did not yet exist one single specimen of the now known species of mammals.[17]

How could this possibly be so unless what the Ancient Commentary says is accurate? As Cremo and Thompson tell us in further support of de Quatrefages:

> Alfred Russell Wallace, who shares with Darwin the credit for formulating the theory of evolution by natural selection, expressed dismay that evidence for anatomically modern humans existing in the Tertiary tended to be attacked with all the weapons of doubt, accusation and ridicule.[18]

Darwin himself also appears to concur with the Ancient Commentary when he says in his *The Descent of Man*:

> It has been known in the vertebrate kingdom [that] one sex bears rudiments of various accessory parts appertaining to the reproductive system which properly belong to the opposite sex ... [Thus] some remote progenitor of the whole vertebrate kingdom appears to have been hermaphrodite or androgynous.[19]

Darwin further amplified this in *The Origin of Species* when he expressed the opinion that humans and apes must have had a *common* mammalian ancestor, which itself could well have lived before the Silurian epoch[20] – well over 400 million years ago (according to orthodox modern dating methods).

The Laws of Evolutionary Development

Blavatsky makes the very firm point that occult philosophy believes in an ancient law of progressive evolutionary development which is, however, subject to an accompanying law of retardation 'which imposes a restriction on the advance of all species when a higher type makes its appearance.'[21] It would appear that, due to the workings of this law, each older Race – in the human case, at least – is partially subsumed within the next later one (by evolutionary development). However, the majority die out or are destroyed either by natural cataclysm or their inability to adapt to changing environmental (including climatic) circumstances. This concept is of particular interest because it ties in exactly with the modern perception of an in-built natural limit to the mutation of species, which I mentioned earlier in the last chapter.

The Secret Doctrine refers to certain modern ethnological types as particularly related to the consciousness of the ancient Root Races. Unfortunately this has been taken by some superficially minded commentators to suggest that Blavatsky and her followers were racists who held darker-skinned and other non-European ethnic groups to be inferior. However, Blavatsky herself explicitly rejected any form of racism outright as thoroughly and ignorantly puerile, so this charge does not hold water. Nevertheless, I should perhaps take a brief moment to explain her viewpoint more fully.

As has already been suggested, the *pure* ancient racial types of Lemuria and Atlantis have disappeared altogether, although certain characteristics are still interestingly to be found amongst *all* modern peoples. For example, the Lemurian 'narrow-headed' (or 'Saturnian') characteristic is just as much to be found amongst today's 'European' type as any other, although the actual face is rarely as long in proportion.

The essence of the physical 'evolutionary' idea as propounded by Blavatsky involved the cyclical appearance of new ethnological human types (involving material reductions in overall body size plus sympathetic changes to the skull and facial appearance) as an effect of the insemination of a new form of consciousness. Once this had appeared, it spread – morphogenetically – with increasing rapidity but in varying degree, *throughout* the human race.

However, *The Secret Doctrine* elsewhere makes the point that the direction and momentum of civilization and culture is constantly shifting (as history clearly shows) through migration, colonization or cataclysmic enforcement, with inevitably consequent cultural intermarriage. The natural shift or movement of cultures from one place to another (along with their supporting technology) then brings about quite naturally – often over vast periods of time – the existence of wholly temporary 'cultural backwaters'. These backwaters, along with associated adaptations (to anthropologists at least) then look as though they support Darwinian theory, although they in fact do no such thing. The next global shift of culture and civilization simply picks up and re-assimilates all or at least most of these ethnological groups left to one side by the last wave of global change, with the result that they too incorporate any other mainstream changes made in the meantime. Thus it is that some such groups tend to 'fade away' quite naturally as their own younger people re-assimilate themselves into the mainstream of world civilization and culture.

It is a perhaps curious characteristic of (at least Western) human culture that anything old or different is used to make us feel more cosy about our present because the past was clearly so quaint – and so much less comfortable. This attitude is unconsciously reinforced by anthropologists and archaeologists, who have so successfully managed to convince themselves that human civilization is only about 12,000 years old, that this overall scenario has not even begun to occur to them as a possibility.

Cataclysms and Gigantism

One notable 'evolutionary' effect upon the forward momentum of each Race is that of cataclysm, as Blavatsky remarks:

> After the Great Flood of the Third Race, men decreased considerably in stature and the duration of their lives was diminished. Having fallen down in godliness, they mixed with animal races and intermarried amongst giants and pigmies.[22]

This latter comment is a reference to the dwarfed remnants of the polar Second Race, the 'heterogeneous mass of monsters' created by Nature at that time. Bearing in mind that *The Secret Doctrine* has the gigantic early Lemurian proto-humans as some 60–70 ft (18–21 m) tall, diminishing to about 30 ft (9.1 m) by the end of the Third Race, we can perhaps gain some understanding of the idea that, in those days, the Earth had still not shrunk (or consolidated) to anything like its present size. Hence it was that many of the species of the Plant kingdom – witness some of the giant ferns of New Zealand and the super-giant redwood and eucalyptus trees of California and Australia – were of correspondingly huge size.

The great size of the various species of dinosaurs and other creatures alive at that time is of course already well known to palaeontological science. It is also worth remembering, however, that the process of densification of all body forms had still not, by this time, reached its natural cyclical summation, only doing so by the middle of the Atlantean (Fourth Race) period. Consequently, at the beginning of the Lemurian period – over 50 million years before that – *all* body forms would have been considerably lighter in weight and of a more 'plastic' nature, the skeleton having still not hardened by then.

For those who find it difficult to entertain the idea of proto-humanoids originally 60–70 ft tall, decreasing gradually by over 50 per cent in size, there is a completely straightforward logic behind it. In essence, as the Mind principle developed more fully within the various kingdoms of Nature on our planet, expressing itself as natural intelligence, so did the capacity for attentiveness, or concentration of consciousness.

As we saw earlier, consciousness is itself the form-building principle in universal Nature. So the faculty of increasing concentration of consciousness naturally led to the forms diminishing in size as terrestrial Nature responded with the appropriate 'clothing', using an appropriately greater densification and technical complexity of matter. That in turn led, *pro rata*, to all body forms becoming not only smaller but also increasingly much heavier.

The First 'Sin of the Mindless'

The other part of Blavatsky's statement, concerning the subsequent inter-racial mating of the Third Race types – at that time just beginning to evolve gender differentiation and the associated sexual urge – is of particular interest for another reason which we should address as follows.

The Secret Doctrine refers to this inter-Race liaison as 'the sin of the mindless' – a reference to the fact that it was accidental and quite definitely not intended. The apparent result of the union was a dumb sub-race of semi-human, ape-like monstrosities, the far distant progenitors of the anthropoids. However, the present-day apes (the orang-utang, gorilla, chimpanzee and baboon) were supposedly the product of a much later repetition of this illicit liaison, in Atlantean times, as we shall see in due course. Whilst the original ape-like monstrosities became progressively sterile and hence eventually died out completely, the later anthropoids of the Fourth Race are said to have become imbued with a small spark of (psycho-spiritual) humanity – for reasons which we shall again enlarge upon later – and thus continued to evolve as definite species in their own right, right up to the present day. Blavatsky describes the matter in rather more detail as follows:

> The bestiality of the primeval mindless races resulted in the production of huge, man-like monsters, the offspring of human and animal parents. As time rolled on and the still semi-astral forms consolidated into the physical, the descendants of these creatures were modified by external conditions until the breed, dwindling in size, culminated in the lower apes of the Miocene period. With these the later Atlanteans renewed the 'sin of the mindless' – this time with full responsibility.[23]

On the issue of the first 'Sin of the Mindless' it is interesting to note that the modern anthropologist's *Dryopithecus* – 'an ape-like hominid species', apparently some 4–5 ft (1.22–1.52 m) tall, existed (by current dating at least) some 15–20 million years ago. According to Blavatsky, the Ancient Commentary says of the product of the original, illicit liaison that 'they bred monsters (wicked demons male and female) and also Dakini with little minds.'[24] The latter group is elsewhere described as 'having human shape but having the lower extremities, from the waist down, covered with hair'[25] – which brings to mind the satyrs of Greek myth.

The Ancient Commentary also provides us with a description of

> red-haired swarthy men, going on all fours, who bend and unbend [stand erect and fall on their hands again] who speak as their forefathers and run on their hands as their giant foremothers.[26]

The description immediately brings to mind the modern orang-utan which, these days, is to be found only in the jungles of Southeast Asia, lands which once formed part of the giant continent of Lemuria, extending between Madagascar and the eastern Pacific.

Rather interestingly, Cremo and Thompson have this to say about the ancestors of *Dryopithecus*:

> What if, for example, fossils of anatomically modern humans turned up in strata older than those in which *Dryopithecus* were found? … In fact, such evidence has already been found, but it has since been suppressed or conveniently forgotten.[27]

The Appearance of Gender and Self-Consciousness

With regard to the further evolution of the Third Race, Blavatsky makes the following suggestion:

> It was in the fifth sub-race of the Third Root Race that mankind first began to separate into sexes and then also that the first human was born in the manner common today.[28]

This seems to have occurred some 18–20 million years ago, at the beginning of the Cretaceous period.

The idea that humankind lived quite so long ago would be scoffed at by most scientists today. Yet, several 16-inch (46-cm) long human footprints have been found (and filmed for television during their finding) in the Cretaceous limestone on the banks of the Peluxi River, at Glenrose in Texas. Furthermore, they were found right next to dinosaur footprints going in exactly the same direction – which means that either one was hunting and tracking the other through the same soft ground, or they were travelling together as master and animal pet/servant. The size of the footprint suggests that the human being must himself have been over 20 ft (6.1 m) tall. By Blavatsky's dating, this human being would have been living around 10–15 million years ago.

The Russian newspaper *Komsomolskaya Pravda* of 31 January 1995 rather startlingly confirmed the same sort of thing when it reported the finding of thousands of dinosaur footprints on the plateau of Turkmenistan, one of the former Soviet republics. In the middle of these footprints were human footprints as well, of precisely the same age.

These suggestions might strike some as absurd, were it not for other supporting evidence which clearly shows that the early human race not only existed at the same time as the dinosaurs but had also already begun to develop creatively aesthetic cultural tendencies. As Cremo and Thompson tell us,

> Semi-ovoid metallic tubes of identical shape but of varied size were found at St Jean de Livet in France in 1968, in a chalk bed which indicated an age of 65 million years.[29]

A century earlier, in 1877, a Mr J. H. Neale of the Montezuma Tunnel Company found a mortar and pestle deep underground within gravel beds in California, 'indicating that they were 33–35 million years old.' [30]

Appearance of the Seasons and the First Anthropoids

It would appear that the first 'Sin of the Mindless' occurred at a time – around 20–25 million years ago – when the 'humankind' of the time was emerging from a hermaphrodite and thus bisexual state. At this stage, however, it was still lacking the 'spark' of self-conscious mental intelligence which would enable it to bring about self-control over its elemental nature and its purely instinctive urges. That is said only to have occurred after the next great evolutionary change, which took place in the consciousness of the Third Race.

Prior to that occurrence, Blavatsky's ancient source states that

When the Third Race separated and fell into sin by breeding men-animals, these became ferocious and men and they became mutually destructive. Till then there was no sin, no life taken ... [Then] the eternal Spring became constant change and seasons succeeded. Cold forced men to build shelters and devise clothing.[31]

It was then, as explained a few pages ago, that:

The axle of the Wheel tilted and people knew snow, ice and frost, and men, plants and animals were [again] dwarfed in their growth. Those that did not perish remained as half-grown babes in size and intellect.[32]

On Certain Astrophysical Cycles and Their Effects

As we saw earlier, 'the axle of the Wheel' appears (by reference to other ancient traditions) to mean the constellation of Ursa Minor. Its 'tilt' (relative to the Earth's pole) seems to indicate that at this point (possibly some 20–25 million years ago) in the cyclic orbital movement of our solar system within its greater parent system, Ursa Minor appeared at its furthest point away from the northern Pole Star position which it occupies today. The importance of this relative to climatic and perhaps other changes on Earth is undoubtedly critical, if for no other reason than that its influence had apparently never been felt before – even though its cyclic movements seem to have gone on recurring right up to our present day.

The essence of what seems to have been involved takes into consideration the orbital movement of our immediate system around the Equinoctial Pole, which lies just behind the 'head' of the circumpolar constellation of Draco, the Dragon. The 'gods' who reputedly descended to Earth in ancient times were esoterically known as 'Sons of the Fire Mist', or 'Sons of the Dragon'. It would thus appear that the astronomical position of Earth relative to Draco and Ursa Minor (probably also including Ursa Major) 'triggered' the next major event in Earth's history.

On the subject of the Great Sidereal Year (the 25,920-year cycle of precession) and its effects Blavatsky says:

> At the close of each 'great year' … and which consists of six sars,[33] our planet is subjected to a thoroughly physical revolution. The polar and equatorial climates gradually exchange places, the former moving slowly towards the line and the tropical zone, with its exuberant vegetation and swarming animal life, replacing the forbidding wastes of the icy poles. This change of climate is necessarily attended by cataclysms, earthquakes and other cosmical throes. As the beds of the oceans are displaced at the end of every decimillennium and about one neros [i.e. about 10,600 years in all][34] a semi-universal deluge like the Noachian Flood is brought about.[35]

However, regarding this and other later cataclysms and deluges, we shall hear rather more in the next few chapters.

Chapter Eleven

•

LEMURIA AND 'THE DESCENT OF THE GODS'

'Nature, seeing the beauty of the form of God, smiled with insatiate love of Man, showing the reflection of that most beautiful form in the water and its shadow on the Earth. And he, seeing this form, a form like unto his own, in earth and water, loved it and willed to dwell there. And the deed followed close on the design and he took up his abode in matter devoid of Reason. And Nature, when she had got him with whom she was in love, wrapped him in her clasp and they were mingled in one.'[1]

In order to understand this next piece of the evolutionary jigsaw puzzle, we shall need to approach the subject from a somewhat different angle of reference to those already adopted. That angle comes in part from the Bible, which tells us:

> There were giants on the Earth in those days [i.e. of the Second and early Third Root Races]; and also after that, when the Sons of God [b'ne-Aleim] came into the daughters of man and they bore children unto them. The same became mighty men which were of old [the] men of renown [i.e. heroes].[2]

It also comes (although later, during the late Fourth to early Fifth Race period) from the most ancient of the Indian Vedic texts, the *Vedas* and *Puranas*, which again refer to giant races and their amours and battles with one another. All of these have been assumed by modern scholarship to be a catalogue of mere myth and fantasy. But the Ancient Commentary insists that such is not in fact the case. There is, supposedly a quasi-historical basis to them, for the simple reason that they involved the unfolding and interaction of spiritual and material forces *before* humankind had evolved sufficiently to develop self-consciousness and self-will.

What we are told is that the first part of the evolutionary process on Earth involved the natural *and simultaneously progressive* unfolding, from an altogether ethereal genesis, of the Elements, plus the forms of the Mineral, Plant and Animal kingdoms – the latter including already developing 'Animal-Man'. However, another far more spiritual (or rather, divine) element had been retained 'in archaic genesis', as *The Secret Doctrine* puts it. This was a semi-dormant state of being and consciousness ready for later insemination into the most evolved groups of Third (Lemurian) Race 'proto-humankind', at that stage when the evolution of the latter could progress no further without help from some external influence.

This yet again highlights the suggestion that each species (and thus also each group of species) has a natural, *subjective* limit to its evolutionary development. Therefore, any further 'upward' movement has either to involve a fundamental change (not merely a local adaptation) to its *spiritual* or subjective archetype, or, alternatively, that same spiritual archetype has to instil into the objective entity something further of its own as yet unfulfilled nature. In other words, the spiritual archetype is only able to project sequential aspects of itself down into the material world in incremental fashion, according to due cycle.

Hence it is that every cycle of development would necessitate the prior determination of a point of relative achievement for the species or ethnological type in question. Thereafter, a further infusion of *subjective* potential would become necessary for further advancement. Thus any individual or individual group achieving such an evolutionary cut-off point in advance of the others would have to wait for the rest to catch up. Some, however, would not make the grade at all in this cycle and would thus have to wait for the next one, in exactly the same way as a school system might operate. By virtue of the world system being organized and run by a hierarchy of spiritually advanced Intelligences, one would surely expect no less in the way of what we might regard as 'forward planning'.

What exactly does the word 'archetype' mean in this context? Is it the Jungian archetype, or is it something different? As the essence of the idea is that there is a spiritual (soul) entity which is trying to bring about the manifestation of its own self-expression, through projection of its influence from a higher state down into the matter of the lower world, the answer is surely clear. The archetypal entity presents a sort of reflection of itself in the lower world by holographic projection simply because it cannot itself descend further. That is so by virtue of its own achieved evolutionary status, precluding what would effectively involve going backwards. But it can project a *partial* element of its own nature, which does indeed thus 'fall'. This influential energy is the *lesser* 'spirit' which animates the psycho-physical human being and provides it with the 'motor' behind its elemental nature.

The 'Fall' as the Very Basis of the Evolutionary Process

As indicated at the outset, the idea of a spirit being able to ascend or descend from one realm (that is, a soul-group realm) to another is not a new one, although the philosophy and metaphysics of what is actually involved have been largely forgotten. But what is even less commonly understood is that it is the influence of the descended spirit which itself causes the whole process of evolution to take place – for the simple reason that it is endeavouring to return to its own state of origin. However, in order to do so, it must first of all bring about the evolutionary development (through discipline) of those lesser entities amongst which it has 'fallen', so that they may join in its sense of purpose and thus cease to obstruct its return passage through the psycho-spiritual chaos and 'drag' caused by their instinctive elemental natures. In ancient Egypt, this was allegorically symbolized by the repetitive cycle of Ra's nightly passage down through the Underworld (Duat) and back again to the horizon at sunrise.

Thus the whole point of Man being a 'fallen spirit' – which, as symbolically described in the first chapters of the biblical Genesis, has been completely misunderstood – is that he (as an aspect of the Divine Mind) is a predetermined and necessary self-sacrifice. It is that same sacrifice which enables the varied denizens of the lower orders in Nature also progressively to ascend to higher degrees of evolutionary potential. That then progressively results in the yet higher Self-realization of the greater Intelligence (Logos) of which they *all* form a part.

When we consider the issue of evolutionary development in general on our planet, we apply the very same principles, for there must necessarily exist those spirits which deliberately invoke spirits from higher realms into their own midst. Correspondingly, there will be amongst these latter 'fallen' spirits those which are prepared, self-sacrificially, to give of their own nature temporarily in order to further the development of consciousness and higher sensory faculties in the even lower orders of Nature. Thus I may suggest that our world scheme had its own divine hierarchy of beings of a certain evolutionary status long before primitive humanity even appeared. Hence it would have been the invocatory activity of these which caused the descent from a yet higher (kosmic) soul-realm of a unified hierarchy of Beings representing the furtherance of Divine Purpose. This, so the ancient tradition has it, occurred some two-thirds of the way through the Lemurian era.

This higher divine stream of Intelligence, which thus 'descended' into the Oversoul of our world scheme and then differentiated into a hierarchy of semi-divine beings, *The Secret Doctrine* calls by the name '*Kumaras*'. These are the origin of the shadowy 'Khmers' of Southeast Asian antiquity, also referred to in Greek legend as the 'Kimmerioi', or Cimmerians, who supposedly lived 'at the edge of the world'. They were also the 'Nephilim' (probably derived from the compound Kneph-El-im) referred to in the biblical Book of Genesis, as well as the 'Sons of the Fire Mist' of oriental mysticism. It is they who – as yet unbeknown to science – came to constitute the archetypal fifth, sixth and seventh kingdoms in our planetary Nature. It is thus towards these kingdoms that modern humankind is said to be progressively evolving, for the latter contains something of their nature within itself. But more of that shortly.

The very idea of 'gods' descending or 'falling' from celestial realms above our Earth state is one that tends to appal modern rationalists, on the grounds of being supposedly superstitious nonsense. However, one has to say that it seems largely that (a) they have not properly understood the concept and (b) it has not been clearly or rationally presented in the first place. But even those who do believe in the concept usually have little or no clue as to the associated 'celestial mechanics and dynamics', of which the Ancients at least were aware. The rest of this chapter is therefore dedicated not only to explaining the rationale, but also to showing how it applies specifically in relation to the appearance of self-conscious humanity on this planet in Lemurian times, nearly 20 million years ago.

Lucifer and the 'Fall From Grace'

Before we go any further, let us endeavour to put in its correct perspective the concept behind the initial 'Fall from Grace' described in the biblical Old Testament. Sadly, the real meaning has been completely mangled by Christian (and other) theologians and twisted to support a completely and perniciously false concept of 'Good' and 'Evil'. Thus in the biblical tradition we have the story of Lucifer, the highest of all the archangels apparently proclaiming that he intends to be greater than God Himself. He does so in such a vainglorious manner that God Almighty (whose favourite he is) slings him down to Hell in a blaze of 'sparks', there to create the Underworld and somehow to mutate into the devilish 'Satan'. The biblical God appears a most capricious being (even with his own favourites) simply because the story is purely allegorical.

To begin with, the 'God' mentioned in the text is not the Universal Deity (which the Ancients in any case regarded as inconceivable) but rather the demiurgic Logos of our local universe. Lucifer – 'Son of the Morning' (Isaiah 14:12) and traditionally, before his fall, the greatest of all the Archangels – is actually symbolically representative of that self-conscious element in the kosmic Nature of the Logos which believes that evolutionary betterment is possible. Thus whilst the remainder of the Archangels merely follow the instinctively repetitive status quo (which is thus referred to as 'The Law',

Lucifer and his followers 'rebel'. This makes it quite clear that they are repre-sentative of the principle of *kosmic* Imagination and are thus but a metaphor for (kosmic) Man himself – the 'Divine Spark'.

As Imagination has to act as the vanguard of Creation, so Lucifer and his group are (again symbolically) depicted as being thrown headlong down into the oblivion of kosmic Chaos, there to create worlds. The fact that Lucifer is himself described as disappearing 'in a shower of sparks' is but indicative of the same idea that we find in the Vedic tradition where the great flame of Agni, the supreme god of fire and light, is described as being full of 'countless sparks'. Contrary to popular Christian theology, these same 'sparks' are then the kosmic monads which in their various orders later develop self-conscious planetary humanity out of their own nature – hence the ancient idea that the *inner* human is inherently a god 'in potential'.

It is also interesting to note that certain of these 'sons of Mind' emanated by the consciousness of the Logos (symbolized by the Agni principle) are called, in the Vedic texts, 'Agni-Shaitans'. In due course of time – through culturally ignorant Christian theologians picking up loose ends of other spiritual tradit-ions – the word 'Shaitan' mutated into 'Satan'. Hence the 'fallen angels' or higher *daimones*, emanated by the kosmic Mind to redeem the lesser consciousness of the lower world system, inadvertently became prey to the unhealthy fixations of early Christian theologians with their ideas of the Underworld being inhab-ited by 'devils'. Indeed it is, but as *this* world is the Underworld (*see* Chapter 1), they are actually human devils – led by theologians, politicians, social analysts, and other self-proclaimed 'opinion formers'.

Adam and the Elohim

The story of Adam (and of the human soul too) as a 'special creation' is another biblical tradition which has also been taken literally and therefore completely misunderstood. The name 'Ad-am' merely means 'primordial – being'. The fact that he is effectively a body of 'dust' put together by the Elohim (again, not by the Universal Deity), renders him no more than the similar-sounding Egyptian 'Atum', who was correspondingly described as a 'mound of earth'. Both the 'dust' and the 'earth' are esoteric metaphors for the latent ethereal matter of kosmic Space, out of which the *objective* universe has to be formed. Ad-am is thus a metaphor for the highest soul principle from which is removed a one-eighth part – representing the next lower soul octave and symbolically described as a 'rib' from which Eve is created. However, the whole 'Garden of Eden' story is an allegory describing a merely intermediate heaven world state (not a place on Earth) from which the cycle of incarnation into the lesser Underworld takes place. Hence we have the ejection of the dualistic

Adam and Eve (the divine and spiritual souls) from this intermediate world together with the serpent, the latter representing the terrestrial soul. The latter then merely symbolizes the re-awakening of the sense of duality and choice which leads to what we call 'Good' and 'Evil'.

The biblical tradition of Genesis also of course describes the whole process of Universal Creation by the seven groups of Elohim within the space of seven days. However, this is yet one more esoteric metaphor for a grand cycle involving seven sub-cycles, in line with the sevenfold nature of everything in the universe which we find in all other ancient traditions. Interestingly, the term B'ne Aleim (those who 'create' human beings 'in their own image' was a name common to the 'Malachim' or 'Molochim', (the angelic messengers) and the 'Ischim', (the supposedly 'lower angels') – in a kosmic sense.

The chief of the Ischim was Azazel, believed by some scholars to be the Chaldeo-Semitic version of Prometheus but certainly one of the *seven* chiefs of the rebellious angels who were said to have descended upon Mount Armon (borrowed from the Egyptian deity Amon). Meanwhile, the 'As' or 'Az' in Az-az-el is also the root of the Egyptian names As'r and As't (Osiris and Isis) and actually refers to a semi-divine state of being.[3] The duplication of 'As' in the name Azazel indicates that the semi-divine state is *twice* removed from the divine (that is, kosmic) state and thus becomes an Underworld, or merely planetary deity.

The way in which these esoteric allegories and metaphors have been simplistically travestied by ignorant medieval theologians and then allowed to maintain their existence by modern 'creationists' causes nothing but confusion. The fact that these distortions are currently regarded as the only alternative to Darwinism and its theory of evolution by chaotic natural selection, shows just how far modern understanding both of Nature's workings and of ancient philosophical teaching technique has gone astray. But anyway, let us now turn our attention to the process of Creation as *properly* understood by the Ancients.

We start with a set of clearly stated assumptions – firstly that there are planes or states of being and consciousness other than those of which we humans are generally aware. The second is that a state of being and a state of consciousness are not necessarily to be regarded as precisely the same. For example, we and the animals and plants and minerals all exist within the same objective, terrestrial state of being; but humans both experience and rationalize higher states of consciousness which the other kingdoms cannot access. The third assumption is that whilst a state of consciousness may require some form of bodily organism in order to perceive and experience it, that bodily form and its faculties must be appropriate to the associated state(s) of being within which the consciousness itself exists.

As I have previously described, the Ancients took the view that the universe was not only of sevenfold construction (within the octave of the soul organism), it was also concentrically organized – hence the lesser organism existed within a greater one – something which, in relation to the solar world, symbolized by the sun god, was depicted in progressive mathematical sequences to the power of 10, hence:

1. 1,000,000 – the divine state (the upper celestial heaven world)

2. 100,000 – the semi-divine state

3. 10,000 – the pure spiritual state

4. 1,000 – the state of spiritual soul (the intermediate heaven world)

5. 100 – the psychological state (that of the mind)

6. 10 – the psychic state (that of the emotions and desires)

7. 1 – the objective physical state

The Seven and Ten

One might ask, if the structure of the universe is sevenfold, why should the concentric principle be tenfold in nature? The answer – which is the key to the evolutionary process itself – is provided in figure 8 (*see* page 56), in which we saw the microcosmic septenary organization of states within its macrocosmic parent. In every case, the lowest or seventh state *objectively* replicates the system *in toto*, but on a lesser scale, in exactly the same way that we find in the *Doh* of the harmonic scale.

However, it is the intermediate fourth principle in the greater organism which initiates the overall process of kosmic *emanation*, followed by a 'progressive' 'fall' through three lesser kosmic states – those of kosmic Thought, Desire and Objectivity. These three then become the source of all trinitarian religious doctrines, as the Will-to-Be, the Will-to-Know and the Will-to-Create, which we mentioned earlier in Chapter 3.[4]

Hence it is that we have the three planes within the macrocosmic continuum, plus the seven planes within the microcosmic continuum, making a total of ten altogether. The same principle is to be found in the sacred Tetraktys of the Pythagoreans, where the three corner points represent the three greater or kosmic states. Thus that which 'falls' from the intermediate kosmic heaven world (in response to a yet greater influence) emanates as a Mind impulse which fragments, like the refraction of light. This thereafter has to be reconstituted *within the octave of the lower world scheme* before it can re-ascend to its place of origin – thereafter to begin a yet higher evolutionary climb.

In the system of the Ancients – reproduced in the modern Theosophical system – the archetypal impulse to creative expression in the 'Underworld' emerges downwards from the fourth kosmic plane (the intermediate heaven world of the greater system) in response to invocative desire from the kosmic Underworld state. It takes its first phenomenal form within the fifth state, counting downwards (that of the Kosmic Mind).

As the Mind principle was universally known in ancient times as *m(a)n*, *m(e)n* or *m(o)n* – as reflected in the Sanskrit word *manas* (meaning the mind principle), and related terms in other Indo-Germanic languages, such as Latin *mens* and the English *mind* itself – that which emerged from the kosmic Mind then became A-men (hence the Egyptian god figure 'Amon'). This, as the philosopher Iamblichus tells us, then mutated into the Ptah principle[5] (the Egyptianized form of Buddha), who represented kosmic Desire for self-expression. Ptah (actually a kosmic hierarchy of creator-spirits called 'Dhyani Buddhas') then generated the World Oversoul through enfolding a portion of Space within his field of consciousness – which is symbolically represented as a crystal sphere. Hence it was within this that the final unfoldment of our local solar scheme was thereafter to take place – yet again in a sevenfold sequence.

The Appearance of Deities

One of the questions usually asked by 'rational' scientists and other sceptics on the subject of 'gods' and 'angels', and so on, is that if they actually exist, why do most of us never apparently see them?[6] The question is rather disingenuous because one could say the same about atoms, particles and even germs *in their own state*. We never see them either, nor does even the most powerful electron microscope. However, there is actually good and logical reason for one field of perception not being directly accessible from another, although it is very poorly understood and hence almost never explained properly. So let us spend a few moments examining the subject in slightly more detail before we go on.

First of all, appreciably lower *and* higher forms of life involve far less complexity, thus resulting in far greater subtlety of their bodily organization. Secondly, if we accept the ancient tradition that the spiritual and divine natures are immensely more powerful or potent than the purely physical and psychic ones, we can perhaps conceive of why this should preclude them from being generally able to appear all at once, in any one environment, other than as an overshadowing or germinal influence. That must be so, even within the highest of Nature's objective lower forms – the human being.

It has of course long been known that the mystic seeking direct 'union with God' has to undergo a prolonged period of self-abnegatory discipline and subjective withdrawal before such an experience of higher self-realization becomes possible. However, it was well known to the Ancients and practised in their Mystery Schools. Here it was also understood that the 'god' thus experienced was actually the divinity in man's own 'Higher Self', rather than (as commonly imagined today) the Universal Deity.[7]

Practical common sense should in any case tell us that the power of such a divinity making even a fraction of its presence felt within an unprepared individual nature would result in no less than immediate disintegration of all that person's faculties of sensory perception – if nothing else. As Euripides is reputed to have said, 'Those whom the gods wish to destroy [for their arrogance], they first make mad.' Even in the potential case of the gods appearing in the vicinity of ordinary mortals for any length of time for supposedly beneficial reasons, we would anticipate psychologically disruptive side effects.

The Electrifying Influence of Deity

It is commonly imagined by the majority of people that just because a being is far more evolved spiritually, its nature must be all sweetness and light and thus a permanent joy to be in contact with all the time. However, there is no rational justification for this entirely simplistic viewpoint. The psychic power and influence in any ordinary person's aura becomes supercharged through either intensity of subjective focus or simple enthusiasm. It is due to this that the infectiously magnetic nature of open enthusiasm or of flaming oratory is capable of developing in others a sense of group purpose and involvement – and this for either good or evil. Charisma is a very double-edged faculty.

But just imagine to what degree a *really* advanced being's presence would be expected to produce automatic side-effects in a less powerful aura. It would be equivalent to that of a small-scale generator put right in the immediate vicinity of a powerful electro-magnetic force field; in other words, complete disorientation and 'electrical overload'. Thus, one of the major effects of spiritual development involves an inevitably commensurate increase in psycho-spiritual power which needs to be approached (or used) very carefully. It is thus not altogether surprising that the consciousness of Lemurian pre-human 'human-kind' had to be adequately prepared before being able to absorb anything of the considerably greater power and mental illumination of the divine *kumara* – a kosmic being in its own right.

The other point to be taken into consideration is that the enhanced power in the aura is entirely due to the (literally) electrifying 'presence' of consciousness; hence the enhanced 'electrical' connection made between the terrestrial soul and the spiritual soul in the case of the real spiritually evolved type. As the consciousness of the individual extends progressively further from the objective self (with a resultant increase in self-less-ness), so the higher consciousness and its power automatically feed through to the physical organism.

Inevitably, as spiritual development progresses, the main focus and proportion of the individual's self-consciousness tends to remain in the higher soul-organism rather than returning to the lower. Eventually, it reaches a point where such a return to the lower organism involving a physical body is no longer necessary and the individual then passes out of the fourth (human) kingdom of Nature altogether, into the fifth kingdom. Thereafter, there is supposedly a free choice as to whether or not to make a reappearance in human form for purposes of specific evolutionary assistance to humankind.

The Significance of Ritual

Fortunately, the philosophy of the Ancients recognized that there are distinctively different psychic, spiritual and divine hierarchies. Therefore, any religious or magical invocation of a higher influence had to be carefully approached using all the correctly sympathetic paraphernalia of due ritual, in order to attract the attention of the correct order of spirits – and then, in continuing safety, to make them depart. Similarly, the Mystery Schools (*see* Chapter 1) taught the individual, through discipline, how progressively to recognize their own inner spiritual and divine natures and how to become progressively assimilated into them, thereby gaining access in *full Self-consciousness* to the higher planes or states of reality.

Few seem to recognize the distinction between being aware *of* the spiritual state and being aware *in* the spiritual state. However, that distinction is fundamental to progressive spiritual development and Self-realization; for the associated transition of consciousness eventually takes man out of the fourth kingdom in Nature into the fifth.

The Fifth and Sixth Kingdoms in Nature

The idea of a fifth and even a sixth and seventh kingdom in Nature, superior to the fourth – the human – is something we rarely comes across. Yet it is perfectly logical and self-consistent with the hierarchically sequential order in which Nature works. It also makes far more sense than the suggestion of their being 'gods' or 'demigods' *per se*, even if the characteristics and powers of these more evolved beings are as far beyond ours as ours are beyond those of the Animal and Plant kingdoms. It is also unsurprising that they are as rarely to be found mixing with human beings as human beings are to be found mixing with wild animals. Just as we tend to consort only with domesticated animals, which we can trust, so it is said that only the spiritually self-conscious and harmless amongst men (of whom there are few indeed) are able to have direct access to them – in accordance with *their* choice.

The ancient tradition had it that there was an absolute break between the soul nature of each kingdom in Nature – hence there could never be any such thing as the objective 'missing evolutionary link' which Darwinian evolutionists hope to find. In the same way that the electrical synapse or gap exists in the human brain in order to force electrical energy to jump (thereby producing a pulse action), so it would appear Nature uses the same principle throughout its field of Creation. The acquisition of real spiritual consciousness requires a corresponding 'leap of faith' and once made, there is no going back.

Spiritual Advancement and Regression

Contrary to what some think, the ancient Wisdom Tradition wholly rejects the idea of an evolutionary regression involving human beings being reborn as animals, or anything else of a lower nature. As the *Hermetica* assures us:

> It is not permitted that a human soul should fall so low as to enter the body of an irrational animal ... A soul then may rise to a higher grade of being, but cannot sink to a lower grade.[8]

And for good measure it adds:

> All human souls are immortal. But souls are not all of one kind; different souls have been created in different fashions; for souls differ in quality.[9]

The achievement of spiritual *Self*-consciousness traditionally (and quite logically) liberates man from the 'captivity' of the cycle of human reincarnation, thereby making of him an 'Adept', or 'Master Soul'. Understandably, just as our considerably expanded consciousness gives us access to perspectives of possibility of which the Animal kingdom does not even begin to be aware, so the spiritual Adept – having made an equivalent onward transition – is said to have access to a range of faculty and inclusively wider perception of which we can only be aware in theory, or by virtue of descriptions passed down. However, something of it has been perceived by humans in fragmentary moments of deep mystic introspection.

Remembering that it is the soul which is the *fons et origo* of all consciousness and also that the soul is essentially a *group* of spirits with a common sense of their own self-hood, it makes absolute sense that the 'divine spark' in man, when passing from a lower state into a higher one, has to forego and thus leave behind the lesser one in order to gain access into the higher. Once he has attained to the latter state, he must himself appropriate (hence 'individualize') something of the substance of the latter for his own use. This then is the basis of the 'leap of faith', itself based upon growing certainty that the higher soul state exists and that access to it is worth the sacrifice of the 'old' consciousness which has to be given up. Hence the mystic idea that 'we must die in order to live' – in this 'kingdom of Heaven'.

More on the *Kumaras*

The eventual transition into the sixth and seventh kingdoms of Nature would necessarily appear to involve a similar 'leap' plus a similar expansion of self-consciousness and range of faculty. There is not a great deal of point in speculating on these, however, because they are so far beyond our present range of human evolution that we could hardly begin to conceive of them. However, it needs to be made perfectly clear that tradition has the *kumaras* themselves having passed through the stage of human evolution in the long distant past and that we ourselves will do the same for a future humanity. All we are told in the meantime – via sparse fragments of information passed down – is that such a range of developed consciousness and faculty becomes solar (or inter-planetary) in context and nature.

It is also said that such spiritual advancement puts the individual in direct contact with his own emanating source – which is, again that of the *kumara*, the 'ever-virgin youth' of ancient mystic poesy. The phrase 'ever-virgin' derives from the fact that the *kumaras* – as monadic 'sons of the kosmic Mind' – are said to be capable of self-regeneration by an act of will. They are therefore immortal and eternal (that is, celestial) Monads. Thus the *state* in which they have their essential being is the 'fount of eternal youth' – another esoteric metaphor which has sent men on wild goose chases around the planet, trying to find 'Shangri-La'.

It naturally follows that the *kumaras* themselves must in due course follow the higher evolution as well, firstly by ascent into that sphere of consciousness combining the essences of all the solar states. This thereby puts them on a par with the very archangels of the solar scheme who, in their totality, constitute the instinctual intelligence of the local Demiurge. Then, they must ascend yet higher through the lower kosmic planes of consciousness until they attain direct re-union with the kosmic Mind, their own initiating Source. That, however, is the basis of the misunderstood allegory involving Lucifer becoming greater than 'God'. The same idea is to be found in the Egyptian allegorical tradition where the demi-god Unas is symbolically depicted as eating the very entrails of the gods who originally created him.

The Achievement of 'Human' Consciousness

The *kumaras*, having appeared on Earth, so we are told, some 20 million years ago or more, thus became the teachers and spiritual guides of the later Lemurians.[10] In the same way that humankind has tamed and domesticated various sections of the Animal kingdom, so they are said to have progressively brought the more evolved parts of proto-humankind under their aegis, with the aim of assisting their evolution. Thus, as the emanation of the semi-divine nature is that of spirit-energy, so their direct influence 'pollinated' the developing mental consciousness of Lemurian animal-man and thereby developed in them an attraction to spiritual ideas and concepts. The duality of consciousness which that engendered thus eventually generated the faculty of *self*-consciousness in humankind some 18.6 million years ago.

The consequential effect of that direct influence over a prolonged period of time (several million years, so it would appear) was, one might suggest, akin to the flame of one candle eventually lighting the flame of another candle through an influence derived from sheer proximity and/or physical insemination. Thus increasing numbers of the more evolved Lemurian types received and developed (*within their soul nature*) a donated 'spark' of self-conscious individuality which is the true hallmark of the human being. It is for this reason that esoteric philosophy flatly denies the Darwinian idea that 'man is but an evolved animal'.

As mentioned in a previous chapter, the ancient mystery traditions had it that the spirit of Man was born in the Pleiades. This spirit, however, is the highest aspect of man – what the ancients called the 'Divine Spark' – which was otherwise said to have arrived on Earth as a single mysterious entity which then (just like the human spermatozoon which penetrates the ovum) diversified by itself into several lesser hierarchies of being. By virtue of these great Intelligences having supposedly originated in the Pleiades and by further virtue of the Pleiades being part of the constellation of Taurus, they were represented in the Chaldeo-Babylonian Mysteries as winged bulls, or Kabiri, examples of which can still be seen at the British Museum in London (*see* figure 21).

The name 'Kabir' or 'Khabir' (hence also 'Hebrew', from 'Khabiru') otherwise mutated, in the ancient Egyptian tradition, into 'Kheper', the self-regenerating scarab god – Kheper-Ra. The 'dark alluvial stream' of celestial divinity from which the Kabiri originally emerged was itself the source of the ancient Egyptian god 'Khem' (the source of *al-khem-ea*, our modern 'alchemy'), which itself also changed phonetically into 'Khem-er' or 'Khmer', which thus became the origin of the term '*kumara*' – representative of the 'ever-virgin divine youth' of supposed Hindu myth, as also mentioned earlier.

Figure 21. The Assyrio-Babylonian winged kabiri-*bull*

The original 'divine spark' of nascent spirituality inseminated into the consciousness of Lemurian humankind by the *kumaras*[11] is thus the very source and nature of our own human faculty of self-conscious intelligence. But it remains a spiritual (and thus solar) entity in its own right and most definitely not a terrestrial one. Thus the 'animal' form and behaviour which man adopts for the external vehicle of his consciousness does not make man an animal, any more than the hirsute coverings of the animal render it part of the plant kingdom.[12]

The fact of the human and anthropoid body form looking distinctively similar is, as already described, due (as *The Secret Doctrine* has it) to the evolutionary development (literally hundreds of millions of years ago) of pre-human 'animal-man' which entirely lacked the 'spark' of self-consciousness. However, because *some* of the *kumaras* decided that the personal sacrifice of uniting their essence with that of the Lemurians was necessary to engender a sense of natural continuity within the Lemurian psyche itself, the prototypal 'hairless ape-man' continued and improved, whilst the rest reverted to type.

The Development of Lemurian Civilization and Culture

Now it might be thought that, due to the vast time spans involved since the main stock of Lemurian humanity actually existed – literally over ten million years ago – it would by now be absolutely impossible to know or discover anything of any true historic value about its culture and civilization. However, such is not the case, for there are at least a few general traditions which have been passed down to us, as I shall now endeavour to show.

So we are told by *The Secret Doctrine*, by the time of their sixth sub-race, under the supervision of the *kumaras*, the Lemurians were building 'the first large cyclopean cities [out of volcanic rock] which ... appeared on that region of the continent which is [now] known as the island of Madagascar'.[13] As *The Secret Doctrine* also says: 'They built large cities, cultivated arts and sciences and knew astronomy, architecture and mathematics.[14]

Madagascar – now a large island off the east coast of Africa, within the Indian Ocean – is originally supposed to have formed part of the western area of the giant ancient continent which stretched westwards from the Pacific to the Atlantic at a time when the vast majority of modern Africa did not yet exist. It is also of course well known to science as the home of a most extraordinary range of animals and plants, many of which are to be found nowhere else on the planet – not even in Africa, notwithstanding its proximity. It is now extensively covered by jungle (although this is decreasing at an alarming rate); but one can well imagine how this may perhaps hide as many secrets as the jungles of Central America did until only a few decades ago when the cultures of the Mayans and Toltecs came to light.

It otherwise appears that the advent of the *kumaras* is the source of the Chaldeo-Babylonian story of Oannes or Dagon, the half-fish god, who emerged from the 'waters' (of Space) and brought all the knowledge of the arts and sciences to humanity. It is also apparent in the Greek 'myth' of Prometheus, who – so the story goes – brought the 'heavenly fire' (of Mind) down from Olympus to humankind on Earth.

Australia and the Aboriginal 'Dream Time'

Of the details of that apparently idyllic period, when these 'gods' literally 'walked amongst men', there is very little that has been passed down. That is perhaps unsurprising given the fact that it is usually bad or cataclysmically unfortunate news which remains stark in the individual or racial memory. However, it is specifically remembered in the vivid 'Dream Time' culture of the Australian aboriginal people, who are quite certain as to this having been a real prehistoric period when the 'gods' literally walked amongst men. Australia, according to *The Secret Doctrine*, was originally an inland part of the great Lemurian continent and only became an island as a result of the vast cataclysms which destroyed the vast majority of it so many millions of years ago. Other traces of this great primordial continent can also still be seen today in the multitude of south-east asian islands to the north of Australia, as well as those of Polynesia and Melanesia, extending all the way to Easter Island.

Early Forms of Language

We are told by *The Secret Doctrine* that the creatures of the later Second Root Race (one could hardly call them 'human-kind') had only developed the capacity to use chant-like sounds composed entirely of vowels. Prior to this, communication was entirely telepathic. However, the Third Race – by its end – was able to converse in monosyllabic speech, agglutinatively mixing vowels with consonants – hence their capacity to produce a distinctive civilization and culture. By way of confirming this, the occult Ancient Commentary from which Blavatsky drew her knowledge makes the point that these late Lemurians were a highly intelligent and even cultured race.[15]

Concerning the 'Third Eye'

Blavatsky adds that the last three main sub-races of the Lemurians (those living 10–20 million years ago) were the 'one-eyed Cyclopes' of Greek myth, the 'one eye' referring to the 'Wisdom Eye', related to the pituitary gland, 'for the two front eyes were fully developed as physical organs only in the beginning of the Fourth Race.' She otherwise mentions, in relation to the story of Ulysses putting out the eye of the cyclopean giant Polyphemus with a burning brand, that this was an allegory based upon the atrophy of the 'Third Eye', Ulysses being a metaphor for the hero type of the early Fourth Root Race.[16]

It is interesting to note that some cave paintings have been found around the world which depict giant beings with a single eye in the middle of the forehead as well as the two normal eyes – and with auras around their heads. This seems to indicate that they were in fact representations of early Atlantean race types.

The Sequence of Evolutionary Development

So ancient esoteric philosophy tells us, the evolutionary development of humankind in the round – like everything else in universal Nature – progresses according to a sevenfold plan and sequence, which – man being the microcosm of the macrocosm – is paralleled by an individual human development today that proceeds as follows:

Age 1–7   The learning of complete control over the bodily mechanism and senses and the development of a sense of physical individuality

Age 7–14   The learning of complete control over the personal feeling functions and senses and the development of a sense of emotional individuality

Age 14–21   The learning of the full range of the intellectual faculty and senses and the development of a sense of mental individuality

Just as in today's child we see the quite sudden emergence of a definite sense of self in the fifth to sixth year, and an even stronger sense of individuality in the seventh year, the same principle, so it is said, applied to Lemurian humankind. The first definite signs of *self*-consciousness appeared in their fifth–sixth sub-races, whilst by the end of their seventh sub-race, something between 8–10 million years ago, a general sense of personal individuality was evident, preparatory to the next stage of evolutionary development. This involved the unfolding and extension of the personal feeling sense, of urges, emotions and ideals. These, so we are told, were the predominant psychological stimuli of the Fourth Race epoch, and its whole civilization and culture were increasingly based upon them and reflected them.

It is perhaps very difficult for us to imagine an adult humankind some 30 feet tall with a consciousness which – amongst its intelligentsia at least – was childishly impressionable yet sufficiently developed in intelligence to understand astronomy and mathematics as taught to them. This is despite the fact that they were apparently not in the least 'intellectual' in our modern sense. Yet the more naturally intelligent of the population must have been highly and intelligently creative otherwise they could hardly have been responsive to the education and direction provided by the *kumaras*, the guardians of the human race.[17] But the masses of the giant population had seemingly not yet reached quite such an evolved stage of development and were merely like our average children today – playful, often naturally irresponsible, but still intelligently curious with a definitely developing and quite intelligent sense of their own selfhood. It also appears from some of the artefacts rediscovered by Cremo and Thompson and dating back to the era of about 10 million years ago, that they had discovered how to play games, because circularly indented spherical balls have been found in stratified subsoils of this age.

Evidence of Third Race Civilization

There appear to be a variety of indications of Lemurian civilization and culture, some of which we have already mentioned earlier in the chapter. However, perhaps the most obvious ones are those associated with giant walled buildings. According to Blavatsky's sources, the Lemurians first started building cave cities out of the volcanic rock in places like Madagascar during their mid-late period. Only much later did the humankind of the time construct huge and intricately cut stone-walled edifices such as those already well known to us at Ollantaytambo and Sacsayhuaman in Peru, Tiryns (Tyhrens) in Greece, Commagene in Turkey and in the so-called sun temples of Malta.

Here, we find carefully dressed stone slabs of more than 500 or even 1,000 tonnes in weight, often brought great distances and engineered to fit with other stone blocks to tolerances of fractions of a millimetre. Nobody is going to start cutting and preparing huge lumps of stone in this way unless they have some definite sort of building project in mind in which they can be sure of being able to transport and manipulate such stones into position. The builders therefore clearly had both the knowledge and the technology.

One can perhaps imagine Lemurian or Atlantean giants of over 20 ft (6.1 m) in height each manhandling stone slabs of say a tonne in weight, in direct correspondence to an extremely strong man today manhandling say one-tenth of that. But the manhandling or other moving or transportation of weights of 500 and 1,000 tonnes defies description, as it would require the capacities of today's most powerful cranes. So it is difficult to imagine even large groups of Lemurians or Atlanteans being able to handle them without some form of technology being involved. However, when one takes into consideration my earlier suggestion that, in those days, everything was much lighter in weight, *pro rata* – the Earth not having by then fully condensed to its present density – the idea becomes at least slightly more rational.

The Use of Sound as an Engineering Technique

There is, however, one other potential technique involved in the raising and manipulation of great weights, known since ancient times amongst the adept initiates of the Mystery Schools around the world: the harnessing of sound. Whilst a little of what is involved is known within the laws of modern physics, such at present only really involves either the transmission of sound by certain (very limited) means or otherwise its destructive nature and effects. Without attempting to go into serious detail, the ancient Mystery Schools seem to have possessed a 'science of sound' (something still practised in some oriental temples today), the basis of which involved a knowledge of the properties of the absurdly discredited 'ether' of science, which has now been renamed as 'the quantum fluid'.[18]

This knowledge – the unconscious application of which is actually to be found in the West in Gregorian chants and church bell manufacture and ringing – involved using rhythm and amplitude in combination with simple geometry to produce what to us would be the startling phenomenal effect of moving physical objects. (Gregorian chanting, for example, only moves our emotions and can thus be considered only a *psychic* engine, notwithstanding its beauty.)

The great inventor Nikolai Tesla (1856–1943) was able to learn and demonstrate various wonderful phenomena involving this technique in his practical research, through an understanding of sonic amplitudes, but even he did not fully appreciate all of the principles involved. Others understood them not at all and were so frightened by Tesla's capacity to increase amplitudes to levels that literally threatened the structural coherence of buildings, that they managed to put an end to his work altogether.

Sound – or at least extremes of sound – are well known by modern science to have extremely disruptive effects on plant, animal and human organisms. For example, J.H. Brennan cited a Professor Gavraud as having found, during his own research in this field during the 1970s, that a basic infrasound rhythm of seven cycles per second made him feel extremely unwell, whereas other amplitudes made him feel much better and reinvigorated.[19] There have also been many successful experiments over recent decades using musical sound with animals and plants to stimulate productivity, as for example described in the book *The Secret Life of Plants*.

For example, Luther Burbank in California was able during the early part of the 20th century to show amazed colleagues and scientists that he could not only select the correct plants (at great speed) for mutation, using his own psychic sensitivity, but that – using music and light playing in and around the plants – he could achieve those same mutations in an extraordinarily short space of time, which normal methods just could not begin to consider as remotely possible.

The still young science of cymatics deals with phenomena arising out of vibrational sound producing not only two-dimensional images on a plane surface, but also three-dimensional images in particular aeriform or liquid/plasmic states. Liquid crystallography (as found in modern computer technology) reproduces similar phenomena as a result of electrical impulses which are themselves but sonic packages. But these are, of course, only small-scale phenomena.

The problem for science in accepting that huge weights can be levitated by mere sound is not that of understanding how amplitude can be hugely increased by making sound waves coincide.[20] This is already well known. What our science as yet fails to appreciate is the principle that *every* form in Nature is fundamentally composed of *qualitative* aggregations of the ether/quantum fluid (crystallized as light) and that every associated structure is the result of geometrically organized sound and the resonance produced by it.

Thus we can logically suggest, with due reason, that sympathy and antipathy are the results of harmony and disharmony between the natural sonic amplitudes of different materials or forms – or the consciousnesses inhabiting them. One of the manifestations of a harmonic vitality, for example, is simple surface tension. One might perhaps be forgiven for thinking that a lump of stone has no surface tension – but it can be induced, by resonance; and, once induced, it can be utilized to offset the natural inertia between materials which otherwise makes traction so difficult.

To the world of orthodox science, this might sound like 'New Age' pseudo-magical flim-flam. But that is only because science's knowledge of the fundamentals behind the laws of physics are still rather crude, no matter what scientists might believe to the contrary. The fact remains, however, that the Ancients knew of this particular science and were able to use it, when important and necessary, in their construction techniques. Thus, by looking at the huge interlocking masonry of the Sphinx temple, for example, we can with some justification suggest that sonic levitation may well have been employed (even though in rather more recent historic times). It seems likely that the very same knowledge enabled the ancient Lemurian builders to build their huge walls at Ollantaytambo, Sacsayhuaman, Commagene and Tiryns.

The Demise of the Third Race and Its Culture

However, given the fact that further information about their culture is decidedly nebulous or non-existent at present, we may as well move on to the eventual demise of the Third Race. At this time – so we are led to understand from the available ancient traditions – the *kumaras* withdrew from even occasional contact with humanity. From their original base in what is now northern South America, they instead took up eventual residence to the north of the Himalayas, on the fabled distant island of Shambala, located somewhere within the vicinity of where the Karakorum and Gobi Deserts now stand, close to Russia's Lake Baikal.[21]

The Ancient Commentary, as cited by Blavatsky, tells us that:

In the Eocene age [i.e. roughly 9–10 million years ago], even in its very first part, the great cycle of the [early] Fourth Race men, the [Lemuro-] Atlanteans, had already reached its highest point of civilization and the great continent, the father of nearly all the present continents, showed the first symptoms of sinking.[22]

These elements of *The Secret Doctrine* were drawn from one of the Adept letters in *The Mahatma Letters*, in which we read that the last lands of Lemuria 'perished about 700,000 years before the beginning of the Tertiary period', and also that

> Lemuria can no more be confounded with the Atlantic continent than Europe with America. Both sank and were drowned with their high civilizations and 'gods', yet between the two catastrophes a short period of about 700,000 years elapsed, Lemuria flourishing and ending her career just at about that trifling lapse of time before the early part of the Eocene Age.[23]

Notwithstanding the fact that their continental homeland had almost entirely disappeared under the waves, the most evolved of the late Lemurians had already found a new home on a continental landmass in the centre of what is now our modern Atlantic Ocean – and there we shall rejoin them in the next chapter.

Chapter Twelve

·

GREATER ATLANTIS AND ITS HEIRS

'One of the most ancient legends of India, preserved in the temples by oral and written tradition, relates that several hundred thousand years ago there existed in the Pacific Ocean, an immense continent which was destroyed by geological upheaval, the fragments of which must be sought for in Madagascar, Ceylon, Sumatra, Java, Borneo and the principal islands of Polynesia'.[1]

Lest there be any further lingering confusion between the two continents and civilizations of Lemuria[2] and Atlantis, let us bear in mind what *The Secret Doctrine* has to say on the subject, as follows:

The Atlantean portion of Lemuria was the geological basis of what is known as Atlantis. The latter indeed, must be regarded rather as a development of the Atlantic prolongation of Lemuria, than as an entirely new mass of land upheaved to meet the special requirements of the Fourth Root Race. Just as in the case of race-evolution, so in that of the shifting and re-shifting of continental masses, no hard and fast line can be drawn where an old order ends and another begins. Continuity in natural process is never broken. Thus the Fourth Race Atlanteans were developed from a nucleus of Lemurian Third Race men centred, roughly speaking, towards a point of land in what is now the mid-Atlantic Ocean.[3]

The Language, Social Organization and Religion of the Atlanteans

Whereas the late Lemurians had apparently developed a quite sophisticated method of vocal communication, involving the use of a mixture of vowels and consonants to produce 'root words', the new Atlantean form of consciousness began to evolve the first proper language. This was the 'agglutinative' – which involved stringing root words together in different orders and sequences to produce a sense of differential quality and force. That in turn seems to have accompanied the development of powers of intelligent reasoning and the perception of right from wrong – in other words, of subjective discrimination and even of forms of analytical consideration. Blavatsky tells us that this agglutinative language of the Fourth Race was called 'Rakshasi bhasa' in old Sanskrit works, and she claims that traces of it still survive although 'limited to the aboriginal tribes of America.'⁴ Other agglutinative languages are, however, still to be found all around the world today (for example Hungarian, Finnish and Turkish).

It is interesting to note the general tendency of children of seven and over today to form definite self-interest groups, which thereby tend to initiate the natural internal separation of society. Well, so the tradition has it, the Fourth Race followed the same principle. As a consequence of this, the *tribal family* principle first came into being – the remains of this being visible even today in Africa and the Americas, for example. (This is despite the North and South American systems having been largely decimated by European immigrants and conquerors over the last four or five centuries.)

The other major characteristic of the Fourth Race is the type of general religion which they practised – ancestor worship – some or other form of which is still practised widely around the world today. But it is important to note what it was all about in the first place or we shall put it anthropologically in the wrong context – which is what mainstream anthropology has managed to do almost right across the board. However, we shall deal with this subject in fuller detail in Chapter 16.

Atlantean Geography

As we have already seen, the first Atlanteans of the Fourth Root Race were derived from a group of the most evolved of the 'narrow-headed', seventh sub-race Lemurians. Whilst the giant Lemurian super-continent was already in a general state of fragmentation into smaller island continents, these first members of the early Fourth Race type found a home for themselves (seemingly about 9–10 million years ago) on a landmass somewhere in the present mid-Atlantic Ocean area. This was probably quite close to where the present Cape Verde island group is located – some 200 miles (320 km) west of Senegal. Long before this time, so the tradition has it, these proto-Atlanteans' evolutionary mentors, the *kumaras*, had already set up their own base in the nearby region of what is now northern South America.

It appears that, at this stage, before the founding of the Fourth Race, the central and northern Atlantic Ocean connected directly with the Indian Ocean, because Blavatsky tells us:

> The area between [the] Atlas [Mountains] and Madagascar was occupied by the ocean waters till about the early part of Atlantis, when Africa emerged from the bottom of the ocean and Atlas was half sunk.⁵

She also mentions that 'the most archaic Sanskrit and Tamil works teem with references to both [the Atlantean and Lemurian] continents', and that 'most of the correct names of the countries and islands of both continents are given in the *Puranas*.'[6]

However, during this same era – and evidently for several million years afterwards, the landmass on which the first Atlanteans lived stretched from present-day Africa to the mainland of northern South America; for as the same source confirms:

> A pilgrim could perform a journey [by land] from what is in our days termed the Sahara Desert, to the lands which now rest in dreamless sleep at the bottom of the waters of the Gulf of Mexico and the Caribbean Sea.[7]

We are elsewhere told, in a manner clearly following in Plato's tracks, of an extract from the writer Theophrastus, written during the days of Alexander the Great (356–323BC), and preserved by the Roman writer Aelian. The extract, Blavatsky says,

> is a dialogue between [King] Midas the Phrygian and Silenus. The former is told of a continent that had once existed in times of old, so immense that Asia, Europe and Africa seemed like poor islands compared with it. It was the last to produce animals and plants of gigantic magnitudes. There, said Silenus, men grew to double the size of the tallest man in his time and they lived to twice as old an age.[8]

In fact, the main Atlantean continent left over from the original Lemurian super-continent, seems to have stretched from Newfoundland to the Scilly Islands in the north and from Brazil to southern West Africa in the south. Here, on this land, the early Atlanteans seem to have developed side by side with the remaining Third Race types. From here also they eventually spread out in all directions until the first really major planetary cataclysms occurred – almost certainly during the fourth Atlantean sub-race period, about 4–5 million years ago, after which central and southern Africa first appeared.

The Second 'Sin of the Mindless'

It appears to have been slightly prior to this that members of the third or fourth sub-race of the Atlanteans re-committed the 'sin of the mindless', with some of their male numbers mating with the dumb female monster-ape types left over from the mid-Lemurian period. However, whereas the lesser 'spark of divinity' had not been present in the consciousness of the mid-Lemurian types, it was in the mid-Atlantean types. Consequently, so *The Secret Doctrine* tell us, this 'spark' was passed on to the new breed of semi-human monsters, which did not die out. Instead they began to mutate and, in so doing, devolved (rather than evolved) into the ancestors of our present day anthropoids – the gorillas, orang-utans, chimpanzees and baboons. As Blavatsky confirms from her oriental sources:

> The pithecoids … do descend from the animalized fourth human Root Race, being the product of man and an extinct species of mammals (whose remote ancestors were themselves the products of Lemurian bestiality) which lived in the Miocene Age.

She adds:

> The anthropoids of our day have not existed at any time since the middle of the Miocene period when, like all cross-breeds, they began to show a tendency – much more marked as time went on – to revert to the type of their first parent, the black and yellow gigantic Lemuro-Atlanteans.[9]

And again:

> The real anthropoids … came far later in the closing times of Atlantis. The orang-utan, gorilla, chimpanzee and cynocephalus are the latest and purely physical evolutions from lower anthropoid mammalians. They have a spark of the purely human essence in them. Man on the other hand has not one drop of pithecoid blood in his veins. Thus saith the old wisdom and universal tradition.[10]

Rather interestingly, scientists in the field of molecular biology, from research carried out on modern anthropoids, have come to the conclusion that the divergence of man from the ape line actually took place about 5–6 million years ago. Bearing in mind that the mid-Atlantean Root Race period must have been about 4.5–5.5 million years ago, this ties in quite well chronologically with what Blavatsky's source, the Ancient Commentary, has to say about when the second 'sin of the mindless' took place. The distinction is of course that whilst mainstream anthropology still sees man as derived from the anthropoid, esoteric philosophy says quite categorically that modern science is looking down the wrong end of the telescope.

In other words, the anthropoid is quite clearly to be classified as a degenerate species derived (at least in part) from humankind. From this one might infer that the earlier *Dryopithecus* and the later, 4-ft (122-cm) high *Australopithecus* (the so-called 'Lucy' type, discovered in East Africa and dated at between 2–4 million years ago) are in fact two such ancestors of either the much later chimpanzee or gorilla – but not of humans. The suggestion that *Australopithecus* is 'near human' is in fact (as indeed many scientists and anthropologists agree) absurd and based on mere wishful thinking.

The Mid-Atlantean Deluge

The main planetary cataclysm of the Fourth Race cycle also seems to have coincided with the fourth Atlantean sub-race, during the Miocene period, some 4.5 million years ago, when the central part of the main Atlantean continent was submerged. However, it seems to have had nothing to do with this second round of primeval bestiality; for, as Blavatsky advises us:

> The secret teachings show that the 'Deluge' overtook the fourth giant race not on account of their depravity, or because they had become 'black with sin', but simply because such is the fate of every continent.[11]

This latter point is something which needs to be taken on board in relation to the supposed nature of plate tectonic theory.

Not very much more in the way of detail is given as to the extent of the cataclysm other than that it was due to a shift in the Earth's poles and that 'the final disappearance of the largest continent of Atlantis was an event coincident with the elevation of the Alps.'[12] However, it certainly seems to have been of a worldwide nature, because Blavatsky mentions that Easter Island was occupied

> by some Atlanteans who, having escaped from the cataclysm which befell their own land [location unspecified], settled on that remnant of Lemuria only to perish thereon when destroyed in one day by its volcanic fires and lava.[13]

However, these planetary cataclysms last for millennia and there was evidently more than enough time for the refugees to rebuild their culture on the island, as confirmed by the huge sculpted heads still seen there (*see* figure 22). Of these Blavatsky says:

> The Easter Island relics are, for instance, the most astonishing and eloquent memorials of the primeval giants ... One has but to examine the heads of the colossal statues ... to recognize in them at a glance the features of the type and character attributed to the Fourth Race giants.[14]

The Facial Features of the Atlantean Type

Now this last statement is a particularly interesting one because, when we look closely at the long and narrow Easter Island carved heads, they bear a striking resemblance also to the heads which we still find extensively today being carved by some African tribes and also by a few American tribes (*see again* figure 17). Modern anthropologists and archaeologists have taken for granted that this form of carving was merely a stylistic technique and no more. However, it would appear that it is, in fact, a deliberate (although now quite unconscious) reminder of the 'narrow-headed' Lemuro-Atlanteans.

Figure 22. A group of the huge Atlantean sculpted heads still standing on Easter Island

The Evolutionary Sequence

The way in which the evolutionary development of consciousness works within the universal sevenfold system appears to be that the first half of each cycle sees the gradually physical expression of the previous cycle's experiential achievements. The second half then sees that expression put to use in a largely new range of subjective (and often environmental) experience. Thus each racial type becomes subsumed in its successor. Consequently, in the first half of the Atlantean Fourth Race cycle, there appeared a marked change in the human *form* generally, although the instinctual consciousness of the mass of the population remained distinctively (late) Lemurian in nature. The leading intelligences of the time, however, were already beginning to develop powers of emotional and mental discrimination.

Similarly, we might say, with the transition between the Fourth Race and our own Fifth Race. The latter has a significantly different appearance (facially) to the former, whilst still retaining a largely Atlantean type of consciousness, which is only now (in the latter half of the Fifth Race cycle) beginning to move on to its next stage of development. The more advanced, however, are beginning to develop the principle of abstract mental and spiritually intuitive sensitivity which will themselves result in later mutations of the head and face.

The Polynesian Peoples

The 18th-century explorer and anthropologist Jacolliot wrote that

> The aborigines of the Sandwich islands, of Viti [Fiji], of New Zealand, of the central groups of Samoa, Tahiti, etc. had never known each other, had never heard of each other before the arrival of the Europeans. And yet, each of these peoples maintained that their island had at one time formed a part of an immense stretch of land which extended towards the West, on the side of Asia [i.e. in the Indian Ocean]. And all brought together were found to speak the same language, to have the same usages, the same customs, the same religious belief. And all to the question 'Where is the cradle of your race?' for sole response, extended their hand towards the setting sun.[15]

By confirming that the ancient centre of their civilization and culture had been in the West, these Polynesian peoples – whose islands are scattered across immense distances (thousands of miles) all over the central and southern Pacific – made it quite clear that they meant Atlantis, at a time when central Africa still did not exist because the Indian Ocean connected directly with the Atlantic, right over the top of it.

Modern anthropologists have gone out of their way to try to show that the Polynesians – commonly acknowledged as great oceanic sailors who guided their passage by reference to the stars – could indeed have travelled these great distances, each of over a thousand miles, to create new migrant communities. But if so, how is it that they all, without exception, told the Europeans that they knew nothing of each others' existence? What strange sort of social logic would have induced them to do so? It would seem that modern anthropology is trying to invent a prehistory to suit itself.

The Meso-American Peoples

Bearing in mind that the core of *original* Atlantean continental civilization appears to have been located in the area between the Equator and the Tropic of Cancer, it is perhaps interesting to pause here for a moment to consider some of the traditions of the still existing native peoples of this area. Particularly interesting are those of the peoples of the Antilles, because examination of the local geography indicates that this long curving group of islands, which stretches all the way northwards from Venezuela almost to Haiti, was once attached to and formed part of what is now the modern South American mainland.

The French author Paul Gaffarel wrote in 1892 that the native Carib Indians of the southern Caribbean had told the invading Spaniards that the Antilles had once formed part of a single great landmass.[16] According to them, this landmass had suddenly become internally divided by the oceanic waters (now the Caribbean Sea) – which clearly indicates that some areas had been subject to submersion due to violent earthquake activity. Sir James Frazer confirms the very same local tradition.[17]

The inhabitants of the island of Tobago, slightly to the south, correspondingly have a tradition that their island was once part of a large continental landmass – inhabited by giants.[18] The association with giant inhabitants in ancient times is also found on Cuba. In 1898 David Brinton, an American archaeologist, described huge human-like forms carved out of the rock faces in the river valleys of central Cuba.[19]

As confirmed by the 19th-century explorer and anthropologist Abbé Brasseur de Bourbourg, the 'myths' of the pre-Mayan Toltec peoples of Central America also mention a race of giants. Human skeletons, 12 ft (3.65 m) tall and with six toes have been found in California and Arizona. Giants are to be seen in what might appear to be the definitely later Atlantean type indicated by the huge Olmec statuary found in Central America. However, nobody knows who, or what, the Toltecs and Olmecs actually were, or where they came from – or, in truth, how long ago.

The facial features of the Olmec monuments are strikingly dissimilar to those of any Native North or Central American, as archaeologists have had to admit. Instead, with their combination of broad, flat nose and thick lips the statues look distinctly African, but Africans, supposedly, should not have been known of on the west side of the Atlantic at the time the statues were created. However, the wider, flatter nose alone is found in several American tribes, as well as among the Polynesians and some northern Chinese, perhaps suggesting an ethnic relationship. (However, many Polynesians – at least those of today – have slightly more prominent nasal bridges and are on average much taller than the peoples of Southeast Asia, China and Mongolia.)

The Great Atlantean Planetary Cataclysms

Several decades before geological science became aware of the fact, Blavatsky wrote of the great and extended planetary cataclysm which had begun some 850,000 years ago and lasted for about 150,000 years. As a result of this, as she tells us:

The Secret Doctrine declares that most of the later islander Atlanteans perished in the interval between 850,000 and 700,000 years ago and that [the early Fifth Race] were 200,000 years old when the first great island or continent was submerged.[20]

After the mid-Atlantean planetary cataclysm of about 4.5 million years ago, there appear to have remained only two large continental islands in the possession of the Fourth Race. 'Ruta', in the south, was apparently located in or very close to the Gulf of Mexico and probably incorporated Bolivia and northern Peru as well as the whole of Central America and Mexico. 'Daitya', in the northern Atlantic, seemingly incorporated the Azores, the Canaries and Madeira chains, the Maghreb and the Iberian peninsula, as well, possibly, as southern France, Switzerland and Italy. These, as just confirmed, are said to have continued in existence for several million years until the next main cycle of planetary cataclysms, commencing around 1.5 million years ago, as we shall see in a moment.

These cataclysms seemingly resulted in the general destruction and submersion of Ruta. Daitya, apparently, survived intact until about 270,000 years ago, when further earthquake and volcanic activity destroyed its centre. It appears to have been this which led to the flooding of the Tyrrhenian Plain, as a result of the forced opening of what subsequently became known as 'the Pillars of Herakles'. Rather interestingly, Blavatsky comments that:

> The pure Atlantean stocks – of which the tall Quaternary cave-men were, in part, the direct descendants – immigrated into Europe long prior to the glacial period, in fact as far back as Pliocene and Miocene times, in the Tertiary.[21]

The Great Atlantean Exodus

As the late Tertiary ended about 4–5 million years ago, this seems to tie in with the earlier description of the mid-Fourth Race planetary cataclysm and deluge period leading to mass evacuations and migrations of lesser Atlantean giants from gradually submerging lands in the tropics to other lands in the north. As the only available lands in the northern regions comprised the island continent of Daitya – incorporating the Azores, Iberia and the Maghreb – the suggestion is that it was to the latter that these refugees fled. However, the sheer distances which they would have had to travel otherwise indicates that they must have had some sort of ocean-going craft to carry them, which again would have necessitated a high degree of civilization.

It would appear that some at least of these mid-Atlantean giants managed to migrate as far as what now constitutes the eastern Mediterranean and the Middle East, because some of their cyclopean architecture is still to be found there as well.[22] For example, the huge terrace of giant heads at Baalbek in the Lebanon, which are not dissimilar in style from the Olmec heads of Central America – has some foundation stones over 1,000 tonnes in weight. Those found at Tiryns (Tyrhens) in Greece are not much smaller. Although nothing like the size of these examples, the masonry of the 'palaeolithic' temple found in Malta – which was then part of greater eastern Tyrrenhia, extending between Italy and the Tunisian Atlas – is also of colossal dimensions. Legends of ancient giants in northwest Africa are themselves well known.

In addition, of course, we have the gigantic carved stone walls of Ollantay-tambo and Sacsayhuaman in Peru, the constructional style of which is similar to that found in the temple in front of the Egyptian Sphinx. The walls of the Sphinx temple contain carved stone blocks of well over 250 tonnes in weight, which even the most powerful modern crane could hardly swing into position, even though it might be able to lift them. This is still a hugely puzzling and unsolved mystery for modern science.

The Black and White Magicians of Atlantis

We now come to the sequence of events leading to the eventual demise of the Fourth Race and the genesis of the Fifth Race. This is something which appears to have happened in two main phases, because the Ancient Commentary says that there were two huge and prolonged planetary cataclysms between which an intervening period of only some 700,000 years elapsed.[23] It is known for certain that the second of these commenced about 850,000 years ago, at a time when the Fifth Race was already several hundred thousand years old – something which I shall deal with in greater detail in a moment. So, by simple deduction, the first great cataclysm must have taken place about 1.55 million years ago, and it is this which would appear to have been the origin of the Exodus from Egypt described in the Old Testament.

However, it would appear that the Exodus *as described in the biblical tradition* never actually took place. The real story (borrowed from and described in the Vedic *Mahabharata*) seems to have involved the epic final showdown on the southern continental island of Ruta between the forces of good and evil in Atlantean times, where the ideals of the opposing magi of the 'Right-Hand Path' (white magicians) and the 'Left Hand Path' (black magicians) and their respective followers created some sort of serious schism in Atlantean society. Although the full details are not given, it is clear that the materialistic tendencies of a major part of the population – that associated with the self-centred and self-indulgent nature of the 'Left Hand Path' – had brought about some sort of really serious crisis affecting the elemental forces of our planetary Nature.

Blavatsky says of the Atlantean black magicians that they not only tried to control the subterranean elemental spirits, but that they were so arrogant that they even tried to command or harness the powers of the Sun (a suggestion of nuclear fusion perhaps?) and when this failed, they cursed it.[24] Bearing in mind what I said in Chapter 2 about the relationship between the Sun and the ionosphere and our planetary core, it is just conceivable that this sort of psycho-physical interference between the natural workings of these planetary forces could, in response, have set in train a calamitous sequence of (eventually) geological events. Just what sort of interference will become clearer in Chapter 17 on the nature of Atlantean magic. There is a modern parallel, however.

It is known that in the 1950s and 1960s, in the wake of Nikola Tesla's extraordinary electrical engineering research, military paranoia induced certain US government agencies to look seriously into the question of trying to harness the powers of the ionosphere as a potential weapon in the Cold War against the USSR. This came to nothing (fortunately for us all), but nevertheless it does show the extent of human arrogance and folly in the paranoid pursuit of greater power.

The Great Migration to Asia

It would appear that some sort of prolonged series of cataclysms – perhaps of a pan-planetary nature – overtook the black magicians of Ruta, thereby isolating and destroying their power for good. Some of the fleeing Atlanteans (traditionally led by magi of the 'Right-Hand Path') then migrated to Daitya, whilst others, so it would appear, migrated to the high plateau of Central Asia, to the north of present-day Tibet and the Himalayan mountains. Here these Atlanteans are said to have remained for another 150,000–200,000 years, evolving out of themselves and their culture the new Fifth Race type. The place where this genesis took place was described by Blavatsky as follows:

> Arga Varsha – the 'land of libations' – is the mystery name of that region which extends from the Kailas Mountains nearly to the Schamo [Gobi] Desert ... The Airyana-Varsedya of the Zoroastrians, as a locality, is identical with it. It is now said to have been situated between the Sea of Aral, Battistan, and Little Tibet [Ladakh]; but in olden times, its area was far larger.[25]

This same area is of course in the immediate vicinity of where the fabled 'Shambhala' is or was supposed to be. Thus the migrant body of Atlanteans – from which the seed of the new (Fifth) Root Race was to be drawn, were clearly brought into close proximity with the *kumaras* for the very purpose of guiding and supervising their evolutionary development at close quarters. This is somewhat akin to a modern gardener who would take cuttings from his garden and keep them safely in a protected greenhouse during their formative rooting period.

The Atlantean Refugees

Of the refugees themselves, *The Secret Doctrine* has this to say:

> The land which they fled to was no other than Central Asia. There [their descendants] lived and died until the separation of the nation ... Nearly two-thirds of one million years have elapsed since that period. The yellow-faced giants of the post-Atlantean day had ample time throughout this forced confinement to one part of the world and with the same racial blood and without any fresh infusion or admixture in it, to branch off during a period of nearly 700,000 years into the most heterogeneous and diversified types.[26]

The Secret Doctrine then hints that the same principle had applied in relation to the period subsequent to the founding of the Fourth Race by adding:

> The same is shown in Africa; nowhere does a more extraordinary variability of [human] types exist ... because of their forced isolation [on] their continent for several hundreds of thousands of years[27]

– at least, not until the last 11,000 years or so, in the aftermath of the Poseidonian cataclysm.

The Genesis of the Fifth Race

Anyway, some 150,000–250,000 years after the birth of this first sub-race of the new Fifth Root Race, which Blavatsky referred to as the 'Airyan' or 'Aryan' – from which the Irish derived their 'Eireann', or 'Erin'), they appeared to have moved westwards from the Tibetan Plateau area and settled in the lower-lying lands of the Caucasus. Here, a wide variety of nations then developed.

This was at a time when the oceanic waters covering the face of the future Europe were already beginning to recede. Once the new European lands had sufficiently dried out (several hundred thousand years later, one imagines), the early Aryo-Caucasians began to disperse. Some of them migrated westwards into Europe and the eastern end of what is now the Mediterranean; some went southwards into the lands of the Middle East and India, where they seem to have intermixed with other late Atlanteans in the Indian Ocean area.

This all seems to have occurred at a time when the Atlanteans of Daitya began to explore the new lands of Europe and the northern Mediterranean from the west. Inevitably this led to friction, for as Blavatsky tells us:

From the first appearance of the Aryan [Fifth Root] race, when the Pliocene portions of the once great Atlantis began gradually sinking and other continents to appear on the surface, down to the final disappearance of Plato's small island of Atlantis, the Aryan [i.e. modern human] races never ceased to fight with the descendants of the first giant races. This war lasted till nearly the close of the age, which preceded the Kali Yug and was the Mahabharatean war so famous in Indian history.[28]

It is reasonably clear from this that the final break-up and submersion of the remaining major Atlantean islands (except Daitya) commenced about 850,000 years ago as a direct result of astrophysical changes of the time affecting our planet. These seem to have lasted about 150,000 years. They not only destroyed many landmasses in the tropical regions, but also raised others in the temperate regions (including modern continental Europe) and so caused the more southerly Atlanteans to migrate northwards, looking for new lands to settle. However, by this stage, the first sub-races of the new northerly Root Race had already begun to move southwards and westwards. Inter-racial conflict was almost inevitable.

The Distinctive Consciousnesses of the Two Races

As a prelude to what was to happen much later on, it might be worth at this point trying to highlight the differences between the two Race types. On the one hand there were the Fourth Race Atlantean giants, some of them probably still well in excess of 20 ft (6.1 m) tall, whose consciousness was still entirely driven by emotions and idealistic passions, plus a Lemurian sensitivity to Nature. On the other was the relatively new Fifth Race type, probably about 15 ft (4.6 m) in height and beginning to develop the faculty of purely intellectual reasoning, yet still prone to Atlantean emotional intensity.

As I suggested a little earlier, the consciousness of the Atlantean Race had distinct parallels with that of a modern child between the ages of 7 and 14, whilst our modern Fifth Race consciousness is parallelled by that of a young person between the ages of 14 and 21. This puts our own present level of human evolution (of those with the as yet most advanced types of consciousness) as having an equivalent age of about 18 or 19.

Now, let one thing be made perfectly clear, lest there be any unfortunate misunderstanding about what I refer to as the relative 'advancement' in consciousness among different human groups today. From the viewpoint of esoteric philosophy, it is the leading intelligences in *all* of today's many ethnological types who possess and express the most evolved qualities of consciousness. Correspondingly, we find the lowest qualities of human consciousness simultaneously expressing themselves in all human types. Consciousness, as I have said before, is an expression of the soul entity and it is the soul type and age *alone* which define its outward expression in the innate capacities and subjective behaviour of the human individual. It is most unequivocally not a question of one ethnological type being 'more advanced' than another.

Ancient Emigrants and Refugees

Not surprisingly perhaps, despite the extensive and bitter wars fought between the two groups, as related by Vedic texts, intermarriage between the two great Fourth and Fifth Race types eventually occurred. This thereby resulted in the appearance of various hybrid sub-races in western Europe. Thus we have, on the one hand, the Atlantean island continent of Daitya finding itself annexed to a newly emergent northern landmass and seeking to colonize it. On the other, we have the same emergent landmass attaching itself to the area of the Caucasus, from where the expanding new Fifth Race types began their gradual westward migrations, raising dolmens and menhirs as they went on their way.

The Secret Doctrine suggests that also as a result of the great cataclysms that took place between 700,000 and 850,000 years ago, what we now know as Egypt, Sudan and Ethiopia gradually came into existence.[29] Thus it was, so *The Secret Doctrine* tells us, that migrant Atlanteans from Daitya in the west later came and settled there, commencing about 400,000 years ago. Meanwhile, others – known to modern anthropology as 'Cro-Magnon man' – had already escaped into southern Europe, en route producing some of the beautifully subtle cave paintings found by modern archaeologists in southern France and Spain, such as those at Lascaux. However, we shall take a look at the eastern Atlanteans, their territories and the cataclysms affecting them in rather greater detail in the next chapter.

Chapter Thirteen

·

THE POST-DILUVIAN WORLD

'All historians agree with Philostratus and admit that commercial intercourse did exist between Egypt and India. Nay more, Eusebius asserts that in
the reign of Memnon, king of Ethiopia, a body of Ethiopians from about the
countries of the Indus River migrated and settled in the valley of the Nile.'[1]

In the aftermath of the last really great world cataclysms, between 850,000
and 700,000 years ago – leading to the progressive raising of the European
continent as we know it today – three major migrations of the early Aryo-
Caucasians seem to have taken place. One of these was to the west, into mainland Europe, a second southward into Afghanistan, northern India and Persia,
and a third (rather later) from the Maghreb area of northwest Africa to Egypt
involving a mixed Atlanto-Aryan hybrid race. Of the first of these, the *Secret
Doctrine* has this to say:

> The archaic records show the initiates of the second sub-race of the Aryan family
> moving from one land to another for the purposes of supervising the building of
> menhirs and dolmens, of colossal zodiacs in stone and places of sepulchre to serve
> as receptacles for the ashes of generations to come. When was it? The fact of their
> crossing from France to Great Britain by land may give an idea of the date when
> such a journey could have been performed on *terra firma*.[2]

The Druids and the Great 'Neolithic' Monuments of Antiquity

It was once believed that many of the great prehistoric stone monuments
of Europe were built by early Druids. As the above quote confirms, however,
sites such as Stonehenge (figure 23) are in reality far older, and were built as
monumental zodiacs. In contradiction of this idea, Blavatsky adds:

> They are not druidical ... Nor did the Druids build them, for they were only the
> heirs to the cyclopean lore left to them by generations of mighty builders and
> magicians, both good and bad.

Figure 23. The zodiacal temple of Stonehenge in England

and then again:

> [The Druid] priests were the descendants of the last Atlanteans and what is
> known of them is sufficient to allow the inference that they were eastern priests,
> akin to the Chaldeans and Indians, although little more.[3]

There is a clear phonetic similarity between the word 'Druid' and 'Dravid' (that
is, Dravidian). As the Basque language has been confirmed to have at least
some direct correlations with the Dravidian language,[4] it seems quite clear
that, at some time between 500,000–100,000 years ago, mixed Aryo-Atlantean
Dravidians from ancient India – whether as a sub-race or a merchant colony,
including their priests – actually migrated to and subsequently lived in western Europe. As Blavatsky adds:

> Palaeolithic man of the Miocene and Pliocene times was a pure Atlantean, as we
> have previously stated. The Basques are of course of a much later date than this
> but their affinities, as here shown, go far to prove the original extraction of their
> remote ancestors. The mysterious 'affinity' between their tongue and that of the
> Dravidian races of India will be understood by those who have followed our
> outline of continental formations and shiftings.[5]

Notwithstanding the fact that it was the Aryo-Caucasian initiates of their own
second sub-race which had built dolmens and menhirs right across Europe,
Blavatsky states quite categorically of the majority of so-called 'neolithic' caves
and conical menhirs in Morbihan and Brittany – and even the giant 'tombs' in

Sardinia – that they were actually built 'by Cro-Magnon man of the escaping Atlantean type.'[6]

The Great Southward Migration

The Vedic records of India today still speak of the Aryan peoples who originally descended from the north and conquered the native Dravidian peoples of India and Ceylon (modern Sri Lanka). The great Dravidian empire and civilization at that time seems to have extended all the way to modern Cambodia and Thailand, as well as to modern Iraq. The *original* Dravidians, however, appear to have been members of a purely Atlantean sub-race who absorbed the Brahmanistic culture of the incoming Caucasians into their own animistic religious culture. This thereby created the highly colourful but spiritually paradoxical version of modern Hinduism, with its ancient caste system and its panoply of human and animal-headed gods and goddesses on the one hand and its deep metaphysical esotericism on the other. As Dr David Frawley says:

> By the traditional accounts of the Dravidians themselves, their [present] culture originated from Vedic Aryans who migrated from northern India ... They became a strong maritime culture and spread Aryan culture to southeast Asia and perhaps further east and to the west. They have an old and massive literature and appear to be amongst the earliest people of the ancient world.[7]

He also adds:

> The [present-day] Dravidian language also appears intermediate between the Semitic and the Indo-Aryan in terms of sound and word formation.[8]

As an adjunct to this, intermarriage between the two ethnological groups may well have been what led to the generation of the Semitic peoples, from whom were derived the ancestors of both the Hebrews and the Arabs in the ancient civilization of Harappa – hence the origin of the word 'Arab'. As has already been suggested, both the Hebrews and the Phoenicians appear originally to have been of a common ethnic (Dravido-Caucasian) stock and to have originated in northwestern India, in the area of the Punjab and to the immediate south of the Indus Delta.

Modern history, alas, can tell us very little about when this southward Indo-Vedic incursion took place, but the esoteric records appear to suggest that it was again some considerable time after the great world cataclysms of 850,000–700,00 years ago, once the world's geography had begun to settle down again. Therefore it would seem that the remains of the civilization of India and Indo-Persia (buried under other much more recent ruins) have to be seen as immensely older than modern archaeology is prepared even to consider.

The First Great Migration to Egypt

Of the Maghrebian migrants into Egypt, the *Secret Doctrine* says that 'the Guanches of the Canary Islands were [also] lineal descendants of the Atlanteans'; to which Blavatsky adds:

> The earliest Egyptians had been separated from the latest Atlanteans for ages upon ages. They were themselves descended from an alien race [i.e. one which had interbred with the new Fifth Race types] and had settled in Egypt some 400,000 years before, but their initiates had preserved all their records. Even as late as the time of Herodotus they still had in their possession the statues of 341 kings who had reigned over their little Atlanto-Aryan sub-race.[9]

From this it is clear that the earliest sub-races of the Fifth Race had migrated as far westwards as the Atlantic Ocean. Here they (like their southward-moving brethren in India) had already had time to intermarry with the 'lineally descended' Atlanteans of Daitya – the by then still huge continental island which incorporated the Maghreb, the Canarias and Madeira islands as well as the Iberian peninsula, Tyrrhenia and modern Italy (*see* Chapter 12). Elsewhere Blavatsky adds:

> Egypt is far older than Europe as now traced on the map. Atlanto-Aryan tribes began to settle on it when the British islands and France were not even in existence. It is well known that the 'tongue' of the Egyptian sea, or the Delta of lower Egypt, became firm land very gradually and followed the highlands of Abyssinia. Unlike the latter, which arose very suddenly, comparatively speaking, it was very slowly formed through long ages from successive layers of sea-slime and mud deposited annually by the soil brought down by a larger river, the present Nile. Yet even the Delta as a firm and fertile land has been inhabited for more than 100,000 years.[10]

In support of the quotation at the beginning of this chapter, Blavatsky then goes on to mention Egypt's later colonization by Fifth Race Indo-Caucasians from the northeast.[11]

The Second Great Egyptian Immigration

It is quite clear from what Blavatsky and others have to say on this issue that the new immigrants were in fact from that great country which, in prehistoric times, seems to have incorporated Chaldea, Assyria, Babylonia and Cusha (modern Iraq, Iran, Arabia, northwestern India and Afghanistan). In the volumes of the 19th-century *Asiatic Researches*, the journal of the Royal Asiatic Society in London, we find several mentions of this great (Indo-Dravidian) kingdom and its connections with Ethiopia-Abyssinia. For example:

As I am informed, a tribe of them [the Palis] has the appellation of 'Haritas'. They are now considered as outcasts, yet are acknowledged to have possessed a dominion in ancient times from the Indus to the eastern limits of Bengal and even as far as Siam ... They were supplanted by the Rajaputras.[12]

In fact these 'Palis' (clearly a mixture of Indo-Dravidian and later Indo-Caucasian peoples) seem also to have been the original founders of 'Palistan' – modern Palestine – as well as of Ethiopia-Abyssinia, concerning which there are also linguistic connections by way of further proof of ancient association.

Ethiopia and the Land of Kush

According to the records of the Royal Asiatic Society,

The written Abyssinian language which we call 'Ethiopic' is a dialect of old Chaldean and sister of Arabic and Hebrew, we know with certainty, not only from the great multitude of identical words but (which is a far longer proof) from the familiar grammatical arrangement of the several idioms. We know at the same time that it is written, like all the Indian characters, from the left hand to the right and that the vowels are annexed, as in Devanagri, to the consonants.[13]

The eastern part of this great kingdom appears to have been named 'Cusha-dwipa', after the contiguous mountain range which we now know as the 'Hindu Kush'. Unsurprisingly, the land of Ethiopia to which these expatriate Palis first migrated, they renamed as the kingdom of what Egyptologists now call 'Kesh'. As the vowel was largely silent in the languages of greater Indo-Persia, we are able to say quite categorically that 'Cush', 'Kush' and 'Kesh' are one and the same, although Egyptologists have mistakenly attributed to the Ethiopian colony a merely recent commencement, at c1500BC.

In a report to the Royal Asiatic Society, one 19th-century member, Colonel Wilford, mentions that

Cusha-dwipa without is Abyssinia and Ethiopia; and the Brahmans account plausibly enough for its name by asserting that the descendants of Cusha, being obliged to leave their native country (by them called Cusha-dwipa within) migrated into Sancha-dwipa and gave to their new settlement the name of their ancestor.[14]

'Sancha-dwipa' was the ancient name given to the kingdom settled by the Poseidonian Egyptians – as the *Puranas* also confirm. So here we have confirmation of the fact that northwestern Africa – incorporating Egypt and Sudan – was in fact already in the hands of Atlantean peoples.

The report in *Asiatic Researches* continues:

These Indian emigrants are described in the Puranas as a blameless, pious and even a sacred race; which is exactly the character given by the Ancients to the genuine Ethiopians, who are said by Stephanus of Byzantium, by Eusebius, by Philostratus, by Eustathius and others to have originally come from India.[15]

The Dating of the Second Great Egyptian Migration

Of these migrating conquerors of the early Atlantean Egyptians, Blavatsky has this to say in support:

Under the reign of Visvamitra, first king of the dynasty of Soma-Vanga ... Manu Vina (the Egyptian Menes) heir of the ancient kings, being abandoned by the Brahmans, emigrated with all his companions, passing through Arya (Persia) and the countries of Barra (Arabia) till he came to the shores of Masra (Egypt).[16]

But when was it that these latter migrants came to Egypt and took up residence in the Delta, the first part of the country which they occupied? Blavatsky again answers us:

History is silent upon the subject. Fortunately, we have the Dendera Zodiac ... which records the fact. This zodiac with its three mysterious Virgos between the Lion and Libra ... justifies the truthfulness of those priests who told Herodotus that (a) the poles of the Earth and the Ecliptic had formerly coincided and (b) that even since their first zodiacal records were commenced, the Poles had been three times within the plane of the Ecliptic.[17]

Given that the Great Sidereal Year is some 25,920 Earth years in length, it is quite clear from the above quotation, that the second invasion of Egypt must have taken place at least 80,000 years ago![18] Despite this, Blavatsky adds,

The civilization of the Atlanteans was greater even than that of the Egyptians. It is their degenerate descendants, the nation of Plato's Atlantis, which built the first pyramid in the country and that certainly before the advent of the 'eastern Ethiopians'.[19]

These 'eastern Ethiopians' are what Herodotus called the Indo-Persian merchant traders of his own time.

The 'Great Builders'

One notes here that Blavatsky does not say that the 'barbarian' Maghrebian Atlanteans built *all* the pyramids in Egypt – but then she does not categorically say that they did not. However, bearing in mind that as the Mayan pyramids

Figure 24. The zodiac carved on the ceiling of the temple of Dendera in Upper Egypt, as redrawn by Lucy Lamy. This is the more famous of the two Dendera zodiacs. The 'three Virgos' mentioned by Blavatsky are missing here; they are to be found on the other, 'square', zodiac (see Denon's Description de l'Egypte, *reprinted by Benedikt Taschen, 1994, pp.398–399).*

appear to have been more in the ziggurat style, whereas the Egyptian ones were generally smooth-sided, it seems quite possible that the Indo-Caucasian initiates, with their complete focus on astronomical and astrological issues, may actually have been responsible for their at least partial rebuilding.

Certainly, the passageways in the various pyramids are rather more of a height and size to suit more modern human racial types than the 'Atlantean giants',[20] at whose prowess the newer cultures marvelled and of whom it was said that

> Their physical strength was extraordinary, the earth sometimes shaking under their tread. Whatever they did was done speedily … They were wise and communicated their wisdom to men.[21]

Notwithstanding this, the Indians have their own very ancient tradition of huge temple architecture and stonemasonry which was always religious in nature and orientated upon particular stars or star groups – like Angkor Wat and the temple of the Khmers at Borobudur. At the very least therefore, it is possible that the 'Cushitic' invaders took over an already existing pyramid culture and refined it as well as possibly also extending it. The modern

Egyptological idea that the pyramids and Sphinx were built only over the last 4,500 years and merely as 'tombs' for pharaohs is patently absurd. Egyptological scholars do themselves and their research no favours by seeking to perpetuate it in the face of increasingly solid evidence to the contrary.

Modern Versus Ancient Anthropology

By this stage of the second invasion of Egypt, the Indo-Caucasian humankind of the day must have been of a height not that dissimilar to that of the above-average male American or Australian physique of today – in other words, something well over 6 ft 6 in (2 m). Blavatsky mentions that 'man's height was reduced from 15 to 10 or 12 feet ever since the third sub-race of the Aryan stock. … Since then it has been steadily decreasing.'[22] As the third Indo-Caucasian sub-race must have commenced its existence about 550,000–600,000 years ago, with the succeeding fourth sub-race commencing about 300,000–350,000 years ago, we can see that the (still current) fifth sub-race had its evolutionary genesis about 50,000–100,000 years ago. However, that is just a little more recent than modern anthropology is prepared to agree for *homo sapiens* making its very first appearance upon our planet (some 180,000 years ago). The discrepancy between the two chronologies is somewhat more than marked.

Rather interestingly, given that the original Atlanto-Aryans of the Maghreb were supposed to be giants, we find that there is some archaeological evidence to support the idea. In the early 20th century, a French army captain called La Fanchère discovered in Morocco a cache of several hundred double-edged axes, each weighing some 17 lb 8 oz (7.9 kg). The sheer weight and size of these is such that it has been calculated that it would have required a giant of not less than 13 ft (4 m) in height to lift and wield one properly. The Roman writer Tertullian (cAD155–230) wrote that in his day the skeletons of a number of giants were found at Carthage, and in 1858 European scientific journals mentioned the finding by archaeologists, also at Carthage, of a sarcophagus full of giant skeletons. (As far as I am aware they are not preserved, or at least not on display – they would be a perpetual embarrassment to modern archaeologists and have probably been well 'filed'.) In the face of this, it is rather remarkable that modern scholars pay the subject such little heed.

Ancient Maps and Cartographical Technology

In the last part of this chapter, I will turn to the geography and geology of the period coinciding with Plato's chronology – in other words with the period of the last great 'crustal displacement' which geologists now acknowledge as having taken place about 12,000 years ago. By way of reference, let me turn again to Professor Charles Hapgood's reconstituted 1513 map of the Turkish admiral Piri Re'is (*see again* Figure 19 in Chapter 8). The original map is quite remarkable in many ways, its characteristics having already been dealt with at some length in Hapgood's *Maps of the Ancient Sea Kings*. Probably the most extraordinary aspect of the cartography – apart from its minute attention to detail – is the fact that it must have been done using spherical trigonometry, which requires an absolutely and reliably accurate clock mechanism to define longitude.

As the first such clock was, to the knowledge of historians, only made in the mid-18th century, in England, there have as yet been no useful conjectures as to quite how the ancient maps were put together. However, it is known that the Ancients (quite apart from having a good working knowledge of compass magnetism) used a form of astronomically based navigational computer technology, because a multi-functional and multi-geared mechanical device (called by the Greeks an *antikythera* and now located in the National Museum in Athens) was discovered about a century ago in an at least 2,000-year-old wreck off Crete. Unfortunately, the method of its use has never been worked out, but its sheer complexity suggests that it may well have been a calculator of longitude.

The original 1513 map was apparently a composite put together by Piri Re'is from various ancient 'portolans' (navigational charts used by medieval sailors), some at least of which he believed to have originated in ancient Alexandria and which, even in his day, were thus nearly 2,000 years old. The implication therefore is that even these ancient portolan maps were based upon yet older maps and ancillary cartographic data. That too raises all sorts of further questions about the sophistication of ancient ships, theodolites, telescopes, and so on, although space does not permit an examination of such matters here.[23] The fact remains, nevertheless, that in terms of sophistication some aspects of ancient technology appear to have been on a virtual par with our own. It would certainly appear that the Ancients were familiar with the spherical trigonometry needed to allow for the Earth's curvature in the preparation of maps, as Hapgood suggests.

The Earth's Ancient Cartographic Centre

As can be seen from the original Piri Re'is map, shown in Hapgood's book, ancient cartography used a system of spherical loci from which radiated straight lines in 16 or 32 directions.[24] These foci were not randomly placed but were arranged in arcs of a circle, the centre of that circle having been confirmed by Charles Hapgood's team as being in Egypt.

As I suggested in my previous book, *Egypt, Child of Atlantis*, that same Egyptian centre appears to have been at Arsinoe in the Faiyum, just to the southwest of Giza[25] – traditionally regarded as the place where the god Ra 'first rose in the First Time.' The name 'Arsinoe' is, however, derived from 'Alcynoe' which is itself a corruption of 'Alcyone', the latter being the central and brightest star in the Pleiades, the 'eldest' of the 'seven sisters'; and as suggested in an earlier chapter, our local celestial system appears to have been regarded by the Ancients as part of the Pleiades nebula. So, it makes complete sense that the Ancients – who were insistent that the celestial organization should be mirrored on Earth – should have regarded Alcyone as the star around which our own solar system orbited and thus named its mirror location on the ground after it. Thereafter, the radially circular positioning of both major cities, temples and cartographic points would have been quite straightforward – using spherical trigonometry.

The use of 16 or even 32 radial directions was, rather interestingly, the system used by the Etruscans over 500 years BC and, as we shall see in Chapter 15, they and the Carthaginians seem to have derived their knowledge and culture from even more ancient sources. Consequently, we can suggest with some logic that the portolan maps from which Piri Re'is made up his own map, may well have been of Etruscan or Carthaginian origin.

Other Noteworthy Features in the Map

In trying to establish just how old the Piri Re'is map data (as shown) actually is, there are three main areas of focus, the first of these being the western Mediterranean. As we can see, there is not only one strait (that is, Gibraltar) between northern Africa and Spain; there are two, the other resulting from the existence in ancient times of a very large promontory, extending northwards from the area of Oran in northwestern Algeria almost to Almeria at the eastern extremity of the Costa del Sol in southern Spain. So the far western Mediterranean at the time was effectively an inland sea (like the Black Sea) but with two access points, one at either end. As we know from today's map, the more easterly promontory no longer exists, having undoubtedly been despatched to a watery grave by local earthquakes (of which there are many, even today), as occurred further along the southern Mediterranean coast at Egyptian Alexandria in Roman times.

The Mediterranean is of course now clear of obstructions in the area. In ancient times, however, the navigation through the Balearics to the inner strait would probably have been quite hazardous. One thus wonders if the story of Odysseus's voyage through the 'clashing cliffs' might in fact derive from a true historical memory of one or other of the two original straits, as a result of the constantly shifting earthquake activity of the time causing the cliffs on the two sides of the strait constantly to shake and thus appear to move towards each other.

The second feature worthy of note in the Piri Re'is map is the fact that the island chains of the Canaries, Madeira and Azores already then existed as island groups, although there were clearly several more islands in each group at the time and all of them were far bigger than they are now. Figure 25 shows a copy of Charles Hapgood's comparison of the 'then and now', which shows to scale just how much subsidence and submersion has taken place in the Azores group since the original map was drawn. That the Azores were once actually part of a far greater landmass was shown in the 1970s by the geologist Christian O'Brien, who claimed that it must have been roughly the size of Spain, with mountain ranges rising to over 12,000 feet above see level.[26]

Similar subsidence and submersion seems to have taken place in the area of the Atlantic directly between the projections of West Africa and South America, because the 1737 Phillippe Buache map (*see* figure 26) shows a number of quite large island groups (immediately to the south and southwest of the present Cape Verde group) which no longer exist but which otherwise confirm the Piri Re'is map details. As these islands and the Azores lie directly over the highly volcanic Mid-Atlantic Ridge, there seems to be some direct relationship involved in their gradual disappearance. What is also worth mentioning about the drawing (as Charles Hapgood noted) is the extraordinary bathymetric section of the Atlantic Ocean seabed – which could not possibly have been worked out by soundings in 1737.

Whilst the Azores were evidently once part of the same landmass as the Canaries and Madeira, neither they nor Madeira were found to have any population whatsoever when the Portuguese and Spaniards arrived. So, if our

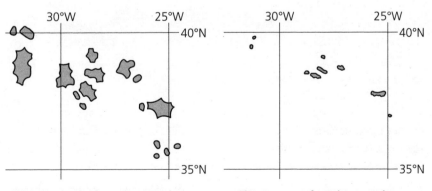

The Azores before the cataclysm   The Azores after the cataclysm

Figure 25. Charles Hapgood's comparison of the Azores before the ancient cataclysm that submerged them (left, taken from the Piri Re'is map) and as they are today (right)

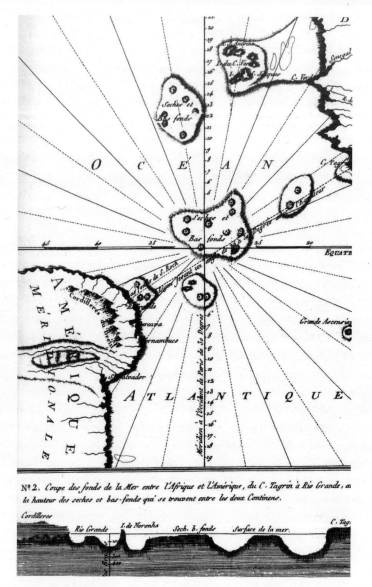

Figure 26. Detail of the Philippe Buache map drawn in 1737, showing no longer existing islands south and southwest of the Cape Verde group

overall hypothesis is correct as to Madeira and the Canary Islands being the scattered last remains of Plato's Poseidonis, the Piri Re'is map must date to the period *after* the cataclysm which, Plato tells us, occurred c9500BC. How long after it is of course impossible to say. However, as Blavatsky tells us, the fact that the ancient sailors of Indo-Persia knew of the islands (which they referred to, in the *Puranas*, as 'Atala') is indicative not only of the fact that the *Puranas* and Indian navigation pre-date the Poseidonian cataclysm, but also that they were sufficiently well known for them to be able to use exactly the same name for them as the Greeks of Plato's time.[27]

Now, although it has been made quite clear why this book takes the view that Plato's island was where we now find the Canaries and Madeira,[28] we should perhaps spend a moment looking at the other side of the Atlantic Ocean. The reason for that is because, due to the sheer size of the Poseidonian cataclysm, there should perhaps be evidence there of further cataclysmic destruction at around the same time.

The Ancient Geography of the Western Atlantic

To begin with, the issue is even more interesting because of the land configuration on the Piri Re'is map on the western side of the Atlantic (*see again* figure 19). As we can see, whilst the Antilles clearly existed at the time, the original coastline of central America seems to have extended virtually due north from a point between Panama and the Yucatan peninsula in the south to Florida in the north. At this time, so it seems, there was no 'Gulf of Mexico' *per se*.

Now, whereas Charles Hapgood and his cartographic team seem to have taken the view that the original maps were perhaps poorly put together by either Piri Re'is or his predecessors, because they were based upon a partial use of straight rather than spherical trigonometry, the sheer detail of the coastline and islands in this area seems to make this look increasingly unlikely. If the Ancients could map small island groups like the Antilles so clearly, and so obviously in line with modern maps, why should they have suddenly made such colossal errors in relation to far larger landmasses which were in the same vicinity?

So if the Gulf of Mexico did not exist at the time, why didn't it? One possible answer seems to be provided by the *Troano Codex* containing the Mayan sacred epic, the *Popol Vuh*. This was translated by the explorer Brasseur de Bourbourg[29] in the 19th century, his translation being as follows:

> In the year 6 Kan, on the 11th Muluc in the month Zac, there occurred terrible earthquakes which continued without interruption until the 13th Chuen. The country of the hills of mud-clay, the land of Mu, was sacrificed; being twice upheaved, it suddenly disappeared during the night, the basin continually being shaken by the volcanic forces. Being confined, these caused the land to sink and to rise several times in various places. At last the surface gave way and ten countries were torn asunder and scattered. Unable to stand the force of the convulsion, they sank with their 64 million inhabitants 8,060 years before the writing of this book.[30]

This amazingly graphic account, claiming the submersion of a gigantic landmass and the consequent drowning of the 64 million people in ten countries who inhabited it, cannot be taken anything other than very seriously. Now, 64 million people is equivalent to the whole population of Great Britain, or 20 per cent of the population of the US. So, given that the people of the time might possibly have lived in such dense urbanization as we find in some modern cities today, the suggestion that the original landmass where the Gulf of Mexico now stands was home to such numbers seems, at the very least, quite possible.

De Bourbourg is written off by modern scholars as something of a fantasist as far as his translations are concerned. However, as many modern archaeo-logical scholars – Egyptologists being the perfect example – are so clearly and utterly incapable of understanding the nature of ancient allegory and metaphor, one has to question whether their own interpretations of Mayan and other Central American traditions even begin to approach the true facts. However, let us not rely entirely upon de Bourbourg. Let us see if any other avenues of reportage and general scientific research appear to back up what he has to say.

Other circumstantial evidence is certainly available from Native American Indian sources. For example, J.B. Mahan describes[31] a conversation with the chief of the Yuchi tribe, which is today located in Oklahoma. The chief confirmed, however, that the tribe's original homeland was an island in the Atlantic and that the Bahamas (east of Florida) were the remnants of this island. Furthermore, so the tradition had been passed down, the main mass of the island had been destroyed by cataclysm long (unspecified) ages before. When questioned further the chief described how the land was destroyed 'by fires and clouds of different colours which came from the west and north'– which clearly suggests cataclysmic volcanic activity in the Gulf of Mexico area. But the same cataclysms seem to have extended all the way south, past the Yucatan peninsula, to the Caribbean Sea.

Local Geological Evidence

The oceanographic authors of *The Geology of the Atlantic Ocean* confirm for us that

> in the Caribbean Sea [crustal] thicknesses reach more than 14 kilometres just west of the Beata Ridge and more than 12 kilometres just west of the Aves Ridge. Both ridges thus appear to be massive piles of volcanic rocks more related to local plate tectonics than to the typical layer 3 of the Atlantic Ocean [seabed][32]

– which is itself stated as being between 3 and 4 kilometres thick. To find a vol-canic overlay with a thickness of 8–10 *kilometres* above the Earth's crust, one must logically come to the conclusion that the volcanic activity that produced it must have been of truly gigantic proportions. Quite clearly then, the geological evidence supports the case for the most almighty of cataclysms in this area.

The fact of a huge mass of islands of widely varying sizes in the ocean immediately to the east and southeast of the Gulf of Mexico also clearly indicates that there was an original continental landmass here too, whether an island or whether somehow formerly attached to the main north and south American landmasses – which looks the more likely from the geographical configuration of the island archipelago. As Professor B.C. Heezen of the Lamont Docherty Marine Observatory observed regarding the geology of the Ares Ridge near the Virgin Islands (following a Duke University marine expedition):

> Up to now, geologists generally believed that light granite or acid igneous rocks were confined to the continents and that the crust of the Earth beneath the sea is composed of heavier, dark-coloured basaltic rock ... Thus the occurrence of light coloured granitic rocks may support an old theory that a continent formerly existed in the region of the eastern Caribbean and that these rocks may represent the core of that subsided lost continent.[33]

In June 1960 there appeared an interestingly corresponding article in *The American Journal of Science* in which Heezen, with his Lamont Docherty observatory colleagues W.S. Broecker and M. Ewing, put forward a really groundbreaking theory. They had uncovered clear and extensive evidence 'for an abrupt change in climate close to 11,000 years ago'[34] in the same general area. Other scientists, whilst confirming the dramatic climate change in the area, have come up with variations in the timing of up to 1,000 years, although in practical terms this might be considered 'nitpicking'.

Asteroidal Catastrophe Theory

As I have previously mentioned, some scientists have of course theorized that a great asteroid or meteor plunged into the Gulf of Mexico, just off Yucatan, some 65 million years ago. Their theory is based upon the discovery of a 'sharp and brief but widespread increase in iridium and other trace elements in sedimentary rocks at the Cretaceous-Cenozoic boundary',[35] due to 'fallout' producing a thick veil of dust. However, nothing else has been found but a vast undersea crater over 150 kilometres in diameter, which could just conceivably be the remains of a vast, sunken volcanic super-caldera. Trace elements of the type described could just as easily have been produced by prodigious volcanic activity of the sort which we have just suggested. In reality, there is no need to bring an entirely speculative falling comet or asteroid into the equation.

Notwithstanding this, the area seems to be a veritable magnet for such spontaneous celestial visitors. Further suggestions have been made as to yet another comet or asteroid supposedly having fallen into the northern Gulf of Mexico area 'around 9000 BC' and having given rise to what are called the 'Carolina Bays' – masses of oddly shaped indentations in the ground over several hundred kilometres – which are supposedly the result of cometary or asteroidal 'shrapnel'. However, there is again no proof in the form of the actual 'shrapnel' having been found – and several other quite different theories have anyway been put forward for these phenomena.

Evidence of the Great Cataclysm

It is true that some of the native legends in the area speak of 'a great serpent of fire' which appeared in the sky, followed by a gigantic cataclysm and terrible floods, plus unending rain, leading to the death of the whole population other than those who managed to escape to the mountains and other high ground. Some commentators have automatically assumed that the 'serpent of fire' had to be a comet or blazing asteroid; but there are other possible explanations of this phenomenon which have hardly been considered. For example, whilst there may have been a comet in the sky at or around the same time, there is no explicit suggestion in the legends of it having actually 'fallen to Earth'. Altern-atively, it is just possible that a huge fireball could have been ejected into the sky by a particularly large and powerful volcano. Mega-lightning could also have been the source of the tradition.

However, quite apart from all this, there is direct native evidence of the cataclysms having been caused by volcanic and earthquake activity rather than anything else. The picture taken by Mayan scholar Teobert Maler (1842–1917) in the late 19th century from a wall frieze of an unknown Mayan temple (*see* figure 27) clearly shows the large blocks of building masonry of a high ziggurat collapsing into the sea on the left, whilst a large volcano emerges from under the sea in the centre and spews out vast plumes of smoke and ash, plus magma. In the lower half we see a woman drowning, whilst under her the Earth's crust has split laterally and vertically. On the right, a native priest is paddling his canoe, which perhaps suggests efforts at rescue – or merely of the fact that at least a few individual survivors lived to tell the tale.

The whole area is of course highly volcanic and also subject to local earth-quake activity – and probably always has been, for many millions of years at least. Consequently, the native population would have been as used to such activity and would have paid it as little attention as they generally do even today. However, what we see in the wall frieze is the result of a singular and obviously highly memorable event which the priests who escaped would have

Figure 27. Detail of a Mayan wall painting, from a photograph by Teobert Maler, who himself claimed that it depicted the destruction of Atlantis

wanted to ensure remained permanently in their historical records, as well as in the folk memory of the tribe. I suggest, therefore, that the wall frieze could well be confirming in pictures what the *Popol Vuh*, as presented in the *Troano Codex*, is saying to us in words.

If this Central American cataclysm were to have coincided with that affecting Plato's Poseidonis (where we place it) – which is located at pretty well the same latitude – the timing provided by the Maya would look quite realistic. It suggests that the *Popol Vuh* was written c1000–2000BC, when Mayan civilization and culture were still extant. It would also tend to explain why the Toltecs and the foreign-looking (that is, non-Mesoamerican) Olmecs disappeared so suddenly.

The fact that the surrounding landmasses of Mexico (including the Yucatan), Guatemala and smaller adjacent modern Central American states are peppered with notable sacred sites, such as Chichen Itza, Tenochtitlan Xochicalco and Teotihuacan, involving ziggurats and other temples, is surely the clearest of indications that a coherent, large and very widespread civilization once existed in these parts. The much later Aztecs encountered (and butchered in their tens of thousands) by Cortez and his gangs of military thugs, made it quite clear that they had merely taken over the temple buildings constructed by a previous civilization (that is, the early Maya or the pre-Maya Toltecs) of which they themselves knew nothing. However, that does not mean that that predecessor civilization was 'Atlantean' *per se*.

It would follow quite logically that, if the centre of an original great civilization were torn out and destroyed in the way described, with the vast mass of the people being killed in the general cataclysm and its aftermath, the existing culture would cease to exist in any strength at all. Some temples and even temple complexes might have survived but would have had no population to tend or use them. They would thus have lain empty until the Aztecs or the invading Spaniards or other later Europeans found them.

The Sudden Demise of the Dinosaurs

There has been so much speculation in recent years that the massive seabed crater under the Gulf of Mexico was caused by an asteroid or comet which crashed into the earth some 60 million years ago, that this has now 'evolved' into mainstream scientific orthodoxy. This is along with the further theory, also mentioned earlier, that the same falling celestial body caused the almost instant demise of the world's dinosaur population. But this idea is based upon sheer speculation without any real supporting proof whatsoever, whereas the Mayan tradition does at least provide strong circumstantial evidence of a purely terrestrial cataclysm.

It is otherwise worth mentioning that the end of the Pleistocene era (also the end of the last ice age) is currently set by scientists at c9000BC – again roughly the time of Plato's island cataclysm. However, at this same period, we find a recurrence of the same type of rapid mass destruction that supposedly killed off the dinosaurs. It took the form of the very sudden and violent death, in Alaska and Siberia, of literally millions of animals of all shapes and sizes. The animals' bodies – many literally torn apart and mangled by some huge but as yet unexplained force in Nature – were found tangled up together in a deep layer of mud, along with the remains of all sorts of vegetation, including trees which had been uprooted and splintered into matchwood. Some of the animals were found with vegetation still in their mouths, indicating just how sudden was the nature of the cataclysm.

It should otherwise be obvious by now that if such sudden and violent cataclysms occurred pretty well simultaneously around the planet about 11,000 years ago (give or take 1,000 years on the basis of scientific argument), there is fair reason to suppose that they might well have had a common cause. If so, and given that the asteroid/comet theory has been shown to be very hypothetical, one must also suggest the possibility of an astrophysical *cycle* being involved, as described in a previous chapter. The fact that the Maya and Inca seem to have had a clear sense of the world ending amidst cataclysms *in due cycle*, also leads in the same general direction. However, there are one or two issues concerning the supposed origins of the native peoples of Central and South America which we ought also to touch on before closing this chapter.

The Origins of the Meso-American Peoples

The native peoples of the Yucatan told the invading Spaniards that their ancestors believed their own land to have first been colonized by an ancient and
unknown race which had come from the east and built the temples which they
themselves now occupied. The tradition had it that God himself had helped
this ancient people by opening up 12 great pathways through the great Ocean.
However, this appears to be a straightforward allegory with a clear zodiacal
reference, even though the natives of the Yucatan may by then have come to
believe in the story literally.

The Aztecs similarly told the Spaniards that their own race had originated
on a large island called 'Aztlan', which lay in the ocean to the east. Now this too
could well be a literal interpretation of an ancient esoteric metaphor, because
the name appears to be derived from 'As't-Llan', the *As* or *As't* being the same
divine or celestial state of being and consciousness which we find in many esoteric traditions throughout the Middle and Far East. For example, As't is the
Egyptian version of the name of the goddess Isis. 'Llan', however, resembles a
similar word found in the Welsh and other Celtic languages – and is thus much
closer to a supposed Atlantean origin. But, although the origin of Aztlan
appears to be found in the sense of a 'divine land' or 'divine state', it is nevertheless possible that it was latterly used for (and thus became synonymous
with) one or other of the real Atlantean island-continents.

Notwithstanding all this, there is no adequate evidence – circumstantial or
otherwise – to suggest that the native peoples of Central and South America
were, at the time of Plato's island cataclysm still bona fide 'Atlanteans'. The
ancient tradition has it that virtually the whole of the southern Atlantic *island*
continent was destroyed several hundred thousand years ago and that the
remaining nuclei of truly Atlantean culture and civilization (together with its
still giant population) had already migrated northwards. All that remained
behind were local Atlantean 'backwaters' which were themselves reoccupied
(again, over hundreds of thousands of years) by later and very different ethnological sub-races, from both east and west. It is accordingly these which appear
to have given rise to the Inca, Toltecs, Olmecs, Maya, Aztecs and other peoples
of modern history.

The Geography of the Southern Atlantic

The eastward extension of South America as shown in the Piri Re'is map was
regarded by Charles Hapgood and his colleagues as yet another cartographical
aberration, this time involving the supposed missing out of a long length of
coastline – probably due to misaligning two or more of the ancient portolan

maps. He therefore ascribed this now non-evident landmass as the original eastward extension of Tierra del Fuego, at the foot of South America, extending across to the Falkland Islands and South Georgia. However, given the amount of detail on the map, this speculative assessment cannot be considered by any means absolutely certain.

In addition, when we look at the complete Heezen-Tharp bathyspheric map of the Atlantic, we find that there are indeed submarine mountainous areas extending several thousand feet up from the ocean bed in a curved line extending eastwards from a point roughly 200 miles south of Rio de Janeiro in Brazil. The line extends right the way across the Rio Grande Rise to the Tristan da Cunha group (which lies almost astride the Mid-Atlantic Ridge) and finishes at a point some 300 miles to the west of Cape Town in South Africa.

If this scenario is correct, it surely lends weight to Blavatsky's submission that the original Lemuro-Atlantean super-continent extended in a horseshoe shape down through the Atlantic, around the Cape of Good Hope and then northwards into the Indian Ocean, with what are now the sub-oceanic ridges then playing the part of a spinal mountain chain. But it also suggests that some at least of these lands may themselves have disappeared *after* the truly vast cataclysm of between 11,000 and 12,000 years ago which destroyed so much of the land masses in the Gulf of Mexico, the Caribbean and the northeastern Atlantic. That must be so, unless they accompanied it and the map itself had just not been up-dated. However, this southern part of the Atlantic is not our immediate concern. Nor is the Gulf of Mexico or the Caribbean, because neither of these comes anywhere close to fitting the locational description attributed by Plato to his Atlantean island. We shall therefore return in the next chapter to the subject of his island – immediately facing the Pillars of Herakles.

Chapter Fourteen

•

THE DESTRUCTION OF POSEIDONIS
AND THE PILLARS OF HERAKLES

'These histories tell of a mighty power which, unprovoked, made an expedition against the whole of Europe and Asia, and to which your city [Athens] put an end. This power came forth out of the Atlantic Ocean, for in those days, the Atlantic was navigable; and there was an island in front of the straits which are by you called the Pillars of Herakles; the island was larger than Libya and Asia put together ... Of the combatants on the one side, the city of Athens was reported to have been the leader and to have fought out the war; the combatants on the other side were commanded by the kings of Atlantis.'[1]

Thucydides, a contemporary of Plato, discussing cataclysms in *The Peloponnesian Wars*, wrote:

The sea at Orobiai in Euboia, retiring from what was then the line of the coast and rising in a great wave, covered a part of the city and then subsided in some places; but in other places the inundation was permanent and what was formerly land is now sea. The people who could not escape to high ground perished. A similar inundation occurred in the neighbourhood of Atalante, an island on the coast of the Opuntian Locri.[2]

From this it is at least quite clear that Plato was not the only one to know about the Atlantean disaster,[3] although Thucydides does not go into any greater detail.

From Thucydides' and Plato's descriptions, however, there is no doubt that the only really suitable candidates to fill the geographical post of his Atlantean island – 'Poseidonis' – are the island chains of the Canaries and Madeira, plus perhaps those of the Azores. The variously scattered 'skeletal' remains of these do indeed all face the 'Pillars of Herakles' at Gibraltar, quite close on the Atlantic side.[4] However, there is also little doubt that they were once part of one and the same great continental landmass. This would *originally* have included not only modern Portugal and Spain but from there would have extended across southern France, following the line of the Alps up into modern Switzerland and then down through the Italian Apennines, across to Malta and Tunisia, finally extending southwestwards across the southern perimeter of the Atlas Mountains back to the Canary Islands.

In other words, the circuitous mountain ranges of this great continent – still visible to us today in the shape of the North African Atlas, the Spanish Sierra Madre, the Pyrenees, the French Massif Centrale, the Swiss Alps and the Italian Apennines – were all once interconnected. Thus the whole of the western Mediterranean would once have been a great inland plain. It is therefore not surprising to find the Egyptian priest's description of this original island continent as being 'larger than Libya and Asia put together' – a statement which has caused much head-scratching amongst interested researchers and which has also caused modern geologists in the main to discount the whole story.

It has been assumed that in the Egyptian priest's story to Solon, as recounted by Plato, 'Poseidonis' was one and the same as this great island continent. However, it is clear from studying the text carefully that such could not have been the case, particularly when the story has it that all that remained after the cataclysm were the skeletal island 'fragments', bereft of most of their soil. So we can suggest with some reasonable degree of certainty that the island of Poseidonis was itself only a fragmentary part of the originally much greater continental landmass – that of ancient Atlantean Daitya.

In order to put this geographical conundrum in perspective, it needs to be remembered that at this distant time in prehistory, virtually the whole of northwestern Europe was still under oceanic water. In addition, the Atlantic Ocean covered the whole of the Sahara Desert, extending across most of modern Tunisia and Libya to incorporate the whole of the eastern Mediterranean. What we now see in the eastern Mediterranean is quite different to what it was then, for modern Greece not only extended far southwards to incorporate Crete, but was connected to Anatolia (modern western Turkey) as part of the continental landmass which incorporated the whole of the Middle and Far East, plus all of Russia to the east of the Ural Mountains.[5] How long ago was this? Well, seemingly, up to the time of the great and prolonged planetary cataclysms which shook the world to its very foundations between 700,000 and 850,000 years ago.

Prehistoric Geography and Geographers

As indicated in the last chapter, the portolan source maps which gave rise to the Piri Re'is map (*see* figure 19) and others showing the western Mediterranean and Atlantic Ocean areas as very different to today, seemingly did not show the Canaries, Madeira or the Azores as single island landmasses. At that time they were appreciably larger island chains and for the most part much more closely grouped. The same goes for the Cape Verde group, much further to the south. As we can see, the Piri Re'is map also shows the southern half of the South American continent extending eastwards, almost at right angles, from about the location of Rio de Janeiro, across the Rio Grande Rise to the Tristan da Cunha group of islands – which now lie in mid-ocean – across to a point about 300 miles (500 km) south of Cape Town.

The cartographer Charles Hapgood suggested that the southern part of the Piri Re'is map had been faultily put together from various original portolan sources.[6] He did not accept that the South Atlantic landmass (and many other island groups) as shown on it could actually have existed. However, it is this landmass to which the Egyptian priest seems to have been referring (at least in part) when he describes the opposite continent as *surrounding* 'the true ocean'. The North and South American continents, as they stand today, could hardly fit this description with any real degree of accuracy.

Hapgood's view possibly arose because he accepted the generally shared view of his scientific peers that the Mid-Atlantic Ridge was the point of separation of two tectonic plates and that, therefore, the idea of an ancient continental landmass laterally crossing it would be illogical. However, I have reasoned in this book that there are actually no such things as 'tectonic plates' *per se*, so we are not bound by such conceptual limitations. Indeed, the suggestion that a supposed error of such incredibly immense size could have been made by experienced cartographers – necessarily in consultation with experienced navigators – must itself be regarded as rather far-fetched.

For those who find it difficult to believe that ancient cartography was so advanced, Hapgood himself confirmed that the Piri Re'is map could only have been made using spherical trigonometry. However, this capability was not rediscovered by our modern savants until the early 18th century, once reliably accurate clocks had at last been produced, enabling geographical longitude to be confirmed. In addition, as Graham Hancock has described, the portolan maps of the Renaissance era show that the Ancients knew the detailed shape of the actual landmass under the ice pack of Antarctica.[7] Such a thing would have been impossible without the most modern aerial technology, unless the ice pack itself had unfrozen – which could not have been the case during the last 10,000 years at least.

Whichever way one looks at it therefore, there can be no doubt that the source of such ancient cartography extends back into a prehistoric civilization and culture of which modern scholarship and science currently have no knowledge. The fact that such a civilization has been termed 'Atlantean' when it relates to events having taken place in the Atlantic Ocean area is at least reasonably justified. But I shall nevertheless endeavour to justify it even further from a variety of other angles in this chapter and the next.

The Incredible Extent of the Cataclysm

Curiously, *if* Poseidonis finally went down in a gigantic cataclysm some 11,000–12,000 years ago, it would logically follow that the Piri Re'is map must itself be based upon source maps prepared somewhat *after* that period. That is, *unless* it was assumed by the ancient cartographers – who were unable to confirm matters at first hand because the Atlantic was unnavigable for centuries – that the original southern Atlantic continent (of which they were already by then aware) had been unaffected by the northern cataclysms. Whichever of these is true, the massive extent of South Atlantic landmass which has disappeared indicates that the vast cataclysms which destroyed Plato's northern island also (probably rather more progressively) destroyed the mid-southern Atlantic landmass very comprehensively too.

It is at first difficult to imagine that a volcanic eruption (or series of eruptions) could cause such vast damage. However, when considering the various islands within the two groups known to us today as the Azores and the Canaries-Madeira group, we begin to see the full extent of the cataclysm which appears to have blown out the whole of the originally central landmass. Whilst the Azores sit immediately adjacent to or even over the Mid-Atlantic Ridge, the Canaries are located some 120 miles (200 km) east of it, standing on the northwest African continental rise and slope.

The easternmost island of the Canaries (Lanzarote) is about 90 miles (150 km) from the African coastline, its visible landmass however consisting of only 5 per cent of its total bulk. It and Fuerteventura are non-volcanic and lie on a relatively shallow sub-oceanic platform. However the other five islands of the group – Gran Canaria, Tenerife, Gomera, Palma and Hierro – are all active volcanic peaks which rise sharply from the oceanic depths. Madeira, too, is still volcanic.

The Fact of Continuing Destruction

When we carefully compare the Piri Re'is map with a modern map, it quickly becomes obvious that the majority of the islands which formed part of the Azores, Madeira and Canaries chains no longer exist. It is consequently quite clear that the destruction of landmasses in this area is still continuing, the remnants of the original islands being now but sub-oceanic seabed mounts. Some of these are over half a mile (1 km) below the ocean surface and others so far destroyed that they are indistinguishable from the seabed itself. This destruction is immediately evident from Hapgood's comparison of the 'then and now' (*see again* figure 25 in the last chapter) involving the originally 17 islands in the Azores group, according to the Piri Re'is map, as against the much smaller 9 remaining islands which can be seen and visited today.

Around the Azores, the seabed is at a depth of about 3 miles (5 km), whereas around Madeira and the Canaries the depth is around 2 miles (3.2 km), rising on an abyssal slope to the coastline of northwest Africa. Those islands which have disappeared altogether from the Piri Re'is map appear on the Heezen-Tharp bathyspheric map (*see* figure 17 in Chapter 8) as either much smaller sea mounts or just amorphous parts of the ocean floor. This means that their original structures have collapsed by 2–3 miles, one imagines due primarily to earthquake activity, but finished off by huge sub-surface landslides which have destroyed all previous individuality of shape.

It is particularly noteworthy that the whole archipelago of the Canaries group forms a shallow, roughly semicircular arc which is open to the north, with Madeira slightly to the northwest of the central axis. From this it would appear that the whole middle area between the Canaries and Madeira – having a diameter of slightly over 200 miles (320 km) – may actually be a gigantic undersea volcanic caldera (now filled with debris and silt), the centre of which originally exploded mainly northwards – right in the direction of the modern straits of Gibraltar.

A Modern Parallel

There are those who might suggest that a caldera of such size is impossible. However, leaving aside the Gulf of Mexico, there is today another potential caldera lying under Yellowstone National Park, in the western US. This is already recognized as one of the largest active compound volcanic basins in the world, having an internal dimension of 28 by 47 miles (45 by 75 km).[8] Whilst the picturesque surface of this national park is treated currently as a popular tourist wonder, because of the hot springs and geysers and abundantly beautiful scenery, it causes geologists not inconsiderable anxiety because of the fact that it is ringed by a fundamentally volcanic mountain range. It is also subject to daily earthquakes, usually registering between 2 and 3 on the Richter Scale.

Now, were this all to explode in a chain reaction (as one day it almost certainly will), it is likely to produce an even bigger caldera, probably double the size – in other words, some 60 to 90 miles (100 to 150 km) in diameter – very akin to the Canaries-Madeira scenario.

However, Yellowstone National Park is well inland, while the Canaries-Madeira group is very different in one respect because it is located out in the open ocean. Whereas a land-based compound explosion will cause land- and air-based devastation, such an explosion at sea level is even more destructive. That is because the volcanic explosion – as happened with the Indonesian island of Krakatoa in 1883 – allows cold sea waters to pour into the volcanic crater(s). This results in their coming from above into direct confrontational contact with the superheated magma gases still being liberated from below. The consequent cataclysm thus involves an explosion from below sea level which, through producing a far shallower blast zone, effectively rips the top off virtually all landmasses at the same horizontal level. Thus an island could literally disappear from view in a matter of minutes.

Once this gigantic explosion has taken place, the ocean water rushes back into the caldera thus formed, thereby resulting in a false 'ebb tide' on any relatively nearby coastal landmasses. However, that is then followed by the ocean waters resettling themselves, thus producing a series of huge outflowing tsunamis. The ones caused by the destruction of Krakatoa are believed to have been about 200 ft (61 m) in height. The Poseidonian ones would probably have been at least double that size. It is consequently believed, by this author at least, that it may well have been these northward-travelling tsunamis which comprehensively destroyed the original Pillars of Herakles and left the modern and much wider Strait of Gibraltar in their place.

The most recent research concerning the giant tsunamis of Krakatoa indicates that they were in fact initiated by giant pyroclastic flows (that is, made up of volcanic ash and fragments of volcanic rock), which left a sediment on the local ocean floor up to 262 ft (80 m) in depth. However, these same pyroclastic flows, travelling at speeds of up to 200 mph (320 km/h) and initially possessing temperatures up to 500°C, are also known to have travelled right across the adjacent Sunda Strait, a distance of some 50 miles (80 km), and then still caused immense destruction, involving the loss of over 2,000 lives. The Poseidonian cataclysm would have been immeasurably more powerful and destructive.

Modern Vulcanism in the Area

Many of the Canaries islands are still volcanically very active. For example, on the Atlantic side of the island of La Palma stands the huge volcano Cumbre Vieja immediately overlooking the Atlantic Ocean and facing westwards. It is well known by scientists that it is only a matter of time before either severe volcanic or earthquake activity in this immediate area, or both, will see the whole seaward side of the volcano slipping into the ocean. This will create a gigantic tsunami which, gathering speed and height as it crosses the ocean, is likely to devastate several of the main cities on the east coast of the US.

On Tenerife, the gigantic (and also still active) Mt Teide stands at the northern end of the island whilst immediately overlooking a truly vast but now extinct caldera at the very centre of the island. This caldera (Las Canadas) which supposedly collapsed around 170,000 years ago, (but which actually looks much younger) is so big that one can literally drive around inside it for over half an hour looking at smaller volcanic craters to either side. However, the somewhat older and much larger N'goro n'goro crater in Tanzania, has been extensively filled in and has thus become a savannah-based plain, almost unrecognizable for what it originally was.

The magma rivers that flowed out of the vast Las Canadas crater on Tenerife are to be found all over the east, south and west sides of the island. On the west side, the phenomenal effect is most marked of all in the craggy coastal area named Los Gigantes, 'The Giants', because of the huge, towering cliffs, well over 500 ft (152 m) in height, of solidified volcanic lava which rise in sheer formation straight out of the sea. The lava can clearly be seen to have formed in multiple layers, stacked one upon the other – something over 30 of them – many with sandy layers in between.

What has happened is that the island – or at least this part of it – has been subject to a relatively rapid cycle of repeated total submersion and re-elevation over a comparitively short space of time. Quite apart from having wiped out any original flora, fauna and human population in the area, it must have been a shatteringly terrifying experience for those who survived on the other sides of the island. It is hardly surprising that the indigenous Guanche told the first Spaniards that their ancestors believed the whole world to have come to an end when the last cataclysm(s) took place.

But this is merely the description applied to one of the many islands of these two chains and it fails to take into consideration the complete collapse of the original intervening landmass which seemingly once (up to some 12,000 years ago) interconnected them all over a north-to-south distance of some 500 miles (800 km). The collapsed landmasses at the centre of the group of course now form the muddy bed of the ocean surrounding the remaining islands and it is thus impossible to discern any possible man-made structures, even by deep-diving in the area. The ocean bed around here drops to between 12,000 and 15,000 ft (2–3 miles) below sea level; so nothing is going to become apparent until serious seismic activity pushes the ocean floor back up to a level within easy reach of the surface.

The Original Continental Geography

In very ancient times, many tens (if not hundreds) of thousands of years ago, the whole of southwestern and central France (north of the Massif Central) would have been fully submerged under the waters of the northern Atlantic

Ocean. Similarly, the Atlantic would have covered the whole of what we call the Sahara Desert, south of the Maghreb and eastwards as far as the borders of Libya, leaving Egypt, the Sudan and the countries of the Horn of Africa as yet another, quite separate island continent. Thus the *original* northern Atlantean continental island of Daitya, extending all the way from the Pyrenees and Alps in the north to the foot of the Atlas Mountains (in southwestern Morocco) in the south and then westwards out into the Atlantic, would indeed have been seen by its contemporaries as a continent in its own right.

However, by the time of which the Egyptian priest was speaking to Solon, this great continental mass had fragmented very seriously indeed through constant volcanic and earthquake activity. The ensuing result would have involved the separation of the Azores (one larger island of which was later called Antillia) from the island of Poseidonis (originally comprising probably the Canaries and Madeira as one mass). Both these then became detached from the more eastern landmass comprising the Maghreb and also what became the Iberian Peninsula.

This thereby allowed the Atlantic to penetrate through what subsequently became known as the Pillars of Herakles, to flood the whole of the Tyrrhenian Plain. In the process, so it would appear, a small sea or lagoon was formed immediately to the east of Gibraltar, that small local sea being quite clearly still apparent in the northeastern corner of Hapgood's reconstruction of the Piri Re'is map (*see again* figure 19). It is this which was referred to by the Egyptian priest to Solon as merely 'a harbour, having a narrow entrance'.

Some have suggested that the Iberian Peninsula was originally thought by the Ancients to be an island unto itself. However, given the self-evident excellence of their cartography, that seems highly unlikely. Similarly, however, modern geographers and other commentators have assumed that the original continent of which the Egyptian priest spoke must have been based upon the general configuration of the western European and north African landmasses today.

Both these derive from the further assumption that the Ancients were actually not that intellectually or technologically sophisticated and that their history did not go back as far as they believed; hence their ideas must have been generally based upon a mixture of confused folk traditions, superstition and wishful thinking. Well, as we have already shown in previous chapters, the only complete misapprehensions and misinterpretations appear to be the modern ones. Starting from a series of false assumptions and prejudiced preconceptions, it is hardly surprising that many such clues worth following up have, in fact, been completely overlooked.

The Creation of Poseidonis

As I have just endeavoured to describe, the original northern continent of Atlantis contained within its bounds the whole of what we now call the western Mediterranean, but which was then called 'Tyrhennia'. It was only when the outlying mountain chains became fragmented by earthquake activity – at Gibraltar and in the area of Malta – that the ocean poured into the great central Tyrrhenian plain and flooded it. It seems to have been this that (quite naturally) caused the great dispersal of Atlantean Cro-Magnon man northwards into what was to become southern Europe, and also eastwards into what was later to become the land of Egypt.

The geological and geographical separation of the northern and southern parts of this once great Atlantean island continent necessarily resulted in northwest Africa (including the Canaries and Madeira as part of it) becoming an island landmass in its own right. Only later, as the great landmass of what is now the Sahara Desert rose above sea level, did this become geographically connected to the remainder of what are now central and southern Africa. However, further and later earthquake activity in the far northwest eventually seems to have resulted in this southern section of the original Atlantean landmass again fragmenting, with the result that a smaller section – possibly about the size of the British Isles – became an offshore island. It appears to be this island to which Plato's story refers in the strictly geographical sense and it is because of its independence (as well as its association with the god Poseidon in Plato's story) that we have referred to it as 'Poseidonis'.

The idea of the Canary and Madeira island chains comprising the remains of Poseidonis is not a new one. In the 19th century, in the wake of the naval research ship *Challenger*'s discovery of the Mid-Atlantic Ridge and Ignatius Donnelly's book *Atlantis, the Antediluvian Land*, there was general public agreement that it had to be so; and when one actually visits the islands and sees at first hand the full extent of the volcanic activity, it becomes even more obvious why everyone felt the same way. But more of that in a moment. Let us first of all take a look at the known geological history of these various areas and island groups.

The Destruction of the Pillars of Herakles

First of all, the modern Strait of Gibraltar is nearly 20 miles in width. However, the idea that it has always been this wide just does not hold up to scrutiny. Quite apart from the Egyptian priest having been clear that the original area within the Pillars of Herakles was 'only a small harbour with a narrow entrance', it does not take a genius to see that the distance between the Iberian

Peninsula and the North African mainland in those days must have been sufficiently narrow for someone to have called the cliffs on either side by the name
'*Pillars* of Herakles'. Nobody would have done so for landmasses even 5 miles
(8 km) apart. In any case, when we look at the two closest promontories today,
we see that they both involve quite low-lying coastal land. The Rock of Gibraltar on the north side is quite separate and distinct; but it might well originally
have fitted the description of a 'pillar', or at least part of one.

One might add that in the original Greek text, the inner sea within the strait
was called a *pelagos*, which means a small body of sea, whereas a large body of
sea was referred to as a *pontos*.[9] Scholars have assumed that the *pelagos* within
the strait referred to the Mediterranean. However, the sheer size of the
Mediterranean clearly makes that impossible, particularly when we note that
the smaller Black Sea was known in Greek as the *Pontos Euxinos*.

So what is being referred to here is clearly nothing but a medium sized,
inter-oceanic lagoon – which exactly corresponds with what Plato described.
Furthermore, his Egyptian priest's description of the lagoon in the strait
exactly matches that shown on the Piri Re'is map. So it is quite clear that in this
immediate area there has been sufficiently gigantic earthquake activity to
cause the destruction of at least 20 miles (32 km) of landmass between North
Africa and the Iberian Peninsula at some time between the time of Solon
(c600BC) and the Roman era. It is of course known from eyewitness reports
that a major part of Egyptian Alexandria disappeared into the ocean in AD365
as the result of a gigantic earthquake. So the inference is that the original
Pillars of Herakles disappeared several centuries or millennia earlier.

The Resultant Tsunami

Now, if Plato's island (comprising a landmass between the Canary Islands and
the Azores) was destroyed by implosion following intense volcanic activity and
earthquakes c9500BC, we can say with reasonable accuracy that it must have
resulted in a gigantic and hugely powerful tsunami which would have been
remembered by those who survived. The tsunami would have raced northwards towards the gap between the Iberian Peninsula and the Maghreb,
gathering speed and force through tremendous compression between the
narrowing landmasses on either side.

As the hugely compressed force hit the geologically more vulnerable outer
cliffs at the western end of the straits, it would have released itself with
immense destructive power. This would not only have smashed the cliff
promontories to pieces and levelled them on a grand scale, but also – through
natural rotational motion – would have scooped out a great cavity in the ocean
bed immediately on the other side, within the lagoon. The withdrawing waters

would then have generated a seabed landslide to the west, all as shown below (figure 28).

The overall cataclysm, however, would have changed the local geography completely, as suggested here (figure 29).

In the first paragraph of this chapter, I cited Thucydides' confirmation that tsunamis and their deadly effects were well known and that the 'neighbourhood' of the island of 'Atalante' had been hit by one or more. But, by way of further verification, right at the western end of the Mediterranean, there is a huge ocean trench scooped out of the seabed, which comes to a sudden stop just short of the Strait of Gibraltar. This seabed anomaly is quite possibly indicative of tsunami activity.

The seabed between Gibraltar and Algeciras, on the other hand, is very shallow and keeps rising and falling; whilst the seabed on the Atlantic side of the strait merely slopes down to the ocean plain, from which project the surrounding Madeira and Canary island chains. However, it is quite clear from figure 28 that the slope on the Atlantic side is actually the result of major submarine landslides which extend for about 50 miles (80 km) in a westerly and southwesterly direction – again, towards Madeira and the Canaries.

The western Mediterranean ocean floor cavity is still evident (*see again* the bathyspheric map, figure 17 in Chapter 8). So, it is quite clearly the mass

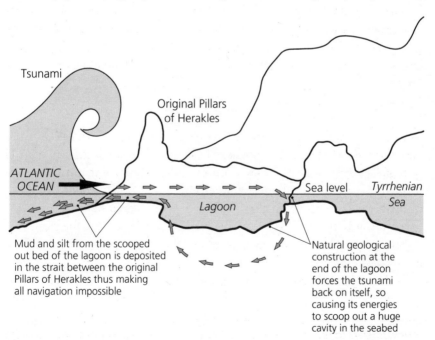

Figure 28. The effects of the tsunami in the region of present-day Gibraltar, the original Pillars of Herakles. The seabed and background landscape are shown in cross-section.

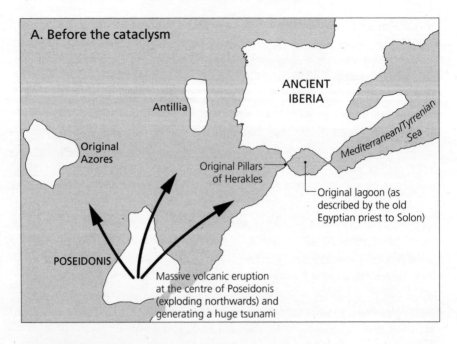

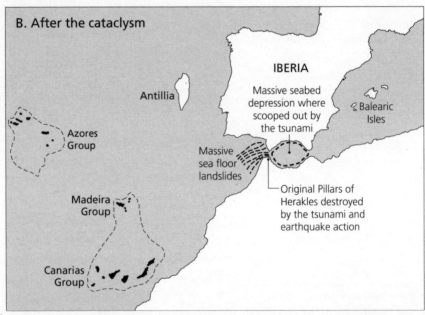

Figure 29. The effects of the ancient cataclysm on the coastlines of the Iberian Peninsula, northwest Africa, and nearby Atlantic islands: (a) shows coastlines before the cataclysm and (b) after

destruction of the original cliffs and immediately adjacent landmasses which would have resulted in the whole of the strait becoming filled up with geological debris. This then made the passage through the strait (and beyond the Canaries) unnavigable for years afterwards, just as the Egyptian priest confirmed to Solon, until oceanic currents from the Atlantic had a chance progressively to wash the debris away. So the scientific logic is clearly able to support Plato's idea after all, notwithstanding previous prejudice to the contrary.

The Destruction of the Greek Fleet

When we remember that in Plato's story the whole of the Greek military force is swallowed up and destroyed in the cataclysm, along with the mass of Poseidonis, it becomes even more evident that a tsunami had to be involved. There is no indication in the story as to where the Greek navy was actually located at the time of the cataclysm, but it seems quite clearly to have been in fairly close formation. It also seems not unlikely that, for tactical reasons, it would probably have been immediately to the east of the lagoon, providing a blockade against any eastward naval insurgency by the Atlanteans.

However, it is quite clear that when the tsunami struck the lagoon, there would have been a follow-on effect on the other side of it, where the Greek navy was probably positioned. That would necessarily have involved a secondary tsunami, with unavoidably disastrous results for the Greek ships lying to the east of the lagoon. It seems highly unlikely that anyone could have survived, although some must have done so in order to have recounted the story for future generations.

When Did the Cataclysm Take Place?

Having dealt with the aftermath of the cataclysm, let us now have a look at what happened to the Atlantic island groups, starting with the Canaries and Madeira. The geological library at the Natural History Museum in London confirms that the last great cataclysm affecting these islands took place approximately 11,000–12,000 years ago; so it seems that Plato's chronology was pretty exact.

As I suggested at the outset, one of the curious things about modern scholarship's technique of avoiding the obvious and/or the unpalatable is its habit of assuming that the Ancients were intellectually sloppy or lacking in literary or mental proficiency. Hence we constantly find them suggesting that whilst the idea of a gigantic cataclysm in the Mediterranean is quite feasible, Plato and others must have got their dating wrong by either unconsciously adding a nought or two on to the number of years stated in the tradition, or by having meant lunar rather than solar cycles.

This attempt to discredit the knowledge of people who were held in the highest regard for their integrity, plus their scrupulous attention to truth and detail, is really rather pathetic. To suggest it of an age when oral tradition necessitated an absolute rigid adherence to retelling each story in the same way, is itself intellectually absurd. But let us see what others of our contemporaries have to say on the subject of prehistoric cataclysms affecting the Canaries group.

> More striking are the very late Pleistocene [volcanic] outbursts, the last. Geolog-
> ically, these were not at all long ago, say contemporary with the last Glaciation in
> the north and they may have continued into the Recent period, which began some
> ten thousand years ago.[10]

Thus comments a geologist writing about the island of Fuerteventura in the Canaries. But that comment is generally applicable to the whole island group and it confirms, yet again, the general acceptance that the volcanic cataclysms which shook the whole area literally to pieces took place around 11,500–12,000 years ago – again, precisely when Plato himself confirmed. But there are other pointers to something very widespread having taken place at the same time.

Zep Tepi and the Celestial Solstice

As mentioned in a previous chapter, modern geological orthodoxy confirms that the last ice age came to a sudden end some 11,000–12,000 years ago – but why? Archaeologists are convinced that at this same time the first move towards building and living in urban environments began – again, why? However, it was also some 10,000–12,000 years ago that the last major crustal displacement took place in the Atlantic and Pacific Oceans, as a result of the roughly 41,000-year cycle noted by modern marine geologists. It was again around the same time that the Earth's polar tilt reached its maximum of 24.4°. In relation to this, an article published in 1976 in the journal *Science* showed that geological and climatic patterns coincide with the periods when the Earth's polar tilt reached its maximum of 24.4°, the last time that this occurred having been, so they confirmed, *c*9600BC.[11]

Rather interestingly, this same period follows on quickly from the primordial Egyptian festival of Zep Tepi, which appears to celebrate the *celestial* winter solstice. This is the period (*c*10,500BC according to Robert Bauval and Graham Hancock[12]) at the end of the 25,920-year cycle of the precession of the equinoxes when the Sun and solar system were at their closest point to the greater star around which our system orbits (*see again* figure 12).

In the face of all this can we really avoid the self-evident implication that this same celestial conjunction possibly had a hand in the phenomenal changes which took place upon the surface of our planet?

Comparable Cataclysmic Effects Elsewhere

It is interesting to note that Tihuanaco, the ancient 'City of the Sun' on the shores of Lake Titicaca in modern Bolivia, appears to have been constructed (or perhaps re-constructed) about 12,000 years ago – which again coincides with the timing of Plato's great Poseidonian cataclysm.[13] Originally at sea level and supposedly (according to the Inca) built by prehistoric giants, Tihuanaco is now some 2 miles (3 km) above it. Similarly, the great animal and bird 'drawings' on the plains of Nazca, about 150 miles (240 km) south of the Peruvian capital, Lima, may have been deserted by the same civilization at around the same time.

It is otherwise interesting to note that the central 'Street of the Dead' in the great pyramid complex at Teotihuacan in modern Mexico points to within one degree of the Pleiades. As 'the dead' is a metaphorical reference to the 'fallen' kosmic spirits which the Egyptians called 'Akhu', and as the 'Akhu' themselves are apparently the progeny of the 'Watchers of Pe' who have their home in the Pleiades (as described in Chapter 5), one can see the obvious correlations between ancient Mayan sacred cosmology and virtually all others in antiquity. Given that there are 49 (7 x 7) other sacred sites in the general area around Tihuanaco, the correspondence with all other septenary systems becomes pretty well irrefutable.

The huge number of mammoths, other wild beasts, sheep and cattle found suddenly frozen in Siberia have been dated to c12,000 years ago. A huge number of mastodon bones were found together by an archaeologist called Braghine near Bogota in Colombia – again dated to c12,000 years ago. As these are lowland animals, it would appear that their death was caused by sudden elevation of the Colombian, Peruvian and Bolivian landmass.

The fact that all these 'coincidences' (affecting both humans and animals quite independently) combine in conjunction with an astronomical event, needs to be examined much more closely by scientists than it has hitherto. Furthermore, it has to be approached on a properly interdisciplinary basis so that the whole scenario and its outcome can be properly gauged and put in context for the sake of future generations.

The most immediately important issue concerns the effects of the two celestial solstices (some 13,000 years apart) within the overall cycle of precession. These appear to involve our planet coming under huge electro-magnetic pressure as our solar system first decelerates when approaching each solstitial turning point and then accelerates away from it, after 'turning the bend'. As described in previous chapters, this must have had a dramatic torsion effect upon the Earth's crust, with consequently devastating results in terms of dramatically increased volcanic and earthquake activity.

In Plato's narrative, the Egyptian priest says to Solon that the cause of cataclysmic floods and volcanic activity 'is a deviation of the bodies that revolve in heaven around the Earth.' However, bearing in mind that this is merely how longer term astronomical movements are noted from Earth, it can only logically be the cycle of precession which appears to cause or result in such clearly noticeable 'deviation'.

It is interesting to note that we are currently approaching the solstice at the other end of the precessionary cycle. Quite logically, therefore, we should anticipate another formidably great change within the next few centuries. Who can say whether it will be of similar magnitude? However, global warming and the slowing down of the planet's axial motion may perhaps be early warning signs.

Chapter Fifteen

THE MEDITERRANEAN COLONIES OF POSEIDONIS

'Solon, the first of the great Athenian law givers and one of the noblest thinkers of the Greeks, studied philosophy in Egypt with Psenophis of Heliopolis and Sonches of Sais, these being the most learned of the priests. By them, Plato affirms, Solon was taught the Atlantean language which he afterwards began to explain in verse.'[1]

Purely historical mention of the Atlantic islands first appears in Roman writings, where they are referred to as 'the Fortunate Islands' or 'the Isles of the Blessed'. However, there appear to be no specific records of their actually having been visited by the Romans, or even by the Phoenicians, those great sailors of antiquity. The latter were rumoured to have circumnavigated Africa well over 2,000 years ago, long before any of the great European sailor-explorers. Nonetheless, for such names to have been attributed to the Canaries, the Romans must certainly have heard about them from other sources. For example, the Roman historian Pliny reports[2] that Juba, the king of Mauretania in northwest Africa (then a vassal state of Rome), sent an expedition to explore the islands, in one of which they found a fierce breed of dogs – hence, Pliny claims, the name 'Canaria' given to the isles by the Romans (from Latin *canis*, 'dog'). However, the native Guanche people seem to have called themselves '*canarii*' – which suggests some prehistoric linguistic connection between the two cultures, since the Guanche worshipped Sirius, the Dog Star.

Irrespective of that, the Canaries today comprise a group of seven islands, which rather interestingly corresponds with the statement in the Sanskrit *Puranas* that the Atlanteans were living on seven islands. As the *Puranas* and *Mahabharata* also refer to the great war between the Atlanteans and the ancient Indo-European ancestors of both the Greeks and the 'eastern Ethiopian' Egyptians, it is quite clear that their associated cultures have to be at the very least 11,500 years old. This is rather more than the mere 4,500–5,000 years suggested by modern scholarship. As H.P. Blavatsky tells us:

Since, in the Puranic accounts, the island is still existing, then those accounts must be older than the 11,000 years elapsed since Sancha Dwipa, or the Poseidonis of Atlantis, disappeared. Is it not barely possible then that the Hindus should have known the island still earlier?[3]

Blavatsky here makes the logical point that, since the Vedic *Puranas* actually describe Plato's Atlantis (as Sancha Dwipa), Vedic civilization and culture must themselves be far older than 11,000 years, whereas modern scholars arbitrarily date them merely to within the last 3,000 years or so. However, notwithstanding the apparent mention of these islands in the *Puranas* and the *Mahabharata*, the first really detailed modern reports and commentaries appear in the wake of the Spanish invasion of the Canary islands during the late 14th century, the Spaniards' sudden appearance having thoroughly astonished the native Guanche people. No indigenous inhabitants of either Madeira or the Azores were ever found by the invading Spaniards or Portuguese.

The Peoples of the Atlantean Continent

It follows quite logically that, if our premise as described is correct, then different social and cultural groups of Atlanteans would have been found on all the islands and other landmasses into which the original island continent fragmented. Therefore – following general anthropological lines – one might reasonably expect those different groups to have produced their own cultural (and linguistic) sub-types.

It also follows that these sub-types could have differed quite markedly due to environmental circumstances and other local cultural factors; and that any truly massive geological catastrophe would have torn the heart out of their civilization. That in turn would have resulted in all the various outlying social groups or colonies necessarily going their own way culturally, albeit probably maintaining some or many of the original traditions.

The Guanche people of the Canaries were found to have traditions which closely matched certain of the descriptions in Plato's story. Probably the most obvious of these was their tribal system of rulership by ten kings (each ruling over different areas of the largest island, Tenerife), one of whom was ruler over all the rest. The Guanche also confirmed to the Spanish that a gigantic cataclysm had taken place thousands of years beforehand. This had totally destroyed their civilization and until the arrival of the Spanish they believed that the rest of humanity must also have been destroyed in the general conflagration and submersion. They had believed themselves to be the only people left alive in the world – which perhaps gives a flavour of just how powerful and far-reaching the cataclysm must have been.

The Guanche Language

In addition to all this, the Guanche were found by the Spaniards to speak a language probably of the Hamitic family[4] which was almost identical to that of the Berber peoples (referred to by the Greeks as the 'barbaroï', or barbarians) of northwest Africa. As Spain itself had been occupied for several hundred years by Islamic invaders from that same area (modern Morocco and Tunisia) it is not surprising that the invaders quickly became familiar with the tongue. In addition, the Guanche were physiologically very different to the Spaniards and the Moroccan Arabs (who were dark and not so tall) but very similar in appearance to the Berbers. The latter were apparently of very tall stature (generally well over 6 ft (1.8 m) in height), light complexion and fair hair with blue eyes – as is the purer Berber stock even today.

The Berber culture today extends throughout the area of the Atlas mountain range, which runs all the way from southern Western Sahara (just opposite the Canaries group in the south) to the tip of Tunisia in the far north – where we find the ancient city of Carthage. So it is a reasonable and logical assumption that they were known to the Romans as living in these same areas over 2,000 years ago.

The Berbers were certainly also known to the Egyptians long before that because of their having extended their presence even as far as the Delta (where they were known as 'Libyans'); but we can say with some certainty that they had been resident over the whole of northwest Africa for several thousand years before that too. For example, the earliest dynastic records refer to a tall, blonde and blue-eyed Libyan tribe called the Temehu, living in the region of Cyrenaica (modern Libya).[5]

It has been assumed by modern scholars that the people of Carthage (in modern Tunisia) were all Semitic-speaking Phoenicians – who were fundamentally merchant traders, mostly by sea. However, it is quite clear that, prior to the Roman and much later Islamic invasions, the *whole* of the Maghreb was already colonized by widespread groups of Berber people. The latter (at least outside the towns) practised a hierarchical tribal system (somewhat out of character with more historically modern seafaring traders) with sophisticated forms of farming, as well as having a quite distinct religious culture.

The Berber Peoples

Ten-thousand-year old cave paintings in the now barren Tassili mountains of Algeria and the Accasus mountains of adjacent Libya show the land of the time as immensely fertile, and populated by all sorts of wild animals. This is confirmed by the Piri Re'is map (*see again* figure 19) which shows the whole of northwest Africa as covered with rivers and lakes that no longer exist. It is also known to modern science that the whole of the area of the Sahara was a luxuriant savannah, roamed by extensive herds of wild animals, until about 4,000 years ago, when a prolonged wet period (lasting several thousand years) suddenly came to an end. This caused terrible drought which, the records show, even affected Egyptian civilization. Before this happened, the currently barren and inhospitable interior of Libya, Tunisia and Morocco was quite different and able to support a much wider civilization and culture.

Although now frequently mixed through intermarriage with Arabs, the Berber peoples still remain naturally tall, often very light-skinned, even blue-eyed. Their social organization consists of tribes – like the Kabyle – and their residential architecture looks very similar to that of the Etruscans. Although their society is male-dominated, Berber women do not as a rule wear the veil and are quite emancipated. They are still able to own property and can divorce their husbands.

It is interesting to note that P. Borchardt, a German explorer, found in 1926 that the Berber tribes of the Shatt el-Hameina in Tunisia were called 'Sons of Attala'. In addition, they have an old tradition that some of their ancestors were refugees from a country to the west which had been destroyed by the sea. As 'Atala' was the name used in the Hindu *Puranas* to describe the Atlantean continent, we have here yet another probable verification that the Berbers are, in fact, the latter-day Atlanteans of Poseidonis.

The 'Sea Peoples'

There can be little doubt in retrospect that the Berber peoples are otherwise one and the same as the ancient Labu' or 'Libyans' known to Egyptologists, Libya being immediately to the west of Egypt. These 'Libyans' began to move into the Nile Delta area during the Middle Kingdom dynasties. This creeping colonization reached its height during the New Kingdom period when the Libyans appear to have taken over politically and ruled as the 22nd and 23rd dynasties from Tanis and Bubastis. However, they were subsequently overcome by the Kushites from the south, who then themselves reigned as the 25th and 26th dynasties.[6]

In the first court of the temple of Medinet Habu, on the west bank at Thebes in southern Egypt, wall reliefs depict scenes of naval battles between the Egyptians and the Libyans and their allies, the 'Sea Peoples' (*see* figure 30) who attempted to invade not only Egypt but also Syria during the 13th century BC. Further wall reliefs are to be found in the temple of Karnak, on the east bank. Archaeologists have never been able to identify who these 'Sea Peoples' really were, assuming them merely to be 'a loose confederation' of relatively minor

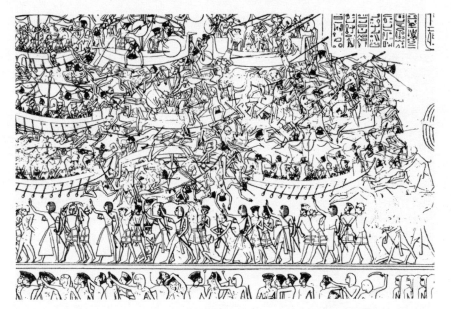

Figure 30. A drawing taken from a relief at the temple of Ramesses III at Medinet Habu, showing a naval battle between Egyptians and the Libyans and their allies, the 'Sea Peoples'

Mediterranean island states. However, no such 'loose confederation' would seriously be able to contemplate overcoming the Egyptian empire or the Syrians either. One is thus forced to the conclusion that they were most likely trained Carthaginian naval forces of Berber origin, acting as mercenaries.

As we saw in the quotation at the very beginning of this chapter, Plato's ancestor Solon, when he stayed with the Egyptians at the temple of Sais in the Delta, was supposedly not only shown details of the wars against the 'Atlanteans', he was also taught the Atlantean language. However, no evidence of any such battles or language have been found in the area – other than those attributed to the 'Libyans' and the 'Sea Peoples', many of whom were taken captive and forcibly made to serve the Egyptians, some as slaves and others as mercenaries. Is it not therefore probable that the language of the Berber-Libyans and that of the Atlanteans were actually one and the same? Bearing in mind that the Libyans were immediate neighbours of the Egyptians, it is entirely logical that the latter would have known their language.

Later in this chapter I will highlight the close historical connections between the Carthaginians and the Etruscans. As I have already shown that the Berbers and Carthaginians are very probably to be identified with the Libyans and Sea Peoples, it would appear that the Etruscans too may have to be brought into the equation *at least* a thousand years (and almost certainly far more) before scholars regard their civilization and culture as having been founded. Such associations have already been suggested. (*See also* Appendix B.)

The Berbers, Carthaginians and Phoenicians

Lewis Spence, a Scottish student of mythology, wrote several books on the subject of Atlantis between 1924 and 1942. He quotes a Dr Badichon, long resident in Algeria and familiar with local ancient traditions, as saying: 'These Atlanteans among the Ancients passed for the favourite children of Neptune ... the Atlanteans were the first known navigators.'[7] If true, this then surely and effectively disputes the modern orthodoxy which holds that the first oceanic merchant mariners in the Mediterranean region were in fact the Phoenicians. But long before even the Romans, the Greeks referred to the 'Tyrrhenoi', the peoples of the western Mediterranean, as the greatest sailors and sea traders, whose naval professionalism and military savagery (hence perhaps the word 'tyrant') made them a force to be feared by everybody else. However, archaeologists have themselves rather interestingly determined that the 'Tyrrhenians' were in fact Etruscans.

Although modern orthodoxy has Carthage being founded by the Phoenicians c800BC (around the time of Homer), it seems extremely illogical that the already sophisticated Berber people would allow a completely (ethnically) different people from the other end of the Mediterranean suddenly to occupy a strategically important part of their land for their own benefit and commercial profit. Particularly as they themselves already had trans-Mediterranean cultural and trading connections. It is rather curious that this simple fact of human nature does not seem to have occurred to some modern researchers, but it is certainly something that we need to take into account here.

It is known that the mother trading city of the Phoenicians was Tyre (in modern Lebanon), and that Carthage was only a staging post for trading in the western Mediterranean – until Tyre was taken by the Assyrians in the late 6th century BC). It thus seems rather more likely that the wealthy Phoenicians (with Carthaginian naval backup) merely resurrected many of the old sea-trading routes which had been abandoned by the Carthaginians for probably centuries, or even several thousand years, as a result of the cataclysm which had blocked the sea passage through the western Mediterranean.[8]

As a consequence of this, I would logically suggest that the Phoenicians' so-called 'founding' of Carthage would only (originally at least) have been a licensed trading operation which revitalized commerce, as was also the case in the Egyptian Delta, by permission of the Egyptians. That the wealthy and influential Phoenicians later became fully integrated into Carthaginian society, thereby appearing to invest it with their own cultural identity, is not altogether surprising bearing in mind the wholesale destruction of their own home bases in Tyre and Sidon by the Assyrians, as just described.

The fact that the Carthaginians were very suddenly able to cement their natural alliance with the Etruscans of the northern Mediterranean coasts *c*530BC, in order to blockade all attempted Greek (and other foreign) trade in the western Mediterranean, also otherwise tends to show just how closely the ancient family contacts between the two must have remained. This blockade proved absolute over the course of the next two hundred years or so, thereby giving Carthage a complete monopoly of trade with its Mediterranean neighbours, in tin and silver in particular. It is recognized by historians that even Alexander the Great was unable to make the slightest dent in this sea-borne commercial barrier.

However, those Etruscans in southern and central Italy seem in the interim to have developed closer and more amicable relations with their Greek neighbours in Magna Graecia (the Greek colonies in southern Italy) and on the Greek mainland – so much so that they eventually decided to go their own independent way and thus evolve into the early Roman nation. This in turn seems to have been what sparked off the family fight with both other Etruscans and also the Carthaginians – the latter turning into what historians call 'the Punic Wars', which commenced in or around 264BC. The whole scenario is paralleled in more recent times by the declaration of independence by the American colonists of both British and French origin.

Scholars know for a fact that Rome was actually founded by the Etruscans and that the earliest kings of Rome were also Etruscans. But why would this have happened unless there was already some political momentum in Italy towards self-government, allied to a completely new social identity with a decidedly Greek cultural orientation?

The Origins of the Phoenicians

As I have suggested elsewhere, it would appear that the Phoenicians or Puni (Puni-cians) were originally seafaring traders from the Punjab in northwestern India.[9] This is an area of ancient Indo-Persia widely known, since time immemorial, for the richness of its agriculture and the herbs and spices grown there. These were exported by merchant traders via land caravans as well as by ship via the immediately adjacent River Indus. Hence the fact that during the second and third millennium BC the Egyptians used to send trading missions by sea to the land of Pun(t) specifically for the purpose of buying spices.[10]

It therefore seems more likely that the Puni-cians actually set up a combined land and sea trading mission in Tyre, itself named by the original founders – Tyrrhenians. Their motive clearly lay with capitalizing on existing land-based trade with Egypt, thereafter to extend trade with the remainder of the Mediterranean. In other words, the Puni (sometimes also known as the Pani or Poeni) were merely expatriate merchants who had their own quarter in Carthage, just as they did in Tyre. They were not natives of the Maghreb at all and nor did they actually found Carthage (or Tyre), despite modern assumptions to the contrary.

It is otherwise worthwhile remembering at this point that the part of the Levant now known as 'Palestine' derives its name from 'Pali-stan', the 'Pali' being an Indo-Ceylonese (Indo-Dravidian) people who spoke a language (of the same name) partly derived from the Sanskrit. Consequently, as the Indo-Persian civilization and culture extended all the way to the shores of the western Mediterranean from western India – and as the peoples of this area have historically been known as perhaps the world's greatest merchants – it is not surprising that they had such strong trading connections all over the Middle East.[11] One should take into further consideration the fact that the Phoenicians are supposed to have been connected ethnically to the Hebrews of Judaea. This latter name, however, itself appears to be derived phonetically from that of the ancient province of Iaothea, immediately to the east of the River Indus and directly to the south of the Punjab. So it is not difficult to see the cultural connections which have caused such perplexity to historians.[12]

That they indeed came from lands to the east, far beyond the Levant, is otherwise confirmed by Herodotus, who tells us:

> The Phoenicians who had formerly dwelt [that is, had a trading post] on the shores of the Erythraean Sea [meaning the northern Indian Ocean, incorporating the Arabian and Persian Gulfs plus the Red Sea], having migrated to the Mediterranean and settled in the parts which they now inhabit, began at once ... to adventure on long voyages, freighting their vessels with the wares of Egypt and Assyria.[13]

Herodotus also has the Phoenicians moving to Tyre only 2,300 years before his own century.[14]

Trading Connections Between the Atlantic Islands, Spain and the Maghreb

It is well known to scholars that, as they earlier did with the Greeks, the Carthaginians made every endeavour to keep the Romans away from their trading routes in the western Mediterranean and out into the Atlantic. They of course knew of the various island groups there (including Britain) and seemed to have paid particular attention to a large one known as Antillia. This lay due west of Portugal and seems to have been a centre of great agricultural fertility, as well as probably having great mineral wealth. However, although that island is shown on the Piri Re'is map (figure 19), it no longer survives, having clearly met a watery end at some time, perhaps during the last 2,000 years. In fact, it seems very likely to have been part of the Azores – before their fragmentation into a small island group.

Now, as I mentioned earlier, the Canaries and Madeira were originally (tens of thousands of years ago) connected by a land bridge to the North African mainland (the Maghreb) and so it is hardly surprising that the islanders' forms of culture and self-government, as well as their physical appearance, closely resembled those of the Berber peoples. However, although the Berbers traditionally have a very democratic system of self-government, they have also always been a quite commercially competitive and even, often, warlike folk.

It is perhaps unsurprising therefore that the great Carthaginian general Hannibal was able to mobilize them into a remarkable and highly professional fighting force. This, with a large herd of elephants, was shipped across to Spain and then led through southern France and across the Alps to terrorize and very nearly defeat the early Roman empire. Such an outstanding achievement just would not have been possible with a nation of mere merchants or farmers or both. These would not, in any case, have maintained herds of elephants (which are not found naturally in northwest Africa) specifically bred and trained for warfare.

It is well worth mentioning as an afternote that the so-called 'Islamic' invasion of Iberia in the early eighth century AD was undertaken not by Arabs but again by Berbers. In fact, the cultural Islamization of Iberia came substantially later and was driven by a caliph from the area of Damascus in modern Syria, whose mother was Iberian. The so-called 'Arabic' culture, which produced the wonderful architecture, town planning, engineering, science and drive towards the expansion of knowledge, also came not from Arabia but from modern Iraq, which had its own origins in an even earlier Indo-Persian civilization and culture which also incorporated Mesopotamia. But that is another story ...

Isolation of the Canary Islands and Madeira

Whilst Tenerife – the nearest island of the Canaries group – is over 50 miles (80 km) from the northwest African mainland, it would seem probable that the distance was nowhere near as great at the time of the cataclysmic submersion of the major part of the island of Poseidonis. However, due to earthquakes and volcanic activity, the huge intervening landmass disappeared, thereby leaving Tenerife and the other islands completely isolated. In addition, the central city of the original Berber/Guanche civilization – situated perhaps somewhere on the main island or on one of the adjacent coasts – seems to have disappeared completely in the cataclysm. This would inevitably have torn the very heart out of their civilization. So, it is unsurprising that the remaining colonies and associated lands scattered across the Iberian Peninsula and the Mahgreb thereafter went their own ways, with little or no further direct contact between many of them for several thousand years.

A major part of the reason behind that has to be the lack of navigability of the western Mediterranean for several thousand years after the Poseidonian cataclysm, as described earlier and as confirmed by the Egyptian priest to Solon. However, there are many other cross-correlations with this information. As K.A. Folliot reminds us, 'Scylla, a contemporary of Plato, reported that stretches of sea beyond Cerne ... were not navigable because of shallow water and too much mud and seaweed.'[15] According to Diodorus Siculus, 'Cerne' was supposedly the capital of Poseidonis and some 12 days' sail from the Pillars of Herakles. Pliny confirms that Cerne lay 'at the extremity of Mauretania ... a mile from the coast.'[16] Even Aristotle, despite apparently disbelieving Plato's story, confirmed (without specifying exactly where) that 'the sea beyond the Pillars of Herakles was muddy, shallow and almost unstirred by the winds.'[17]

The effects of Plato's Atlantean cataclysm seems to have extended far into the Mediterranean. In ancient times, before the flooding of the western Mediterranean (and even for some considerable time after this), there would have existed a mountainous land bridge between Italy and the north African mainland. This appears to have been at a time when Sicily – then possibly already a part of Magna Graecia – was apparently still attached to the 'heel' of Italy. The cataclysmic separation of Sicily from the mainland is commented upon by Philo of Alexandria when, discussing the huge extent of coastal land and coastal cities swallowed up by the sea, he says: 'Who is ignorant of that most sacred Sicilian strait, which in ancient times joined Sicily to the continent of Italy?'[18]

Celtic Connections

Rather interestingly, Diodorus Siculus' mention that the capital city of the 'Atlantioi' was called Cerne, brings to mind the southern English towns of Cerne Abbas in Dorset and Crew*kerne* in Somerset. The word 'cerne' is in fact the same as the Welsh and Cornish *carn* and Gaelic *carn/cairn* meaning a man-made pile of rocks, acting as a cultural gathering centre for the local population. Now, it is known that the southwest regions of Britain down as far as Cornwall (which seemingly takes its name from its pre-English inhabitants, the Cornovii – Carn-people?) were the subject of much interest on the part of seafaring merchant traders from the Mediterranean in ancient times, looking for Cornish tin and Welsh gold. Thus (as occurs with all trade relations) it is perhaps unsurprising that there were commonly used linguistic terms between the two. The idea that the Poseidonians and Carthaginians wanted to keep their trading rights with Britain exclusively to themselves is also hardly surprising.

There are of course other traditions that the Celts who inhabited this part of the British Isles and southern Ireland were themselves expatriate colonists from Atlantis, although little hard evidence has ever been brought forward to prove this.[19] However, both the Pyrenean Basques and the Celts of Brittany have quite closely corresponding creation legends plus traditions of a parent Atlantean island. So, it seems very likely that in the Celtic tradition, 'where there is smoke, there is indeed fire'.

The Etruscan Culture and Civilization

It is known that the Carthaginians latterly (around the time of the Phoenicians' appearance in Carthage c800BC) managed to regain contacts with their colonies on the northern Mediteranean coasts, including Spain. Here the later Poseidonian colonists (the so-called 'Agaric' peoples) operated gold, copper, silver and iron mines using sophisticated forms of hydrological engineering. Some of these mines – such as those on the Rio Tinto – are known by archaeologists and scholars to have existed not less than some 7,000–8,000 years ago, which clearly implies that Carthaginian/Berber culture is much older than modern scholarship in general is yet prepared to acknowledge.

This same civilization and culture also had colonies further eastwards along the northern Mediterranean coasts, extending to Liguria and Etruria (in ancient Italy), whose cultural origins are, even now, a mystery to modern scholars. However, closer examination of the shared cultures and traditions indicates that these too may well themselves have been the progenitors of those people now known to us as the Etruscans. The latter are known to have had a sophisticated poetic and literary culture and also to have been a deeply religious people who originally practised cremation of the dead. They also had a very modern form of social culture. Within this the womenfolk were regarded and treated socially as on a par with the men – just like the Berbers but totally unlike the Greeks and the early Romans, who endeavoured to base much of their culture on that of the Greeks.

Origins of the Etruscans

The Etrurian Etruscans (known by themselves as 'Rasenna') are known to have been a fair (sometimes reddish) complexioned, highly sophisticated and cultured people of clearly Caucasian ethnological type. According to historians, the northern and central Italian culture of Etruria seems rather strangely to have suddenly appeared out of nowhere c750BC, as I have already described. Yet they also occupied the area long before the Latin Romans themselves appeared as a separate nation state in the 3rd century BC.

A highly sophisticated culture and civilization cannot just materialize out of nowhere. It requires centuries of growth, international trade and general development. Therefore, unless the modern dating of this civilization is entirely wrong, it follows that it must itself be a legacy of another, yet greater culture, presumably somewhere else in the Mediterranean.

Counter to the opinion of Herodotus that the Etruscans had originally come from Lydia in what is now Turkey, it was pointed out by the much later Greek historian, Dionysius of Halicarnassus, that the Etruscans did not speak the same language, follow the same laws or worship the same gods as the Lydians.[20] From Dionysius' own viewpoint, the Etruscans were indigenous to Italy – which is precisely what I have suggested here. Charles Berlitz claims that Plato specifically mentions Liguria, the country of the Etruscans, as being a colony of Atlantis. However, I have been unable to confirm this from a specific reference in Plato's writings.

The fact that Italy was largely occupied by Etruscans in pre-Roman times in turn yet again suggests that the Romans were themselves merely ambitiously forward looking Etruscans (perhaps of mixed Greek origin) who wished to create a national identity of their own.[21] It is thus not at all impossible that they had decided to cut off political links with their North African and Iberian counterparts and thereby declare their own independence.

What Did the Etruscans Look Like?

Figure 31 gives some indication, from their own statuary, of what these pre-Roman Etruscans looked like and the way they dressed. As we can see, as well as having fair skin and hair, they (like the Berbers) also have sharply defined and clearly Indo-Caucasian (rather than Semitic) features. However, there are also interestingly striking resemblances (in terms of hair styling) to carved pictures of the Babylonians. But as hair styles are always changing due to cultural fashion, this might just be an indication of a then current Babylonian style becoming known and popular through knowledge derived from merchant trading connections – via Tyre and Sidon perhaps.

Figure 31. An Etruscan couple sculpted in terracotta, from a tomb discovered at Cerveteri in the 19th century

The 'Agaric-Etruscans'

The geographer Strabo says of the southern Iberians:

> They call the country Baetica after the river and also Turdetania after the inhabitants; they call the inhabitants both Turdetanians and Turdulians … The Turdetanians are ranked as the wisest of the Iberians and they make use of an alphabet and possess records of their ancient history, poems and laws written in verse that are 6,000 years old, as they assert.[22]

It is interesting to note that the unusual prefix stem *Turd-* in these names is phonetically the same as the goddess Ta'Urt' (sometimes rendered Taweret and often depicted as a hippopotamus) of the Egyptians and also the Phoenicians of Carthage – a name given to the 'World Mother', or world–soul of our local universe and itself related to the zodiacal 'Taur-us'. It thus seems not impossible that the intention was for the Agarians to regard themselves as (spiritual) 'children of the World Mother' – the 'great river-cow' which was the mate of the Taurean bull.

This same naming principle is to be found elsewhere in ancient times. The blue-veiled Tuareg tribes of the Sahara, immediate neighbours of the Berbers, appear to be ancestors or offshoots of the ancient 'Turkish' peoples, whose place of origin is usually regarded as having been Central Asia, where peoples traditionally wear the same style of headgear – the turban, or 'taur-ban'. The name 'Tuareg' (hence, despite the differently anglicized spelling, the phonetically similar 'Turk') actually appears to be derived from 'Taur-Akh', signifying an association with the constellation of Taur-us plus the ancient Egyptian, Assyrian and Vedic word for a 'fallen celestial spirit' or creative demi-god (*akh*).[23]

Now, as we have just seen, Strabo's comments give 'Agaric' (western Etruscan) culture and civilization an age of at least 8,500 years, and as their history, poems and laws were written down that long ago, it is entirely logical to assume that their origins must have been far older still. That in turn gives further credence to the suggestion that they were indeed Poseidonian colonists. It is also interesting to note that, in support of this proposition, archaeologists have discovered petroglyphs in the Canaries which closely match those of the Agaric peoples, thereby again confirming the prehistoric linkage with a greater Poseidonis, a culture which extended to the Iberian peninsula.

In addition to that, Agaric work has also been found in Sardinia, all along the north Italian coast and even down into Sicily – which archaeologists have assumed to be merchant trading products from other lands. The Egyptian priest confirmed to Solon the same geographical extent of Atlantean influence in the Mediterranean ('they held sway ... over the countries within the Pillars as far as Egypt and Tyrrhenia'[24]). How many more intimations of the prehistoric connections which I have just suggested will it take before mainstream archaeology at last wakes up to the same logical conclusion?

Etruscan Technology

The Etruscans appear to have been technologically, as well as culturally, very advanced. The philosopher-king Numa was reported by Ovid to have learned from the Etruscan adept priests the technique of forcing 'Jupiter Elicius' (lightning or electricity generally) to descend to Earth.[25] In other words, the Etruscan priests seemingly may have known how to generate or harness electricity. Furthermore, Livy describes for us how a prince called Tullius Hostilius later read in the books of Numa how this was done and how, through taking insufficient care in replicating it, he was killed by electrocution in his own palace.[26] One can only infer from this that, if the Etruscans were indeed colonial Atlanteans, then the Atlanteans themselves must have been able to use electricity. But more of that in Chapter 18.

The Carthaginians are known to have developed a sort of production line for building their ships. Huge numbers were made of the various sections of each ship, all being of exactly the same size, such that any damaged section could be very quickly replaced. As the ship's hull was held together with rope which swelled and tightened when in the water – thereby closing up all the joints – the taking apart and reinstating of a ship that had become partially damaged presented no problem at all for the Carthaginian shipwrights. The speed and economy involved in the process thus undoubtedly formed the basis of their navy being so large and powerful. Unfortunately for them, the Etruscan-Romans learned how to develop the same production line technique and later used it to defeat them in battle.

The Etruscan Language

The Etruscan alphabet had a basic 26 letters and seems to have been strongly related to the Greek alphabet. The letters were very similar to our own modern Western lettering – only back to front. However, the Etruscan writing system flowed from right to left, like the Semitic, occasionally departing even from this so that one line would commence under the end of the line immediately preceding it and then depart in the opposite direction, in a sort of serpentine fashion. But even though much is known (from Roman and Greek authors) about the later Etruscan lifestyle and social culture, the actual language has still not been anything like fully deciphered, even today.

It accordingly appears quite possible that, if the Etruscans were indeed originally colonists from Poseidonis, then it might logically follow that the Etruscan written script is very probably that of the Poseidonians themselves – and thus also of the Atlanteans in general. Plato describes the Egyptian priests beginning to teach Solon the Atlantean script, of which nobody in modern times has been able to find any apparent trace – probably because they have been looking for something quite different to what is already staring them in the face.

It is worthy of note that not only Etruscan artefacts, but also variations of the Etruscan language (or other languages with close connections) have been found by modern scholars at a considerable distance from the supposedly parent Etruscan culture. The language spoken and written on the Greek island of Lemnos was particularly close. However, the relationship is also apparent in the Rhaetic language spoken in ancient times in the Swiss Alps. The scholarly Roman emperor Claudius is supposed to have written 20 books (since lost) on Etruscan language and culture, whilst early Roman youths are known to have been schooled in both the Etruscan language and culture before Latin took over. Is there not at least a suggestion in this that Etruscan was acknowledged as the parent language and culture?

Therefore, whilst most modern philologists suggest that the Etruscan language is a completely isolated case, having no evident connections with any of the Indo-European or Semitic languages (or Basque), we can still suggest with complete logic that it was of such a cultural sophistication and magnitude in its own right that it stands alone as having had a highly significant prehistorical origin. That in turn indicates that the original parent culture from which the Etruscan sprang had an even greater and more ancient heritage, of which modern historians are as yet completely unaware.

The Suggested Origin of Our Western Alphabet

The Etruscan alphabet is very similar in form to our own.[27] As noted above, it was, however, usually written back to front and from right to left, as shown at figure 32 (taken from an Internet example). It seems not impossible, therefore, that the new cultural influence of Sanskrit-based (left to right) language which came with the Greeks, resulted in the old Etruscan alphabet being retained by the new Roman empire – *but reversed* in form to convey its complete change of loyalty to a brand new (Indo-Caucasian) culture. This is not quite so bizarre as it perhaps might appear.

One remembers that, in ancient times, movement to the left indicated a directional motivation towards the material world (the Underworld, hence *sinister*, from the Latin for 'left') whilst movement to the right (Latin *dexter*) indicated a directional motivation towards the spiritual world. In the same way that Dr Samuel Johnson codified the English language in the 18th century out of a mass of differently originating dialectical usages, so it would have been quite logical for the early Romans – in wishing to secede completely from western Mediterranean (that is, Atlantean based) culture – to have done exactly the same.

If this suggestion is anything like correct, it would perhaps explain why modern scholarship has found it so difficult to establish a connection between the Etruscan-Poseidonian languages and the Indo-European Greek and Roman languages. The new Latinate culture of the Romans – deeply infused with Greek ideas – would understandably have sought its independence on all fronts possible. They therefore adopted, I suggest, a mixture of the Oscan ('old' Etruscan-Latin) and the Greek, then later recodified it in a new and formal vocabulary and grammatical structure, to create the classical Latin language with which modern historians and scholars generally are thoroughly familiar.

Notwithstanding this, it seems very likely that the grammatical structure also quite closely followed that of the Etruscan.[28] Although Latin is regarded by philologists as a language related to Sanskrit, it looks increasingly likely that it was merely a bastard tongue derived from a fusion of the Etruscan and the Greek, the latter however being truly related to Sanskrit. The parallel suggestion (mentioned in an earlier note) that the Guanche tongue also had Dravidian origins makes it look increasingly suggestive that all the prehistoric peoples of the whole of the western Mediterranean and northwest Africa spoke a common family of languages.

Original Etruscan	Transliteration
𐌀𐌁·𐌂𐌀𐌃𐌉·𐌀𐌉𐌌𐌕·𐌀𐌕𐌋	ita.tmia.icac.he
𐌀𐌋𐌀𐌉𐌕𐌀𐌅·𐌀𐌅𐌀𐌌𐌀𐌓	ramasva.vatieKe
𐌉𐌌𐌀𐌏·𐌆𐌀𐌅𐌕𐌆𐌀𐌋𐌀𐌉𐌇𐌅	unial.astres.ðemia
𐌀𐌁𐌆𐌏·𐌀𐌕𐌅𐌏·𐌋𐌀𐌌·𐌀𐌆	sa.meK.ðuta.ðefa
𐌋𐌀𐌆·𐌆𐌀𐌇𐌀𐌉𐌆𐌀𐌅·𐌉𐌀𐌉𐌓	riei.velianas.sal
𐌅𐌒𐌅𐌕·𐌆𐌀𐌉𐌇𐌀𐌅𐌅𐌋𐌂	cluvenias.turu
𐌆𐌀𐌅𐌅𐌏·𐌆𐌀𐌕𐌆𐌉𐌇𐌅𐌌𐌀𐌂	ce.munistas.ðuvas
·𐌀𐌀𐌂𐌀𐌅𐌋·𐌀𐌂𐌆𐌀𐌒𐌀𐌌𐌀𐌕	tameresca.ilacve.
𐌉𐌀𐌀·𐌉𐌂·𐌂𐌀𐌇·𐌀𐌆𐌀𐌒𐌀𐌋𐌅𐌕	tulerase.nac.ci.avi
𐌕𐌉𐌀𐌌𐌀𐌉𐌁𐌀𐌕·𐌒𐌀𐌒𐌒𐌅𐌋·𐌋	l.Kurvar.tesiameit
𐌀𐌆𐌀𐌁𐌋𐌀·𐌀𐌀𐌂𐌀𐌅𐌉·𐌀𐌋𐌀	ale.ilacve.alsase
𐌂𐌀𐌅𐌋𐌕·𐌆𐌀𐌇𐌀𐌒𐌕𐌀·𐌂𐌀𐌇	nac.atranes.zilac
𐌅𐌁𐌀𐌇𐌂𐌀·𐌀𐌋𐌀𐌕𐌉𐌀𐌋𐌀𐌆·𐌋𐌀	al.seleitala.acnasv
𐌌𐌀𐌒𐌀𐌁·𐌌𐌉𐌇𐌀𐌕𐌉·𐌆𐌒𐌀	ers.itanim.heram
𐌋𐌅𐌕·𐌀𐌂𐌀𐌉𐌇𐌀·𐌋𐌉𐌀𐌀·𐌀𐌅	ve.avil.eniaca.pul
𐌀𐌀𐌋𐌌𐌅	umKva.

Rough translation

This temple and [this] statue have been deicated to Uni/Astarte. Thefariei Velianas, head of the community, donated it for the worship of our peoples. This gift of this temple and sanctuary and the consecration of its boundaries during his three-year term in the month of Xurvar [June?] in this way, and in Alsase [July?] this record together with the divinity/statue shall thus be buried by order of the Zilach that the years may outlast the stars.

Figure 32. An example of the Etruscan script, transcribed from the first Pyrgi Tablet. In the transliteration, the capital letter K represents an Etruscan letter with the guttural sound ch as in Scottish loch or German bach. The symbol ð (eth) represents a letter with the same sound as the Greek theta (θ) or English th in thing. Above is an attempted translation, based on a number of sources.
(Thanks to www.mysteriousetruscans.com/language.html.)

The Languages of the Western Mediterranean

It is worthwhile mentioning here in parallel the 'Occitan', or 'Oc' script and culture of the Languedoc region in southwestern France, because this also conceivably dates back to a time when the remnants of Agaric-Etruscan colonies would have been found in the area. There are in fact two schools of thought as regards the issue of the various languages found in the Occitan area, which extended all the way from northeastern Spain, across the Pyrenees to the Loire in the north and northwestern Italy in the east. One school says that the seven languages of the area – Auvergnat, Gascon, Limousin, Languedocian, Provençal, Alpine-Provencal and Shuadit – are all quite different members of a language family, whereas the other says that they all derive from different dialects of one and the same language. Furthermore, the Catalan language spoken in northeastern Spain (centred around Barcelona) and southern France is understandable also by speakers of Occitan.

Although it may be no more than a coincidence, it is curious to note, in passing, that there are *seven* dialects in this particular linguistic family. As we have seen earlier, seven was considered in ancient times to be the very basis of all structures, even where language was concerned. For example, the septenary goddess Seshat in Egypt was herself considered to be the guardian of language and literature, as well as of all building construction.

Whether or not any more open-minded philologists have actually explored the possible correlations between the Occitan-Catalan languages and the Etruscan, however, I have not been able to confirm, although it is clear that Occitan also looks like a form of Latin. Latin seems to have been derived from the ancient (prehistoric) Etruscan family of languages which spread at least as far north as Switzerland and almost certainly covered (at one time, perhaps also prehistorically) the whole area of Iberia and south and central France, as well as the whole of Italy, down to Sicily. Thus Occitan and Latin would essentially derive from one pre-Romano-Etruscan source. However, it is a fact that the Romans called much of this linguistic area – incorporating the cultures of northern Iberia and southwest France – by the single name 'Aquitania' – which is clearly a corruption of 'Occitan-ia'. Why would they do so unless there were cultural correlations between the two? (All this is in radically direct contra-diction to modern linguistic orthodoxy.)

The Etruscan Religious System

It is otherwise known that the (solar) religious system of the Etruscans was astronomically and astrologically based, their system – like most others in the ancient world – involving a heaven world and an underworld separated by an intervening 'Middle Earth' world, associated with the colour green. The celestial universe was itself separated into 16 quadrants over which 14 different gods ruled, there otherwise being – as in the Greek tradition – a group of kosmic Titan gods (the *Dei Superiores*) and a lesser celestial group in which the main trinity comprised Tinia, Uni and Menrva.[29] The main Etruscan solar deity was, however, called 'Catha'. Hence perhaps the origin of the name 'Cathar', plus the associated cultural and spiritual connections with the southwest of France, which would thus have pre-dated (by a long way) the advent of the cult of the Slavic Bogomils.

The Etruscans took their religion and its celestial associations so seriously that they even designed their temples and cities to follow the same numerologically consistent basis of 16 quadrants. But this is consistent with the most ancient traditions elsewhere as well, most obviously in Egypt, where all temples and pyramids were astronomically orientated and representative. We otherwise know from Charles Hapgood's researches, mentioned earlier, that the Piri Re'is map (*see* figure 19) was based upon 16 quadrants, which may perhaps indicate an Etrusco-Carthaginian provenance.

It seems very probable that the Etruscans had a Gnostic side to their religion as well. Some of the supposed 'tombs' which have been found are much more likely to have been akin to Masonic temples – meeting places in which the Mystery traditions would have been followed. As the Etruscans practised cremation of the dead, there would hardly have been any point in building tombs.

Other Poseidonian Colonies in the Mediterranean

Despite indications of an Iberian origin, the actual provenance of the ancient people of Crete represent as much of an enigma to modern archaeologists as does that of the Etruscans, with whom there again seem to be some clearly apparent historical and commercial trading connections. Here again (as we can see from their domestic architecture and its decoration) we have a clearly sybaritic culture which had the bull at the centre of its social and religious system. Quite apart from the Greek *allegorical* myth of Theseus going to Crete and killing the Minotaur, or man-bull, to stop the annual sacrificial toll of seven male and seven female virgins (another wholly esoteric metaphor and allegory) exacted by the king of Crete on the Athenians, we also know that the Cretans practised 'bull-leaping' (figure 33).

Bull-leaping was a highly gymnastic sport, somewhat in the style of the Spanish *corrida*, or bullfight (but without horses), where young male and female athletes would literally run at the bull and vault or somersault over it, thereby displaying their agility and courage. However, as with the *corrida*, the root of the tradition seems to have been related to the astronomical movements around each other of Taurus and Orion, as I have also elsewhere described,[30] thereby making of it an at least quasi-religious ritual, probably performed at specific times of the year, or cyclically every few years.

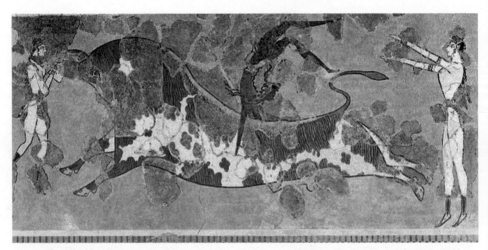

Figure 33. A depiction of the ancient Cretan sport of 'bull-leaping', from the frescoes at the ancient palace of Knossos

Cretan civilization and culture has been calculated by archaeologists as having commenced *c*2500BC and ended *c*1000BC as a result of the cataclysmic volcanic convulsions which blew apart the nearby island of Thera, resulting in the complete burial of the capital city of Knossos under volcanic ash and debris. However, this chronology is based upon very limited and purely circumstantial archaeological evidence. What seems clear from their wall frescoes and vase decorations, however, is that the ancient Cretans were dark-haired people (which distinguishes them somewhat from the Berbers and Etruscans) with at least semi-Indo-European facial features (*see again* figure 33).[31]

Various other ethnic groups found in Greek literature also seem to have had Atlantean origins. For example, H.P. Blavatsky comments in *The Secret Doctrine*: 'The Pelasgians were certainly one of the root-races of future Greece and were a remnant of a sub-race of Atlantis. Plato hints as much in speaking of the latter.'[32]

Although modern historical scholars are inclined to consider the Pelasgians (who were supposedly giants) as probably having emanated from somewhere to the east of Greece, there is no real evidence for this. Herodotus refers to them as having learned something of the Egyptian sacred culture and then having passed it on to the Greeks before becoming absorbed themselves into the newly forming Hellenic nation. That itself suggests that, if indeed Poseidonian in origin, their colony had become very estranged from its parent culture by sheer distance over very prolonged time.

One could doubtless go on almost *ad infinitum* exploring the ethnological and geographical backgrounds of many of the Mediterranean tribes mentioned in Greek and Latin literature and history. However, the available information is so threadbare that the whole exercise rapidly becomes very speculative and thus increasingly unreliable. All that we can perhaps say is that the available evidence – whether proven or merely circumstantial – does seem to indicate that the Poseidonian empire and its associated culture had extended as far as the central (and perhaps even the eastern) Mediterranean, just as Plato's story tells us.

Having said as much as we can say on that issue, therefore, let us turn our attention back to the subject of the Poseidonian homeland itself and its more recent history, with the military advent of the Spaniards in the 14th century and their crushing of native Guanche resistance.

The Re-Annexation of the Canary Islands and Madeira

The Spanish wished to annex the Canary islands, and rather unsurprisingly their more numerous and better-armed troops eventually defeated the native Guanches. Thereafter they carried out (with the support and encouragement of the Catholic church) a disgraceful scheme of virtual genocide. Subsequent to this, very few Guanche remained alive to tell of their traditions. Fortunately, however, something of their culture was noted and written down for posterity before this happened and these records remain extant today.

It was found that the Guanche not only spoke almost exactly the same Hamitic language as the Berber, they also built stepped pyramids – small-scale ziggurats. They also embalmed their dead in the same way as the ancient Egyptians, whilst also worshipping the 'Dog Star' Sirius – hence the islands' name 'Canaria' – isles of the dogs. Not surprisingly, Victorian anthropologists rapidly came to the conclusion that there had to have been an ancient cultural link between the two civilizations. Unfortunately, because of the near-genocide of the Guanche, none of their chiefs or wise men were left alive to pass on more detailed information as to their religious belief systems and general philosophy of life. We are thus left today with little more than the mere 'wrappings' of their culture.

Exploration of the Canaries confirmed that there were (and still are) seven islands – Gran Canaria (inhabited by the Canarii), Tenerife (inhabited by the Guan Chenech), Fuerteventura (inhabited by the Maxos), Lanzarote (inhabited by the Tyterogatra), La Palma (inhabited by the Benahoare), La Gomera (inhabited by the Gomeros) and El Hierro (inhabited by the Bimbaches). As has been mentioned elsewhere in this book, this sevenfold existence provides an immediate correspondence with the Vedic/Hindu Puranic tradition that 'Atala' also had seven islands.

When we look at Madeira and the Canaries on a bathyspheric relief map (*see again* figure 17) it quickly becomes obvious that they must originally have been part of one single landmass (once probably also connected to the Azores), its centre having, however, been utterly destroyed by volcanic activity. That landmass was originally connected to the Maghreb in the area of what are today Morocco and Western Sahara, and research into the geology of the area confirms that the last major volcanic and earthquake activity which affected the area took place some 11,500–12,000 years ago, which fits Plato's chronology perfectly. Here then is yet another bit of evidence supporting Plato's story and historical timing, for his Poseidonis was utterly destroyed, in his words, some 9,000 years before his own time – that is, some 11,500 before the present.

When one looks closely at the topographical map (including the ocean floor) in this general area, it becomes reasonably clear that the Canaries and Madeira chains were not only once connected to the Maghreb – and thus to the Atlas Mountains chain – but also to the Iberian Peninsula. The mountains here connect with the Pyrenees, the chain then passing into the Alps and then the Italian Apennines, before crossing the Mediterranean and rejoining the Atlas in Tunisia. At some stage, literally the whole of this area must have formed one giant continental island landmass – the Mediterranean part of which geologists refer to as 'Tyrrhenia' – before the rest of western Europe appeared above the waves.

Conclusion

To conclude therefore. Plato's island appears to have comprised the Canaries and Madeira and possibly also the Azores as one single landmass, before their cataclysmic fragmentation. If Plato was correct about his Atlantean island being the cultural centre of a great Atlantean empire and civilization, it was at a time when it was also either connected to the Maghreb by a still extant land bridge or otherwise still lay very close to the northwest African mainland. At this time also, a lagoon existed between the then geographically close Pillars of Herakles which were likewise destroyed in the same cataclysm that saw the sinking of Poseidonis. These facts seem to be borne out by the historical memories and traditions of the peoples we have quoted in this and other chapters.

If Plato was right, it also then follows quite logically why the ancestors of the Guanches, Berber and Ibero-Etruscan peoples would all have belonged to one and the same ethnological group or nation. That being so, we have no need to look further for the Atlanteans, for their offspring are to be seen in the faces of all the present-day peoples of the Mediterranean area. But even these are now so thoroughly intermixed with Indo-Caucasian and Hamito-Semitic strains as to have produced a thoroughly cosmopolitan ethnic mix which effectively conceals almost all trace of its original historic provenance.

PART FOUR

.

CULTURE

Chapter Sixteen

·

THE RELIGIOUS CULTURE OF THE ATLANTEANS

'Our interpretations of history follow our social values and beliefs. Our modern interpretation is essentially a commercial and technological one. We see civilisation as developing through the invention of the wheel, writing and so on. It reflects the view of a culture that holds wealth and equipment to be the highest reality and is attached to the outer world of the senses as the truth. Such commercial and technological ideas of humanity do not show much sensitivity to the spiritual view of life. They are economic ideas and reflect the bias of the business class. They are a merchant's view of history and reality ... seeking not so much to understand the world as to dominate it.'[1]

In the earlier part of this book, I spent some time looking at the background of our planet's unfolding development from an initially ethereal to a plastic state, before finally settling down into its present range of densely organized material forms. I also described how, by virtue of all states of matter being synonymous with different qualities of light-substance, consciousness itself had to be considered as synonymous with qualitative states of light. In mystic or religious terms, of course, light has always been regarded as synonymous with spiritual insight. But what I have described here puts this in a very practical context.

The essence of the Ancient Wisdom tradition involves the development of intelligence through a process of gradual individualization of consciousness from the mass. So, in trying to understand Atlantean culture and consciousness as distinct from our own, we need to know something more about the mechanics and dynamics of consciousness itself. Inevitably, some of what we suggest here in this chapter may appear very speculative, particularly in relation to the prehistoric cultures of many hundreds of thousands (or even millions) of years ago. But one can only ask the reader to keep as open a mind as possible in relation to the associated logic and its parallels with modern human experience.

First of all, a civilization and its culture are the products of a major *group* consciousness. So, when discussing the spiritual or intellectual consciousness of any lesser group of human beings, of any historic period, it is very easy to make the mistake of over-generalization. Whilst people inevitably share characteristic family, tribal, national and ethnological forms of consciousness – largely because of the associated traditions which have been developed – the actual range of individual intelligence involved is almost always very wide and frequently inconsistent. That is because the spectrum of developing intelligence is by no means regular. There have always been fools and wise people in every society, just as there have always been leaders and led.

In addition to this, there have always been, on the one hand, those relatively few who were progressively willing and able, under strict discipline, to follow the philosophy of the inner or gnostic Mysteries which stand behind all exoteric religious practice; and on the other hand, the majority who were content merely to watch or follow the outer ceremonial practice with varying degrees of attentiveness, either through a truly devotional nature or otherwise due to a nature tending towards the purely superstitious. These groups, however, constitute the quite natural division of spiritual and material experience.

All traditional religion and all knowledge, like everything else in objective nature, tends towards eventual corruption through either abuse, laziness or forgetfulness. The sustaining of real knowledge requires constant discipline and sustained adherence to cyclical ritual, even down to the simple maintenance of library and other records. This is the case, whether in literary or other more metaphorical and allegorical formats, such as carved artefacts and painted art. It also requires a high degree of respect; for if knowledge is treated as a mere functionality, rather than with due respect, it quickly withers; or it becomes subject to distortion through literalism and subsequent corruption into mere superstition.

In ancient times such respect was inculcated in the general populace by the *lack* of easy availability of real knowledge, except to those who (through the tests of the Mysteries) could prove their determination to acquire it and use it responsibly and altruistically. These then naturally became the wise leaders of that society. However, the understanding that such knowledge was available to all who were prepared to make the effort came with the fact that *all* were made to participate to some or other degree in the cyclical rituals and festivals of that society's spiritual culture. Thus developed the general sense of a coherent community of belief and religious practice.

Modern commentators are fond of ascribing to the ancient priesthoods a largely socio-political attitude, involving the desire to keep the general population 'under their thumb'. This was supposedly by creating a hierarchical system which only allowed further upward progress to those seen to be willing to maintain the system of control, without 'rocking the boat'. However, although it is doubtless what ultimately prevailed in some cultures through the usual processes of psychological corruption to which humanity in general falls prey, this is a complete misapprehension of what was *originally* involved.

Primordial Religious Practice

We have already mentioned that the fundamental *exoteric* religious practice of at least the late Fourth (Atlantean) Race peoples was that of ancestor worship and that this is still to be found all over the globe even today, simply because the vast majority of human consciousness on our planet today is still Atlantean in nature. However, we should perhaps try to put this in some sort of perspective, by seeing it in terms of the development of an evolving consciousness of humanity in the round, as follows.

The larger mass of the later Third (Lemurian) Race, as we have seen, is supposed to have had an ingenuously naive, child-like mentality (because still imbued with its original spirituality) which viewed its environment as a sort of permanent playground. At the same time, however, it is supposed to have involved an instinctive sense of obedience to its spiritual guardians, the *kumaras*, and also – so the tradition has it – to the great *devas* responsible for the very workings of Mother Nature.

It should also be borne in mind that it it this very sense of direct personal association which exists as the foundation of what is commonly called 'sympathetic magic'. The latter involves an absolutely total commitment of the consciousness towards a particular aim, resulting in Nature instinctively and automatically producing a gathering of matter and force in sympathy, to provide an appropriately corresponding form. Hence it is that the effective performance (with positive results) of either religious ritual or 'magic', so called, is entirely relative to the capacity to hold *absolutely* to a particular belief or range of beliefs and to follow it in due sequence.

This is also the real basis of true faith, whether in theurgy or religion. Hence it was, so tradition has it, that the *kumaras*, being divine and wholly imbued with a sense of divine purpose, were able to produce a range of extraordinary creative phenomena by what is called in the Vedic tradition, the power of *kriya-shakti*. This concept extends as far as bodily self-creation by an act of will, involving projected creative thought, out of local light substance.

One has to bear in mind here that the *kumaras*, being of divine stock and thus spiritually Self-conscious from the outset, were already fully aware of their group purpose in Nature and also of their need to work hand-in-glove with the great *devas* in order to achieve it. Mid-to-late Third Race Lemurian human-kind, however, being of the early fourth kingdom in Nature, had to begin with only an intermediate, really quite rudimentary form of self-consciousness. This being essentially (and necessarily at that stage) self-centred,[2] it had no reliably stable sense of spiritual responsibility. Consequently, as with our own children today, it had to be taught that sense in conjunction with the development of a sense of intelligent discrimination and self-discipline.

The Separation of 'Man' from 'Animal Man'

In horticulture, when it is intended to breed a new genus of plant, it is well known that one has to ensure that the new cuttings or seedlings have to be strictly segregated from the others from which they have been derived. Otherwise, there occurs a regression to type. However, the same principle holds good in animal husbandry as well. The essential result of what was being taught in Lemurian times thus initially seems to have involved the segregated development of a (wholly new) fourth kingdom in Nature from the existing third kingdom which, until that time, involved no essential diversity of consciousness between the 'humankind' and 'animalkind' of that era.

The groups of *kumaras* of the sixth kingdom in Nature might thus be seen as akin to spiritual 'gardeners'. They appear to have lived and moved normally amongst the Lemurians, gradually selecting those who were most likely to prove capable of what we might call 'fast track' evolutionary development, the 'fast track', however, still taking many millions of years of sustained effort.

By no means all the Third Race types were selected for the personal attention of the *kumaras* and, consequently, so the ancient tradition has it, not all became imbued with the 'spark' which 'lit the flame' of self-consciousness. So we are told, some of those who did manage to contain the 'spark' eventually let it die out and thus reverted to type – to their original animalistic nature. But sufficient were 'spiritually awakened' to ensure that they became the foundation of the future human race. However, the Ancient Commentary makes it clear that it was not until much later, in early Atlantean times, that one could realistically consider them to be truly recognizable 'human beings'.

It is perhaps worth noting that, in preparation for the development of a fourth kingdom in Nature during the late Third (Lemurian) Race, so in the later Atlantean (Fourth) Race cycle, attention was given to the 'organic' development of a Fifth kingdom in Nature – that of the spiritual Adept Hierarchy[3] – whose role was to help more directly with the evolutionary progress of humankind, although progressively from 'behind the scenes'. That transitionary development has of course continued into the present cycle. However, in strictly logical consistency, our own (Fifth) Race has seen – so we are led to understand – the very first achievements of evolutionary transition of some from the Fifth into the Sixth (semi-divine) kingdom in Nature. This has thereby fulfilled the ancient prophecy of humankind self-consciously re-entering the 'kingdom of God' – albeit not in the extraordinarily limited sense of that expression shared by the Judaic, Christian and Muslim faiths.

In each of these race periods, the necessary (spiritual) evolutionary training took different forms. In mid-Lemurian to mid-Atlantean times, it seems to have taken the form of learning consciously what principles were applied by the *devas* in manipulating elemental Nature to achieve its functional ends. Thus were learned the very principles of magic, involving the use of sound and colour. During the mid-Atlantean to mid-Fifth Race period (that is, until the recent historical past), the educational process, so tradition has it, involved the sequential training provided by the Mystery Schools, all over the planet. This required often ascetic forms of both objective and subjective self-discipline. The intended educational process for the future is, however, as yet unclear.

The Withdrawal of the *Kumaras*

The progress of evolutionary development had evidently progressed suffi-ciently far by or towards the end of the Third Race, so we are told, for the *kumaras* to have largely withdrawn from permanent day-to-day contact with the nascent humanity, whilst still maintaining regular contact by way of cycli-cal rituals and appearances. The apparent and quite logical reason for this withdrawal was that humankind had to learn to develop its own sense of responsible individuality, whilst at the same time being watched over from a distance to ensure that its early efforts led to no accidental harm. The princi-ple is quite normal and understandably similar to what good parenting would involve today. More mundanely, it is also inherent in good gardening practice.

However, it would appear that 'maternal' communion with the *devas*, or Nature spirits (the 'mother' aspect of Nature) continued through the psycho-spiritual capacity inherent in the 'Third Eye', which was still universally functional until close to the middle of the Fourth Race period. By that time, it had closed up (quite naturally, in line with evolutionary development) and later Atlantean humanity's visual capacity functioned entirely through the two eyes which modern humanity uses.

The *Deva* Kingdom in Nature

Now, although we have mentioned the *devas* (the angelic kingdom in Nature) on several occasions in this book, as they are central to *all* religious and other ritualistic practice throughout the world, we should perhaps pause for a moment here to touch on their nature and function in rather greater detail, before moving on. In doing so, I naturally recognize that some readers will find this subject either intellectually repugnant, on the grounds of it being 'unscientific', or mystically self-delusional.

Notwithstanding this, the fact remains – as explained in earlier chapters – that there are clearly intelligent and/or semi-intelligent organizing and building forces present in Nature which cannot be observed by human physical vision under normal circumstances, any more than atoms and germs can. Therefore, we should at least endeavour to listen to what ancient tradition has to say on the subject, before making any precipitate judgements.

The first and most important point to be remembered about this particular kingdom in Nature is that – as the expression of the 'Memory of God' – it is held to be responsible for the universal balance in Nature. It is also responsible for the associated building, maintenance and destruction/renewal of *all* forms and bodies, such work taking place within and strictly according to due celestial cycle. As otherwise already confirmed, the individual *deva* is a hierarchically organized, superior *Nature spirit* with a particular sense of due function.

However, despite having an acute natural intelligence, the *deva* does not have an individualized mind. That is to say, difficult though it may be for us to imagine, it is a genderless being whose consciousness is entirely instinctive and responsive to its own group purpose. Consequently, it is essentially part of a coherently organized body of Nature spirits of some or other order. These in their totality constitute what we call a 'soul' being, whose overall intelligence is, again, of a purely instinctive nature – wholly and unquestioningly responsive to its own hierarchical superior. It is perhaps for this reason in particular that our orthodox science tends to regard plants and the lower animals (both being *deva* forms) as having instinct, but not intelligence.

Both the form and consciousness of the *deva* are concentrically organized; that is to say, their true body form is an aurically organized sphere of light, whilst their consciousness forms a limited part of the consciousness of a greater *deva* parent entity. The latter is said to emanate them from itself (and subsequently withdraws them back into itself) according to its own instinctive response to due cycle. Notwithstanding this, the *deva* may produce (by projection) a form of self-expression *within* its auric sphere, this being what has sometimes become apparent to human vision as a luminescent, human-like entity with 'wings'.

The Elemental World

Distinct from the *deva* is the lesser Nature spirit, the (wholly instinctual) consciousness of these traditionally being associated with the Elements – of Fire, Air, Water and Earth – which thus express their nature. These entities (the salamanders, elves, undines and brownies, etc.) – unlike the *devas* – have no sense of a wider purpose, but merely act to fulfil their own group nature and function wherever possible. They are largely capricious in their instincts; yet those instincts hold them largely if not entirely in thrall to the will of the *devas* who they recognize as their superiors and mentors and whose powers are far greater than theirs. Nevertheless, some of them – like children when their parents are not in the vicinity – can be very quick to get up to mischief, whether intentionally or not. The stories of leprechauns in the traditions of Ireland, for example, thus appear to have a foundation in fact.

It is worthy of note that our own human organism involves a *deva* entity (known to us as the 'terrestrial soul') which contains within itself a vast number of hierarchies of elemental spirits, of immensely varying function and power. These elementals then combine to comprise the very nature and motor of all our instinctual human functions and senses – whether of a purely phys- ical nature, or otherwise involving our emotional feelings and lesser mental capacities. When under firmly disciplined control, they are useful slaves. However, they are unreliable servants and poor friends – as becomes obvious to anyone who engages in any degree of self-indulgence, thereby giving them virtually free rein to run amok.

It is for this reason that the true magus or adept traditionally had to learn – through personal austerity – to forego *all* self-indulgence in or around the practice of his art. For to attempt otherwise would put him in grave danger, just as self-indulgence progressively does to the rest of us, although perhaps to a lesser degree. In a very real (although as yet commonly unrealized) sense, the science of psychology deals with the art of self-control over all these lesser elemental entities within our own nature.

Archangels

Whilst Man (the spirit) is said to be of the 'sixth' of the seven kingdoms in Nature, the seventh and highest is said to be that of the 'archangels'.[4] These traditionally hold an overall planetary responsibility which otherwise literally involves containing Nature itself within their own consciousness. Thus all the lesser Nature spirits – the hierarchically organized *devas* and elementals – are part of their nature and subject to their will, which is itself the source of all planetary cycles, in conformity with greater solar cycles.

The archangelic hierarchs are thus said to be the very source of all *objective* being. They are the demiurgic basis of Nature. In a paradoxical sense, they are at once more powerful than man; yet they are also ultimately subservient to (the divine) Man who is the emanation of the Kosmic Mind and thus the expression of a yet higher sense of Purpose.

All the *devas* are said to be expressions of the 'fifth' Element in Nature –

the Aether. They then separate in their lower functions into four great sub-hierarchies of instinctive knowledge and function. These are the Elemental spirits, which I mentioned above. Thus it is that the greater *devas* (of Fire, Air, Water and Earth) are themselves the primal origin of the four objective elements in Nature, as we know them, each of these, however, having three sub-expressions.

As already indicated, the greater *devas* themselves are regarded as the instigators and architects of all the forms in Nature. The lesser Nature spirits are then the 'craftsmen-builders' or organizers, whilst the elemental spirits are the labourers and materials, in varying degrees of density and volatility.[5] Thus, for example, Water is to be found as vapour, crystal and liquid, whilst Fire is to be found as electricity, flame and frictional heat. The four times three adds up to the twelve associated with the signs of the Zodiac, with which there are said to be directly sympathetic affinities. These numerological associations are of crucial importance in the interaction of the various influences which maintain balance in Nature.

The *Devas* and the Lemurians

As I have suggested, late Lemurian humanity was still capable of learning from the *devas*, whose work in maintaining Nature was tireless and thus continued all around them at all times. Consequently, these first human 'children' learned at first hand how – through forms of ritual – the more evolved *devas* controlled and organized the lesser nature spirits and elemental groups. This resembles the 'Dream Time' of the Australian aboriginal peoples.

As a result of this proximity, the Lemurians themselves learned of the nature of what we now know as 'sympathetic magic'. As we shall see later, this was the source of huge problems in mid-late Atlantean times, due to the accrued sense of self-centredness which had also (quite naturally) developed in the evolving human race by that period. However, in late Lemurian times, the human imagination and will were insufficiently developed even to consider the idea of action consciously independent from their parental guardians, the maternal *devas* and the paternal *kumaras*.

The Development of an Individualizing Group Consciousness

As I have also suggested, Lemurian humankind – when the *kumaras* first appeared amongst them – was of an age comparable to that of our modern child of about four or five and was thus in the first throes of learning a sense of personal independence. The problem for the *kumaras* would have involved weaning nascent humanity away from complete dependence upon the *devas*, whilst at the same time ensuring that they maintained their sense of being part of the human family and of the One Life in Nature as a whole. The parallel today would involve the child learning of its place and duties and disciplines within both the immediate family and society as a whole (that is, Nature in the round).

As a consequence, so tradition has it, different forms of 'religious' ritual were organized, involving both *kumaras* and *devas*, highlighting the distinction between the energies and forces of the Sun and Moon and those of Earth Nature. As a result of this, so it would appear, the first ziggurats (*see*, for example, figure 34) were built in Atlantean times. These provided a recognition (by way of esoteric metaphor) of the steeply stepped path towards the greater heaven world 'above', which at this time would undoubtedly also have involved some perception of the relationship between Man and the stars in the celestial heavens.

We should also realize that (according to the Ancient Commentary) Lemurian humankind at this time, with a still somewhat ethereal consciousness, was still coming to grips with three major aspects of life which it had not encountered before. These were gender, sexual instinct and birth by the normal mammalian method. Death was of course something which they would already have been familiar with, although it probably had as little direct impact as it does with the consciousness of an infant today.

However, the technique of family and family group relationships was something which needed to be inculcated and the disciplined routines related

Figure 34. A Mayan ziggurat at Palenque. Ziggurats represent the (metaphorical) stepped path toward the higher 'heaven world'.

to this undoubtedly took several million years to achieve. It would only have been as a result of this achievement then that the paternal *kumaras* would have felt it safe to leave nascent humanity to its own devices for much of the time. The second stage of this parental distancing would then have taken place in the mid-Fourth Race period when the 'Third Eye' closed up and when, therefore, the by then entirely self-centred Atlanteans were no longer in the main able to see and thus take direct advantage of the maternal *deva* side of Nature.

Now the Fourth Race – developing in parallel to the modern human age range of 7–14 – had to learn of the range of experience to be had through exposure to and involvement in personal sensitivity, involving the interplay of experience between themselves and others. It thus had to do with learning about the faculties associated with the emotional self of humankind. As we can see with youngsters today in the above age range, this must have resulted in all sorts of increasingly independent attitudes (some of them responsible and some others not) together with a definite 'tribal' sense and a tendency towards idealism and associated worship of what was seen as 'heroism' and 'group loyalty'.

Inevitably, however, this led to both extreme hero worship and aggressive antagonisms between groups of different character, as well as some areas of exploratory curiosity of an unhealthy nature which caused many later problems. The most obvious of these involved the already mentioned second 'sin of the mindless' (*see* Chapter 9) at a time when Atlantean humankind was in its mid-cycle period – comparable to our modern child's age of about 10 or 11, just before puberty occurs, when the first stirrings of positive sexual interest take place.

Race Memory

However, as the usual pattern of life had by then taken the same form as remains extant today, there would have developed '*race* memories' of great heroes and sages, as well as personal memories of parents, siblings, friends and family members. This communal form of memory is of great importance because it is the source of all historical karma between human groups. We see it resurfacing even today – for example in the hatred which flared up in the early 1990s between the peoples of former Yugoslavia. The enmity between Christians and Muslims, for example, arose as a result of the invading Turks in the 14th century having literally forced local conversion to Islam at the point of a sword. This created a bitter resentment which – fuelled by further atrocities on all sides in the Second World War – has lasted for centuries, despite being partially concealed below the surface of normal village and town life.[6] But it is a perennial attribute of tribal consciousness.

It is always where essentially self-centred *belief* systems come into contact with each other without a background universal philosophy of Life that we find the greatest conflicts arising. Thus the concept of 'my God and thy god', or 'my tribe and thy tribe', has caused more general antagonism and warfare in this world than anything else – and still does today. But this all seems to have started in mid-Lemurian times when, so it is said, the first 'sin of the mindless' caused the animal consciousness to react strongly in resentment against the early human mentality, thereby resulting in the development of a separative consciousness involving fear. It was then the latter which eventually led to the first brutal taking of life and the full separation of the fourth kingdom of Nature from the third.

The Era of Dual Perception

Notwithstanding all this, the one thing which held everybody together during the early period of human existence was apparently the common perception and memory of the great and powerful Intelligences (the *kumaras* and *devas*) who guided early human evolution and the general workings of Nature respectively. At this stage, because life and death were seen as part and parcel of the same ongoing process, the Third Eye enabled the perception of the spirit merely passing from one state to another. Consequently, there was no fear involved in the process of death because the spirit in man and Nature were seen as eternal. If one was not in incarnation with one set of spirits, one was with other spirits in a parallel field of existence with far fewer restraints.

During the second or third Atlantean sub-races, however, so the tradition goes, the Atlanteans in the main started to lose the 'third eye' faculty, which effectively meant that they began to lose direct contact with the *devas* and the spirit world in general. It would appear, as a direct result of this, that Animism first appeared. However, that statement needs to be explained in somewhat greater detail by reference to another ancient tradition.

As we mentioned in an earlier note, certain *deva* hierarchies – being the creators of the forms of the various animal and bird species – are traditionally regarded as possessing heads and visual appearances akin to each type of species. Hence, the idea of the gods (not just God) creating Nature's forms in their own images. However, the increasing inability of the early Atlanteans to see and directly maintain contact with these spirit guides effectively necessitated their creating a visual counterpart – thus the animal or bird masks and costumes which are still to be found in use in so many apparently animistic religious cultures all over the world even today.

These masks were (and are still) always worn – usually by a shaman – for ritualistic purposes, associated with sympathetic magic. In other words, they are intended to be invocative, allowing the shaman to go into some form of trance so as to be able to make direct contact with the spirit world. However, in some parts of the world such as India, we find that the wearing of clothes and masks representing animals and birds 'in order to honour the gods' in religious ceremonial has become far more general in use over the millennia.

These same forms of originally religious animal or bird regalia are still to be found in North, Central and South America and in the dragon festivals of China and Southeast Asia, although the latter seem to have astronomical associations as well. In ancient India, it would appear that the Dravidians (originally of Atlantean descent) combined their use of such representations by association with the new Vedic deities imposed upon them by the invading Aryan-Caucasians. Consequently, we now find the Hindu pantheon involving all sorts of colourfully potent deities, some with human heads and others with animal or bird heads, in an often bewildering display of apparently animistic religion. However, this is just a hangover. The later Atlantean sub-races appear to have practised a rather different form of religion.

Ancestor Worship

As the spirit world was seen as the 'home world' from which and to which all spirits came and went, the tradition of honouring with ritual one's parents and 'heroes' beside them, not only during their incarnate life but also afterwards, increasingly became the norm. Thus a sensed strength of distinctively human spiritual continuity built up in the later Atlantean consciousness. Unfortunately, however, again as a result of the gradual loss of the Third Eye faculty, this later developed into forms of worship, rather than pure respect. As a result, there appeared separate tribal 'heroes' and 'gods' in totemic form, via the carving of likenesses in both stone and wood and the building of sacred places within which to keep them safely and respectfully. The very fact of later Atlantean humanity not having the functional Third Eye to enable them to see directly and for themselves the inner psycho-spiritual workings of Nature also meant that such phenomenally perceptual insights could only be achieved through appropriate ritual invocation; hence the birth of so-called 'Magic', which originally meant only 'Great Knowledge'.

As the sense of direct association with the spiritual world itself became increasingly more tenuous over countless tens of thousands of years, ancestor worship became even more degenerate and self-centred. This took place because both individual and group began to think of the departed spirit of a relative or hero primarily as a potentially benefic agent for them in the 'afterlife', there to smooth the passage for them not only in their own afterlife but also here as well. Out of this, although much later, all sorts of other degeneracy arose, including the appearance of 'professional' priestly classes, specifically to act as go-betweens and organizers of the associated rituals.

In the first place, these priestly classes would have comprised only those who retained a high degree of psycho-spiritual sensitivity. That in turn (as is known to historians) frequently became the 'specialization' of particular families who then handed down the mantle from one generation to another, irrespective of home-training not necessarily producing quite the same degree of 'quality control' needed to ensure that the gift retained the same high proficiency.[7] As a result, increasingly greater faith was placed on the efficacy of mere ritual – with increasingly patchy results.

This rather understandable but nevertheless tragic development has of course passed right down to our present day and age in the form of the various priests and theologians of our own modern religions and other 'spiritual' belief systems. The problem in the present day is that *very* few priests and theologians actually have any *direct* experience of the spiritual nature *per se* and so, by merely practising established rituals without any true sense of the energies and forces involved, are indeed 'the blind leading the blind'. Furthermore, very few (fortunately) have any sense of the associated powers with which they are blindly dabbling.

Progressive Change in Religion

It is interesting to note, in passing, the progressive development of *general* religious observance from early Atlantean times right up to today. As we have already seen, the early Atlantean sub-races appear to have practised Animism in order to reproduce their lost contact with the spirit world of the *devas*. Animism was then succeeded by anthropomorphic ancestor worship in the second half of the Atlantean race cycle, whilst mere ancestor worship, in turn, was succeeded during the first half of the present Fifth Race cycle by deism, or worship of the solar gods, rather than the *devas* or merely planetary 'gods'. However, what we now have in this second half of the Fifth Race cycle is a further onwards turn towards a commonly shared and *directly experiential* sense of an unitary Deity. But despite this, there are still elements of human consciousness which instinctively hark back to previous religious experience and tradition which involved *outward* forms of worship and supplication.

The Mystery Traditions of Atlantis

We have already suggested that the ziggurat or stepped pyramid (figure 34) was a cultural development of ancient Atlantean mentality. This developed in response to the sensed need for an idealized metaphor depicting the steep heavenward climb required on behalf of the individual wishing to recover his divine heritage.[8] The same applies to the sacred fire maintained on top of the ziggurat and originally produced, so it would appear, by the use of a simple crystal lens focussing sunlight. Quite when the first ziggurat appeared I cannot begin to suggest, and it actually seems to be of little real importance. What *is* of importance is what it signifies in terms of humankind's developing consciousness, as follows.

First of all, ceremonial rituals (if they are to achieve anything) need to be led by those truly adept in the associated science and art. Therefore, it follows logically that there must have been some system of spiritual initiation in existence at the time, led by spiritually orientated initiates of varying degree. Secondly, we may reasonably infer that such an initiatory system or tradition would have been sevenfold in nature, paralleling everything else in Creation. Thirdly, the fact that there were degrees of knowledge and faculty involved means that there were also Mysteries – because of the increasing degree of ignorance of the masses as to true 'inner knowledge'.

Now, as the overall intention of the Guides of the Race (the *kumaras*) was to ensure that humanity as a whole succeeded in attaining conscious spiritual re-attainment, those Mysteries would undoubtedly have been structured accordingly. How? Well, we find certain pointers in the ancient Egyptian and Greek Mystery traditions (and several others), although these are not yet recognized by orthodox scholarship.

The Triple Nature of the Mysteries

Both the Egyptian and Greek Mystery traditions are threefold in nature, even though there is a sevenfold structure of progression involved. Thus each has:

1. A basic allegory of Creation and the attainment of the sense of human individuality

2. An allegory for the development of the individualizing spiritual Ego

3. An allegory for the nature of divine consciousness in Creation

In the Egyptian system, these three allegories are to be found respectively in the stories of (1) Osiris and Isis; (2) Horus and Set; and (3) Ra-Herakte, the winged solar disc. In the Greek tradition, the allegories are found in (1) the Eleusynian Mysteries; (b) the Orphic Mysteries; and (c) the Dionysian Mysteries. Reference to other Mystery traditions however, will confirm that the same trinitarian concept was universal in application.

The Berber and Etruscan Traditions

The Berber religious tradition has become so overwhelmed by the force of Islam over the last 1,200 years or so that it is difficult to establish any coherent idea of the pre-Islamic form of their religion. Despite the fact that there is a current fightback (in Morocco at least) to re-establish Berber culture on its own terms, all that can be said is that the remaining fragments of the ancient Berber religious belief system appear to be closely related to magical concerns which have degenerated, for the most part, into merely superstitious practice. It is for this reason that Islamic theologians short-sightedly regard it as purely degenerate and thus something to be buried.[9]

However, when we look at ancient Carthage, a rather different view emerges, because Carthage was a highly cultured (albeit materialistically orientated) urban environment, whereas the Berber culture today has become almost totally diffused into merely localized pockets of tribal custom. Purely from the architectural viewpoint, however, it becomes obvious that Carthage has strong visual correspondences with the architecture of the Etruscans.

The Etruscan form of religious practice is still not well understood, even though it is known that at least some aspects of their religion appear to have been practised underground, in catacombs – which, by simple association, suggests a Mystery tradition. But this may have comprised only the 'gnostic' side of their belief system, with a separately presented public religion based upon simple worship of the gods – the solar deity Catha in particular. However, from one viewpoint at least, one could conceive of the Etruscan exoteric religious system being little different to that of their immediate neighbours, the Greeks.

It is acknowledged by archaeologists that the Etruscans, from at least 600BC, were so entranced by elements of Greek and Middle Eastern culture, that they began to absorb them wholesale. Etruscan tombs have consequently been found to contain more material belongings from their eastern neighbours than anything else. It is also acknowledged that the Etruscans – whilst having had cultural ties with the Carthaginians from long before – were evidently bored with Carthaginian artefacts, which tended to be much more utilitarian (due to association with pure commerce) and thus lacked the distinctively artistic element of Greek and Middle Eastern ware. One can therefore understand how, over an extended period of time, the Etruscans came to see their *subjective* sympathies and allegiances shifting from one culture to the other in all areas of life, including religion and the Mysteries. But a shift of subjective sympathies (particularly when the object is geographically closer) almost always leads to the eventual appearance of an equivalent objective counterpart.

The Cult of the Bull

One of the most common religious cults to be found all over the ancient world was that of the sacred bull, which I touched on at the beginning of the book. However, it is very poorly understood because it is rarely seen or explained in the proper context. As it appears to have been derived from either late Atlantean or early Indo-Aryan times, it would perhaps be useful to spend a moment or two here briefly reminding ourselves of it, as follows.

The cult itself unsurprisingly derives from the zodiacal constellation of Taurus. However, the details of the association are by no means self-evident. As also mentioned earlier, the *spirits* of humankind were deemed to have originated in the circumpolar stars but to have 'fallen' and thus been 'self-born' in the Pleiades, which is itself a nebula of solar systems within the constellation of Taurus. Hence these spirits were known as '*kabirs*', a name which in the ancient Egyptian mystical system is to be found as *kheper* – an aspect of the solar demiurgic deity Ra. In the kabbalistic tradition, the name mutates into the celestial state 'Geburah' and in the Hebrew biblical tradition as the Gibborim, the ancient 'giants'.

The *kabiri(m)* were themselves depicted in the Mesopotamian religious cults as deific figures with the bodies of winged bulls (*see* figure 21 in Chapter 11) and the heads of priest-kings. In later Fifth Race traditions such as the Mithraic, in an effort to show spiritual man's full evolutionary emergence from his zodiacal nativity, we find the religious cult depicting the death of the bull at man's own hands. This is the originally esoteric basis of the Iberian bull-fighting tradition, which appears to have been derived from the Etruscans.[10] In Egypt, of course, we find the human head emerging from the lion's body, which is basically saying the same thing but in a more advanced, very specific initiatory and astrological context.

The Progressive Nature of the Mystery Tradition

There is every reason to believe that, in ancient times, the progressive sequence found in the Mysteries was followed universally throughout the world, although we are unable to say now quite what sacred allegories and metaphors would have been used at the time. Such allegories and metaphors are devised specifically to appeal to particular areas of evolving necessity in the various race consciousnesses of humanity. Therefore, they necessarily change in focus and emphasis over time. That is because the race consciousness of humanity, as it develops an inward understanding of the 'coded' messages and the associated principles behind them, quite naturally fails to retain its original sense of wonder. Its spiritual orientation thus alters as the individual or group thereby either gets bored with the original concepts or starts to treat them literally as historical fact.

All *esoteric* religious concepts are thus ultimately discardable and all are ultimately discarded, whilst the *esoteric* principles involved are retained in the Race memory. It is for this reason, so we are told, that each sub-racial group has its own prophets and seers to lead it forward. Each such prophet – whether consciously or not – concentrates his attention on a particular need or failing in the consciousness of the group into which he has either been born or otherwise become affiliated by circumstance. This truism operates today with just as much force as it would have done in the mid-late Atlantean era. All world religions have their birth, zenith and eventual demise, some lasting longer than others only because they fulfil a wider need in the greater mass of humanity than that associated with their original 'birth group'. However, something of their original personalities seems to linger in the racial subconscious, their ghostly fingers remaining to tap us occasionally on the shoulder as a reminder.

The Distinctions of Race Consciousness

By now it may have become self-apparent that the fundamental difference in the Mysteries and associated traditions of the Fourth and Fifth Race consciousnesses is that the former were orientated towards the *outer* world order, whereas the latter are (at least by now) orientated towards the *inner* world of reasoned consciousness. The Atlantean nature – correspondingly like that of the early teenager – might be said to have focussed on the objective fulfilment of desires and attainment of satisfaction and pleasure, as well as fascination with devotional idealism and mysticism.

In that sense – using modern terminology – it was much more concerned with God Immanent. The still developing Fifth Race consciousness, on the other hand, is much more concerned with the nature of reasoned understanding and the way in which *subjective* nature operates beyond the constraints of physical Nature. It is thus much more concerned with the nature of God Transcendant.

Trying to distinguish between Fourth and Fifth Race consciousness today on a purely ethnological basis is of course extraordinarily difficult – if not impossible – by virtue of the mixing of the Races generally over the past several hundred thousand years. However, it would appear that at some stage in the far distant past, before that intermixing took place on any great scale, it would have been possible; and it may have been at that stage that much of the sense of ethnic discrimination we see today had its origins. However, in line with the development of the subjective nature of humankind today, most so-called 'racial discrimination' is actually of either a religious or a cultural nature. However, it remains deplorable whatever its basis.

Putting the Ancient Mysteries in Perspective

Now, we have already drawn certain correlations, in general terms, between religious observance through ceremonial and magical invocation by ritual. Is it possible to be more specific? Well the short answer to that must be 'yes', although our concern here is to deal with general principles rather than those specifics of action which, to some, would appear more exciting. It has always been the case that those who are after the excitement provided by mere phenomena are those who most need to be protected from them, lest their own ignorance and self-evident lack of self-control lead them into great danger.

It has always been self-evident to those who have seriously studied the subject, that the essence of the initiations available to humanity irrevocably involves the gradual discarding of self-interest (and proof of the same by increasingly severe and then increasingly subtle test). That is for the simple reason that the individual had to display his dissociation of *personal* interest in (and thus power over) lower and cruder forms of existence in order to safely progress to higher and more subtle ones himself.

One has to remember also that the progressive sequence of initiations involves expansions of consciousness which lead to an increasingly greater sense of *inclusiveness*, rather than of exclusivity. Thus the progression into a higher kingdom of Nature through greater spiritual insight and faculty necessitates a self-sacrificial concern for, or direct sense of responsibility towards, the beings of those lesser kingdoms left behind.

At the same time, it needs to be remembered that initiation involves lib-eration. Hence not only individual human beings take initiation. Groups of beings in the lesser and greater kingdoms of Nature must also do so. Ultimately each kingdom of Nature does so – by the progressive achievement of all those units comprising its soul nature.

The Ancient Mysteries are otherwise believed to have involved the development of knowledge in the field of magical practice. In the next chapter, therefore, we shall take a look at the whole issue of magic and we shall also discuss the principles involved, in relation to some of the known ancient traditions.

Chapter Seventeen

·

ATLANTEAN MAGIC AND MYSTERIES

'Magic then is a mysterious force through which the spiritual and physical universe becomes manifest and hence a force permeating and linking all levels of reality from the highest to the most material. But it is also – and this is an especially important aspect of the way the ancient Egyptians understood magic – the means by which the human being, and ultimately all Creation, returns to the supreme Godhead, the unmanifest Source of all that exists.'[1]

So much has been said and written about supposed Atlantean magic and its associated traditions that a chapter on the subject in general terms is unavoidable. Moreover, since theurgy (supernatural or divine invocation) and thaumaturgy (the performance of magic) feature in biblical and historical writings alike, it would also perhaps be useful to take this opportunity to set some of the background straight and in due perspective. However, I shall deal with the subject here in a fairly generalized way, as going into detail would require a complete book to do it reasonable justice.

First of all, the essential rationale behind all ceremonial and ritual in general – even in orthodox religion today – is magical and intended to evoke sympathetic *memory*. That might perhaps seem strange or even rather simplistic at first, but it is entirely logical. Our own human memory is actually part of the storehouse of Universal Memory. As Pato himself said, 'All is recollection.' Therefore, under the right conditions and using the correct form of invocation, it is possible to re-engage subjectively with the shadows or the potentials of what we rather crudely call 'the 'Past' and the 'Future' or, alternatively (by theurgical or thaumaturgical means), with the as yet untapped powers of the Present.

The Science and Art of Magical Invocation

However, as we have seen, in ancient tradition it was the angelic or *deva* hierarchies in Nature which (as soul-beings) were seen to comprise in their entirety the mass of Universal Memory and its associated functions, whilst also constituting part of our human consciousness. Therefore, in order to regenerate an extra-human memory or supernatural power, a magus had to invoke the correct *deva* or angelic nature, to appear (as a spirit, whether benefic or malefic) within the framework of whatever he was trying to achieve. This is the basis of all so-called 'magic' down the ages, whether in the context of ceremonies of religion or, for example, alchemy or healing practice. It is also the reason why such 'magic' only ever works where there is *total* focus on the question or reason behind the invocatory ceremonial.

As previously described, the *devas* and Nature spirits are regarded as being geared to respond to discipline and control in line with what the magus specifically requires of their instinctual natures. Hence the importance of astrological timing. When such discipline and control are missing, however, they – if already commanded into a cycle of functional re-existence – are said instinctively to look for the nearest alternative through which to channel their energy and force. This they do via the elemental nature which they bring into being and thus command. However, because some of the *devas* and Nature spirits lack a high degree of discrimination, while still capable of generating great power, the associated effects could prove very dangerous for both the individual and the community in general.[2]

It is for this reason that phenomenonalistic magical invocation was (and still is) considered highly dangerous, unless under the stringent but wholly altruistic control of an initiated adept in the art. But even an adept, in ancient times at least, was bound to practise such invocation solely within the grounds of the temple, which had itself been ritually prepared and its magnetism maintained with great care and rigour for that very reason.[3] This is something of which modern religion, and archaeology, are almost totally unaware. It might be added that the present-day phenomenon of the individual Merlin-like magician or shaman is a pure anomaly arising out of the historic corruption and disintegration of ancient religious or magical tradition, the two at that stage being inseparable. But more of that in a moment.

It might also be added that each individual human being, every time he or she *thinks*, practises this very art of invocation, some being more adept at it than others and thus often appearing more 'intellectually' capable. However, the mere invocatory repetition of the past with great organizational clarity and force (in line with many blindly indiscriminate educational systems today) is not particularly clever. Lacking any great degree of discrimination in response to need, it certainly lacks *wisdom*.

The art and science of such invocation – in the sense of its aiding evolutionary development and thereby engendering wisdom – actually involves learning to control the faculty that we call 'intuition'. This, however, is merely the perceptual 'in-sight' of a higher form of (spiritual) memory than that already contained within either the objective consciousness or the subconscious mind of the individual. This is something of which modern psychology is again, as yet, largely unaware.

The Power of Memory

Bearing in mind that the *deva* hierarchies and their sub-hierarchies of Nature and elemental spirits are themselves the expression of Universal Memory, it follows quite naturally that control of all the various forces in Nature is entirely dependent upon both memory *and* discrimination. Without such capacity, individuals are defenceless against the elemental forces which they themselves conjure up through mere desire or emotional reaction, or by other forms of personal association.

Hence it was that in ancient times, the magus was held to be able to control such forces by a process of invocation involving their numbering and naming. This, however, is not a question of applying simple numerological or strange naming principles, as practised today by those playing around with various forms of lesser occultism. By the latter is meant similar divinatory techniques to those involved in card or other systems of 'fortune telling', which also work on the basis of sympathetic association.

Notwithstanding that, in ancient times augury and divination of the future were indeed practised by some priesthoods as part of their religious duties. This frequently involved study of animal or bird entrails – sometimes even human ones in debased societies such as that of the Aztecs.[4] However, that type of activity (and indeed any form of blood sacrifice) merely confirms for us that severe degeneracy had set in, because 'black' magical practices of this type would have been wholly unacceptable to any real esotericist.

The old adage, 'Knowledge is power', still holds true. But in the sense of the practice of invocation and evocation required in true magic,[5] it requires intense focus. Without this – as in general education – nothing can be achieved. That is why almost all liturgical ritual today, in any religion, when pronounced without any sense of its real inner meaning and value is thereby rendered almost entirely useless. Whilst it often manages to achieve the level of making the practitioner feel better – particularly when practised en masse with others – this is a purely personal psychic self-stimulation and has no practical effect in the greater environment. Even when the words used are those originally derived with a knowledge of mantric influence, if they are not accompanied by total focus, they will achieve little or nothing of any practical or lasting value.

Shamanism

The various types of shamanic practice widespread throughout the world today are nothing but the vestigial (and usually much corrupted) remains of prehistoric religions and their varied forms of invocatory practice.[6] Most native shamans are indiscriminately treated in the West with far more reverence than they are generally due. In most other places they are usually tolerated or regarded with fear as (at least potential) practitioners of the 'black arts'. However, as the practice of 'black magic' is one of the various charges levelled at the Atlanteans and regarded as the source of their cataclysmic downfall, it is perhaps worthwhile spending a moment or two in passing to look at what is actually involved in the general run of native or aboriginal shamanism found today – other than the sort of divinatory practice which we have just described.

To begin with, any form of possession of the shaman by a nature spirit or animal entity (for example as in West African or West Indian Voodoo) is indicative of a form of *elemental* regression which the true Mystery Schools would, again, *never* have practised under any circumstances. Not only does it very effectively debase the condition of the human spirit and soul, it also results in the elemental nature gradually taking overall power, thereby destroying the soul's hitherto hard-won evolutionary status. The temporary feeling of power engendered by this type of activity is itself completely illusory and merely glosses over the actual damage which is being caused to the psycho-spiritual organism. The use of animal spirit 'familiars' – notwithstanding the descriptions given by Don Juan in the popular books by Carlos Castañeda – has always been regarded as highly dangerous, not only to the individual, but also to the community at large.

There are grounds for believing – notwithstanding modern scientific and scholarly incredulity at such a possibility – that the Ancients were able to invoke certain types of spirits into statues or simulacra, which thus took on powers of prophecy or prescience. Certainly, one comes across this in biblical tradition and ancient writings generally, and it is the source of many stories – such as that of Aladdin's Lamp – found throughout the Middle and Far East. However, whereas such practice may originally have been pursued solely in the temples, it is clear that they were also followed by degenerate prehistoric groups which sought to utilize such magically invocative powers to enslave elemental forces purely for their own selfish ends. In later Egypt, amulets were used for such purposes. We find traces of this practice even today in the use of 'lucky charms'; but whether the later Atlanteans actually used such practices on a grand scale, as some believe, we shall probably never know for sure.

Magic and the Law of Karma

It is interesting to note that the ancient Egyptians referred to the magical invocatory ritual as '*hekha*'. This is to be found in corrupt fashion in the (eso-terically allegorical) biblical story of 'Hagar', the 'bondswoman' of the entirely metaphorical Abraham, by whom he fathered Ishmael. The very same word is to be found in use today (as '*hakka*') amongst the Maori, having the very same meaning as it did in ancient Egypt.[7] According to the Egyptians, all creative capacity involved *hekha*. Even the appearance of the foundational god Atum – the mound of substance appearing out of the 'waters of Space'[8] – had to be accompanied by the descent of *hekha* in the form of the two Bennu (phoenix) birds, representing the karma and *dharma* of the Past and of the Future.[9] Thus, it is useful to remember the Vedic teaching concerning karma – that all action results in re-action, even where apparently simple thought is concerned. Magic is no exception to this rule.

In the ancient tradition – and we must assume that this applies as much to the understanding of the Atlanteans as it does to ourselves today – the idea of there being a fundamentally instinctive sense of balance in Nature (which only Man upsets) will have been prevalent in their religion. However, the under-standing that Nature will seek that balance by apparent 'karmic retribution', often lasting for generations, again comes back to the issue of there existing then and even today, fundamental forms of group consciousness and race memory. This, regrettably, is not something of which modern politicians take any notice, or of which they even have any awareness – largely because few of them have ever studied history and thus wisely noticed its tendency towards constant repetition.

The Basis of Atlantean Religious Culture

Having provided some background ideas as to the actual rationale behind ancient mystic and magical philosophy and practice in general, I shall now move on to look, in general terms, at the question of how such recognitions might have led to some of the religious forms found in their civilizations. This will be largely concerned with Fourth and Fifth Race civilizations for the simple reason that the Lemurians, by tradition, had the benefit of learning directly from the presence of their instructors. Later humanity, according to tradition, did not. We commence our considerations on this subject, therefore, with the early Fourth Race, at a time when the idealistic and devotional tendencies of the Atlanteans were beginning to gain in strength and when the psycho-spiritual faculty of sight provided by the Third Eye was beginning to be considered of less interest.

To explain why this redundancy of the Third Eye should have happened is a little difficult and one can only cite the fascination of youth with novelty and change as perhaps being at the source of it. Psycho-spiritual vision functions in a state of being where (by virtue of it involving association with a particular quality of light) there is no real change – merely a coming and going of different groups of spirits, as already described. Our ordinary eyesight, however, functions in a three-dimensional world state which is subject to constant change of form, colour and sound – at least partially due to the nature of cycles of birth, ageing and death. In addition, the objective world has its objective problems and pressures which need to be dealt with objectively – or so we usually think.

There is an adage: 'If you don't use it, you lose it.' So the loss of psycho-spiritual faculty – whilst perhaps quite understandable – inevitably led to human consciousness and understanding becoming generally rather coarser in nature, through natural adaptation to a world which was itself still densifying from a previously ethereal state.

The Sevenfold Cycle Again

This in turn may seem somewhat odd and even illogical until we remember that the first three sub-stages in any cycle (under universal Law) are said to be concerned with the re-expression of the achieved consciousness of the previous cycle. Hence in the case of the individual human being, he or she is not to be considered fully re-incarnate until the age of 21 (3 x 7 = 21). It is only then that the new *evolutionary* cycle commences properly. This is why the age of 21 has for so long, in our present era, been traditionally regarded as the 'coming of age' or 'age of consent'. In the previous (Atlantean) cycle, the coming of age would have been connected with the age of 14 and puberty, when humankind is of course able to recreate itself *physically*.[10]

What we are trying to do here is understand the logic and the logical (metaphysical) sequence involved in the way Nature works to reproduce her own memories. By doing so and by comparing it to our physiological and psychological knowledge of humanity today – itself the logical and sequential expression of an ancient memory – we should be able not only to see the general principles involved, but also to speculate more rationally and logically about the ancient civilizations and cultures of the past, rather than trying to pick them 'out of the air'. The latter is what many 'New Age' theorists often seem to do without considering the logical, accompanying necessities of an ever-active evolutionary process, regulated by watching Intelligence.

The Basis of Evolving Consciousness and Faculty

It is one of those perhaps curious paradoxes of life that it is actually impossible ever to understand something fully. All that one can do is to improve one's understanding of what something is *not*. Therefore, one's perception of Nature's potentials is always developing. The process is fundamentally infinite in Universal Nature.

In the ancient tradition, this principle was always well recognized as a simple fact of human experience. Consequently, it is not surprising that through the process of spiritual individualization, the individual and the group come to an increasingly better understanding of the fact of what it is they have, by choice, left behind – and thus also of the (as yet unknown) potential of what they may face in the future.[11] It is for this reason that the spiritual Path has always been associated with the initial recognition of one's own ignorance, followed by a process of renunciation and self-sacrifice. But what is not so obvious is that the individual must go through the full range of objective and subjective effects and functional capacities generated by the causes which they have themselves set in motion, before they can recognize what is no longer necessary and thus move on to the wider field of perception.

For the simple reason that the Lemurian Third Eye faculty provided only a psycho-spiritual range of perception of *planetary* life, it became necessary for that faculty to be left behind, to give way at a later date for its re-animation in conjunction with a higher form of perceptual consciousness. As that higher form of consciousness was regarded as solar, or extra-planetary in nature, the continued use of the third eye for merely mundane purposes would have been a complete educational distraction and bar to further progress. So it had to be put to one side.

On this basis, therefore, we may logically suggest that the general loss in humanity of natural psycho-spiritual faculty must have been foreseen by the Guides of the Race and appropriate measures taken. It would therefore seem likely that the development of formal religious architecture and observance accompanied the change, with a consequently overall change in humankind's social culture by way of (re)directional compensation. However, there are always cultural 'throwbacks' ... .

I have already suggested that the mid-Fourth (Atlantean) Race period occurred about 4.5 million years ago, at a time when a hugely extended series of planetary cataclysms took place. This wiped from the face of the Earth all

remaining Third Race types, thereby encouraging (by necessity) the unhind-
ered forward evolutionary development of Fourth Race consciousness and its
various cultures.[12] It is from here therefore, that we really concern ourselves
with the cultural changes affecting the Atlantean peoples.

The Downfall of Atlantis through Magical Malpractice

One of the most popularly recurrent aspects of stories associated with Atlantis
is that the cataclysms which eventually destroyed it were the result of the
Atlanteans themselves indulging in 'black magic' practices. Part of this story
originates originally from the *Mahabharata* of Vedic India and other sources,
more latterly from the works of Edgar Cayce. The *Mahabharata* catalogues the
bewildering variety of relationships and battles between a mixture of allegorical spirit groups and Atlantean historical groups, the latter involvings forms
of air travel and thus implying a high level of technological brilliance at a time
when modern anthropology has humanity still wandering around with its
knuckles trailing on the ground.

The issue of Atlantean technology, whatever the truth of the matter, has very
little to do with the real nature of the people of the time. However, as I have
already mentioned, elements of the story of the fight between the black and
white magicians of Ruta, and the flight of the latter and their followers to Asia,
in the last chapter, let me try to put that story in perspective, firstly by suggesting that the biblical 'Exodus from Egypt' of the Israelites is actually based
(in part at least) on what happened in Atlantis. That is why modern scholars
have been unable to find any historical verification whatsoever for it in the
Hebraic or other contemporary traditions.

What the story appears to imply is that the 'black' magicians, rather than
simply carrying out great acts of theurgical wizardry, had more prosaically
managed to harness the raw energies of *elemental* Nature, although perhaps
using magical ceremonial to achieve this.[13] They would thereby have availed
themselves of great prestige for their sophistication and socio-political 'nous'
in providing for the material needs and welfare of the general population of
the time.

However, modern scientific and administrative technology is actually
endeavouring to do exactly the same. Although avowedly for the same supposedly philanthropic reasons, its basic rationale involves regarding Nature
as something useful, to be merely exploited for purposes of consumption –
whether humanitarian in nature or otherwise. Again, modern science –
through rejecting the mediating existence of the *deva* – is endeavouring (completely blindly) to harness purely elemental forces via mere technological
expediency. It thus *automatically* creates distortions of which it is completely

unaware. Many examples are to be found today in the fields of allopathic med-icine and genetic engineering. Here, scientific fascination with its (as yet only partial) discoveries is already laying up potentially immense problems for future generations by trying to sideline Nature's natural processes.[14]

Notwithstanding the increasingly general acceptance of the Gaia concept (*see* Chapter 3), any suggestion of Nature in the round possibly having an evo-lutionary Purpose and consciousness of its own is currently regarded in many quarters (in the West) with laughter and disdain as the imagining of cranks. One can therefore imagine the parallel possibility of Atlantean technologists and politicians similarly disregarding the philosophical and spiritual effects of what they were trying to do 'in pursuit of happiness'.

In other words, they also wished artificially to contain elemental Nature to a permanent cycle of restraint which totally disregarded its natural instincts of allegiance to and balanced control by their more evolved counterparts, the hierarchies of *devas*. Fortunately, the *devas* in general seem subsequently to have managed increasingly to distance themselves from open contact with humanity and have thereby escaped both imprisonment and the possibility of being drawn into all sorts of potentially nefarious practice.

Recognizing the Inner Workings of Nature

Modern humankind believes that by merely 'softening' its exploitation of Nature, this will give Nature the time to regenerate itself – and thus to carry on being exploited. That, in principle, might seem a very sensible attitude and cer-tainly one to be followed in the shorter term. However, as we have already explained at some length in previous chapters, Nature has a definite intelli-gence and sense of purpose which lead to its own natural *longer*-term cycles. Humankind in its wilful ignorance of what is involved, can (and does) only interfere with these constantly at its long-term peril; for Nature fights back in order to maintain its instinctively fundamental rule of harmonic balance.

The problem in Atlantean times seems to have derived from the intellectual arrogance of the 'black' magicians in believing that they could completely subjugate Nature to their will, instead of recognizing the need merely to work *with* Nature. But their un-natural intentions would very logically have led to unnatural results, because Nature is the ultimate arbiter of what it will or will not accept.

The modern ecological movement has managed to confirm to some extent how the subtle balance of Nature can be affected in both the short and medium term by human technological intervention. However, political and financial self-interest ignores this as far as it can and spends a huge amount of effort and money in merely trying to find less disputational alternative technological means of achieving the same results – which merely 'puts off the evil day'.

It would appear that the 'white' magicians of Atala or Atlantis, with the benefit of their *unselfishly* orientated 'inner' knowledge as to the subtler work-ings of Nature in the bigger picture,[15] could actually see that 'evil day' coming in their own era, because a point of no return had by then already been reached. Nature was on the point of violent sympathetic reaction – very probably in line with the critical point of a major astrophysical or astrologi-cally-based cycle which would have been seen as providing the natural 'trigger' for an associated geological chain reaction.

According to tradition, the magi of the 'right hand path' thus made due preparation for the mass escape (northwards) of themselves and their follow-ers from the southern Atlantean island continent of Ruta, which seems to have been located around or just to the east of the present Gulf of Mexico. Thus just before the cataclysms struck, the main mass headed for the high plateaux of what now constitutes Central Asia whilst others headed for the northern island continent of Daitya. This at that time (according to what little information is currently available to us) seems to have stretched as far north as a line between modern Newfoundland and Brittany, whilst also incorporating Iberia and the lands in and around the whole of the western Mediterranean.

The Post-Deluge Civilizations and Cultures

The point of mentioning this particular sequence is that it gives us certain clues as to the probable nature of Atlantean civilization and culture *after* the cataclysm of 4.5 million years ago. This was leading up to the time – suppos-edly about 400,000–500,000 years ago – when elements of the interbred (hence Cro-Magnon) early Aryans and Atlantean types migrated eastwards to populate Egypt and thereby provide it with its first civilization and culture. Any civilization which had so forthrightly rejected living under a materialistic cultural regime would almost certainly have tended to move back towards a naturally agrarian type of society, without undue dependence on 'high tech' technology.

That is not to suggest that such a society would have gone back en masse to being simple 'hunter-gatherers'. Having already had a well established and sophisticated urban culture for millions of years, those principles already learned would undoubtedly have been put straight back into practice, but this time in line with a very definitely anti-materialistic religion and social priorities.

The Origins and Practice of Voodoo

As we are told from the available traditions, Ruta was very largely destroyed by an extended period of vast cataclysms beginning some 850,000 years ago, whilst much of Daitya was similarly destroyed about 270,000 years ago. However, Ruta's soubriquet of the 'Dark Island', apparently because of continuing obsession with essentially selfish 'black' magical practices, may well have been the origin of those forms of 'Voodoo' in adjacent West Africa which later translated themselves so easily across the Atlantic with the slave trade during the 18th and 19th centuries and which still exist today in countries like Niger, Benin and Mali.

As described earlier in the chapter, Voodoo is based upon a highly debased form of shamanism in which the lowest types of elemental spirits are conjured through the use of fetishes and blood sacrifice. The principle of the fetish is that it supposedly contains a captive elemental entity which is bound to do the will of the conjuror or shaman. The rationale behind blood sacrifice itself is that the blood carries (some of) the very life of the soul, whilst all power ultimately lies with the soul. However, as earlier suggested, the soul entity is, in reality, the organism of a particular type of *deva*. Hence the black magician adopting this particular type of practice is in a very direct sense endeavouring to conjure the powers in Nature in order to wreak his/her will. The fact that a particular type of animal or bird is used in the sacrifice – usually a cockerel[16] in the voodoo tradition – has to do with the fact that particular deva groups are regarded as directly associated with certain animal species and also with certain functions in Nature. As also mentioned earlier, the latter idea is still to be found in the Islamic tradition even today.

Prehistoric Magical Practice in the Americas

What is known in academia of magical practice in the Americas tends to be somewhat fragmented, by virtue of the knowledge having been handed down within tribal families, largely privately, by word of mouth. Whether or not the tribal shaman was always drawn from the same family (like the hereditary Hebrew Levites and Zadokites), we cannot say; but certainly, every tribe or sub-tribal group had its shaman, without which it could not expect to survive. It would seem that each tribal shaman was also expected to maintain contact with the others in his tribal family nation, of which there was not only a paramount chief, but also a paramount shaman.

Apart from being the source of such ceremonial conjurations as those involved in rain-making or psychically calling the animals into or towards the tribal hunting ground, the tribal shaman in historic times was effectively the all-purpose magician, theologian, doctor and counsellor for the tribe. However, it would seem not unlikely that in previous millennia, where urban civilization existed (as amongst the Toltecs and Maya, for example), a rather more formally organized structure also existed in parallel.

Modern archaeological and anthropological research in Central America has come to the conclusion that the Aztecs and Maya practised blood sacrifice on a wide scale, using human victims.[17] The fact of this practice, by the Aztecs at least, was visually verified by horrified Spanish conquistadores in the 16th century, who then associated it with the seemingly also horrific faces of god-figures found on Mayan and Aztec temple reliefs.[18] However, it seems unlikely that it was by then anything other than another degenerate form of psycho-spiritual practice – degenerate because its practitioners failed to understand original concepts from a previous Toltec and/or Mayan culture. The latter (despite superficially appearing to promulgate such barbaric practices) appear in fact to have been using them purely as graphic religious metaphors, like many other Mysteries-based systems around the world.

One might go so far here as to reiterate the fact that any debased form of magical or pseudo-religious ritual based upon necromancy and blood sacrifice is necessarily the product of a society which, through panic (often in the wake of a period of irreligious materialism), has lost its way psycho-spiritually. Such a society – for some or other reason deprived of a truly spiritually awakened figurehead – has thus fallen into the trap of believing that 'the gods' (or rather the elemental forces in Nature) need to be appeased in this abject manner, through having lost faith in their own essential human divinity. Unfortunately, distortion and misunderstanding of the central principles of sympathetic magical practice often lead ignorant practitioners down this dangerous and ignoble path, even today.

Whilst disenchanted elements of Rutan civilization drifted southwards, westwards and northwards to generate the ancestors of the native 'Indian' tribes and nations of those areas, it also appears that some of them migrated even further westwards and south-westwards to became the ancestors of the modern Polynesian and Dravidian peoples. As parts of the original Polynesian culture still survive relatively intact today, it is perhaps worthwhile briefly considering its own approach to the sacred Mystery Tradition.

Magical Practice in the Polynesian Sacred Tradition

Modern anthropological orthodoxy – following the neo-Darwinian assumption that humankind first emerged from ancient apes of East Africa – believes that the natives of the Americas arrived from Siberia via the islands, or an ice-age landbridge, of the Bering Strait, some 20,000–40,000 years ago. However, the ancient traditions take the very opposite viewpoint – that the peoples of Asia were in fact migrants from Atlantis *via* North America, following the cataclysmic break-up of the main Atlantean civilization some 750,000 years ago. The Polynesian peoples of Oceania, however, appear to be prehistoric Atlantean migrants from the Americas who travelled due west (rather than northwest via the Bering Strait) at an earlier time, when there were still many more landmasses in the Pacific Ocean than there are now.

The Polynesian magical tradition is known as the *huna* – which term seems to have its origin in the common ancient word '*khu*' or plain '*hu*', meaning 'spirit'. Like other basically Atlantean traditions, the traditional Polynesian sees Nature in the round as his or her place of worship and also of invocatory or magical practice. For this reason, every different stone, plant and place is given a different name, because infused with the vitality of accompanying Nature spirits.[19]

The Ancients took the view that to name something properly (that is, with its true psycho-spiritual name) was to command it. Therefore to summon or command Nature with accuracy necessitated a knowledge of names, delivered with proper and directed intent. For this reason, every child was given not only a familiar name, but also a spiritual name which was to be used purely for spiritual purposes. Today of course, the understanding of the potency of names has declined beyond the point of absurdity, due to the lazily misguided Western approach to written and, more particularly, spoken language. It is interesting to note to what degree this abuse has itself led to a basic loss of that common social respect which enables human society to function coherently and happily.

Shamanism

The former shamanic tradition of the Fourth Race consciousness having evolved into the more centrally organized priestly tradition of the Fifth Race consciousness (by evolutionary necessity as much as anything else), shamanism amongst the Indo-Caucasian peoples has become increasingly less apparent – and increasingly more suspect. Consequently, the modern New Age tendency to refer to any form of Nature-orientated invocative tradition as 'shamanistic', is actually somewhat misplaced.

The Druids for example, were *not* shamans, but – like the Brahmans of India and the priesthoods of Egypt and Chaldea and Babylonia – were scholar-priests who practised their rituals in specific locations of gathering (such as Stonehenge or Avebury in England), openly known to the population at large. The shaman, *per se*, does not (and probably never did) use a temple or *constructionally* dedicated place of invocation or worship, even though he may have habitually used a natural one, in conjunction with ritualistic para-phernalia, as some native North Americans did with totem poles.

Astrology

Astrology is commonly regarded by modern scholars as an aspect of ancient superstitious practice, but it is no such thing. Astrology is based upon a combination of astronomical and other scientific knowledge concerning the nature of both sympathetic association and the law of cycles. These are subjects of which mainstream modern science knows virtually nothing, although a few scientists do faintly suspect that there may be more to them than meets the eye.

The Atlanteans were, according to tradition, the first to practise astrology as both a science and an art and it was they who supposedly passed on their knowledge to the real ancient Egyptians and also to the ancestors of the Brahmans of India, who in turn passed it on to the Sumerians, Chaldeans and Assyrians.[20] Whilst astrology was practised throughout the ancient world (and is still practised in India today, even at government levels), it too became degenerate. Instead of its originally intended use, for purposes of determining the best opportunities for spiritual development, it has progressively become a tool for indulging personal self-concerns and aims of material profit, often through mere superstition. Regrettably, however, it is merely the degenerate form to which modern scholarship has turned its critical attention, again using knee-jerk prejudice to cloud its own better long-term judgment.

The Magical Traditions of the Mediterranean Peoples

We might be expected to turn finally to the magical traditions of the neo-Atlanteans – the Guanche, Berbers and Etruscans, as well as the Egyptians. However, little can actually be said of them in detail, other than that these peoples were evidently very aware of the subject of magic and practised it quite extensively in relation to their particular religions. Again, however, archaeologists and anthropologists have laid so much emphasis on the purely negative or corrupted versions of magic practised by these cultures in their latter periods, that it is pretty well impossible (without writing a complete book on the subject) to disentangle the facts from the truth. I am unwilling to add to the mass of misinterpretation and distortions of fact arrived at by past scholarly ignorance by further focussing on merely corrupted versions of magical practice around the globe today. So, having attempted to describe the true basis of magic in the earlier part of this chapter, I shall have to leave this subject here – for the time being at least.

Chapter Eighteen

·

ANCIENT SCIENCE AND TECHNOLOGY

'We explain human civilisation as developing through various practical inventions like pottery, writing or the wheel. This is not based on an understanding of the ancient world, nor is it the view of the Ancients themselves. It is what is convenient to our particular mind-set and our technological and materialistic values. It is important that we examine what the Ancients themselves say and how the statements of different ancient cultures fit together, not how it would appear to us today, as if our values pertained to all of human history ... What it means to be a human being, or what human civilisation means, must be examined in its total context, all of history, not just that of modern man.'[1]

Today's anthropologists are all too keen to tell us how recent human civilization and culture are by suggesting that humankind has 'gone from hunter-gatherer to the Moon' in only a few millennia. But, without denigrating today's scientific and technological achievements, this is a long way from the rather limited actuality of what has really been achieved in that short space of time. As we shall see in this chapter, the *principles* behind what we take for granted as the scientific achievement of the 17th and 18th centuries (and thus subsequently of the industrial revolution of the 18th and 19th centuries) were, seemingly, already well known in ancient times. However, they had long since been forgotten – probably several times over. In addition, the very foundations of all of our modern astrophysical sciences and atomic/quantum theory are themselves actually based upon that ancient knowledge and associated practical expertise.[2]

Despite culture actually having very little in reality to do with technology, we today tend to take it unquestioningly for granted that any society which was not or is not technologically based, must be relatively backward or lacking in cultural (particularly intellectual) advancement. One might be forgiven for thinking that industrial growth was intended to reduce the burden of manual work on society and to make it socially more philanthropic. Yet our techno-logically-orientated society is in fact based upon the primacy of the 'cultural' foundations of commercialism and the profit motive.

Scientific research in the 20th century and today has become almost entirely orientated towards either profitability or political considerations. Industry – these days largely based upon international market and stock market pressures – has become a diffused juggernaut which even the leaders of the world's largest countries find it difficult to control. But, take away these purely com-mercial priorities and there would be left little or no practical incentive for large-scale industrialization and technology, even in our modern civilization.

Added to this, however, we have religious secularism also taken to an extreme. By virtue of an equivalent, reciprocal reaction to religious dogmatism in the West and the Middle East, a scientifically based demi-atheism has taken general hold in the West. This infection is spreading relentlessly towards the East, paradoxically through the central idea of neo-Darwinism (as embodied in the atheistic ideologies of socialism and communism, under which much of Eurasia was governed in the 20th century). It encompasses the belief that, because man has supposedly been evolved from the apes, the concept of Deity – if not altogether redundant – is of secondary or even tertiary consideration and priority.

The Ancient View

When we look at the traditions of the Ancients, it rapidly becomes very clear that at the core of their 'material' concerns (apart from the very basic ones of providing food, drink and shelter) was the constant search for increasingly greater *spiritual* understanding, as well as objective daily expression to associ-ated *spiritual* considerations. Much of this gave rise amongst the masses merely to ritualistically based religious observance in support of leaderships. However, it is clear that amongst the spiritually motivated intelligentsia of ancient times, this search led to the appearance of extraordinarily sophisti-cated and usefully beautiful architecture and engineering projects – based upon a foundational knowledge of universal principles.

These projects (like the pyramids and temples of Egypt) were intended to complement deity (as an outward expression of it) whilst at the same time clearly making life productive for the advancement of human civilization, through communal involvement. However, the very idea of putting mere profitability or technological superiority before *spiritual* concerns would have been greeted by all with shock and horror, as putting man before God, even where Deity was perceived as a subjective 'spark of the divine' within man himself.

Whenever one comes across the idea of science and technology in relation to the name Atlantis, the automatic inference, as far as many are concerned, is that it must have to do with giant energy-producing crystals, death rays and space ships from other star systems. However, these are (almost) all the products of the fevered imagination of 20th-century film makers and novelists, the exception being that of 'the sleeping prophet', Edgar Cayce, who first mentioned such energy crystals.[3] However, this chapter is really concerned only with listing the rather more mundane practicalities of everyday life with which the intelligent (late) Atlantean would have had to deal. As we shall see, technology for them was, again, ever subservient to prior spiritual orientations and considerations.

One might well ask, how do I propose to talk about technologies that must be over 11,000 years old and of which there are no proven archaeological remnants? The answer to that is threefold. First of all, by direct reference, through mention in the historical records of later cultures. Second, by circumstantial evidence and associated inference. Third, by virtue of the fact that some of them, or their products, are actually still visible.

Whilst the first two of these may not be considered entirely satisfactory, they are really all we have to go on in certain cases, for the simple reason that almost all complex technologies and their objective products are the products of the minds of specialists. As specialization involves not only specialist minds but also a chain of supporting services and materials in response to a given set of environmental needs, they are highly vulnerable to changing circumstances and also to simple availability. Not surprisingly, all such materials eventually break up or are otherwise corrupted or re-used by adaptation for something else anyway. For example, over the last millennium even the limestone casing stones of the pyramids have been taken away by locals and used either for building or merely for burning in kilns.

Given this situation, all that I can hope to do is to provide enough generalized information to furnish an equally generalized and retrospective idea of what sort of socio-technological environment the Atlanteans might have created and lived in. But, as we shall see, the available information – although limited – is, when put together, certainly capable of demonstrating a very high level of cultural mentality and technical capability, even in those far-off times.

Whilst I may be criticized for not approaching this subject in more detail from the point of view of how the (necessarily later) Atlanteans and their successors actually dealt with the technical problems which they faced on land and sea (and also in the air, because aerial transport is mentioned by several sources), that cannot be helped. There have been plenty of books and television programmes over recent years which have endeavoured to deal with this issue in relation to the Romans, Egyptians, Chaldeans and even further back into the Palaeolithic era. Whatever evidence is to be mentioned here will necessarily be merely in the form of commenting on either (a) the tools used, or (b) a description of the technology, or (c) the products of that technology, some of which have already been mentioned earlier in the book. So, given that structured approach, let us start with technology in general.

Tools, Instruments and Habitations

It is generally acknowledged by anthropologists that the creative imagination involved in toolmaking is what distinguishes humans from the other higher animals.[4] Without tools, technology is impossible. Leaving aside modern man-made materials such as plastic, tools are normally made of wood, stone or metal; but it is the use of metal which really indicates the highest level of intellectual discrimination needed to sustain an economically viable social system, because it involves an analytical knowledge of metallurgical and chemical processes and how to harness and adapt them.

Notwithstanding this, some natural tools appear to be much more efficient than man-made ones, or otherwise far less expensive or difficult to buy and maintain, or less cumbersome. For example, the ancient Egyptians used immensely sharp and naturally sterile obsidian knives for surgical purposes,[5] whilst the pestle and mortar are fundamentally simple tools and have traditionally been made of wood, even today. Pottery and brickwork have, since time immemorial, involved the use of all sorts of fired clays for different purposes. One thus has to ask, using basic logic, why a naturally organized society would even bother with breakable and difficult-to-replace man-made tools and artefacts if other natural implements could be locally obtained and replaced without undue cost or effort.

As to housing, the popular idea of ancient humans as 'cavemen' is a myth. There is no doubt that in some parts of the world, *some* people lived in caves – but then some few still do so today, for a variety of reasons – including ease (caves are 'ready-made') and comfort, as well as security or a wish for cultural privacy. By virtue of the fact that caves are naturally protected from the ravages of the elements, and often generate their own micro-climates, ancient artefacts and skeletal remains can still frequently be found intact in them today. But this on its own does not mean that ancient humankind must, as a general rule, have lived in caves and used crude stone tools any more than the vast mass of modern humankind could be said as a general rule to live in skyscraper blocks or to use computers or to fly regularly in aeroplanes.

Quite apart from the fact that ancient inhabited settlements were often deserted once the local natural resources ran out – due for example to climatic change or local cataclysms – it has been proved by archaeologists that some of the ruined towns and cities which they have discovered have been built over previous ones, sometimes even three or more previous ones – as is the case, for example, at Tihuanaco in Bolivia. But it has not been possible to confirm just how far back in time the first of these was originally built. Such ruins built on previous ruins and far older foundations are to be found all over the world and they show beyond all shadow of doubt that humankind has been constructing buildings for untold ages, not just the last 10,000–12,000 years.

For example, Michael Cremo and Richard Thompson mention one archaeological find involving block stone walls having been found in 1928 nearly two miles underground in a coal mine in Heavener, Oklahoma.[6] This discovery was roughly dated at over 280 million years. Another such find involved a slate wall, with several lines of hieroglyphs on it, discovered at Hammondville, Ohio in 1868, again deep underground in the middle of a coal seam.[7]

As regards the prehistoric fabrication of metal instruments and other artefacts, Cremo and Thompson's review of old archaeological finds includes metal technology also going back several million years. For example, in 1852 a metallic vase (of silver and other metals) was found at Dorchester, Massachusetts in a Pre-Cambrian rock stratum, which would make it several hundred million years old. In 1891, a gold chain was found (yet again jammed inside a carboniferous coal deposit) in Morrisonville, Illinois – suggesting an age of over 250 million years. Similarly, in 1949 an iron cup was found in Oklahoma, wrapped inside another coal deposit over 300 million years old. In 1968, several metallic tubes were discovered in a chalk deposit at St Jean de Livet in France, indicating an age of some 65 million years.[8]

In purely practical terms, it is not logically possible for archaeological finds to confirm with such consistency man-made relics dating back millions and millions of years *unless* human civilization and technological culture also existed at those times. Mainstream archaeology has never been able to explain these finds in any manner that might be considered remotely logical. Indeed, it has seldom tried. We are therefore forced to accept what the evidence is telling us, even if the dating is slightly out by even a few tens of millions of years. In short, ancient prehistoric humankind possessed sophisticated (although now unknown) technology and was not merely a fabricator and user of stone or wood tools.

Nature's Own Destructive Powers

It needs to be taken into consideration that Nature also frequently and ruthlessly takes back man-made habitations and other artificial structures, such as river levees and bridges, reducing them all to invisibility. The sea has provably claimed townships and even cities all over the world and is still doing so today, either gradually or by the destructive effects of tsunamis and hurricanes, whilst monsoon rains, river floods, volcanoes, earthquakes, forest fires and mountain mudslides have totally obliterated all trace of whole villages and townships, frequently along with their inhabitants.[9] In addition, the further one goes back in time the more apparent it becomes that most prehistoric civilizations routinely used cremation instead of burial, thereby leaving no palaeontological remains whatsoever.

Given the far-reaching and frequent extent to which such natural processes of destruction occur, it is hardly surprising that, over a period of many decimillennia, the whole geography of the planet has changed beyond all recognition. How then, in all seriousness, can modern anthropology expect to find that complete sequence of human civilization and culture which it so fervently seeks? But, in addition, how can it make the assumptions it does about human urban civilization only commencing about 12,000 years ago?

The Heritage of the Most Recent Ancient Civilizations

Our own Western educational system appears to be the product of a mere 5,000 years of accumulated Renaissance, Roman, Greek, Egyptian, Chinese and Indo-Chaldean intellectual and artistic input. However, the ancient Egyptian, Etruscan and Indo-Chaldean systems of 5,000 years ago all appear to have sprung ready-made into existence, which – despite archaeologists' refusal to acknowledge the fact – clearly indicates that they were the legacies of yet earlier and just as sophisticated cultural systems.

As we mentioned earlier, the Etruscans of 2,700 years ago were of the opinion that their own literary culture was at least 8,000 years old. The Egyptians confirmed that their culture went back well over 50,000 years. Yet, as previously mentioned, the Hindu Brahmins regard their own culture as having been over a million years old, whilst the Greeks were openly of the opinion that the Assyrian culture was several hundred thousand years old.

Of the various civilizations and cultures known to history, however, the only ones going back several thousand years that have left reasonably reliable records of their existence and technologies, are those of ancient Egypt and India, which as we have already suggested, were, in any case, closely related. It is therefore on these that we shall tend to concentrate, more particularly on Egypt because of its much greater proximity to the ancient Atlantean civilization which we suggest as having been located in the area of northwest Africa and the Canary Islands. However, much of what we have to say about Egypt will automatically be true of the ancient Indo-Persian culture which generated the civilizations of both Sumer and also Chaldea, as well, probably, as Assyria too.

The Ancient Egyptian Culture

As Diodorus Siculus and Clement of Alexandria confirmed, the Egyptian educational system was based upon the 42 sacred *Books of Tehuti*[10] and the curriculum included mathematics, geometry, optics, principles of engineering, surveying, law and ethics, chemistry and medicine, botany, astronomy and cosmography, geography and cartography, music, theology, drawing and oratory. Now why, it has to be asked, would any civilization have such a broad and highly defined educational system for its more able minds unless there were an essentially practical side to it? Knowledge is based upon practical experience as well as theory and any truly sophisticated educational system must thus of necessity be the product of several thousand years (at least) of cultured thought.

As Herodotus confirmed, the Egyptians were obsessed with the spiritual nature of things down to the very tiniest detail. He consequently drew the distinct impression that their whole culture – including the intellectual side – involved an essentially religious expression of their underlying spiritual belief system. Yet here we are faced with the fact that their highly sophisticated educational institutions also taught essentially practical disciplines, whilst their range of knowledge and the quality of their teachers was the subject of unbounded admiration throughout the ancient world. This, surely, is no paradox. It merely indicates that their religion and philosophy were more thoroughly grounded in general reality than ours are – yet with a much wider spiritual orientation and basis.

Mathematics and Geometry

In the area of mathematics and geometry, the Egyptians clearly understood the principles and applications of Pi, Phi, the laws of perspective and proportion inherent in the Golden Ratio, and the use of algebraic equations to solve complex problems of both an abstract and a practical nature. Euclid was himself an Egyptian and head of the mathematics department at the great university of Alexandria in the 1st century AD. That such knowledge was available several thousand years earlier, however, is implicit in the engineering construction and geometry of millennia-old pyramid and temple structures. So, we can regard the knowledge itself as being far, far older still.

Although the basis of the Egyptians' use of spherical trigonometry appears puzzling to us, there is at least an indication that they used a type of computer for the associated calculations. In the Middle and Far East generally, the use of the abacus has been known for thousands of years; even today, the speed with which a skilled person can use it is quite remarkable and certainly, in most cases, as fast as a modern calculator. As mentioned earlier, the ancient mariners of the Mediterranean area also seem to have used for navigational purposes a multi-geared, astronomical device called by the Greeks an *antikythera*, the sole remaining example of which is now in the Athens Museum.

The mathematical and geometrical knowledge of the Ancients nevertheless had much wider applications. They used it to calculate the size of the Earth and then used spherical trigonometry to produce maps which contained details of both latitude and longitude. Some temple drawings show early replicas of the navigational sextant, by which mariners define their latitudinal position by reference to the Sun and stars.

The Egyptians were of course great geographical surveyors. That they must also have understood the land surveying principles involved in the use of the theodolite is also confirmed because their longer straight lines would have been impossible to achieve without it. The (supposedly later) Etruscans are actually known to have employed a form of theodolite called a *groma* in conjunction with another instrument called a *chorobates*,[11] somewhat similar to a modern spirit level. So it is entirely possible that the use of such instruments was common throughout the ancient world. We also know for a fact that the Egyptians – and almost certainly all others too – used cartographical measurement by triangulation.

Today we use a form of telescope attached to the theodolite. However, as Robert Temple has recently confirmed, the Ancients had telescopes, binoculars and spectacles over 4,500 years ago at least.[12] That they understood the associated principles of optics and the grinding and polishing of natural crystal to form lenses (as well as actually making clear and skilfully engraved glassware), is also now evident. But that in turn necessitates an originating knowledge of the principles of refraction and reflection, plus the associated mathematics. It cannot be done reliably by purely off-the-cuff methods.

The Pharos lighthouse at ancient Alexandria (one of the 'Seven Wonders of the Ancient World') was not only capable of shining a light which could be seen at sea from a distance of many dozens of miles, it apparently also had a reflective dish (probably made of very highly polished copper) which allowed approaching ships apparently to be seen at a distance of over 100 miles (160 km).[13]

Building and Construction

In the above fields, ancient knowledge and experience was considerable and is self-evident even today. Highly sophisticated water supply and underground drainage systems (using clay drainage pipeware) plus associated bathing and toilet facilities, have been found in the ruined townships and cities of such widespread places as Mohenjo Daro on the River Indus, Carthage in northwest Africa and Knossos in Crete. But the same systems have been found in the towns and cities of the Maya and Inca of Central and South America, plus those of the Etruscans of northern Italy, as well as amongst the Romans. The same is just as true of the ancient Egyptians, Babylonians and Chaldeans. Sub-floor warm air central heating – generally used by the Romans in cooler climes – was also known to other nations.

The associated design expertise, involving permanent water flows, some-times over dozens of miles, necessitated extensive surveying knowledge plus the associated technology for calculating gradients, together with the ancillary building expertise for cutting or forming stone channels and building viaducts or underground tunnels. But the sheer amount of work and forethought involved makes it crystal clear that these were considered at the time to be very long-term projects indeed, not subject to the permanently frequent changes induced by our modern markets.[14] The high quality of the workmanship also confirms that these skills and knowledge were not developed merely within the space of a few generations.

Although housebuilding appears always to have followed fairly similar con-struction techniques, using mud/clay bricks and tiles, plus timber and stone, the building of temples and other sacred buildings is another matter, certainly throughout the East and also in the Americas. We have already talked of the altogether gigantic stones to be found in temple walls at such places as Giza, Ollantaytambo, Tiuhuanaco, Tiryns[15] and Commagene, many of these being over 500 tonnes in weight and a few over 1,000 tonnes.

Not only have these huge stones been cut to shape to fit against each other in quirkily odd patterns, with an almost imperceptible joint (containing no mortar) but they have also been somehow manoeuvred into place in a manner that would severely test (if not defy) the capacities of the world's largest mod-ern crane and its driver. Furthermore, the stones have been held in position – against potential earthquake activity – by cast-iron butterfly ties which have self-evidently been poured *in situ* into carefully cut incisions in the stonework. That the butterfly ties were forged *in situ* (thereby necessitating the use of mobile forges), again makes clear that mineral technology and knowledge of building construction techniques were well advanced at a time (probably tens of thousands of years ago) when modern anthropology regards humankind as having still been wandering around in skins as a 'hunter-gatherer'.

The ability of the Egyptians to drill and cut the hardest granite with the accuracy of a modern diamond cutter is yet another inexplicable phenomenon because no tools capable of such work and workmanship have ever been found anywhere in the ancient world, let alone Egypt. It has already been shown that the fineness of the cutting of the internal sides of the sarcophagus in the King's Chamber of the Great Pyramid would have required technology of the quality of modern lasers. However, archaeologists have (perhaps understandably) avoided pursuing this issue very far.

Architecture

So much has already been written about the truly extraordinary scale and design of the architecture of ancient Egypt that one would only be repeating matters to mention them again in detail here. However, one might reiterate in passing the suggestion that the original structures were clearly designed and built in the depths of prehistory, according to a master plan of which modern archaeology knows nothing.

The same is true of the great temple of Teotihuacan in Mexico, with its giant pyramids so reminiscent of Giza. The natives told the invading Spaniards that these great structures had been built by an unknown people long before their own times. They themselves had simply occupied a deserted urban environment. Modern archaeologists have, in the main, merely ignored such remarks without further comment – evidently because of the many other uncomfortable questions which could inevitably arise from pursuing them.

It is a curious fact that the Romans did not start their own really large-scale construction projects until after they had come into direct liaison with the Greeks following Alexander's contact with Egyptian civilization in the 4th century BC. It was shortly after this that the Punic Wars commenced between Rome and Carthage, doubtless because of the secessionary Graeco-Etruscans of Magna Graecia in central and southern Italy deciding that now was the time to strike out for their own independence.

Cranes and Lifting Principles

The general orthodoxy today is that the Ancients used a somewhat *ad hoc* mixture of grease and rollers to move heavy blocks of stone up gradients of piled sand and then swung them into place using levers and some form of small crane. The inevitably ensuing damage to the blocks (particularly with limestone) would, however, be obvious – yet there is no evidence of any such distress to the stonework. Nor is there – except in one single localized (and still questionable) case within the temple of Karnak – any evidence of the literally *millions* of tonnes of sand needed to carry out major construction projects – such as pyramid building – in this way. In fact, the temple of Karnak was, when re-discovered by Europeans in the late 18th century, full of desert sand, stacked by the winds to a height of some 30–40 ft (9–12 m), almost to the top of the temple pillar capitals. Drawings taken at the time and later confirm this situation. So, the suggestion that this particular heap of sand was in fact part of an original construction site is patently ludicrous.[16]

Whilst the Ancients also understood the principles involved in leverage and are known to have used both the A-frame and the block and tackle to lift heavy loads of up to several tonnes in weight and to convey them into position locally, this is a far cry from lifting loads of hundreds of tonnes. Bearing in mind that some of these huge stones have been brought from quarries literally *hundreds* of miles away, with intervening valleys, hills and rivers in between, one can only wonder at how they might have been transported in the depths of prehistory, when our own most sophisticated technology today could not manage it.

Today, we have no knowledge of counterweighted cranes having been used in those days. However, such technical knowledge and expertise must have been available to make such construction work possible. So where today are the remains of their lifting tools?

To listen to archaeologists talk about these and other such matters, one would think that the Ancients, in order to achieve their ends, used merely intelligent guesswork based upon past experience. But any engineer or surveyor will tell you very quickly that such experience would border on unacceptable recklessness, involving immediate and ever-present danger to the lives of all those involved in the project. The early Egyptians, at least, certainly did not use slaves and their care in all matters was legendary. So why should such recklessness and lack of professionalism have been any more acceptable in those times than it is now? On the contrary, as we know, the Egyptians were fixated about detail in every aspect of life; so the chances of their being so slapdash are precisely nil.

Civil and Hydrological Engineering in Egypt

It is of course known that the ancient Egyptians quarried their red granite at Aswan and then used great engineering skills to convey their immensely heavy cargoes (some of them over 100 tonnes) often hundreds of miles down the River Nile. That was achieved using multiple barges in tandem with each other and using the natural forces of buoyancy and hydraulic pressure to counter the loads. However, they must have been able to calculate these loads and buoyancies using the equivalent of algebraic equations, founded on the knowledge of the tolerances of the materials being used. But even after all this, and after also cutting canals from the main river to the areas of the temples, they still had to transport these huge blocks to their final resting places in the temple grounds and then finally manoeuvre them into position (involving lifting) without breaking or otherwise damaging them.

The Egyptians' skills in the field of civil engineering generally are really breathtaking. First of all, I have elsewhere suggested that in order to bring the Nile under a reasonable degree of control, they built cataract dams to slow down its flood waters at various positions along the Upper Nile, from Aswan nearly to Khartoum.[17] The bland and unquestioning assumption by Egypt-ologists that the cataracts were natural is manifestly absurd.

In addition to their known re-engineering of the Nile at Memphis – sup-posedly in the time of 'Menes' (the reputed first pharaoh of Egypt) – the Egyptians appear to have literally re-routed the Nile itself just to the north-east of Aswan at a place called Silsila. As Wallis Budge tells us, the bed of the Nile now flows something like 1 mile (1.6 km) to the west of where it originally lay, the old bed having subsequently been used by the Egyptians for quarries.[18]

Even more amazing than this, however, is the tradition that, of the originally seven mouths of the Nile, only three or four were natural. The others were dug out by hand – a feat involving not only huge manpower, but also the necessary use of very extensively applied coffer dam and pumping technology to stave off collapse whilst the excavation works were in progress. The sheer volume of material needing to be dug out and carried away – millions and millions of tonnes, in the most difficult and hazardous of conditions – is simply awe-inspiring. To undertake such a project today would require vast reserves of manpower, the most sophisticated technology and huge amounts of finance.

Further down the Nile is the gigantic Faiyum Depression, to the southwest of Cairo. This great 'natural' reservoir – originally some 360 miles (579 km) in circumference (the same distance as the length of the original Egyptian Mediterranean coastline) – was very largely dug out by hand in very ancient times, to enable the overflow waters from the Nile, when in flood, to be retained rather than wasted by flowing straight out into the Mediterranean. This great reservoir was connected to the Nile just north of Abydos by a canal roughly 360 miles long and some 66–98 ft (20–30 m) across, which still exists today.

Notwithstanding all this, there is no mention in the ancient Egyptian texts or temple hieroglyphs of anything remotely like it, even by inference. But then, even the building of the Great Pyramid at Giza only rates a mention because of Herodotus having been told an unbelievable old tale about it. The literally dozens of other pyramids in Egypt and the Sphinx also rate no mention. But why? Any modern civilization from Greek or Roman times onwards would have wanted to trumpet such achievements from the housetops and would certainly have left extensive inscriptions on their monuments to remind future generations.[19]

The ancient Egyptians – as we have already seen – possessed very consider-able hydrological engineering knowledge and experience. They understood the power inherent in the current of the River Nile (calling it by the name of the Nile god Hapi) and they knew how to reduce its force (using cataracts) and how to channel it using canalization. If they knew how to contain and make use of the sea breezes for purposes of powering their sailing vessels, it seems somewhat unlikely that their engineers failed to grasp that the same principles could be harnessed in relation to water power in some or other way. We take it for granted that the 'Archimedean screw' did not exist before the time of Archimedes himself. But this is again an assumption, as scholars themselves today admit.

Roman Mechanical Engineering

As we can see from the extant works of the Roman architect Vitruvius, who lived 2,000 years ago at the time of the emperor Augustus, most of our currently known mechanical engineering principles were already highly sophisticated by his time. His tenth book is devoted to describing these principles, which even involved a highly developed understanding of acoustics for theatrical construction purposes.

The Romans were otherwise proficient in the use of syphonic principles to make water travel over difficult obstacles. They also understood that water expands under pressure, specifically when heated, and would undoubtedly have used this knowledge in other functional areas. However, such knowledge also appears to date back to Etruscan times and it could thus extend back several millennia further.

It is well known that the Romans understood the principle of the pump – and thus also of the valve mechanism. These – together with pipework and (natural resin-based or bituminous) joints – form the basis of the science of hydraulics, involving the capacity to lift heavy loads by mechanical means, or to shift water from one place to another.[20] But there is every reason to believe that the Romans again inherited the knowledge and expertise from their predecessors, the Etruscans, or from the Egyptians whose use of bitumen is well established. Modern sceptics would probably suggest that since the pipework and joints have never been found, this is pure supposition. However, although metal pipes corrode faster than virtually all other metal artefacts, some really ancient examples have indeed been found.[21]

Mining Engineering

The fact of mineral technology's use and the capacity to contain vast water pressures whilst digging and removing rocks and soil, is plainly indicative of the fact that the pre-historic Ancients were totally unfazed by the thought of gigantic engineering projects of this sort. However, such confidence only comes from having a very thorough knowledge and experience indeed of everything to do with the associated engineering skills plus specialized knowledge of materials and their capacities and qualities. But again, such skill and knowledge does not materialize from scratch in the space of a few generations, or even a few centuries.

Earlier I mentioned the Rio Tinto mines in southern Spain as being at least 8,000 years old. These mines have been dug to a depth of several hundred feet, with evidently associated hydrological engineering *in situ* to get rid of naturally rising artesian waters. But that in turn must have required at least mechanical pumps and pipework with reliable joints and valve mechanisms.

It is known that the Roman military engineers had these and, one can reasonably assume by association, that they derived their knowledge from their immediate predecessors, the Etruscans, who already knew how to build excellent roads and bridges, as well as how to drain and dredge land very effectively for various purposes. But then, if Egyptian civilization was well over 50,000 years old, and Assyrian and Indo-Persian civilization many hundreds of thousands of years old, as I have previously described, one would have to ask how could it be that such knowledge and expertise were not known to them as well?

Metallurgy

Colin Wilson and Rand Flem-Ath explain how iron smelting techniques were used long before 4000BC and how the ancient Egyptians had used powdered metallurgy.[22] This process involves heating the metal ore to a temperature where it vaporizes, after which it condenses into a powder. However, the temperature required to achieve this would have been in the order of 6,000°C – which suggests that they must also have had knowledge of, and access to, laser technology involving the use of crystals.

It is also known that the Egyptians used certain ores to harden their base metals. For example, copper ore was used with hornblende (a type of volcanic rock) in order to achieve a hardness not far short of modern steel. This might in itself seem remarkable. However, what is even more noteworthy is that such a range of metallurgical knowledge existed at that time.

That the Ancients knew how to contain the energy of fire is apparent in the fact that they understood the qualities and characteristics of asbestos. Furthermore, they understood how to use asbestos to produce ever-burning oil lamps, something which our modern technology only rediscovered in the late 19th century.

Energy Production

On the face of it, there would seem to be no evidence at all that the Ancients understood or practised the principles of energy generation through the use of steam power, or any other means. However, as we shall now see, this assumption too is wide open to question because they certainly knew how to make efficient water heating boilers and, as hot water inevitably involves steam and high pressure, both of which have to be carefully understood in order to be used safely, the circumstantial evidence is that they also knew how to use steam to generate pressure.

Quite apart from this, they knew how to focus the rays of the Sun (for example through crystals) in order to burn materials or to set them alight.[23] It is inconceivable, therefore, that with such knowledge of solar power they did not use it for other practical purposes, for example to light up the interior of underground tunnels and chambers in order for (quite often highly skilled and intricate) work to be carried out in them. It has often been remarked that there is no sign of the soot of oil lamps in the interior of either the Egyptian pyramids or the burial chambers of western Thebes. So artificial light *must* have been used. However, it is known that highly polished copper mirrors were also used to provide additional light by reflection.

As I have already mentioned, the Etruscans certainly seem to have known about electricity and magnetism. However, the Ancients also seem to have understood the relationship between magnetism and light. For example, the Egyptians described their goddess Net[24] as being the only self-generated one, who had existed since the dawn of Time and whose responsibility it was to weave the clothes for the dead. (The name Net, related to the Egyptian verb 'to weave' (*netet*), almost certainly gave rise to the English word 'net'.) However, contrary to orthodox Egyptological interpretation, the expression 'the dead' was an esoteric reference to the 'divine sparks' who had fallen 'naked' from higher states of being into the solar underworld. The reference to 'clothing' therefore (symbolized by the funereal wrappings around the mummified human corpse) was a reference to *light*.

How can all this be proved? Net (herself associated with the Pleiades) is depicted in two ways – either with a bow and a pair of arrows, symbolizing 'shafts'of light, or with what is supposed to be a weaving shuttle on her head (*see* figure 35). However, the abbreviated projections from both ends of the object on her head look remarkably like the curving lines of influence of a magnet. Furthermore, the fact that it is shown on her head denotes its association with consciousness and, as mentioned in an early chapter, a dynamically awakened or energized consciousness is highly attractive – or magnetic.

Now, if the Ancients understood that there was a definite inter-relationship between energy, magnetism and light, as I am suggesting, it seems highly unlikely that their interest would have just stopped there. They would undoubtedly have experimented with it in order to discover the full range of its potentials. This is simple human nature.

As I have elsewhere mentioned, the Etruscans seem to have had some working knowledge of electricity and its means of generation. In Iraq, ancient ceramic jars have been found with copper wires trailing from them, thereby at least suggesting that the principle of the electrical battery was understood. The phenomena of static electricity and magnetism must also have been known to the Ancients, because they are so common. Certainly, the Ancients are known to have used volcanic ebony and amber to produce natural electrical

Figure 35. The Egyptian goddess Net, with the 'magnet' on her head symbolizing energized consciousness

discharges by rubbing them; and they used natural 'lodestone' magnets[25] for navigational compass bearings – undoubtedly by land as well as by sea. The same principles enabled the Ancients to develop their astronomical knowledge.

Quite apart from this, dowsing was very extensively used in the most ancient times for purposes of locating water. We now know that the human sensitivity involved in dowsing enables the really skilled operator to dowse for other materials as well. So why would the Ancients not have followed the same principles?

Transport Systems

Modern archaeologists are of the opinion that humans only domesticated the horse about 10,000 years ago and then devised the wheel about 5,000 years ago. However, that opinion looks appreciably 'off the wall' given the probability, outlined earlier in this book, that human civilization and culture are actually many millions of years old – and particularly in view of Cremo and Thompson's 'rediscoveries'. There can be little doubt that in distant 'prehistoric' times wheeled vehicles would have been used, pulled by both horses and oxen (if not other animals as well; for example the use of reindeer in some regions is of deep antiquity). If ancient humankind understood the principle of the astronomically and astrologically turning wheel several hundred thousand years ago, as I have already described, there can be no doubt whatever that people adapted the same principle for transport purposes, at least on land.

Edgar Cayce talked about Atlantean 'flying machines', but he was certainly not the first to do so. The Vedic writings also talk about them in relation to the final days of the original Atlantean continent, where they describe both the 'black' and 'white' magicians possessing '*vimanas*' in which some escaped and some were pursued.[26] In the biblical Exodus tradition these *vimanas* of course mutate into the 'chariots' of the pursuing pharaoh's forces, most of which were destroyed by the waters of the 'Red Sea' as they closed over them after Moses had withdrawn his power.

However, the aerial vehicles of the Atlanteans[27] appear, according to tradition, to have been 'powered', although there is no indication as to what the power source might have been. Now how could a supposedly 4,000-year-old culture which had only quite recently learned how to domesticate the horse, even begin to conceive of airships – and powered ones at that?

Even if the 'flying machines' in question were simple dirigible airships, the knowledge of how to build them was certainly not simple. It involved an understanding of how to generate and collect lighter-than-air gas, how to keep it in safe housings, how actually to design and build an aircraft and then how to conceive of the technology of propulsion by the use of even a simple motor and associated controls. It would involve considerable expertise resulting from theory plus prolonged trial and error. The time of the Montgolfier brothers' first hot-air balloons in 1783 to the production of the first passenger-carrying Zeppelin in 1900 was only a little over a century, but it was a century that saw the full arrival across Europe of the industrial age, with its array of 'new' discoveries and technologies. However, if this were possible in such a short term, why could not the Ancients, with equivalent theoretical knowledge, perhaps have done the same?

Although the ancient Chinese understood the power of the wind and used it to fly kites – some bearing human observers in battle situations – there is no known mention of wind-power as a direct source of energy (for example, in the form of windmills) other than in relation to sea and river sailing craft. However, the phenomenon of flight by birds and some mammals and reptiles would of course have been known to the Ancients and, with their thirst for knowledge, it seems unlikely that they would not have experimented, at the very least, with associated ideas. This is even more likely in terms of warfare, because times of war always inspire more technological creativity than periods of peace. War machines then become adapted only subsequently for peaceful purposes.

The earliest known records of sea travel deal with sail technology for trade and commerce, plus the use of multiple-oared ships – triremes, with three

banks of oars, and even quinquiremes, with five – for purposes largely of warfare, because of their humanly augmented speed. Again, there is no explicit
mention anywhere of any other sort of power being used. When industrialization was essentially low-key, this is perhaps hardly surprising. However, it now
seems clear that ancient humans, even before the Phoenicians, were highly
accomplished trans-oceanic sailors, navigators and merchants, using natural
means. So mechanical power was hardly to be considered necessary, because it
was too expensive and energy-consuming.

Optics

As Robert Temple explains, the Ancients understood the principles of optics
thousands of years before our era and used them to create magnifying glasses,
spectacles and telescopes, the latter of course being of significant use in astronomy and land surveying.[28] However, they also understood and used the
principle of the camera oscura, involving the fact that light curves (in a mathematically calculable manner) and thus produces inverted virtual images. This
also led to the Ancients' great understanding of the principle of perspective
and its use in both art and temple architecture.

As Robert Temple also confirms, the Ancients also used optical lenses as
microscopes, thereby producing artistic carvings which are so small and
detailed in some cases that the unaided human eye cannot make them out.[29] But
if they used lenses for artistic purposes and in telescopes, they would also
undoubtedly have used them for scientific research as well. To suggest otherwise
in the face of the Ancients' other self-evident scientific interests – even if there
is no remaining evidence or written testimony of the fact – would be illogical.

Astronomy, Horology and Numeracy

It has long been acknowledged that we entirely owe to the Ancients our
modern sexagesimal system of hours, minutes and seconds, plus the 360° of
arc in a circle. Without these it would be impossible to make any architectural,
engineering, astronomical or navigational calculations. However, the fact that
such a system was already in common and widespread use at least 5,000 years
ago, along with water clocks, surely indicates that it had been thoroughly
thought out and practised long before that.

Notwithstanding this, there is no historical record, evidence or suggestion
of when such discoveries were made. By definition, therefore, such knowledge
was a legacy from the prehistoric past. How could one in all seriousness
endeavour to argue to the contrary? In fact, most scholars do not. They merely
avoid the issue altogether.

Whilst the Brahmans of India were believed by the Ancients to have the old-est and best astronomical records, they themselves have a tradition that all their knowledge on the subject derived from the Atlantean astronomer-adept Asura Maya – evidently some many hundreds of thousands of years ago – and that they in turn gave it to the cultures of Sumeria, Chaldea and Assyria.[30] The accu-racy of their recorded data and calculations going back over tens of thousands of years has already been confirmed as being on a par with modern technol-ogy; yet there are no examples of ancient Brahmanic technology in support.

The exactitude of the Mayan calendar on the other side of the world is again quite extraordinary. Yet here again there is no immediately apparent evidence of the Maya's ancient technology. How then did they acquire such scientific information, and over how many centuries, or millennia?

Notwithstanding this, the ruins of ancient astronomical observatories – astoundingly similar in shape to some of our own today – are to be found in both India and Central America. But if the Ancients of the Middle East and India are known to have understood the principles of optics and to have used telescopes as well – and were also great ocean voyagers – why should it be assumed that the astronomical telescope was unknown in Central America? A straightforward combination of common sense and circumstantial evidence should tell us that such a view cannot be correct.

Modern commentators – whilst believing in the popular modern hunter-gatherer theory of humankind's limited and superstition-based anthropo-logical development – have not yet been able to come up with any clear idea of *why* the Ancients should have gathered astronomical data going back over hundreds of thousands of years. This is notwithstanding the fact that such data would appear to have no practical value to societies concerned merely with agriculture and their own immediate political or personal futures. The ability to predict cyclical solar and lunar eclipses is one thing, but to have a detailed interest in, and a working knowledge of, the 25,920-year cycle of precession (as the Ancients clearly did) is quite another altogether.

The Brahmans[31] were concerned with even longer cycles of hundreds of thousands of years, by virtue of their interest in the whole process of our planetary evolution. But why should they have been interested in the issue of evolution in the first place? Is this not basically as scientific an interest in pure knowledge as that of today's anthropologist?

The sophisticated numeracy of the ancient Vedic culture is another point of note. Our modern Western system of numbers (including the use of the zero) is known to have been in use in the Indus Valley and in southern India well before 2500BC. It was used by Phoenician merchants as a matter of course and was transmitted by them, via Arabic-speaking Muslims, to Europe – which, at the time (the 10th century) was still struggling with Roman numbers.

Conclusion

As I said at the very outset of this book, *homo sapiens* of a type indistinguishable from modern humankind (other than being on average taller and having a larger brain capacity) was generated by Nature well over a million years ago – perhaps even many millions of years before even that. Nature had unquestionably done so in order to fulfil its own requirements and potentials at that time. However, to suggest (on the basis of serial unproven assumptions that humans at that time had no technological sense) that Nature would have generated this being without good reason, or without incorporating the limitless powers of adaptive reasoning which we ourselves possess, is patently ludicrous. It has no remote relationship with even basic deductive logic.

The current view held by scientists is based entirely upon the assumption that the Ancients, in general, were so hidebound by superstition that they must have been incapable of scientifically rational processes of thought and would certainly have been incapable of trial-and-error tests under laboratory conditions.[32] Yet the fact is that, notwithstanding the evident existence of superstition in those days on the part of many, there were plenty of others with brilliant minds who were capable not only of conceiving of great scientific, architectural and engineering projects, but also of carrying them out.

There can now be no doubt whatever that the Ancients practised science and technology in a very sophisticated manner, and that their ancestors had done so for untold thousands of years. That they subsumed scientific knowledge within the term 'philosophy' was because, *in their system of value judgments*, they saw 'science' as being of more than just utilitarian application. Knowledge was a sacred power and function and its wise use, in sympathy with (a) divine ordinance and (b) the environment, was of the first importance. That is why the word philosophy was derived in the first place – because *philo-sophia* means, literally, the love of wisdom, *not* the love of knowledge.

Apart from anything else that has been suggested here, because the Ancients understood the principles behind the practice of *occult* science, we are told that their initiated adepts were able to see and do things through the use of powers which science today regards, at best, as science fiction. Yet, one might point to those imaginatively original scientists of the late 19th and early 20th century who were convinced (through experimentation) that spiritualism worked and that other states of existence could be accessed. It was these same individuals who designed, adapted and built the very foundations of our modern telephone, radio and television systems of communication. But this was in the face of other contemporary scientists (many of them of great stature, like Faraday) who said that such ideas of 'ethereal' communication were absurd and had no scientifically rational basis.

It is a simple fact that our modern technological age is barely three centuries old. Yet in that short space of time, human intelligence has been capable of turning the age-old existing theories of mathematics, physics and chemistry into a host of applied technologies of communication as well as of energy production and distribution. These, in conjunction with corporate application, have completely transformed the culture of humanity. Yet corporatism and its crassly materialistic approach to life have also been the main destroyers of family life and human values, something which the Ancients considered to be sacred (notwithstanding, or perhaps demonstrated by, their own apparent cold-blooded brutality in warfare).

Already we are talking about whether technology and general consumerism have gone too far. We acknowledge that they have caused too much damage to the environment, and perhaps need to be scaled down or even replaced with more 'natural' technology which does not put such a strain upon the world's resources as well as upon basic human health and happiness. This has been accompanied by a growing call for ecological awareness so that we are not overcome by a general devastation arising out of our own ignorance and greed. But *why* do we so unquestioningly assume that this same scenario could not have happened before, when it is quite clear from history that the Ancients too made similar ecological mistakes, even though they were very skilled observers of Nature's processes?

Whilst it may ultimately be impossible to prove (with evidence in the shape of ancient artefacts or written records) that all the technical knowledge and skills which I have mentioned in this chapter were generated as far back as the original Atlantean era, there can now be no serious doubt that they *were* already extant in some degree in very distant prehistoric times. That conclusion in turn surely provides the strongest possible circumstantial evidence that immensely sophisticated civilizations and intellectually based cultures must have existed before anything known to recorded history. This is irrespective of the claim by modern archaeologists that we have no knowledge of any civilization and culture before those of Sumeria, Egypt, Chaldea and the Indus Valley. But that in turn merely confirms beyond any shadow of doubt that our modern archaeological orthodoxy still has a long way to go before it catches up with the simple, albeit uncomfortable, truth that there is indeed 'nothing new in recorded history'.

EPILOGUE

·

LOOKING TOWARDS THE FUTURE

Whilst this book has primarily concentrated on the subject of Plato's Atlantis, it has obviously extended its general remit far further. In order to put Atlantis in the correct context, it has also dealt with the general anthropology and ethnology of the human race on either side of the Atlantean period, whilst also looking at the basis of what actually causes global cataclysms. As a result, it should have become self-evident that our planetary world is a place of continuing, dynamic change. It is not the cosily safe place which most people would prefer it to be, nor has it ever been anything of the sort. Humankind's continuing place on it may perhaps be assured, but that assuredness is overridingly conditional on our own progressive psycho-spiritual, evolutionary development.

The Ancient Wisdom traditions which have been cited as a background to this work make it very clear that there is Intelligent Purpose behind all Nature. There is no question of it being merely subject to the vagaries of a purely chaotic impulse – or to the purely arbitrary actions of a wholly theoretical God who is to be followed in blind subservience. Humankind's own nature has a very critical part to play in the planet's overall development of consciousness and discriminating intelligence. However, there is no part in it for the tendency, found so frequently in human society today, towards local 'racial' or any other form of purely social discrimination based on personal 'like and dislike'.

Nature will use whatever forms and influences are most available and suitable to promote the train of evolution of our planetary consciousness *as a whole and at any time*. The rest Nature will evidently dispense with. Therefore, were the forms and developed consciousness of the Fifth Race type to prove inadequate for her requirements, Nature would merely adapt the nearest, although perhaps older ethnological types and bring them up to date for the same evolutionary purposes. Thus, as Blavatsky said, the idea that one racial group is somehow 'better' than another, is wholly unsupportable and merely 'falls to the ground'.

The Principle of Discrimination

If the ancient perception of Man as a soul which takes a body for purposes of incarnation had not fallen by the wayside over the last few centuries as a result of (a) religious prejudice and (b) scientific and academic myopia, such 'racial discrimination' would never have had a chance to proliferate in the way it has, particularly in the West. However, religious and ethnic prejudice have never been far from the armoury of humankind's ignorance and stupidity. Unfortunately, the swing of so-called 'political correctness' just as far in the opposite direction over the last 30 years or so, has made the problem even worse, through creating an atmosphere of fear in response to perfectly normal and reasonable social commentary. It works in a very insidious manner against scientific objectivity and rational discussion.

The situation has been further compounded by the arguments both for and against Darwinian 'natural selection' theory, as though Darwinism and Creationism were the only possible options for consideration in dealing with the question of evolution. However, as we have seen, both of them suffer from the same problems – intellectual stasis and literalism – which are the death of all real perception. Not surprisingly perhaps, the two supporting 'camps' of Western religion and science have turned this subject into a crisis of mere belief.

Creationists – whilst with justification believing in the existence of superior Divinity – have, in their own blindly literal pursuit of biblical theology, almost completely disregarded the laws of Nature as pursued by scientific research. Orthodox science, on the other hand, rejecting the possibility of Divinity without even trying to understand the principles involved, has instead pursued an evolutionary 'March hare'. Strangely, however, there are some scientists whose beliefs are so rigid that they could only be considered to be following some form of religious creed of their own.

The Equality of Man

Another quite serious problem which has arisen from a combination of Darwinism and modern political 'democracy' is the idea that 'all people are equal' when (as the 19th-century Indian sage Vivekananda pointed out) they are manifestly not – except when they are dead. In absolute terms, there is no doubt that some spirits and souls are more advanced than others in terms of their range of subjective development and their capacity to bring that development into responsible equilibrium with the 'equipment' provided by their human bodily form and senses in any one lifetime. It is as a consequence of this that we find some of the most advanced beings on Earth taking incarnation in some of the oldest ethnological types of body forms, whilst there are self-evidently plenty of very *unadvanced* human spirits incarnating in the most modern Fifth Race human body forms. Mere parentage is no adequate indicator of anything.

It has been said many times before by ancient Eastern philosophy that we are all friends and companions in the 'fellowship of spirit'. If this is indeed so, it should then become obvious that the more advanced the individual, the greater the responsibility he or she bears for any less advanced fellow traveller as a 'younger brother' or 'sister'. Unfortunately, 'advancement' in the modern era has become synonymous with 'self-advancement' of the primarily materialistic type, which has generated an atmosphere of spiritual sterility wherever it has laid its coldly ungenerous hand.

The Dangers of Technology

This sort of foolishness has, however, extended very dangerously into an altogether unholy union of scientifically based technology and politics. We saw in earlier chapters how the Atlanteans seemingly came to depend upon their capacity to manipulate elemental entities and nature spirits for their own selfish ends. What we see today sadly involves a mere repetition of the same stupidity. However, it is currently driven by an intellectual perception of man as the most evolved organism in (blind) Creation and of (equally blind) Nature as thus there to be exploited at will. This exploitation is supposedly for humankind's benefit but it has actually been made to coincide with purely political and commercial desires. As a direct consequence of this, today's fascination with biotechnology and 'high-tech' commerce, amidst foolishly relaxed ethics, is in many ways an even more dangerous juggernaut than the Atlantean attitude proved to be. Fortunately, there have arisen two crusading antagonists to counter these forms of materialistic terrorism. The one is the science of Ecology and the second is the so-called 'New Age' movement.

As yet, neither of these two youthful movements has developed anything other than fairly general philosophies, although there can be no doubt that both were, in origin, spiritually based. The ecological movement is concerned about terrestrial Nature as a whole in terms of a supposedly 'normal' balance, whilst the 'New Age' movement is (as yet) almost entirely anthropocentric in its concerns for spiritual development. However, both have their ingenuously reductive and self-limiting sides which regretfully seek at times to trade on little more than public anxiety and fear of the unknown.

For example, the New Age movement has somehow managed to allow its own subversion within the last two decades to such an extent that the major part of it has now seemingly turned into a mere 'personal lifestyle' movement.

In this, spirituality is bizarrely seen as synonymous with physical health, plus the need to feel good about oneself and otherwise do well in life without being overly competitive. The ecological movement, on the other hand, more often than not seems to take it for granted that Nature could actually be destroyed by humankind. It frequently fails to take into account that Nature itself is far more likely to be the larger-scale destroyer, if humans go too far in their attempts to exploit it – and that this reaction will take place long before we have a real chance to cause any serious long-term problems.

The Powers of Nature

Nature is neither blind nor deaf and its organic power and reach are far greater than any weapon of mass destruction of which humans have so far been able to conceive – or build. This is now beginning to be recognized by science; but science (particularly Western science) has some way to go before it comes to a parallel recognition of the fact that our planetary Nature has a definite guiding intelligence behind and within it. Conversely, however, that part of the New Age movement which sees in Nature only the all-guiding 'Mother' principle, also misses the mark somewhat and often seems to pursue a path which would lead straight back into the mystic mists of blind superstition. The idea of a permanently halcyon 'natural' environment – not far short of the biblical Eden – is completely un-natural, and this is where rational science's input is so very important for us all.

Rather than indiscriminately accepting the (wholly false) idea that all the powers of Nature are more powerful than those of humankind and thus making grovelling, superstitious obeisance to them via generally blind ritual (which always degenerates into superstition), we need to know more about those powers, their natures, qualities and cyclical functions. But this must be done from an objectively considerate viewpoint, which is where the ecological sense comes in. However, neither the mystic nor the scientist can achieve this alone.

Research and Education

Because such an investigation into Nature's powers will involve research into consciousness itself, it necessitates the multi-disciplinary approach of those who can combine both the scientific and mystic approaches *as operative techniques*. But both must be operated simultaneously within the individual's own nature, thereby producing a high and reliably balanced degree of subjective and objective perceptual faculty. This, however, requires a commensurately high degree of self-discipline, involving a parallel degree of reduction in even subtle self-indulgence. That is precisely why the Ancients recognized the need for the proving grounds of progressive 'Mystery Schools'. However, whilst modern education continues to be regarded merely as an adjunct to commerce, or as as means of entry to a business career, or as a training ground for following a particular religion, this very different viewpoint is unlikely to prevail. The development of an across-the-board spiritually orientated intelligence could hardly derive from any of these.

Opinion today about the ancient level of intelligence is largely polarized between those on the one side blindly following Darwin and those on the other just as blindly following Creationism. The Darwinists believe that culturally domesticated, but still entirely superstition-ridden, *homo sapiens sapiens* only appeared 10,000 or perhaps 20,000 years ago. The Creationists – still obtusely following the 17th-century Bishop Usher in the belief that the world appeared only in 4004BC – regard humanity as not needing to evolve *per se*, but needing merely to improve its behaviour and follow some or other religious creed. However, there are also those who, whilst seeing the human discriminative intelligence as almost ageless in its potential, because of its essentially spiritual nature, believe that humanity must somehow move on, unconditioned by mere belief systems.

But the time has come, surely, for a more imaginative overall perspective to be considered, based on a recognition that it is in fact intelligence itself which evolves, throughout *all* the kingdoms of Nature. Thus intelligence drives change in consciousness, the latter only subsequently producing changes in its outward forms of self-expression. We also need to understand, however, that Nature can only achieve this through a process of intelligently purposeful recycling of outmoded forms – and that the spirit within humankind is an active participant in this, even if humankind itself is generally unconscious of the fact.

Humankind may feel committed to this process either consciously or unconsciously – depending upon our level of intelligence and sense of common responsibility to the rest of Nature. But only those who accept the need for absolute scientific objectivity and absolute subjective probity – and then endeavour to translate these into actual faculty – will understand just how difficult such self-training actually is. It is not for the faint-hearted or for those lacking in determination. That is why pure, selfless courage, allied to harmlessness, was one of the characteristics which had to be demonstrated in the true Mystery traditions of the Ancients before any real sacred knowledge could be imparted.

Today, we have come to expect that all knowledge is ours as of right. However, this is not the case without due qualification and can never be so in practice. Real knowledge is a *qualitatively based* characteristic of consciousness. Therefore, if the perceptual consciousness of the individual is of low quality, the knowledge itself will become commensurately degraded. It is for this reason that the education and training of children in natural ethics, by following unselfish adult example, is so vitally important. Consciousness needs to be carefully raised and appropriately balanced in quality *before* any advanced educational practice is attempted. As long as our Western educational systems pay insufficient attention to this principle, anti-social problems among modern youth will inevitably continue.

The Future of Humanity

As regards the future, our own Fifth Race type will itself undoubtedly pass into history in due course of cyclical time, as have the Lemurians and Atlanteans before us. One can therefore envisage a period – perhaps tens or even hundreds of thousands of years from now – when the new Sixth Race of humanity (whatever it turns out to look like) will find amongst its midst widespread groups of by then ethnologically degenerate Fifth Race types. Just as happened with previous races, these will either willingly be absorbed into the new ethnological stream or they will otherwise die out by a process of attrition. In addition, the landmasses of that far-off day will doubtless be quite different to what currently exists.

It is already apparent to scientists that various parts of the world's geographical areas are threatened even now by Mother Nature's own cyclical reclamations or variations and that this will itself have a dramatic effect upon the distribution of populations around the globe. For example, it is accepted that large areas of Japan (including Tokyo) will disappear ere long due to earthquakes; that the man-made levees of the southern states of the USA cannot long protect them from permanent oceanic submersion; that the British Isles are tipping westwards and will eventually (some thousands of years hence) sink into oceanic oblivion, the greater part of central London and other surrounding suburban areas having disappeared long before then, perhaps in a matter of centuries; that parts of Greece are already sinking by the metre every year; that Manhattan and other parts of New York, plus some areas of California, including San Francisco, will also disappear in the not too distant future, due to oceanic submersion and earthquake activity.

Long before that, however, the cyclical return of rising oceanic levels, due to melting of the polar ice caps, will cause some 20 per cent of the planet's inhabited areas – including whole countries like Holland and Bangladesh, plus extensive parts of China – to disappear altogether. At the same time, large areas of Siberian Russia, northern Canada, Alaska and Greenland, for example, which have been frozen and largely uninhabitable for thousands of years, will return to general agricultural fertility. These facts alone will potentially lead to immense political and cultural changes, plus worldwide population movements of as yet unimaginable magnitude. But politicians have not even begun to wake up to this forthcoming scenario despite the fact that the process of global change is now quite clearly irreversible.

Within the last 300 years we have seen noticeable population shifts taking place, largely from Europe to the continents of Australasia and North and South America, but also from Asia to Europe. It is generally assumed that such migrations have been purely the historical result of human desire for social betterment or the wish to move away from religious or political and social persecution in existing environments. But, Nature has a curious way of providing quietly in advance for its own future development. One wonders therefore whether human activities are subliminally made to coincide with Nature's own desires and purpose, rather than the other way around as humankind so often fondly seems to imagine.

Imminent Global Change

The immensely severe and widespread flooding which has taken place in Central Europe in recent years, plus the accelerating melting of glaciers, polar icecaps and the Siberian and Alaskan permafrost, are all indicative of the fact that the geography of the whole planet is itself *already* in an advanced process of great change. Within the next five centuries or so, we can perhaps reasonably expect low-lying areas west of the Urals to be under seawater – again – which will completely change European civilization as currently known.

Further south, the fact that the seabed in the Strait of Gibraltar is rising and may well within a few centuries make navigation through it, in and out of the Mediterranean, impossible to large shipping, has huge implications for southern European and North African civilization in general. The probability of large- scale volcanic and earthquake activity in western North America will undoubtedly result in vast changes there too. Long-term droughts, pestilence and famine all over Africa are already constant phenomena, but rising oceanic waters will alter present low-lying coastlines there beyond all recognition as well.

Science also tells us that potentially deadly pandemics will, within the immediately foreseeable future, sweep the world, killing tens of millions; that Nature itself is responding to chemical immunization by fighting back to produce genetic mutations in germs and insects, at a speed which we cannot counter. But, one must ask, why is Nature doing so? Is it perhaps because something about humankind's own 'high-tech' approach is itself un-Natural? Or is it because Nature is merely intent on reducing human numbers in due cycle?

Divine Retribution

There are of course those who would say that all this is due to humankind having displeased 'God' (or 'the gods') by its lack of spirituality, in such a manner that Deity is being forced to exact retribution. However, this is purely the result of blindly fearful religious superstition and it is absolutely right that modern science rejects it outright for what it is. Nevertheless, the universal Law of Cause and Effect (karma) *does* exist in Nature, as a matter of established fact. Thus modern science will not satisfy the majority of humanity as to its own approach until it has itself begun to take into active consideration the nature and function of the psycho-spiritual worlds which drive Nature itself from the *inner* side.

Whether we like it or not, we live in a time in which great change is imminent, just as faced by the Atlanteans of different historic eras. The 'Age of Aquarius' and the celestial solstice are imminent, although whether the new era turns out to be quite so halcyon as some people would like to think, remains to be seen. Professor James Lovelock has recently gone public, in his book *The Revenge of Gaia*, with his opinion that global climatic change has already moved beyond the critical point and is now to be considered 'irreversible'. It is clear from this and also from other scientific reports, that general oceanic levels are likely to rise anything from 20 ft (6.1 m) in the next century to in excess of 200 ft (61 m) thereafter. As we saw earlier, our planet's axial movement is already slowing down and global warming is accelerating, although scientists have not yet linked the two phenomena. The Mayan calendar, so we are told, predicts the end of a great world cycle in 2012.[1]

In conclusion, we are left wondering what the next century or two may bring in the way of potential worldwide cataclysms, rising oceanic levels, extremes of weather and other supposed harbingers of doom and gloom. Of course there is no point in worrying unduly, because it is all part of Nature's cyclical processes, and the spirit itself is immortal; but one is inevitably reminded of the old Chinese curse: '*May you live in interesting times.*'

APPENDIX A

THE ORIGINS AND EVOLUTION
OF DARWINISM

Modern Darwinism bears only a passing relationship to the Darwinism of Charles Darwin himself. In order to understand the modern form in due perspective, we have to take an at least brief look at how the original form came about – involving some issues which may well surprise the reader of this book.

To begin with, Darwin's family was financially comfortable and socially well known. This was in part due to his grandfather Erasmus Darwin, an early proponent of the concept of evolution and a radical humanist who wrote inflammatory poetry at the time of the French Revolution. Charles Darwin also married into the Wedgwood family of industrialists, who were also radically orientated humanists, particularly where slavery and any form of human persecution were involved. Darwin himself was a very sensitive type who suffered periodically from anxiety-induced bouts of illness. He was not a scientist. In fact, he failed medicine and therefore, when going up to Cambridge, studied for a degree in divinity.

As James Moore and Adrian Desmond point out in their very informative introduction to their recent edition of Darwin's *The Descent of Man* (upon which these various comments are based), whereas the Church of his day took an entirely anthropocentric view of the universe, as having been made for humankind, Darwin went to the other extreme by anthropomorphizing Nature in general. Anthropomorphism was thus central to his way of thinking. The vigorous anti-slavery of his family also fundamentally conditioned his views at a time when native peoples around the world were often regarded as no better than animals. From his view that the blood-line between animals and all types of human must be the same and that the anthropoids at least could be seen at London Zoo doing some things which humans themselves do, resulted his perception that evolution would 'level things up'. Since the worst aspects of human nature had been shown in the way some Europeans treated their slaves, he had already come to the conclusion that man himself (at least of the lower classes) must be an animal or only in the process of emerging from the animal state.

It is interesting to note that, like many others of his class and period, Darwin took the view that because women were intuitive and imitative – these supposedly being indications of an earlier, lower form of civilization – womankind did not evolve. Women were also less evolved than men because, as Darwin saw it, of men's capacities for intellectual self-development. This level of chauvinism demonstrates a very superficial perception of the real nature of the human type. It also shows just how little psychological perception Darwin possessed.

Darwin's real interests specifically lay in relation to racial diversity and sexual selection – the latter more in relation to animals than to man. However, as a result of watching male animals and birds competing for the attention of females, for example through more colourful plumage and supremacist behaviour, he conceived the idea that aesthetic choice was involved in sexual selection. This thereafter also completely conditioned his whole thinking on evolution. In other words, his whole perception was based upon an unthinking assumption that the whole process of human interaction (at least amongst the lower classes) was a materialistically based one. Despite being religious himself, he – again like many others of his period – took the bizarre view that religion and the material world view had to be kept separate

It is interesting to note how Darwin's perspective regarding human social development coalesced with others' of the time – notably that of Malthus, whose view it was that human and animal existence alike were based entirely upon the principles of competition and struggle, leading to 'survival of the fittest'. But Darwin modified this slightly for humans by suggesting a form of 'reciprocal altruism for the sake of survival' – a sort of commercially and materialistically enlightened attitude which thus necessarily underlay the workings of a successful urban society.

Today, we would regard Darwin's social views as crass and superficial in the extreme. The fact that he was extremely wary of airing his evolutionary ideas because of the effects this might have on his social standing, further highlights his psychological limitations. The additional fact that (like the Church in general at the time) he apparently had no idea of what psycho-spiritual existence might perhaps involve in practical terms, leads one directly to the fact that his general perspective on Nature's potential in planes other than the material were almost non-existent. Descartes, several centuries before, had of course concluded that animals possessed no soul, a view that influenced theology down to the 18th and 19th centuries. This anti-Renaissance perception – likewise based upon facile and materialistic reasoning – must have caused at least some early evolutionists some serious problems when considering man as merely a more evolved aspect of the animal kingdom. It still unthinkingly conditions 21st-century scientific research and thought to an absurd degree.

It is interesting to note, in concluding, that Alfred Russell Wallace, who came out with a very similar theory of evolution at exactly the same time as Darwin (who published first, however), and who was a socialist who had actually lived amongst native peoples, eventually became a spiritualist.

APPENDIX B

THE 'SEA PEOPLES'

Writing of ancient Persia's unsuccessful war against Egypt in the 12th century BC,[1] Diodorus Siculus says:

> The army was commanded by Pharanbazus and Iphicrates the Athenian (the great Greek tactician), the barbarians by Pharnabazus and 20,000 mercenaries by Iphicrates ... When the (Persian) king's forces came to Aces in Syria and were there mustered, there were found 200,000 barbarians, to be under the command of Pharnabazus and twenty thousand Grecians, under the command of Iphicrates. (Diodorus XV, 3)

Diodorus then says of the naval force put together out of the same military grouping: 'About the beginning of the spring, the officers with all the forces both at sea and land, made for Egypt.' (Diodorus XV, 5.)

In ancient times the meaning of the term 'barbarian' was very specific. It derives from the name 'Berber', meaning the tribes of people who occupied northwest Africa from Libya in the east to the far end of the Atlas Mountains in the west. The name – as *barbarii* – was used first by the Egyptians and then the Greeks to refer to invading Libyans. It was also later applied by the Romans to the Carthaginian forces, and subsequently became a generalized derogatory Roman term for any foreign tribal system with which the Romans came into contact.

From these quotes by Diodorus, it is quite clear that a very substantial force of Berbers formed the greater part of the Persian army. However, bearing in mind that the Carthaginians were also great sailors and navigators (they had been feared by the Greeks as seagoing marauders for centuries) it is more than likely that the naval part of the force also comprised a preponderance of Berbers, if it was not made up entirely of them.

In the Egyptian temple of Medinet Habu, on the west bank at Luxor, the wall reliefs (of Rameses III, the pharaoh who built the temple) refer to the same naval force by the name 'the Sea People' and also as 'the Peoples of the Isles'. It has been assumed by scholars that 'the Isles' had to be the Greek islands of the Aegean. However, it is just as possible that they were actually a reference to the tribal peoples of the Canary Isles or possibly the Balearics. Another interesting quote pointing in this direction comes from the Old Testament (Jeremiah 25:22), which refers to 'All the kings of Tyrus and all the kings of Zidon and the kings of the isles which are beyond the sea.'

'Tyrus' and 'Zidon' might be taken simply to mean the two trading city-ports of Tyre and Sidon in modern Lebanon. However, it is highly improbable that there would be 'numerous' kings of each as the text indicates. 'The sea' referred to, however, is clearly the Mediterranean, which was *the* sea as far as the peoples of the Near East were concerned. 'Tyrus', on the other hand, is then undoubtedly the contemporary name for the lands surrounding the Tyrrhenian Sea (the western end of the Mediterranean) which, as we know from other sources, was completely under the naval control of the Carthaginians and their allies, the Etruscans. The same is no doubt true of 'Zidon', since both city-ports were almost certainly named after western kingdoms of a similar name. Thus, by simple deduction, the same 'islands beyond the sea' cannot be other than a reference to the Canaries, beyond the 'Pillars of Herakes'.

It is known that Rameses III, in referring to this campaign, also mentioned the immensely long swords of the Sea peoples as 'five cubits long'. Five cubits is equivalent to a modern length of about 7 ft 6 in (2.3 m) and it would obviously take an extremely tall and powerful man indeed to wield such a weapon, even if he used both hands, as with some of the later broadswords of medieval times, the longest of which were about 6 ft (1.83 m) long. However, it is known that Berber men (even up to quite recent times) were very tall indeed, often up to 7 ft in height, while the biblical Philistine Goliath was supposedly some 9 ft tall.

NOTES

PREFACE

1. Blavatsky openly admitted that her information came from an ancient 'Esoteric School' based in the foothills of the Himalayas, on the borders of Tibet and northern India. Although regarded by some even today as merely a hoax, this school was known of well over 2,000 years ago. Auguste le Plongeon writes of 'a secret society of wise and learned men, whose object is the study of philosophy in all its branches, but particularly the spiritual development of man. The leading fraternity is established in Tibet ... They are known throughout India by the name of Mahatmas.' (*Sacred Mysteries among the Mayans and the Quiche*, pp.29ff.)
2. V. Harrison. *H.P. Blavatsky and the Society for Psychical Research* (*see also: Journal of the SPR* 53, no.803, pp.286–310)

INTRODUCTION

1. J. Naydler. *Shamanic Wisdom in the Pyramid Texts*, p.30
2. The fact that we have intellectual giants around today does not preclude similar men and women of genius having existed tens of thousands of years ago, in quite different social, religious or philosophical environments.

CHAPTER ONE

1. G. de Santillana and H. von Dechend. *Hamlet's Mill*, p.209
2. Among Plato's late works, the *Timaeus* and *Critias* are two of a projected trilogy of dialogues, although Plato never wrote the third, *Hermocrates*, and left *Critias* unfinished. The two dialogues are sometimes referred to as a single work, 'the *Timaeus* and *Critias*', or '*Timaeus-Critias*'.
3. According to Diodorus Siculus, Homer visited Egypt at least 200 years before Thales. Plato later sent his own pupils there too, for example, Eudoxus of Cnidus, the famous astronomer, geographer and mathematician. *See* Diodorus Siculus, book 1, p.327.
4. Following Socrates' death, Plato left Athens and went with other disciples of Socrates to Megara to study under Euclid and thence to Cyrene in North Africa to study mathematics under Theodorus – and only then on to Egypt.
5. Herodotus. *The Histories*, pp.149–152
6. J. Naydler. *Shamanic Wisdom in the Pyramid Texts*, p.29
7. Ammianus Marcellinus. *Roman History*, book 22, xvi
8. This I describe at greater length in my book *Khemmea*, dealing with the Egyptian mystic tradition and how it is dramatically different from the current popular view of it.
9. As the authors of *Hamlet's Mill* confirm: 'There is good reason to assume that he [Hipparchus] actually rediscovered this, that it had been known some thousand years previously

and that on it the Archaic Age based its long range computation of time' (G. de Santillana and H. von Dechend. *Hamlet's Mill*, p.66). In fact, other evidence suggests it as far older still.

10. Herodotus. *The Histories*, p.186
11. Iamblichus. *The Egyptian Mysteries*, p.269. *See also The Secret Doctrine* vol.2 , p.1048. Epigenes also confirms (Pliny, *Historia Naturalis*, book 7, ch.56) that the Chaldeans' astronomical calculations extended back over 720,000 years.
12. Diodorus Siculus, book 2, p.457
13. K.A. Folliot. *Atlantis Revisited*, p.92
14. G. de Santillana and H. von Dechend. *Hamlet's Mill*, p.311. This is actually a little wide of the mark. What we regard as 'reality' was always philosophically regarded as illusory by the ancients. Myth was always originally intended to provide a memorable visual parallel which concealed the route to esoteric knowledge, ever available to those who understood the key. Thus what appeared fantastic or even absurd to the rational mind of the uninitiated always contained within itself a deliberately disguised thread of truth.

CHAPTER TWO

1. G. de Santillana and H. von Dechend. *Hamlet's Mill*, p.311
2. Plato. *Critias*
3. *Ibid.*
4. *Ibid.*
5. Hence Acheron derives from the Egyptian Aker, 'guardian of the ways', the name of a deity. Hence also the divine spirits of humankind, called *akhu* by the Egyptians, and *ahu* by others. The lesser primordial system into which they thus fell – known in the ancient metaphysical system simply by the term *as* – thus mutated in Vedic Indo-Persia into the *Akas*, anglicized as today's *Akasa*.
6. G. de Santillana and H. von Dechend. *Hamlet's Mill*, p.292
7. As *cleito-* appears to mean 'hill' in Greek, the paradoxical idea of a hill within or generated by the mountain of Evenor and Leucippe sounds like an intended esoteric metaphor, almost suggestive of the mound of pregnancy. If Cleito symbolizes the semi-divine solar state (itself the product of an insemination from a yet higher kosmic state), this ties in with the overall concept described earlier.
8. Plato. *Critias*
9. A palace 'in the habitation of the god and their (divine) ancestors' clearly indicates that this was no physical palace.
10. *Ibid.*
11. *Ibid.*
12. The builders of the ancient Phoenician port at Carthage designed it with an inner harbour surrounded by two outer harbours, evidently for security reasons. They did not use this system at any other Mediterranean port, so I suggest it was not a Phoenician design but rather an indigenous Carthaginian one.
13. Proclus. *Commentary on the Timaeus*, book 2, p.661
14. Plato. *Critias*
15. *Ibid.*
16. Hence the killing of the bull by the hero in several ancient traditions (such as the Mithraic) signified the 'death' of the original spiritual nature, with the semi-divine human emerging from its nature as a result.
17. Berosus, a Babylonian priest, wrote in Greek for Alexander the Great the traditions and some of the astronomical knowledge of the Chaldeo-Babylonian priesthood, covering a period of some 200,000 years. However, Epigenes (according to Pliny's *Natural History*, book 8, chapter 56) and Plato (*Timaeus*, book 1) confirm the astronomical calculations of the Chaldeo-Babylonians as extending back over 720,000 years.

326 NOTES TO PAGES 38–52

CHAPTER THREE

1. Philo. *The Works of Philo*, pp.16–18
2. As Stephen Wolinsky says: 'If [the scientist David] Bohm is correct and the universe is a gigantic multi-dimensional hologram, [it] would have profound implications for many of our other common sense notions about reality. For example, … Time and Space would no longer be viewed as fundamentals.' (S. Wolinsky, *Quantum Consciousness*, p.128.) In my view, though, (kosmic) Space is certainly fundamental.
3. R. Milton. *Shattering the Myths of Darwinism*, p.234
4. F. Hoyle and C. Wickramsinghe. *Evolution from Space*, p.xv
5. J. Lovelock, *The Ages of Gaia*
6. Without the dozens of electrical storms constantly circling our globe and re-charging the lower atmosphere, it seems highly unlikely that any organic forms within the planetary atmosphere could survive. There is a clear implication in this that all these sub-organisms are part and parcel of one gigantic electro-magnetic process, all sub-organisms exchanging vital energy with one another.
7. David Bohm recognized this as a universal principle in his work *Wholeness and the Implicate Order*, of which his fellow scientist Peter Russell commented: 'Bohm's theory of implicate order suggests that the physical universe may be like a hologram, with the whole of Space and Time somehow encoded in every part of it. This implicate order is never perceived directly. What we see is the explicate order – specific forms which are generated from the underlying implicate order. Ultimately, concludes Bohm, the entire universe has to be understood as a single undivided whole.' (P. Russell, *The Awakening Earth*, pp.127ff.)
8. Sir W. Scott, trans. *Hermetica*, p.183
9. *Ibid.* p.195
10. *Ibid.* pp.217–219
11. Such an attitude is akin to suggesting that every colour has only one shade and that every musical note is contained within the same octave, which is self-evidently absurd.
12. Hence 'an idea is a being incorporeal which has no substance of itself but which gives figure and form unto shapeless matter and [so] becomes the cause of its manifestation.' (Plutarch, *De Placitis Philosophorum*.)
13. However, the Ancients would not have accepted Einstein's idea that nothing could move faster than the speed of light (Mind does) or that the speed of light is an invariable.
14. The word 'involutionary' signifies the downward movement into matter from the ethereal world of spirit. Hence 'involution' involves the sequential process of unfolding Creation, whilst 'evolution' means the reverse process, through ultimate liberation from form.
15. Hence the concept of the 'DemiUrgos', or demiurge, found in the various writings of the Gnostics. However, this concept has been generally misunderstood in the rush to work out the nature and origins of so-called 'Good and Evil'.
16. Sir W. Scott, trans. *Hermetica*, p.177
17. The name 'Ormazd' is derived from Aur-mazd, meaning the enmeshed sphere of light, symbolized by the serpent biting its own tail.
18. Iamblichus. *The Egyptian Mysteries*, p.259
19. Tobias Churton (*Gnostic Philosophy*, p.1) says that very same imagery lies at the centre of one of the rituals in the Ancient and Accepted Rite of Freemasonry.
20. Such immortality was, however, conditional. It depended entirely upon the soul's capacity to adhere to the dictates of the higher 'Word', thereby consolidating and advancing its own evolution.

CHAPTER FOUR

1. Sir W. Scott, trans. *Hermetica*, p.205
2. This idea is found in Islamic theology. As Wallis Budge confirms: 'Muhammadan theolo-

gians declare that the angels are created of a simple substance of light … ; their obedience is absolute.' (E.W. Budge, *The Gods of the Ancient Egyptians*, vol.1, p.5.)

3. Thus, we might suggest, there is a close correlation between the *quality* of a field of light and the ability of an entity to access it or, with even greater difficulty, to manifest within it. Hence, the whole evolutionary process must necessarily (and quite logically) involve sequential progression through a series of different qualities of light.

4. In the Christian tradition, this became the 'Saviour' – a concept found in the New Testament in the form of 'the rider on a white horse', equated with Christ though originally having much wider connotations.

5. Unfortunately humankind has a habit of eventually distorting almost every usefully good or spiritual idea that comes its way, through blind or wilful ignorance, superstition, or straight-forward selfishness. Many religions founder on the rocks of theological literalism and many philosophies are corrupted by pernicious intellectual sectarianism.

6. Hence, in Vedic philosophy, the allegorical concept that Vishnu lies asleep 'at the bottom of the great ocean' on the great seven-headed kosmic serpent until the cycle of manifestation commences with a lotus flower emerging from his navel and unfolding to produce the Creator-god Brahma. Vishnu later awakes as the avatar-god Krishna who then (in the *Bhaghavad Gita*) explains to his disciple Arjuna the nature system in which humankind finds itself and how we must overcome our lower nature in order to rediscover our ancient divinity.

7. This is the basis as the much misunderstood Christian doctrine of the Trinity. E. J. Dingwall cites the Tibetan scholar Lama Kazi Dawa-Samdup: 'In the boundless panorama of the existing and visible universe, whatever shapes appear, whatever sounds vibrate, whatever radiances illuminate, or whatever consciousnesses cognise, all are the play or manifestation of the Tri-Kaya, the threefold principle of the Cause of all Causes, the Primordial Trinity.' (A.E. Dingwall, *Ghosts and Spirits in the Ancient World*.)

8. As outlined in my book *Khemmea*.

9. In several of the ancient Mystery systems, the lower world system was metaphorically described as a reflective surface (e.g. a pool of water) on the surface of which the god's own reflection serves to entrance him and draw him down into the lower world system. In the Hermetic tradition, Nature, in the lower world, is entranced by the god (a metaphor for the spirit in Man), who responds in kind and thus unconsciously becomes enfolded, or temporarily 'entombed', in Nature's embrace. However, the 'god' also represents the spiritual consciousness of humankind in general.

10. About a century ago, scientists tried to disprove the existence of the 'ether' in what came to be known as the 'Michelson-Morley experiment'. However, science today has been forced to accept the existence of a 'quantum fluid', but still tries to suggest that this is quite different from the 'ether'!

11. Which, only *within* the solar universe, became 'Amun-Ra' – a fact not yet recognized by Egyptologists.

12. The name 'Kadmon' appears to derive from the compound (A)kh-Ad-Mn, signifying: divine spirit – primordial – mind.

13. As Iamblichus says: 'The soul, being moulded and formed by the Mind and itself moulding and forming the body by encompassing it on every side, receives from it impression and form.' (*The Egyptian Mysteries*, p.259.)

14. Hence in central and southern Africa, for example, the initial development (during this particular historic cycle) of a sense of *national* consciousness could only have been induced by colonial imposition.

15. One might also take into consideration that the three 'fallen divine sparks' are themselves the expression in parallel (within the imagination of the Logos) of the Will-to-Be, the Will-to-Know and the Will-to-Create. The lowest of these – to be found traditionally in the human heart – is concerned with developing quality and force in the functionally integrated capac-ity of the objective body senses. Correspondingly, the second spark (the 'Higher Ego') is

concerned, in parallel, with developing the Will-to-Know in man, thereby producing the principle of increasing self-knowledge and self-consciousness. But only when we come to a dawning perception of our own inner divinity does the third and highest 'spark' begin to manifest its influence and force within our overall consciousness, thereby eventually making of the human being a veritable planetary god incarnate, the full outward expression of his parent Logos and a member of the sixth kingdom in planetary Nature.

CHAPTER FIVE

1. Sir W. Scott, trans. *Hermetica*, p.317 and pp.328ff.
2. *Ibid.* p.48
3. It thus becomes possible for differently evolved groups of entities to coexist in parallel dimensions or states of being on our planet, whilst unfolding their nature from an archetypal state, yet without necessarily being in any way aware of each other, or even in sensory contact with each other.
4. Sir W. Scott, trans. *Hermetica*
5. The Aeon, like the Greek god Kronos (Saturn) is specifically associated with Time or Duration for the simple reason that the Aeon is the Demi-Urgos which literally contains the whole system within its consciousness and thus acts as the lesser field of expression for a greater Intelligence.
6. H.P. Blavatsky. *The Secret Doctrine*, vol.1, p.2
7. *Ibid.* p.102
8. However, whereas orthodox science regards plasma as 'ionized gas', esoteric philosophy says that this is back-to-front. Electro-magnetic plasma *precedes* gas in the process of unfolding. It mutates first into generalized protoplasm and then into cytoplasm – the cell (or atom) without a nucleus, the latter only manifesting later in the sequence.
9. R. Temple. *The Crystal Sun*, p.268
10. This corresponds rather interestingly with the 'spark' in the human Base-of-the-Spine *chakra*. Just as the activity within the Sun's matrix is believed to generate atoms, so from here are said to emanate into the objective world state those energies which give rise to the appearance of the blood cells – and thus to the human skeleton.
11. H.P. Blavatsky. *The Secret Doctrine*, vol.2, pp.289ff.
12. T. Taylor. *Hymns and Initiations*, pp.10–11
13. Cited in H.P. Blavatsky. *The Secret Doctrine*, vol.2, p.360
14. Hence as Plato says, the very first principle in Creation is privation – the isolation of a field of potential thought within the consciousness. The same principle applies in the Vedic tradition, where Shiva the 'Creator-Destroyer' god is referred to as 'the Great Ascetic'.
15. Interestingly, as Wallis Budge says when referring to the angels in Islamic theology: 'Curiously, some are said to have the forms of animals.' (E.W. Budge, *Gods of the Ancient Egyptians*, vol.1, p.5.)
16. However, early Islam appears to have believed in a female aspect of deity, by the name of 'Allat'.
17. P. Russell. *The Awakening Earth*, p.216
18. Thomas Taylor, the great translator of Greek philosophy, says: 'It is here necessary to observe that they (the Ancients) did not promiscuously call all souls descending into the whirl of generation bees, but only those who, whilst residing in this fluctuating region, acted justly and who after being in a manner acceptable to the divinities, returned to their pristine felicity.' (T. Taylor, *Oracles and Mysteries*, p.214.)
19. It would appear from the ancient Greek allegory of Sisyphus and the penance placed upon him that the 'missing' Merope is actually our own solar system. According to the Ancients, the Pleiades were stationed at the centre of our local universe – hence the misconception of the last two millennia that the universe revolves around our planet. However, the Pleiades

are part of the zodiacal constellation of Taurus, which is itself part of a bigger system, following the Hermetic principle of 'as above, so below'.

20. There are biblical correspondences here. In the Old Testament (Genesis 6:4) we read: 'There were giants [Nephilim] in the earth in those days; and also after that when the Sons of God ['B'ne Aleim'] came in unto the daughters of men, and they bore children to them. The same became mighty men [Gibborim] which were of old [the] men of renown.' 'Neph' or 'Kneph' (the Greek 'Cnophis') is an Egyptian word, denoting what was esoterically depicted as a serpent god, whilst the Nephilim (or 'Kneph-Elohim') were the offspring of a prior hierarchy of beings called 'the Watchers' and were also known as 'sons of A-nak' (i.e. the Anakim) who were themselves described as 'giants'.

21. Thomas Taylor quotes Porphyry: 'The soul does not exist on the Earth … in the same manner as bodies accede to the Earth, but a subsistence of the soul on the Earth signifies its presiding over terrene bodies. Thus also the soul is said to be in Hades when it presides over its image.' (*Oracles and Mysteries*, p.196.) Porphyry is here, however, talking about the spiritual soul of man not existing on Earth, whilst its projection – his terrestrial soul – which is overshadowed and guided by it in the manner of a puppet, does indeed do so.

22. As *The Secret Doctrine* describes it: 'In those early ages, astral evolution was alone in progress and the two planes – the astral and physical – though developing on parallel lines, had no direct point of contact with one another.' (H.P. Blavatsky, *The Secret Doctrine*, vol.2, p.157.)

CHAPTER SIX

1. P. Russell. *The Awakening Earth*, p.6
2. This appears to be wrought by a combination of both the descending polar lights (the aurorae borealis and australis) and also by 'mega-lightning' above the cloud base.
3. Cited in H.P. Blavatsky, *The Secret Doctrine*, vol.2, p.557
4. This is also the basis of what we call 'entropy'.
5. In esoteric philosophy there is no such thing as a vacuum. When all the gases have been removed from a container an isolated mass of pure etheric substance remains, the 'astral light' of the Hermeticists and 'dark matter' of science.
6. As Ptolemy says: 'A certain power, derived from the aetherial nature, is diffused over and pervades the whole atmosphere of the Earth … Fire and air … are encompassed and altered by the motions of the aether. These elements in their turn encompass all inferior matter and [act] on earth and water, on plants and animals.' (*Tetrabiblios*, p.2.)
7. B. Greene. *The Elegant Universe*, p.6
8. *Ibid*. p.14
9. For those who still refuse to believe in the existence of both spirit and soul, on the grounds that neither can actually be seen, one might perhaps point out that nobody has yet seen an electron, or even an atom, although both are now generally accepted as 'real'.
10. R.Hinckley Allen. *Star Names and their Meanings*, p.392
11. *Ibid*. p.393
12. J.S. Gordon. *Khemmea*, p.65
13. *Ibid*. p.127
14. On the assumption that the Earth's core is made of iron, the further assumption has arisen that the North and South poles are geographically at the top and bottom of the planet's surface. But if one accepts instead that the ionosphere determines the Earth's polarity (and gravity), the actual poles must necessarily exist some miles *above* the terrestrial surface. Interestingly, the Ancients believed Earth to be 'suspended in Space between two magnets'.
15. In fact, the just under 82,000-year obliquity cycle is equivalent to the precessionary cycle multiplied by *pi*. (*See* my book *Khemmea*, p.38.)
16. This is the same, symbolically speaking, as the 'broken pillar' of the Masonic tradition.
17. Sir W. Scott, trans. *Hermetica*, p.363

CHAPTER SEVEN

1. R. Milton. *Shattering the Myths of Darwinism*, p.275
2. Some of these species remain with us today – for example, the Californian redwood, some forms of Australian eucalyptus, and the giant fern forests of New Zealand. The places where these species grow supposedly formed part of the original Lemurian continental landmasses.
3. Within this previsioned Purpose choice exists (in humankind's nature) according to the field of limitation of an individual's consciousness.
4. Hoyle and Wickramsinghe were proponents of the 'Steady State' theory of cosmic unfolding, as opposed to the current 'Big Bang' theory.
5. F. Hoyle and C. Wickramsinghe. *Evolution from Space*, p.xxii
6. *Ibid.*
7. At least, not in this present objective cycle of the planet's existence.
8. It might be suggested that the consciousness of the Plant kingdom is actually involved in developing 'the senses' – of touch, taste, hearing, sight, mobility, and so on – that we see in coordinated function in the Animal kingdom, the next in the sequence of evolutionary progression.
9. In ancient tradition, this Aether (pure spirit) instinctively produced a circulatory motion, isolating the local matter of Space and causing it to adopt a spheroidal form – hence the ancient concept of the 'egg of the universe' being formed by the (kosmic Intelligence).
10. F. Hoyle and C. Wickramsinghe. *Evolution from Space*, p.28
11. *Ibid.* p.30
12. H.P. Blavatsky. *The Secret Doctrine*, vol.2, p.626
13. Modern science looks at this through the wrong end of the telescope, as it were. Instead of seeing objective matter as a condensate from an originally ethereal state (of light), it starts out with the idea that the quantum particles comprising the future atomic building blocks are the foundational material out of which everything develops in a compounding *upward* cycle – thus that liquid is the second state of matter, gas the third and plasma the fourth.
14. A 'Round' might perhaps be defined as the sevenfold cycle of Time which it takes for the evolving Life Wave to pass through all the four lower states of light substance of which our planetary nature is constituted, and thence back to its point of origin. According to Vedanta philosophy, this greater cycle involves hundreds of millions of years. For details, *see* Blavatsky's *The Secret Doctrine*.
15. H.P. Blavatsky. *The Secret Doctrine*, vol.2, p.68
16. R. Milton. *Shattering the Myths of Darwinism*, pp.38–39
17. As the *Encyclopaedia Britannica* (1985, p.779) admits, the geological column is a mental abstraction, or paradigm construct. The whole subject is currently in a state of intense discussion, even amongst professional geologists.
18. R. Milton. *Shattering the Myths of Darwinism*, p.21
19. *Ibid.*, pp.28–29
20. H.P. Blavatsky. *The Secret Doctrine*, vol.2, p.710
21. R. Milton. *Shattering the Myths of Darwinism*, p.78
22. This book has intentionally kept away from the subject of Creationism for the simple reason that its conceptually simplistic foundation derives entirely from a complete misinterpretation of the biblical Old Testament. Anyone with even the rudiments of objectivity, plus an understanding of the well-known fact that the Ancients dressed up all their cosmological philosophies in mystical allegory, would immediately see that the biblical Creation as described is no more than an over-simplified gloss.

CHAPTER EIGHT

1. P. Russell. *The Awakening Earth*, p.18
2. R. Milton. *Shattering the Myths of Darwinism*, p.61

3. K.O. Emery and E. Uchupi. *Geology of the Atlantic Ocean*, p.206
4. R. Milton. *Shattering the Myths of Darwinism*, p.63
5. K.O. Emery and E. Uchupi. *The Geology of the Atlantic Ocean*, pp.207–208
6. *Ibid.*
7. H.P. Blavatsky. *The Secret Doctrine*, vol.2, pp.333ff.
8. I have regrettably been unable to track down the reference for this statement.
9. J.S. Gordon. *Khemmea*, p.40. We know of Zep Tepi from later Egyptian references; obviously there is no extant contemporary description of a festival held 12,000 years ago.
10. Joshua 10:12–13
11. A 'valley of vulcanism' is a phenomenon found, for example, in Iceland, where a stretch of the Earth's crust several miles long has split open, producing a gigantic lava river.
12. Plato. *Timaeus* and *Critias*

CHAPTER NINE

1. M. Cremo and R. Thompson. *The Hidden History of the Human Race*, p.xvii
2. *Ibid.* p.11
3. From *Hommes Fossiles et Hommes Sauvages* (1884) by Armand de Quatrefages, a member of the French Academy of Sciences and a professor at the Museum of Natural History in Paris; cited in M. Cremo and R. Thompson, *The Hidden History of the Human Race*, p.13.
4. This comes back to the idea that our planet is, in toto, an organism, all its different flora, fauna and mineral forms being merely different expressions of the One Life, temporarily inhabiting a compound appearance which is itself based upon a condensation of (local) light substance, or 'ether'.
5. Man being the sole distinction by virtue of the fact that the human soul entity is said to have 'individualized' a particular form or quality of consciousness *within* its parent group, thereby producing in the outer man the senses of duality and of 'self'.
6. R. Milton. *Shattering the Myths of Darwinism*, p.99
7. *Ibid.* p.104
8. *Ibid.* p.137
9. F. Hoyle and C. Wickramsinghe. *Evolution from Space*, p.91
10. *Ibid.* p.101
11. *Ibid.* p.30
12. *Ibid.* p.31
13. M. Cremo and R. Thompson. *The Hidden History of the Human Race*, p.266
14. *Ibid.* p.4
15. Modern Darwinian theory suggests that the DNA of humans and primates are pretty well the same. In fact, as Richard Milton recently confirmed to me from his own researches, there are three different types of DNA and the one in humans that constitutes approximately 98 per cent of the mass of chromosomes is *completely* unlike that of the primate. Yet this idea, although a complete fallacy, is commonly used (even by scientists) to support the idea of Darwinian evolution and of humans and apes having a common ancestor.
16. But even Neanderthal man would not look that different from some modern human males.
17. H.P. Blavatsky. *The Secret Doctrine*, vol.1, pp.170ff. *See also* A.P. Sinnett, *Esoteric Buddhism*.
18. The time frames relating to the various races and sub-races etc. vary immensely, reducing very considerably as time goes on. The unfolding of consciousness is very slow in the early stages but accelerates rapidly once self-conscious humanity appears.
19. R. Milton. *Shattering the Myths of Darwinism*, p.23
20. M. Cremo and R. Thompson. *The Hidden History of the Human Race*, p.9
21. *Ibid.* pp.103ff.
22. One question which constantly arises in relation to the subject of archaeological artefacts is, if *Homo sapiens* is as old as I am suggesting here, why are so few artefacts to be found scattered around the place? Almost all great cultures and civilizations are founded around

towns and cities built at strategic points either on coastlines or on rivers. However, coastlines and rivers are far more vulnerable to Nature's ravages than most other places. Consequently, most cities and towns in such locations could not reasonably be expected to last for more than a few thousand years at the very outside. Most would disappear, along with all their cultural artefacts.

23. In the Ancient Wisdom tradition, Truth (and also accuracy) was regarded as of paramount importance because it permitted access into the Mind of Deity and was thus the sole basis of all possible spiritual evolution.

CHAPTER TEN

1. D. Frawley. *Gods, Sages and Kings*, p.298
2. *Ibid.*
3. H.P. Blavatsky. *The Secret Doctrine*, vol.2, pp.323ff.
4. *Ibid.* p.327
5. *Ibid.* p.333
6. *Ibid.* pp.401ff.
7. *Ibid.* p.138
8. *Ibid.* p.294
9. The contemporary dinosaurs would have been examples of the 'most heterogeneous' gigantic monsters, in parallel with the remainder of Nature's creative efforts at the time.
10. H.P. Blavatsky. *The Secret Doctrine*, vol.2, p.324
11. *Ibid.* p.329
12. *Ibid.* p.327
13. M. Cremo and R. Thompson. *The Hidden History of the Human Race*, p.212
14. H.P. Blavatsky. *The Secret Doctrine*, vol.2, p.327
15. *Ibid.* p.314
16. *Ibid.* p.324
17. A. de Quatrefages. *Introduction a l'Etude des Races Humaines* (*Introduction to the Study of the Human Races*)
18. M. Cremo and R. Thompson. *The Hidden History of the Human Race*, p.101
19. C. Darwin. *The Descent of Man*, pp.188–189
20. C. Darwin. *The Origin of Species*, pp.484ff.
21. H.P. Blavatsky. *The Secret Doctrine*, vol.2, p.172
22. *Ibid.* p.195
23. *Ibid.* p.331
24. *Ibid.* p.689
25. *Ibid.* p.287
26. *Ibid.* p.192
27. M. Cremo and R Thompson. *The Hidden History of the Human Race*, p.7
28. H.P. Blavatsky. *The Secret Doctrine*, vol.2, p.715
29. M. Cremo and R. Thompson. *The Hidden History of the Human Race*, p.97
30. *Ibid.*
31. H.P. Blavatsky. *The Secret Doctrine*, vol.2, p.201
32. *Ibid.* p.329
33. The Great Year divided by six would produce *sar* cycles of 4,320 years, each equivalent to a Vedic *yuga* cycle. The Chaldean system of calculation worked on the basis of the sixfold principle, whilst the Vedic system also worked on the basis of sevenfold cycles. However odd it might seem, the two are not mutually inconsistent.
34. *The Secret Doctrine* (vol.2, p.330) associates this with an astronomical cycle of just over 21,000 years.
35. H.P. Blavatsky. *Isis Unveiled*, vol.1, p.31 (referring to *Of the Chaldean Kings and the Deluge* by Berossus of Abydenus)

CHAPTER ELEVEN

1. Sir W. Scott, trans. *Hermetica*, p.49
2. Genesis 6:4. (Also cited in Chapter 5, note 20, above.)
3. 'As' in Sanskrit means the essence or 'throne' of being and consciousness.
4. Hence also the kabbalistic Ain, Ain-Soph and Ain-Soph-Aur.
5. Iamblichus. *The Egyptian Mysteries*, p.254
6. Some people do of course, by virtue of their natural clairvoyant ability. However, as mainstream science considers this subject from a basis of disbelief, rational objectivity is in very short supply.
7. A common misinterpretation found today, even amongst Jews, Christians and Muslims.
8. *Hermetica*, pp.82ff.
9. *Ibid.* p.116
10. Bearing in mind that the Lemurians were members of the Third 'Root Race', as Blavatsky terms it, it is interesting to note that the ancient Meso-American tradition follows suit. In the 16th century one Don Fernando de Alva Ixtlilxochitl wrote a history ('*Relaciones*') of the myths of the Nahua people which stated that proper human beings only emerged into the world during the third solar Age of the five so far made manifest.
11. So *The Secret Doctrine* says: 'The Watchers reign over man ... down to the beginning of the Third Race, after which it is the Patriarchs, Heroes and the Manes ... of a lower order.' (H.P. Blavatsky, *The Secret Doctrine*, vol.2, p.267.) As 'the Watchers' are the Dhyani Buddhas responsible for our solar system, it would appear that the *kumaras* are their progeny.
12. Some modern 'New Age' authors claim that intelligent humanity was some sort of genetic experiment by inter-planetary or even inter-galactic visitors who came to Earth by spacecraft some thousands or even millions of years ago. This is a sad travesty of the sacred ancient teaching.
13. H.P. Blavatsky. *The Secret Doctrine*, vol.2, p.317
14. *Ibid.* p.317
15. *Ibid.* pp.198–9
16. *Ibid.* p.769
17. There is an old tradition that the first 'home-base' of the *kumaras* on Earth amongst the later Lemurians was in northern South America. It was apparently only much later that they moved close to Lake Baikal in Russia, in the area subsequently known to oriental tradition as 'Shambala' (*see* D. Frawley, *Gods, Sages and Kings*, p.295). Hence, perhaps, the Fifth Root Race had its 'nursery' next door on the Tibetan Plateau, before being later moved westwards to the Caucasus.
18. Ptolemy of Alexandria reportedly wrote a treatise on sound.
19. J.H. Brennan. *Occult Tibet*, p.26
20. But *see also* my *Egypt, Child of Atlantis* (Appendix Q).
21. This lake is the deepest in the world and is said to contain 20 per cent of the world's fresh water.
22. H.P. Blavatsky. *The Secret Doctrine*, vol.2, p.433
23. T. Barker (ed.). *The Mahatma Letters to A.P. Sinnett*, p.148

CHAPTER TWELVE

1. H.P. Blavatsky. *Isis Unveiled*, vol.1, p.595, citing *Histoire des Vierges: Les Peuples et les Continents Disparus* by the 19th-century explorer and anthropologist Louis Jacolliot.
2. Even today, the Polynesians of Hawaii refer to Lemuria as 'Mu'.
3. H.P. Blavatsky. *The Secret Doctrine*, vol.2, pp.333ff.
4. *Ibid.* p.199
5. *Ibid.* p.264
6. *Ibid.* p.324

7. *Ibid.* p.424
8. *Ibid.* p.760
9. *Ibid.* p.683
10. *Ibid.* p.193
11. *Ibid.* p.350
12. *Ibid.* p.751
13. *Ibid.* p.326
14. *Ibid.* p.224
15. Louis Jacolliot. *Histoire des Vierges: Les Peuples et Les Continents Disparus*, p.308
16. P. Gaffarel. *History of the Discovery of America*, vol.1, p.18
17. Sir J. Frazer. *Folk Lore of the Old Testament*, vol.1, p.281
18. H.T. Wilkins. *Secret Cities of Old South America: Atlantis Unveiled*, p.112
19. D. Brinton. 'Archaeology of Cuba' in *American Anthropologist* (journal), vol. 10, pp.231ff.
20. H.P. Blavatsky. *The Secret Doctrine* vol.2, p.395
21. *Ibid.* p.740
22. Deuteronomy 3.11 says that 'only Og, king of Bashan, remained of the remnant of giants', and his bed measured 9 by 4 cubits (1 cubit is about 18 inches, or 450 mm).
23. H.P. Blavatsky. *The Secret Doctrine*, vol.2, p.313. Such cataclysms, however, took place not over the space of a few days or weeks, but over thousands or even tens of thousands of years.
24. *Ibid.* p.761
25. *Ibid.* p.416
26. *Ibid.* p.425
27. *Ibid.*
28. *Ibid.* p.395
29. *Ibid.* p.368. In fact, these countries and the 'Horn of Africa' in general appear to have commenced as a large island the size of Australia. Only later did this connect with the rest of Africa as a result of rising ocean beds – not plate tectonics.

CHAPTER THIRTEEN

1. A. Le Plongeon. *Sacred Mysteries among the Maya and the Quiche*, p.57. The migrant 'Ethiopians' were in fact from the Indian subcontinent and effectively took over an ancient Egyptian culture already in a state of decline.
2. H.P. Blavatsky. *The Secret Doctrine*, vol.2, p.750
3. *Ibid.* p.754
4. See also N. Lahovary's *Dravidian Origins and the West* and my own *Egypt, Child of Atlantis* (p.216)
5. H.P. Blavatsky. *The Secret Doctrine*, vol.2, p.790
6. *Ibid.* pp.352 and 740
7. D. Frawley. *Gods, Sages and Kings*, p.285
8. *Ibid.* p.286
9. H.P. Blavatsky. *The Secret Doctrine*, vol.2, p.750
10. *Ibid.* p.746
11. *Ibid.*
12. *Asiatic Researches*, vol.3, p.319
13. *Ibid.* p.4
14. *Ibid.* p.302
15. *Ibid.* p.328
16. H.P. Blavatsky. *Isis Unveiled*, vol.1, p.627. As *The Secret Doctrine* says, the Akkadians, so-called, were simply emigrants on their way to Asia Minor from India (or rather, from ancient Indo-Persia), from where the Babylonian culture was also originally imported (H.P. Blavatsky. *The Secret Doctrine*, vol.2, p.203.)
17. H.P. Blavatsky. *The Secret Doctrine*, vol.2, p.368

18. It has already been acknowledged by archaeologists that the Punjab and Rajasthan have been inhabited by humans for at least 400,000 years. But this is entirely in line with the Brahmanic tradition, which alone has the area already occupied by a highly sophisticated culture by then.

19. H.P. Blavatsky. *The Secret Doctrine*, vol.2, p.429

20. But by 50,000 years ago, even the tallest humans (on average) would undoubtedly have shrunk to perhaps little more than about 8 ft (2.5 m) in height), the sort of height attributed to the early Berbers and Guanche men, among others.

21. H.P. Blavatsky. *The Secret Doctrine*, vol.2, p.753

22. *Ibid.*

23. But *see* Robert Temple's book *The Crystal Sun*

24. Apparently unaware of the existence of the *antikythera*, Charles Hapgood says: 'The evident knowledge of longitude implies a people unknown to us, a nation of seafarers with instruments for finding longitude undreamed of by the Greeks and, so far as we know, not possessed by the Phoenicians either.' (C. Hapgood, *Maps of the Ancient Sea Kings*, p.36.)

25. J.S. Gordon. *Egypt, Child of Atlantis*, pp.234–236

26. B. O'Brien. *The Shining Ones*, pp.438ff.

27. H.P. Blavatsky. *The Secret Doctrine*, vol.2, p.402

28. The Roman historian Aelian also confirms the general location when he says that 'the inhabitants of the shores [of the Atlantic] tell us that in former times, the kings of Atlantis, descendants of Poseidon, wore on their heads as a mark of power the headbands of the male sea-ram [i.e. walrus tusks, from a creature not found in the Mediterranean].' (Aelian, *On Animals*, ch.xv. 2.)

29. This is rather interesting given the popular hypothesis that the Gulf of Mexico was created some 65 million years ago by a huge asteroid hitting the Earth, thereby giving rise to the mass demise of the dinosaurs. If the original landmass was still there at the time of the map's creation, the hypothesis looks distinctly inaccurate.

30. B. de Bourbourg. *Mayan Troano Codex*

31. J.B. Mahan. *American World History Before Columbus*, p.5

32. K.O. Emery and E. Uchupi. *The Geology of the Atlantic Ocean*, p.196

33. I have been unable to confirm this quotation from original sources but it is mentioned in Berlitz, *The Mystery of Atlantis*, p.69 and elsewhere.

34. *The American Journal of Science*, vol.258, p.429

35. *Ibid.* p.196

CHAPTER FOURTEEN

1. Plato. *Timaeus*.

2. Thucydides. *The Peloponnesian Wars*, book 3, ch.LXXXIX, p.157. (Loeb Classical Library.)

3. According to the Greek historian Proclus, Plato's disciple Kantor visited Sais in Egypt and was shown priests' columns with inscribed hieroglyphs detailing the history of Atlantis (Proclus, *Commentary on the Timaeus*, vol.1, p.64). Proclus also quotes a much earlier source which referred to 'the islands of the ocean beyond the Pillars of Herakles', one of which had a tradition of having belonged to an extremely large island called Atlantis, which ruled over the whole Atlantic Ocean, including parts of the opposite continent – that is, the Americas.

4. Diodorus Siculus mentions the 'fair isle' as having been some three days' sail out into the Atlantic from the Pillars of Herakles (*Diodorus Siculus*, vol.1, p.147).

5. Thus the Black Sea at this time was an inland sea – as is already acknowledged by modern science. Some scientists have conjectured the date of the seismic activity which connected it to the Mediterranean as c12,000–13,000 years ago.

6. C. Hapgood. *Maps of the Ancient Sea Kings*, ch.2

7. G. Hancock. *Fingerprints of the Gods*, p.15–20

8. The N'goro n'goro crater in Tanzania – the world's largest known terrestrial caldera – is a

mere 11 miles (17 km) in diameter. But how many others lie buried beneath the oceans, or camouflaged by later geological activity?

9. K.A. Folliot. *Atlantis Revisited*, p.59
10. J. Mercer. *Canary Is: Fuerteventura*, p.15
11. J.D. Hays, J. Imbrie and N.J. Shackleton. 'Variations in the Earth's Orbit: Pacemaker of the Ice Ages.' *Science*, vol. 194, pp.121–3
12. R. Bauval and G. Hancock. *Keeper of Genesis*, p.79
13. 'The archaeologist Professor Neil Steede, who studied in Tihuanaco for many years, concluded that the sacred city was built around 12,000 years ago. And more surprisingly, so does Dr Osvaldo Rivera, the Director of the Bolivian Institute of Archaeology.' (C. Wilson and R. Flem-Ath, *The Atlantis Blueprint*, p.138.) It is worthy of note, however, that the ruins of Tihuanaco are themselves built on the ruins of at least four previous cities.

CHAPTER FIFTEEN

1. M.P. Hall. *Freemasonry of the Ancient Egyptians*, p.55
2. Pliny. *Historia Naturalis*, vol.6, v. 197, p.487
3. H.P. Blavatsky. *The Secret Doctrine*, vol.2, p.407
4. There is still disagreement amongst linguists as to the origins of the Guanche tongue. The majority agree that it is related to Berber, an alternative theory is that – like Basque– it is of Dravidian origin, i.e. from India (*see* for example www.atlan.org/articles/dravida/).
5. A. Fahkri. *Siwa Oasis*, p.23 (1944)
6. Egyptologists regard the Kushites as a completely new socio-political group, with its origins in Ethiopia in the mid-2nd millennium BC. However, as I have suggested, the name Kush derives from the land of Kesh or Kush in ancient northwestern Indo-Persia, possibly including modern Afghanistan. It would appear that the Kushites were expatriate Indo-Persians who had originally captured Egypt from the Poseidonians (reputedly c100,000BC).
7. L. Spence. *History of Atlantis*, p.209
8. Modern scholars have suggested that the sudden and unexplained appearance of a fully vibrant Etruscan culture in Italy c750BC might represent a resurgence of an existing local civilization. It seems highly coincidental, however, with the appearance, a mere 50 years before, of the Phoenicians in Carthage, just across the Mediterranean. My suggestion, therefore, is that the one led to the other.
9. J.S. Gordon. *Khemmea*, p.189
10. Modern Egyptologists believe that Punt lay in Ethiopia, but there is little actual justification for this. As earlier Egyptologists maintained, it is far more likely that *India* was in fact the source of the famous spices of the land of Pun(t).
11. The *Royal Masonic Cyclopaedia* describes the original Palestinians as those 'whose fate was to be banished from the Sacred Five Rivers of India'. (K. Mackenzie, The *Royal Masonic Cyclopaedia*, p.541.) One wonders, therefore, whether the supposedly 'Phoenician' trading city of Tyre was in fact originally named by Etrusco-Carthaginian merchants after their own sea – the Tyr-hennian. If so, it might indicate that the Etruscans had very influential trading operations in the Middle East well back into prehistoric times.
12. The popular idea that the Phoenicians were a Semitic-speaking people of the same lineage as the Hebrews makes little sense unless one looks for the common origin of both in a rather larger culture. In fact, the province of Iaothea (hence 'Judaea') was originally part of the great Dravidian civilization and empire, which extended to seafaring colonies on the coasts of both the Atlantic and Mediterranean. Before adopting Sanskrit and Vedic culture, the Dravidians used a right-to-left writing style, like the Phoenicians.
13. Herodotus. *The Histories*, book I, p.1
14. *Ibid.* p.111
15. K.A. Folliot. *Atlantis Revisited*, p.99

16. Pliny. *Historia Naturalis*, book VI, ch. v, p.196
17. Aristotle. *Meteorologica*
18. Philo, trans. C.D. Yonge. *Works*, p.723
19. According to the 4th-century AD historian Ammianus Marcellinus, the 1st-century BC Greek historian Timagenes recorded that the Gauls had a tradition of having been invaded by survivors of an Atlantic island which had sunk in a cataclysm (C. Berlitz, *The Mystery of Atlantis*, p.38).
20. Dionysius of Halicarnassus. *Roman Antiquities*, book 1, ch.30, pp.1–3
21. Interestingly, the Roman tradition of their state having been founded by Romulus, who as an infant with his brother Remus was suckled by a she-wolf or jackal, is a straight crib from the ancient esoteric tradition – shared by both the Atlanteans and Egyptians – that humankind was spiritually overshadowed and nurtured in its evolution by great kosmic Intelligences from the star system of the Dog, that is, Sirius.
22. Strabo, trans. Jones–Sterret. *Geographia*, vol.3, p.6.
23. It has been acknowledged by scholars that of the many tribes which comprised the 'Sea Peoples' one at least (the Sikels) came from and gave their name to the island of Sicily, and may have been connected to the Etruscans. Sicily – midway between Carthage and Italy – was clearly a shared Carthaginian-Etruscan stronghold. In fact, it was ownership of Sicily above all which sparked off the Punic Wars between Rome and Carthage.
24. Plato. *Timaeus*, p.37. 'Tyrrhenia' meant ancient Italy, the western Mediterranean in general being known as the Tyrrhenian Sea. But, as we have already seen, the Greeks referred to the Etruscans in exactly the same way as Solon's Egyptian priest referred to the Atlanteans.
25. Ovid. *Fasti*, book 3, vv. 285–346
26. *Ibid.*, book 1, ch.31
27. There is conjecture that Etruscan (like Basque) had its origins in Dravidian (*see* www.verbix.com/documents/etruscan-dravidian.htm).
28. Which also suggests that our Western alphabet was, in origin, Etruscan, rather than derived from the Phoenician as scholars currently believe. In fact, the Phoenicians may have derived their writing style from the Carthaginians, who already used the same alphabet as the Etruscans.
29. It seems that Tinia nevertheless had to govern by consultation with other superior divinities.
30. See my book *Khemmea*, dealing with the real nature of ancient Egyptian spiritual culture.
31. It is interesting to note that some reliefs of a distinctively Cretan type have been found in the temples of Thebes in Egypt, suggesting a cultural connection.
32. H.P. Blavatsky. *The Secret Doctrine*, vol.2, p.774.

CHAPTER SIXTEEN

1. D. Frawley. *Gods, Sages and Kings*, p.40
2. Hence it was said that the early-to-mid Third Race proto-humans were 'immensely strong and prodigiously ambitious'.
3. The original priest-kings, or 'Piru'- from which the Egyptians derived their name 'pharaoh'.
4. In the eastern tradition, these are known (collectively) as 'Dhyanis' or 'Buddhas' – either of a planetary or a solar nature.
5. Dense matter might thus be defined as the accretion of a lesser quality of light substance, which has not yet evolved a perceptually apparent form of even elemental group consciousness.
6. But it is something which Christianity itself has done, for example in Central and Southern America in particular, where the aboriginal consciousness still lies very close beneath the surface of present-day culture.
7. Thus the 'seventh son of a seventh son' in some cultures (like the Celtic) was regarded as having automatic psycho-spiritual powers.

8. However, the Egyptian pyramid *internalizes* the allegorical ascents and descents of consciousness followed by the individual initiate, making it intensely personal and deeply esoteric.

9. Islam – having no priesthood *per se* – is very largely based upon Sharia law. This, although built around the Koran, involves a set of moral and ethical concepts and precepts passed down by a series of acknowledged theologians and philosophers, in direct succession from the teachings of Muhammad himself.

10. Which in turn suggests that there was a close relationship between the Etruscan and Mithraic esoteric traditions.

CHAPTER SEVENTEEN

1. J. Naydler. *Temple of the Cosmos*, p.127

2. As Blavatsky comments: 'The Ancients, unlike ourselves, could "try" the spirits and discern the difference between the good and evil ones, the human and elemental. They also knew that unregulated spirit intercourse brought ruin upon the individual and disaster to the community.' (H.P. Blavatsky, *Isis Unveiled*, vol.1, p.490.)

3. In ancient Egypt and Greece, the priestesses were seemingly only involved in passive aspects of magical practice, involving divinatory mediumship, for example. But they were much more fully involved in the Mysteries generally.

4. It is worth mentioning here that such practices are always the result of materialistically based hope and/or fear arising out of spiritual ignorance. All of these lead inevitably to the dark and gloomy halls of superstition.

5. The very word 'magic' is derived from the Sanskrit, meaning the 'Great Knowledge' (of how inner Nature works). The word 'shaman', on the other hand, derives from '*shu*' (light) and '*man*' (mind).

6. From a misinterpretation of the ancient texts, it has been suggested, wrongly, that ancient Egyptian ritual magic was based upon shamanism.

7. The Polynesians and Egyptians also used the same name (Ra) for the solar deity.

8. An esoteric metaphor for the self-emanation of the soul entity from a prior state of pure subjectivity.

9. J.S. Gordon. *Khemmea*, p.75

10. We still find this being celebrated in our own era – for example in the Jewish and Islamic coming of age traditions at around this age, and also in the Christian rite of confirmation.

11. We see the past and future (subjectively) all the time in our 'mind's eye', using the powers of 'memory' and 'imagination'. Unlike the animal, such inner vision provides us with the faculty of choosing (at least to some extent) what sort of future we wish to pursue. The rest is down to our will in following our vision and making it so.

12. The same would have been true of our modern Fifth Race cycle's middle period – hence perhaps the great cataclysms of c250,000–300,000 years ago which destroyed the single remaining Atlantean island continent of Daitya, in the northern Atlantic (the fragments of which are the Azores).

13. Although they were doubtless capable of great feats of theurgical wizardry as well.

14. For example, by using medicinal remedies which are out of context. Thus, modern biochemical companies, having discovered a natural remedy in the plant kingdom, try to mass-produce a synthetic chemical equivalent using materials from the mineral kingdom. But the essences of the *mineral* kingdom are not as evolved as the essences of the plant kingdom, so this cannot work in the same way.

15. It naturally follows that the 'black' magicians' wish to contain planetary Nature according to their own will automatically resulted in their restricting their own inner vision, thereby blinding themselves to the potential wider eventualities. The 'white' magicians, however, their inner vision unrestricted by merely parochial planetary concerns, were able to foresee the inevitable dead-end unconsciously pursued by their misguided brethren and were able to take evasive action.

16. The cockerel is also used in the Mazdean spiritual tradition, although in a completely different manner to that employed in Voodoo.

17. Archaeologists find purported examples of human blood sacrifice all over the world, often supposedly involving children. They then use such interpretation to confirm their preconceptions of the ancient world as generally barbarous. But a majority of such 'finds' actually seem to be based upon little other than pure speculation.

18. Interestingly, the fierce spirits depicted in the Mayan tradition are very similar to those found in the traditions of China and Southeast Asia, right up into Bhutan and Tibet. There is a reason for wondering whether there was once a close cultural connection (perhaps through prehistoric colonization) between these parts of the world.

19. Despite the conversion of many Polynesians to Christianity, traditional beliefs and practices are by no means forgotten. Many Polynesian islands are off-limits to Westerners and here in particular they still follow the old traditions.

20. *The Secret Doctrine* says that the Atlantean high priest and scholar Asura-Maya took the knowledge of ancient astrology with him when he and others fled to what is now the high plateau of Tibet, to escape the destruction of Ruta.

CHAPTER EIGHTEEN

1. D. Frawley. *Gods, Sages and Kings*, p.27

2. Perhaps unsurprising when one considers the late 19th- to mid-20th-century generation of science graduates who became familiar with Eastern philosophy at the same time.

3. Seemingly comparable to modern laser technology. However, Cayce only rather unspecifically mentioned these crystals being gathered by Atlanteans, without suggesting any sort of centrally organized system or government agency. It is true that the *Mahabharata* has descriptions of airships apparently taking the shape of nebulous, bluish eggs, or luminous globes, supposedly propelled by some unspecified ethereal force.

4. Some of us would regard this view as the typical parochial logic of the arch-materialist.

5. However, the tools used by the Egyptians to cut and work the hardest granite – for example, the sarcophagus in the King's Chamber of the Great Pyramid – are still unknown. Specialists have surmised that it would take modern diamond and laser drilling technology to achieve such remarkable precision.

6. M. Cremo and R. Thompson. *Hidden History of the Human Race*, p.116. This book is a version of the same authors' *Forbidden Archaeology*, intended for a wider audience.

7. *Ibid*. See also Chapter 6

8. *Ibid*.

9. The stratospheric jetstreams some 40,000 feet (7.6 miles/12 km) above the Earth's surface have caused the problem through having recently changed their direction of flow. This has caused repeated widespread flooding in Central Europe yet at the same time causing terrible drought in Southern Europe, leading to extensive forest fires. But why should such 'freaks' of climate not have happened before?

10. J.S. Gordon. *Khemmea*, p.246. But *see also* E.W. Budge *The Civilisation of the Ancient Egyptians*, p.15, and *The Dwellers on the Nile*, pp.169ff. Tehuti (Djehuty), was Hellenized as 'Thoth'.

11. Archaeologists have assumed that these instruments were originally obtained by the Etruscans from the Greeks. Yet the Greeks merely obtained their technology from others, including the Egyptians and the civilizations of the Middle East. It would seem more than likely that the Etruscans used such instruments for millennia before the 'ancient' Greeks.

12. R. Temple. *The Crystal Sun*, chs. 2 and 4, and p.443

13. *Ibid*. p.167.

14. That is not to suggest that the Ancients did not produce and sell technology. They clearly did and at times, as records show, were highly successful. But religious considerations nearly always came first.

15. The ancient Greek name Tiryns (modern Tiryntha), most probably derives from *Tyrhens*, because of the site's many clear associations with the Tyrrhenians.
16. However, the ancient Egyptians did use the characteristics of sand as a means of construction in the raising of obelisks.
17. J.S. Gordon. *Khemmea*, p.139
18. E.W. Budge. *The Nile*, p.140
19. It is true that Rameses II left inscriptions all over Egyptian architecture, from south to north, of his supposed accomplishments. But then Rameses was a great usurper of older royal monuments, substituting his own names and titles for those of his predecessors.
20. The application of bituminous materials for waterproofing was also a well-known ancient practice.
21. The Romans (and probably the Etruscans) certainly used lead pipes, one example still being in use at the Roman baths at Bath in the west of England.
22. C. Wilson and R. Flem-Ath. *The Atlantis Blueprint*, p.117
23. Archimedes used such knowledge to destroy Roman ships before they even neared the coast of his country, Sicily. But it seems clear that much of Archimedes' knowledge was culled from Egypt and the Middle East.
24. Hellenized as Neith.
25. Referred to in Egypt as 'the bones of Osiris' and frequently derived from meteorites.
26. Some of the Vedic texts also refer to projectiles hurled from these *vimanas* in warfare and producing explosive effects not dissimilar from modern nuclear bombs (*see* H.P. Blavatsky. *The Secret Doctrine*, vol.2, p.563).
27. 'It is from them [the Fourth Race Atlanteans] that they [the early Aryans] learned aeronautics ... and therefore also their great arts of meteorography and meteorology.' (H.P. Blavatsky, *The Secret Doctrine*, vol.2, p.426.)
28. R. Temple. *The Crystal Sun*, chs. 2 and 4
29. *Ibid*. ch.2.
30. H.P. Blavatsky. *The Secret Doctrine*, vol.2, pp.618ff.
31. Here as elsewhere, 'Brahmans' are not to be confused with 'Brahmins'. The former were ancient followers of Brahma, the latter are simply the highest of the four castes of the general Hindu system.
32. Probably because such tests are entirely unnatural. Nature itself was the laboratory of the Ancients and all that they had to do involved deduction from universal principles plus local replication or adaptation according to those same principles. The Ancients were not interested in abstract hypotheses that did not fit into their one-world perception of Nature's processes.

EPILOGUE

1. See, for example, G. Hancock's *Fingerprints of the Gods*, p.499

APPENDIX B

1. With regard to this date, the Egyptological jury is still out. Three or four decades ago, it was felt certain that the New Kingdom did not commence until after 1200BC, at which date Rameses III of the 19th Dynasty is supposed to have come to the throne. However, by the end of the 20th century, the commencement of the New Kingdom had been pushed back to about 1550BC. The modern view is that Rameses III reigned from 1184 to 1153BC within the later New Kingdom period.

BIBLIOGRAPHY

Adams, W. Marsham, *The Book of the Master of the Hidden Places*, Search
  Publishing, London, 1933
Aelian, *Historical Miscellany*, trans. N.G. Wilson, Harvard University Press,
  Cambridge, Mass, 1997
Berlitz, C., *The Mystery of Atlantis*, Souvenir Press, London, 1977
Berriman, A.E., *Historical Metrology*, Dent Dutton, London, 1953
Blavatsky, H.P., *Isis Unveiled*, Theosophy Company, Los Angeles, 1931
—— *The Secret Doctrine*, Theosophical Publishing House, Los Angeles, 1947
Brennan, J.H., *Occult Tibet*, Llewellyn Publications, USA, 1997
Budge, W.W., *The Dwellers on the Nile*, The Religious Tract Society, London,
  1926
Chatterji, J.C., *The Wisdom of the Vedas*, Quest Books, Wheaton, Ill., 1973
Churton, T., *Gnostic Philosophy*, Inner Traditions, Rochester, Vt, 2005
Collins, A., *Gateway to Atlantis*, Headline Books, London, 2000
Cottrell, A. (ed.), *The Penguin Encyclopaedia of Ancient Civilizations*, Penguin
  Books, London, 1980
Countryman, J., *Atlantis and the Seven Stars*, Robert Hale, London, 1979
Cremo, M.A., and Thompson, R., *The Hidden History of the Human Race*,
  Bhaktivedanta Book Publishing, 2001
Darwin, C., *The Descent of Man*, first pub. 1871, Penguin Classics, London,
  2004
—— *The Origin of Species*, first pub. 1859, Penguin Classics, London, 1982
Dingwall, E.J., *Ghosts and Spirits in the Ancient World*, Kegan Paul, London,
  1930
Donnelly, I., *Atlantis, the Antediluvian World*, Dover Books, New York, 1976
Emery, K.O., and Uchupi, E., *The Geology of the Atlantic Ocean*, Springer,
  New York, 1984
Fakhri, A., *Siwa Oasis*, American University in Cairo Press, London, 1990
Flem-Ath, R., and Wilson, C., *The Atlantis Blueprint*, Little, Brown, London,
  2000

Folliot, K.A., *Atlantis Revisited*, Professional Books, Oxford, 1984

Fox, H., *Gods of the Cataclysm*, 1976

Frawley, D., *Gods, Sages and Kings*, Passage Press, Salt Lake City, 1991

Frazer, Sir J., *Folk Lore in the Old Testament*, Macmillan, London, 1919

Gaffarel, P., *Histoire de la découverte de l'Amérique depuis les origines jusqu'à la mort de Christophe Colomb*, Société Bourguignonne de Géographie et d'Histoire, Paris, 1892

Gordon, J.S., *Egypt, Child of Atlantis*, Inner Traditions, Rochester, Vt, 2004

—— *Khemmea*, Orpheus Publishing House, Guildford, 2003

Gosse, A. Bothwell, *The Civilisation of the Ancient Egyptians*, T.C. & E.C. Jack, London, 1915

Greene, B., *The Elegant Universe*, Vintage (Random House), New York, 2000

Hamblin, D.J., *The Etruscans*, Time Life Books, London, 1976

Hapgood, C.H., *Maps of the Ancient Sea Kings*, Turnstone Press, London, 1979

Herodotus, *The Histories*, trans. A. De Selincourt, Penguin Classics, London, 1954

Hoyle, F., and Wickramsinghe, C., *Evolution From Space*, Paladin Books, London, 1983

Iamblichos, *Theurgia (The Egyptian Mysteries)*, trans. A. Wilder, Rider, London, 1911

Jacolliot, L., *Occult Science in India*, W.O. Felt, London, 1874

—— *The Bible in India*, Pannini Office, Allahabad, India, 1869

Lahovary, N., *Dravidian Origins and the West*, Orient Longmans, London, 1963

Le Plongeon, A., *Sacred Mysteries Among the Maya and the Quiche*, Wizards Bookshelf, San Diego, 1994

Lomas, R., and Knight, C., *Uriel's Machine*, Century Publishing, London, 2001

Lovelock, J.E., *The Ages of Gaia*, W.W. Norton, London, rev. ed. 1995

Maclellan, A., *The Lost World of Agherti*, Souvenir Press, London, 1982

Mercer, J., *Canary Islands: Fuerteventura*, David & Charles, Newton Abbot, 1973

Morrell, R.A., *The Sacred Power of Huna*, Inner Traditions, Rochester, Vt, 2005

Naydler, J., *Shamanic Wisdom in the Pyramid Texts*, Inner Traditions, Rochester, Vt, 2005

—— *Temple of the Cosmos*, Inner Traditions, Rochester, Vt, 1996

O'Brien, B.J. and C., *The Shining Ones*, Dianthus Publishing, Cirencester, 1997

Plato, *The Timaeus and Critias*, trans. H.D.P. Lee, Penguin Classics, Harmondsworth, England, 1965

Posnansky, A., *Tihuanaco, the Cradle of American Man*, trans. J. Shearer, J.J. Augustin, New York, 1945

Ptolemy, *Tetrabiblios*, trans. F.E. Robbins, Heinemann (Loeb Classical Library no. 435), London, 1980

Quatrefages, A. de, *Histoire des Vierges*, A. Lacroix & Cie, Paris, 1879

Russell, P., *The Awakening Earth*, Routledge and Kegan Paul, London, 1982

Santillana, G. de, and Dechend, H. von, *Hamlet's Mill*, D.R. Godine, Boston, 1992

Scott, Sir Walter (trans.), *The Hermetica*, first pub. 1924–36, Solos Press, Shaftesbury, 1993

Spence, L., *Atlantis in America*, Ernest Benn, London, 1925

—— *The History of Atlantis*, Rider, London, rev. ed. 1995

—— *The Magic and Mysteries of Mexico*, Rider, London, 1932

Taylor, T., *Hymns and Initiations*, Prometheus Trust, Frome, 1994

—— *Oracles and Mysteries*, Prometheus Trust, Frome, 1994

Temple, R., *The Crystal Sun*, Century, London, 2000

Tompkins, P., *Mysteries of the Mexican Pyramids*, Thames and Hudson, London, 1987

—— and Bird, C., *The Secret Life of Plants*, Penguin Books, London, 1973

Warren, W. F., *Paradise Found: The Cradle of the Human Race at the North Pole*, Boston, 1885

West, J.A., *Serpent in the Sky*, Quest Books, Wheaton, Ill., 1993

Wilford, Col. J., *Asiatic Researches*, Royal Asiatic Society, London, 1806

Wilkins, H.T., *Secret Cities of Old South America: Atlantis Unveiled*, Rider, London, 1952

Yonge, C.D. (trans.), *Philo: Works*, Hendrickson Publishers, USA, 1993

INDEX